Confronting Gouldner

Studies in Critical Social Sciences Book Series

Haymarket Books is proud to be working with Brill Academic Publishers (www.brill.nl) to republish the *Studies in Critical Social Sciences* book series in paperback editions. This peer-reviewed book series offers insights into our current reality by exploring the content and consequences of power relationships under capitalism, and by considering the spaces of opposition and resistance to these changes that have been defining our new age. Our full catalog of *SCSS* volumes can be viewed at www.haymarketbooks.org/category/scss-series.

Series Editor
David Fasenfest, Wayne State University

Editorial Board
Eduardo Bonilla-Silva (Duke University)
Chris Chase-Dunn (University of California–Riverside)
William Carroll (University of Victoria)
Raewyn Connell (University of Sydney)
Kimberlé W. Crenshaw (University of California–LA, and Columbia University)
Heidi Gottfried (Wayne State University)
Karin Gottschall (University of Bremen)
Mary Romero (Arizona State University)
Alfredo Saad Filho (University of London)
Chizuko Ueno (University of Tokyo)
Sylvia Walby (Lancaster University)

Confronting Gouldner

Sociology and Political Activism

James J. Chriss

Haymarket
Books
Chicago, IL

First published in 2015 by Brill Academic Publishers, The Netherlands.
© 2015 Koninklijke Brill NV, Leiden, The Netherlands

Published in paperback in 2016 by
Haymarket Books
P.O. Box 180165
Chicago, IL 60618
773-583-7884
www.haymarketbooks.org

ISBN: 978-1-60846-643-6

Trade distribution:
In the U.S. through Consortium Book Sales, www.cbsd.com
In the UK, Turnaround Publisher Services, www.turnaround-uk.com
In all other countries by Publishers Group Worldwide, www.pgw.com

Cover design by Jamie Kerry of Belle Étoile Studios and Ragina Johnson.

This book was published with the generous support of Lannan Foundation and the Wallace Action Fund.

Printed in Canada by union labor.

10 9 8 7 6 5 4 3 2 1

Library of Congress Cataloging-in-Publication Data is available.

Contents

Foreword by Richard Lee Deaton
*The Two Masks of Alvin Ward Gouldner: Angry Outsider and
Intellectual Street Fighter – Reflections of an Undutiful Son* VII
Acknowledgments XXXIV
List of Figures XXXV

1 The Classics and Beyond 1

2 Intellectuals and Radical Sociology 18

3 Crime and Deviance 36

4 Bourdieu and Reflexive Sociology 68

5 Radical Politics and Soviet Sociology 89

6 Religion and Critical Theory 125

7 Social Justice, Politics, and Religion 153

8 Locals, Cosmopolitans, and the Politics of a Global Humanity 171

9 Mao and the Communist Horizon 194

References 213
Index 236

Foreword
The Two Masks of Alvin Ward Gouldner: Angry Outsider and Intellectual Street Fighter—Reflections of an Undutiful Son*

A Jewish father has mercy upon his children.
  The Talmud

The past is a foreign country.
  L. P. HARTLEY

There is no good father, that's the rule.
  Les Mots

I come not to praise Caesar, but to bury him.
  SHAKESPEARE

I have tried to be objective. I do not claim to be detached.
  C. WRIGHT MILLS

Acknowledgments

I am more than flattered that Professor James Chriss has asked me to write this foreword to complement his second study of Professor Alvin W. Gouldner (Chriss 1999c). He has generously given me *carte blanche* with respect to this essay. His kind gesture and trust is most appreciated. Hopefully, our collaboration of some eight years has been mutually interesting and beneficial. Each of us has retained his own independent perspective and conclusions regarding the main character of this study. For me this has been a true participant-observer collaboration.

Introduction

C. Wright Mills and Alvin Ward Gouldner were arguably the greatest sociologists of their generation and were undoubtedly the most influential and

---

* The author gratefully acknowledges the considerable editorial and stylistic contribution of Mrs. Eleanor Hora for bringing coherence and intelligibility to this foreword.

controversial sociologists of the post-World War Two period. Their originality, theoretical insights and craftsmanship as applied to various subjects and issues made them true scholars and public intellectuals. They dared ask the difficult questions and sought unpleasant truths about the nature of power, ideas, and their own profession. Although they were not always personally popular, Mills and Gouldner inspired an entire generation of young sociologists and social scientists and the issues they studied. Most importantly, they were responsible for creating what is now known as critical or radical sociology.

Circumstance and my own personal history have belatedly cast me in the unintentional role of the prodigal son who demands a fair hearing for his father's reputation and achievements. As his estranged son I can hardly claim to have been close to Professor Alvin Ward Gouldner. For reasons outlined and elaborated upon in this essay, our lives took different directions. Now I am in the unusual, if not suspect and awkward, position of trying to bring some balance and perspective to any assessment of his life and work. Alas, being my father's son, I see something of him, intellectually and personally, in myself. But it is axiomatic that personal and family histories are complex.

Immediately, I am placed in a double bind or Catch-22 situation. On the one hand, if I am disparaging towards my late father, I will invariably be dismissed or accused of being unfair or harbouring a grudge as the alienated son. On the other hand, if I am laudatory or sympathetic, I will undoubtedly be accused of being a hagiographer or uncritical because of the family connection. In this "no-win" situation, I can only do my best to be honest and fair.

A strong caveat is necessary to emphasize that I am not writing this essay out of malice as Professor Gouldner's distanced son. Contrary to the imagery of Goya's *Saturn Devouring His Son,* I certainly haven't spent my life shadow boxing or competing academically with his ghost. Nor is this a form of belated psychological catharsis, despite the opportunity this exercise has afforded me to engage in considerable introspection, and a chance to contemplate a number of personal and intellectual issues. Hopefully, the background information presented here will expand our understanding of Alvin Ward Gouldner, both as a person and as a scholar. As C. Wright Mills said in another context, "I have tried to be objective. I do not claim to be detached."

Alvin W. Gouldner: Methodology of Intellectual Biography

What I expect of any scholar or academic producing a well-researched intellectual biography of Professor Gouldner is that their work conforms to at least three criteria. First, it must be accurate with respect to the biographical facts and details of his personal and family life, as well as his academic career.

Second, in interpreting his personal motives, ideologically-based politics, and intellectual work there should be a sense of fairness and balance. Third, and perhaps the most difficult of all in any intellectual biography such as this, it must establish the linkage or connection between the man and his intellectual work, at least in rough contour. In short, doing the job properly requires balanced craftsmanship in order to produce a full and nuanced intellectual biography (for example: Hobsbawm 2003).

My father's work and ideas were not produced in a vacuum; they must be contextualized, personally and historically. Thus, the intellectual biographer must, or should, establish the interaction between the person and his work and integrate the two to have a picture of the whole. A full and rounded evaluation of a person's intellectual contribution must take into account the person himself, his background, and those formative or determinative forces acting on him, not just a limited analysis or assessment of their abstract or rarified theories or ideas.

Professional biographers and writers have endlessly debated the relationship between a person and their work, and whether any biographical background or history is necessary in order to assess or appreciate their work. Where the balance or emphasis should lie between biography and intellectual history will be interminably debated. The issue is difficult, but at least recognizing that it exists helps to inform the subject. All the more so, when the personality under study is as controversial and "difficult" as Professor Gouldner.

Those wanting to satisfy their prurient curiosity, expecting or wanting a tell-all "hatchet job" revealing family secrets, or an opportunity to indulge their *schadenfreude*, may be sadly disappointed by what follows here. Many things are often best left unsaid, and we all have issues that we would prefer to forget or to remain private. Some of Professor Gouldner's former colleagues and detractors should remember that they, too, may have skeletons rattling around in closets, or bedrooms. Over the years I have often wondered to what extent personal rancor and professional jealousy have played a part in, or coloured, their assessment of Gouldner.

For myself, I prefer to be generous and take the high road and be pensive and introspective, rather than polemical. What are presented here are some personal memories, family history, stories, and incidents that, hopefully, will offer a better—and more balanced—understanding of the man and his work.

Alvin W. Gouldner: Overview

Who, then, was my birth father, Alvin Ward Gouldner? Why, after so many years, is his intellectual contribution to sociology still remembered? Why does his ghost still cast a shadow over the discipline? Was his work seminal? Is he still relevant? Why is he considered such a controversial personality? And why does his name provoke such a visceral reaction among some people? Unfortunately, at times, Professor Gouldner's *persona* was as controversial as his work. Who was this person, or *"graying eminence,"* as he once called himself?

Alvin W. Gouldner was an academic, critical sociologist, social theorist, scholar and Marxologist. He was also a father, a husband, and a man. He was an iconoclast and gadfly, and was both a "non-Jewish Jew" and a "tough Jew"; as well, he was very much a maverick. He was also a product of his times. Much to his credit, he asked difficult questions and sought unpleasant truths as a sociologist and social scientist, while many of his contemporaries and colleagues took the easy way out and failed to deal with the critical issues of their times. He challenged his colleagues and his profession to be engaged and do more, even if he was accused of being "subjective," "lacking objectivity" or being "rhetorical" (Obituary. 1981). He was a brilliant, controversial and hypersensitive "outsider" to the sociological establishment. This undoubtedly rankled and hurt him; he was, he once told me, *"respected, but not liked."*

Will Professor Gouldner's intellectual legacy to sociology survive? The world of academic or intellectual ideas, like great art and music, must satisfy the criteria of universality and timeliness, and, in this instance, be viewed against the litmus test of historical reality. Does Gouldner's work meet those criteria? Perhaps. But the Muse of History is demanding and is not always kind.

What personality characteristics describe Professor Gouldner, the academic, the man and the father? Many people, including myself, would say he was: brilliant, prolific, demanding, angry, ill-tempered, aloof, egotistical, intolerant, insecure, brilliant, opinionated, overbearing, aggressive, argumentative, original, outspoken, arrogant, thin-skinned, abrasive, abusive, disciplined, caustic, hardworking, competitive, combative, charming, intelligent, provocative, impatient, original, bullying, scholarly, stimulating, unhappy, occasionally generous, and at times pugnacious. In short, as a code word, Professor Gouldner was often referred to as a "difficult," "flawed" or "tragic" person, although they are not necessarily the same thing.

To put things in perspective, while Professor Gouldner was often referred to as being "difficult" by many, C. Wright Mills earned that same reputation before him. One reviewer concluded that Mills "was a kind of difficult genius whose vices...[were] integral to his virtues." Mills, before Gouldner, earned a reputation for his "legendary combativeness towards his colleagues." Mills even went so far as to refer to the "sociological brawl at Columbia," where Gouldner was completing his doctoral work at about the same time Mills joined the faculty there (Judis 2000). Gouldner was the intellectual provocateur and social theorist, Mills was the public intellectual and social critic. There are, in retrospect, some uncanny similarities between Mills and Gouldner as personality types. Both were battle-hardened, opinionated and outspoken academics with complicated personalities; both were married three times, enjoyed *haut cuisine,* and died of heart attacks.

Given Professor Gouldner's ghetto reflexes, ideological world view, mercurial temperament and notorious temper, it is fair to say that he didn't suffer fools gladly, or tolerate academic infighting easily. Sadly, Professor Gouldner is often remembered only for being abrasive or being a bully. Interpersonal relations were not his strength; some would suggest that he was a prime candidate for an anger management course. The stories about him, real, exaggerated, mistaken, or imaginary, are legendary and certainly add to his mystique as the "Outlaw Marxist." (Chriss 1999c: 23–27)

Alvin W. Gouldner: Background Influences

Some family background and a disclaimer are necessary to establish my relationship to Alvin Ward Gouldner. Both my parents were left-wing New York City intellectuals: brilliant, involved, competitive and aloof, and in many ways products of their times. My father went to CCNY's Bernard Baruch [Business] College for his undergraduate B.B.A. degree and then to Columbia University for his M.A. and Ph.D. in Sociology. My mother, Helen Ruth Sattler (nee), went to the newly created Brooklyn College in NYC, then to Oberlin College for graduate work in labour economics; she worked as an organizer for Local 65 in NYC and then for the National Labour Relations Board (NLRB) during WW II. Both my parents were children of the Great Depression and knew poverty. Both were secular, if not anti-religious, Jews. Both were members of the Communist Party of the USA (CPUSA, or CP), and both were ultimately expelled in the early 1950s for Browderism, an alleged political "deviation" which advocated adapting Marxism to American conditions.

Notwithstanding my father's considerable academic success, my mother was every bit his intellectual equal and they had an active intellectual, social and political life together. We were a family of four including my younger brother, Alan (Lan), and myself. At home I remember my father often being abrasive, short tempered, irritable, and impatient, but my mother gave as good as she got. My parents divorced in 1955 when I was nine years old. It was not, as they say, a "friendly" divorce, and it was quite traumatic for my brother and me. The custody and child support battle went on for years until my father relinquished visitation rights in exchange for the cessation of child support payments. My brother and I saw him only for summer vacations until I was age twelve. After the legal arrangements were finalized in September, 1960, he phoned me, on what was my first day of high school, and dramatically said, *"I pronounce you dead."*

After this declaration we rarely received any correspondence or gifts from him. He basically disappeared from our lives and had little direct influence on my brother or me, or on our upbringing during our formative years. I did not see him again for 16 years until I was aged 28.

Both my parents quickly remarried. My mother married one of my father's graduate students, Robert Brooks Deaton, who was her junior and became in every practical way, emotionally and legally, my real father. From the age of nine until he died I called him "Dad," and referred to Alvin Gouldner as "AWG." It was Deaton who tried to teach me to read, took me to baseball games, read to me, helped me with my math homework, took the time to talk to me about anything and everything, introduced me to classical music, history and politics, and paid my way through university. He also adopted me; over the years the name change would serve as a shield against Gouldner's notoriety.

Later he was instrumental in my decision to come to Canada during the Vietnam War. (Dickerson 1999) The reality is that my move to Canada afforded me the opportunity to develop personally, politically and career-wise in ways that never would have been possible had I stayed in the U.S. given its political culture.

My step-father was a progressive who had been a trade union organizer, a campaign worker for Vito Marcantonio, an activist involved in the early civil rights movement in the mid-1950s, turned criminologist (specializing in Soviet juvenile delinquency), turned stockbroker. I was brought up on John L. Lewis, Spanish civil war songs, Dr. Norman Bethune, Joe Hill ballads, John Steinbeck, Pete Seeger folk songs, Jackie Robinson, Bill Russell, SANE, and CORE—an unabashed "red diaper baby." In high school I was known as the class Red, much to the consternation of my parents. I have never regretted that upbringing. (Cf. Bernstein 1989; Laxer 2005)

I myself became a Marxist at an early age and have retained that world view over my lifetime, notwithstanding recent seismic events. Like many of my generation I was, in part, a product of the 1960s and was influenced by the civil rights movement and the war in Vietnam, although my political outlook was firmly established before that time. I went to the University of Wisconsin-Madison for my undergraduate work from 1964–68, majoring in economics (with minors in history and sociology) during the zenith of radical student politics. There is no doubt, based on a number of incidents, that Gouldner occasionally tracked or kept tabs on me through colleagues while I was at university.

Many years later as a so-called "mature student" I went to the University of Warwick, UK, to earn my doctorate in Industrial Relations and Business Studies (1986), and subsequently graduated from the University of Ottawa law school (1999). As a well-trained social scientist and political economist, I have written in these fields and have had an eclectic and stimulating career (Deaton 1973; Deaton 1989).

Our family life before my parents' divorce revolved around Gouldner's position as an esteemed faculty member; it was highly intellectual and conventional. The word "fun" was not in our family's vocabulary. As a faculty couple, my parents entertained his colleagues fairly regularly. Progressive faculty members, especially at mid-western universities, tended to cling together for support. Book and film reviews, and of course faculty gossip, were the intellectual medium of exchange. At home I never saw any affection displayed between my parents, and I never remember either of my parents ever hugging or reading to me when I was a young boy, or taking any interest in my activities. It is questionable whether they should have become parents at all.

In retrospect, there is no doubt in my mind that my mother, for her own reasons, did everything within her power to discourage or sabotage any relationship that my brother or I might have had with our birth father after their divorce. She was undoubtedly partially responsible for my anxiety and negative feelings about him. As an austere and cerebral NYC intellectual with a life-long subscription to *The New Yorker*, who also faithfully read *The Ladies Home Journal* and had an avid interest in literature and the theatre, she was a formidable and, in many ways, formative influence on me. My mother undoubtedly had her own axes to grind, especially when it came to ex-husband, Alvin Gouldner.

Full disclosure: Many of the stories and incidents related here about Alvin Ward Gouldner were told to me over the years by my mother, usually on more than one occasion. Notwithstanding her biases and considerable antipathy towards Gouldner, I have little reason to doubt what she told me, but obviously this information is open to interpretation. As well, I witnessed some of those events first hand and therefore have personal knowledge of them. Subsequently, Alvin Gouldner himself corroborated many of these stories and incidents at a later date, as explained below. Thus, the information related here is true and accurate to the best of my knowledge and belief.

The next time that I saw Gouldner, was in Amsterdam, Holland, after a 16 year hiatus, over the holidays between late December 1974 and early January 1975 when I invited myself to see him to possibly effect a reconciliation and establish a new personal connection. Things did not go well. Perhaps I was naïve to expect otherwise. By this time he was working on his third marriage, to Janet Walker Gouldner, and had a so-called blended family. He was teaching at the University of Amsterdam. We discussed a wide range of subjects, personal, family, marriages, careers, and, of course, politics; some sightseeing was thrown in as well. Not surprisingly, there was a low grade tension between us; we were guarded and did not interact easily or freely.

Nothing was resolved at an interpersonal, father-son level. Too much time and personal history had transpired, and our personal experiences and outlook on life and the world were considerably different. During my stay he read one of my best-known political-scholarly articles and paid me the only compliment that I ever remember receiving from him when he said, "You are a natural writer." After all the years of neglect it really didn't matter.

Symbolically, towards the end of my stay he gave me three books as a remembrance, each with a dedication. The first was a pictorial biography of Trotsky with the inscription, "For Richard, the seeker." In his *Patterns of Industrial Bureaucracy* he wrote, "For Dick, With more good wishes than I can find words for." And in a hardbound edition of his *For Sociology* he wrote this interesting dedication, "To Richard Deaton, In memory of a Pleasant Amsterdam Summit Meeting, his father, the author, A.W.G." That said it all about the state of our relationship.

Interestingly, the night before I was to fly back to Ottawa we all went out for an elegant farewell dinner and then began to argue about ideologically based politics. The fight escalated, becoming more ugly and acrimonious, especially after we returned to his home. The next afternoon he declined to take me to the airport and called a taxi for me. I felt disappointed and raw. To this day I am convinced that he deliberately provoked our fight as a way of re-establishing an emotional distance and an arms- length relationship between us. In many ways it was the easiest thing for us both. Whether this was calculated or subconscious on his part is an interesting question.

During my trip to Amsterdam I met my step-brother and step-sister, technically speaking, for the first and last time. Gouldner and his second wife, Helen Pat, adopted Andrew, his third child, Alessandra, his fourth and youngest child, was his daughter by his third wife, Janet, who was my hostess in Amsterdam. We never maintained any relationship and have never seen or contacted each other again. I have no idea what has happened to any of them. Gouldner told me then, *"You were my trial."* I don't know how he related to his other children, but hopefully he learned from his "trial." Notwithstanding my own limitations, I'd like to think that I have treated my (now adult) twin daughters in a more emotive and decent manner.

Our Amsterdam meeting was the last time I saw Alvin Ward Gouldner. We exchanged two perfunctory notes later that spring, but never communicated again. I didn't even bother to inform him in May 1979 that he had become a grandfather of my twin daughters, Emmanuelle and Shoshanah, although I have always felt ambivalent about my handling of that situation (my late wife however, took considerable exception to my approach). He died a year later in Madrid on December 15, 1980. And that was that.

Alvin W. Gouldner: The Father

Was Alvin W. Gouldner a good father? What was it like to be his son? It is perhaps best to start at the beginning. He was, to be blunt, far from being an ideal warm, nurturing father, at least to me. He was aloof, demanding, ill tempered, impatient, and at times verbally and physically abusive. He was certainly too self-absorbed to be an involved parent, especially by today's child-centric standards.

I do not remember him with particular fondness, and have few pleasant memories of him. What I do remember is being continuously anxious and of my stomach tightening into a knot and churning because I was afraid of his anger or disapproval. But it is unlikely that any child could satisfy his expectations or earn his approval. He was not a warm, fuzzy parent figure. Some of the important memories that have stayed with me over the years are briefly noted here.

Oscar Lewis, the well-known anthropologist, lived next store to us when my father was teaching at the University of Illinois – Urbana, and was a serious amateur opera singer who aspired to be a professional. He once told my mother, "*The word around town is that Gouldner is hard on his kids.*" Clearly, others must have been aware of the pervasive tension around our house. Only later did I learn that this was, in part, a result of the political tensions related to the McCarthy era, but it was also largely attributable to the long simmering marital problems between my parents.

Our family moved twice a year so that my father could climb the academic ladder: once in September for the regular academic year and again for the summer school session at another university. The constant moving and setting up of a new household, like a military family, undoubtedly placed a real strain on my parents. I never went to the same school for two consecutive years until after my parents divorced.

Not surprisingly, my father was not involved in household management. Packing for our constant moves, cleaning and cooking were left to my mother. The one exception that I remember was when he was teaching at Antioch College in Yellow Springs, Ohio. Early one stinking hot summer's night I found him in the kitchen sweating away at an old-fashioned manual food grinder, grating orange peels for crepe suzettes for a faculty dinner party at our ranch-style bungalow.

One of my earliest unpleasant memories of Gouldner was when I was in the third grade in Urbana, Illinois, and he was teaching at the university there. I had badly flunked a third grade spelling test and had to have it signed by my parents. After I brought it to the dinner table for their perusal, I remember him yelling loudly and calling me "stupid," and saying it again and again and again: "stupid, stupid, stupid." It was a stinging rebuke, which made me more than self-conscious, and something that I have never forgotten. Even to this day I cringe at the memory of that incident. Many years later I was diagnosed as being dyslectic.

Early one morning the following spring, he found me sitting on the floor of the den playing with his poker chips. He raised his foot, putting it on my shoulder and pushing me into the floor, yelled, "What are you doing? Who said you could play with those?" He then took his right foot and kept jabbing it into my stomach. Hard. He didn't stop until my mother walked in. Later, on an early summer's night in 1955, after my parents had decided to divorce, my five year old brother Lan was misbehaving at the dinner table. Gouldner smacked him so hard across the side of his head that he fell off his chair; my mother went crying into the kitchen.

What I remember most about my father was that he was rarely around. We seldom did anything together. He never took me to Cub Scouts or my Little League games; my mother did that. He was rarely generous or emotive with me. Over the years I only remember him once ever buying me a coke or a hot chocolate; he once gave me change for a movie and years later he took me to a St. Louis Cardinals game. I don't ever remember him saying anything encouraging to me.

On the other hand, there were also occasional good times, when, for example, my brother and I stayed with him and his second wife, Helen Pat, for the summer in Urbana, and we all went swimming every afternoon at a large public pool; we snacked when we came home while he read pulp mysteries and science fiction. He was always highly competitive with me. I remember that same summer we often played ping pong after lunch at the Illini Student Union. He gave no quarter and that entire summer I won only 2 or 3 games out of the dozens that we played. But he could also be unexpectedly nice, such as the time he took me out for pizza with his graduate students after an evening seminar. Life with father certainly had its anxiety-inducing ups and downs.

Alvin W. Gouldner: The Man

What drove Alvin W. Gouldner, the man? He was a product of his times and contributed to them as well. To have a full intellectual and personal appreciation of him requires us, as a minimum, to identify those forces which had a formative impact on him. Three forces or influences, in my opinion, seem to have shaped and permeated Professor Gouldner's life and career.

First, he was a "non-Jewish Jew" to use Isaac Deutscher's phrase (1968). Second, he was a so-called "tough Jew," and third, he was deeply influenced by Marxism as a university student and early in his academic career, resulting in his life-long identification with the underdog. These three elements are interwoven and interrelated, and are crucial to understanding the character, career, and work of Alvin W. Gouldner.

Being a "non-Jewish Jew" is shorthand, or code, for being an outsider. In the broadest sense, the Jew has historically been an outsider in western society, "in" but not "of" a particular society. And no matter what the Jew does, historically, he will not fit in or be accepted; he will always be an outsider looking in regardless of the lengths he goes to integrate himself into the broader predominantly Christian society. Jean-Paul Sartre (1968) referred to the Jewish outsider as The Other, the non-us. One does not have to be Jewish to be The Other, of course, as history has sadly shown. The "non-Jewish Jew" is also a person who asks the difficult and unpopular questions in the tradition of the rebellious-questioning fourth son at the Passover Seder. Being an outsider, however, often results in a person internalizing a certain outlook, way of thinking, and reaction to events.

Gouldner always felt himself to be an outsider because of his social, and, possibly, his ethnic background; and this was re-enforced by his intellectual work, which failed to conform to the accepted dominant paradigm of the sociological establishment. And by temperament he was very much a maverick. Professor Gouldner as the proverbial outsider, intellectual provocateur, and contrarian often seemed to relish (perhaps a bit too much) his role as a snarling lone wolf.

Gouldner came from a secular, that is, non-religious or non-practicing, Jewish family. His father, Louis (Lee) Gouldner, originally came from Galicia in 1902 at the age of 2 and was a sample salesman who died of a heart attack at age 45. He rarely spoke of his parents to me, and only then with considerable reticence and awkwardness. My middle name, Lee, was his father's nickname. Because his parents were secular and not observant in anyway, to the best of my knowledge, he was never *bar mitzvahed*. He never celebrated any of the Jewish holidays such as Passover or the religious High Holy Days.

Throughout my childhood we always celebrated Christmas, and I distinctly remember our family, including my very secular parents, always having a Christmas tree in Kew Gardens in NYC, in Buffalo, Yellow Springs and Urbana; years later Gouldner had one in his Amsterdam living room. And we didn't temporize by calling our Christmas tree a "Hanukkah bush," as is now popular is some circles. (Maynard 1985) Neither my brother nor I ever received any religious instruction, celebrated any Jewish holidays, nor were we *bar mitzvahed*. I suspect that his later children, Andrew and Alessandra, never had any Jewish upbringing either, or were observant in any way. Only one of his wives, my mother, was Jewish by birth. His second wife, Helen Pat, converted to Judaism when they lived in Urbana; his third wife, Janet, was a Gentile.

When I asked my mother about our upbringing many years later, she told me that Gouldner was of the very strong view that he wanted his children *"to feel as if they belonged."* This statement and its meaning are self-evident. In short, he didn't want his children to be outsiders, as he evidently felt he was, and he wanted us to fit into the broader society, rather than being narrowly ethnocentrically defined. This was a true sociological approach to child- rearing.

Re-enforcing this were my mother's strong anti-religious feelings which were triggered during the Depression when her family was impoverished and her mother was refused admittance to High Holy Day services at their modern Orthodox synagogue because they couldn't afford the tickets. This resulted in my grandmother repudiating her Judaism, and in her subsequent left-wing political radicalization, but that's another story. We never celebrated any Jewish holidays at home until I was in high school, and then only occasionally for educational purposes.

Being Jewish in America during the 1930s and 1940s was a struggle. Jews, like blacks, were marginalized and outsiders to the so-called American Dream. Discrimination against Jews was common, such as the quota system in medical and law schools, while ignorance and poverty were rampant within the Jewish community. Being Jewish was not something to be celebrated. It was a decided social handicap; indeed, it was something to be forgotten or ignored, especially if one came from the lower class and straitened financial circumstances. The Judaism of the ghetto was increasingly viewed as backward and an impediment to social advancement in the New World by the children of Eastern European immigrants from the *shtetl* and was abandoned (Schoener 1967; Howe 1976; Sklare 1958; Richler 1955).

Education was a way out of the Jewish ghetto for bright and ambitious young people, be it the lower east side of New York City or the Bronx, as in Gouldner's case. Understandably, Gouldner like many other Jews, and other immigrant groups as well, used the education system as an escalator for upward social mobility out of the ethnic ghetto into the newly emerging post-war middle class. For Gouldner, becoming a secular Jew was not altogether unique. It may be argued that it was very much a generational phenomenon among some Jewish sociologists, particularly those of the Depression and Second World War eras, such as Goffman, Stein, Lipset, Bell, Merton and others (Bell 1980: especially chapter 6.)

What was unique and defining for that up-and-coming generation of young Jewish intellectuals, scholars, and sociologists, was the compelling idea that one had to study either Torah or Marx. Those who studied Torah stayed in the Jewish ghetto with the *haredim* and stagnated; alternatively, those who advanced themselves by getting a higher education escaped the ghetto, often using Marxism as an intellectual framework to explain their social situation during the Depression. Being a "Jewish atheist," a non-Jewish Jew, a left-wing radical, or being involved in the labour movement was integral to the Jewish identity and experience in places like New York City. (Gold 1948)

Within this context, the Young Communist League (YCL) and the Communist Party of the United States (CPUSA, or CP) and their activities had considerable legitimacy on university campuses throughout the 1930s until the beginning of the Cold War in the late 1940s. During the Great Depression, with its mass unemployment, wide-spread poverty and social unrest, Marxism as an ideology and method of socio-economic analysis provided a holistic world view which allowed people to understand what was going on around them and channeled their political energies.

In short, Marxism allowed for intellectual comprehension and political hope. Its appeal was real and powerful, especially among intellectuals and students, and to a lesser extent, workers. And for those studying sociology during the Depression there must have been an even stronger attraction to Marxism because Marx was considered to be one of the great classical sociologists.

Joining the YCL or the CP (USA) meant doing something concrete to change the world. Marxism was a politics based on action. Interestingly, while attending CCNY as an undergraduate, Gouldner paid his expenses, *he told me*, by schlepping clothing trolleys in the NYC garment district during the summer. With some bitterness he said it was *"hot, hard work."* For him, being poor was real and he clearly remembered those experiences. By his own account he "was educated in the streets and schools of New York." (Gouldner 1979b)

At CCNY during the 1930s and early 40s, the political and personal split between the members of the Soviet oriented Communist Party (CPUSA) and the Trotskyists in the Socialist Workers Party (SWP, followers of Leon Trotsky who was expelled from the Soviet Union in 1924) was vicious and unrelenting.

(Howe and Coser 1962; Wald 1987) At the student union cafeteria at CCNY the CPers (Stalinists or "Stals" in the political jargon) sat at one table and the Trotskyists (or "Trots") sat at another. They did not talk to one another, or otherwise socialize, on pain of expulsion from their respective parties. Both of my parents remembered this atmosphere and some of the personalities quite well. It was here, for example, that Gouldner met Lipset and Bell (or *"Danny"* as he later called him in Amsterdam) for the first time.

Both of my parents became members of the Communist Party (CP, or CPUSA). Gouldner, I believe, was first a member of the YCL at CCNY and later joined the CP. My mother had been active in various student study groups while in high school in NYC and joined the party while at the new Brooklyn College she told me; she was quite active when at Oberlin College. Both remained members of the CP until the early-mid- 1950s when Gouldner was teaching at the University of Buffalo (then a private university). As a young child I always wondered what those small gatherings of people in our living room were all about; now I know they were political meetings of one sort or another.

My parents, according to my mother, were expelled from the CP for Browderism, which advocated adapting Marxism to concrete American circumstances. During the 1948 presidential election, Henry Wallace, the Progressive Party candidate, stayed overnight at our home in Buffalo during a speaking engagement.

The second formative influence, which defined Alvin Ward Gouldner's character, was that he was a "tough Jew." The term "tough Jew" refers to a personality type, and is *not* intended or used as an ethnic slur or slight. The phrase in popular parlance generally refers to a combative or aggressive personality. The term is used by historians, as well as by other writers. (Breines 1990; Cohen 1999) Alvin Gouldner was the Norman Mailer of the sociology set; both were cut from the same abrasive ethnic cloth, and both had the same, distanced, relationship with their children.

Being a non-Jewish Jew and a tough Jew are often the flip sides of the same ethnic coin. The non-Jewish Jew wants to forget or distance himself from his Jewishness for whatever reason, while a tough Jew is "in your face" with their aggressiveness or combativeness. Being a tough Jew is one's public *persona*. In effect, a tough Jew is saying to the world, "This is who I am—no one tells me what to do, or pushes me around. And if you don't like it, "fuck off." Indeed, the fact that Gouldner referred to being "educated in the streets of New York," suggests that he had very much internalized that self-image. (Gouldner 1979b)

In this regard, my mother once told me the story, albeit with its pop psychology overtones, that when Gouldner was a young teenager he broke his nose playing stick ball and because his parents were poor they couldn't afford to have it set properly. During his convalescence he withdrew into the world of pulp science fiction. As a result of this mishap, she maintained, he was very self-conscious about this minor physical defect and his appearance. Disfigurement however, is one of the theoretical pillars of Adlerian psychology with its emphasis on how people compensate for a sense of inferiority. Adler himself used the example of Cyrano de Bergerac and his nose. (Adler 2009)

This situation may, depending on circumstance, lower a person's self-esteem. And it can be argued that being a tough Jew—that is, being aggressive or abrasive is an over-compensatory coping mechanism for feeling inferior. This is not to suggest that poor self-esteem justifies an explosive temper, but rather it offers a possible explanation.

One of the most dramatic and revealing incidents reflecting Gouldner's outlook as a tough Jew, with a pugnacious personality, occurred towards the end of the Second World War when both of my parents were working in Washington, D.C. At that time, news was just beginning to filter out about the extent of the Holocaust. One night after work my parents went to a corner convenience store that had an old-fashioned soda counter with stools, where ice cream and soft drinks were served. My parents each ordered a Coke. The soda jerk mixed their Cokes and placed them down on the counter, but Gouldner asked him to fill his glass to the top. The soda jerk objected strongly, resulting in a heated exchange between them; he then called Gouldner "a cheap Jew." Gouldner's reaction was visceral, immediate, and explosive. According to my mother, a particularly ugly fistfight ensued.

While some may be taken aback by this story or say that this is "vintage Gouldner," or portended future events, I for one understand his reaction all too well in this instance. In the mid-1960s when I was in high school on Staten Island, NYC, on two occasions I was called a "Jew bastard." My reaction was reflexive and pugnacious as well, notwithstanding my secular upbringing. Those were the only times that I have ever been in a fistfight. And at a deep, instinctive, gut level I understand Gouldner's reaction. In that sense I am truly my father's son.

Within this context, it is a well-known fact that Professor Gouldner had a temper, which was exhibited inside and outside the classroom. That, too, forms part of his legacy as an academic and scholar.

Alvin W. Gouldner: The Scholar

But what of Alvin W. Gouldner, the scholar? For my part, I would like to focus on Gouldner the teacher and academic craftsman, and then briefly comment on some of his scholarly work. Throughout his academic career, as in his personal life, Alvin Gouldner was plagued by and known for his bad temper. The first notable instance of this was when he was a graduate student at Columbia University. My mother related to me that he got into a *"terrible fight"* with Merton, his doctoral dissertation advisor, when finishing his graduate work. She was unusually guarded and evasive about the reason for the fight, but did say that Merton expressed his concern about Gouldner's temper. I find it highly unlikely, however, that she didn't know the full story. What did come out of this verbal altercation was Merton's promise to Gouldner that he would never teach at Columbia. And he never did, except for one summer school session in 1957 or 1958. That summer, my brother and I stayed with him in Engelwood, NJ, with his second wife, Helen Pat, whom he meet at UCLA in the summer of 1955 immediately after my parents' split. Interestingly, notwithstanding this story, Gouldner and Merton from all accounts had a life-long professional friendship and correspondence.

After completing his doctoral work at Columbia University, Gouldner went on to teach at a number of universities and colleges. However, early in his university career he was confronted, given his political orientation and background, with the challenge of surviving the McCarthy period's witch hunts. The rise of right-wing McCarthyism in the post-war period, with its associated hysteria and paranoia, permeated American political life and university campuses. It was an attempt to destroy independent thinking and the progressive political movement that had emerged in the 1930s and 40s in order to launch the Cold War with its re-alignment of American foreign policy (Horowitz 1965; LaFeber 1975)

The witch hunt atmosphere fomented by Senator Joseph McCarthy, J. Edgar Hoover, and the House Un-American Committee (HUAC), with their alleged lists of radicals supplied by informers, affected people in all walks of life from Hollywood to unions to universities. The McCarthy era created an atmosphere of fear and suspicion on university campuses across the U.S. Self-censorship was common. When Gouldner taught at the University of Buffalo between 1947–51, for example, the head of the sociology department told him to reduce or eliminate the readings of Karl Marx from his courses. As well, when at the University of Buffalo, according to my mother, he was interviewed twice by the FBI, once in a car in front of our house; this was later confirmed by Gouldner to me. It is well established that many academics during this period were kept under FBI surveillance and had security files, as later occurred during the Vietnam War. (Lasch 1968)

Casting a shadow over the McCarthy period was the trial of Julius and Ethel Rosenberg on charges of espionage, and their subsequent executions on June 19, 1953. This re-enforced the hysteria of the McCarthy era and created paranoia and insecurity within the Jewish community. Many were afraid of being

FOREWORD   XXIII

accused of being un-American or "fifth columnists," while some were worried this would trigger a new series of pogroms. For the most part, the Jewish community felt threatened and remained silent. Nevertheless, a close (maternal) uncle of mine joined the legal team that later defended another Rosenberg family member accused of similar charges.

The summer of the Rosenberg executions, we drove from Antioch College in Yellow Springs, Ohio, to Dartmouth College in Hanover, NH, where Professor Gouldner was working as a research fellow during the summer school session. On the way, we stopped in Baltimore to visit some distant relatives of his. We only stayed two days because there were, evidently, some acrimonious discussions about the Rosenberg case. His relatives fell back on the time-worn adage, "Is this good for the Jews?" This myopic and narrow ethnic outlook to the issue, my mother later told me, infuriated Gouldner.

My parents' left-wing politics and anti-religious feelings merged during the McCarthy period when the US Pledge of Allegiance was changed in 1954 to include the phrase "under God." This raised a number of religious, political and constitutional issues which are still reverberating. We were living in Urbana at the time and I was in the third grade. The Cold War was in full swing. My parents told me not to recite the offending phrase "under God," during the daily Pledge of Allegiance, and I complied. My mother was called into school (my father was busy, as I recall) for a meeting with the principal and my teacher. I was never told what transpired, but I was never required to recite that passage. The subsequent jurisprudence on the issue has vindicated my parents.

As a professor and faculty member, Gouldner could be opinionated and outspoken, as well as demanding and a bully. When his newly published *Wildcat Strike* received a mediocre review in a major professional journal right after we moved to Urbana, he phoned the reviewer to vent his displeasure. In 1956, he taught summer school at Harvard. It was the first summer we spent with him and his second wife, Helen Pat, after my parents' divorce. We lived in Gloucester where he commuted into Boston every day by train. One day he brought me along to his seminar. I remember a large room with about 20 students sitting around an enormous oval wood table. At some point, a female graduate student incurred his wrath for some reason. He went at her and kept at her, and brow beat her, and bore down on her, and interrogated her until she finally broke down and cried. Throughout the ordeal the other students were silent; I didn't know how to react. His behavior would be totally unacceptable by today's academic standards.

Later, his well-publicized physical altercations at Washington University with two graduate students, one a clergyman, became the stuff of academic legend and gossip. And when he taught at the University of Amsterdam years later, the graduate students launched a formal grievance against him for his purportedly "excessive" workload and reading lists, which, by my calculation, actually resulted in *one-third fewer hours worked* than the average undergraduate at the University of Wisconsin. He was quite sullen and piqued by their grievance and called the Dutch students "lazy."

Whatever else may be said about Professor Gouldner, he worked hard and was a disciplined academic and scholar. His prolific and intellectually extensive output of books and articles over the years (eight books and dozens of articles), innumerable international speaking engagements and visiting professorships, clearly indicate, despite his controversial status, that he was a serious scholar and an intellectual force to be reckoned with by the sociology profession. After *The Coming Crisis of Western Sociology* (1970a) made him an academic superstar, he enjoyed playing the role to the hilt. Gouldner's career, in many ways, parallels or mirrors the transition of universities from the cloistered world of Mr. Chips to that of academic grantsmanship and entrepreneurship.

Gouldner took his craftsmanship seriously. I remember, for instance, the summer when he was at the University of Illinois readying his manuscript for *Enter Plato* (long before computers, library data bases, and word processing) how he went to the university library stacks to manually check, double check, and sometimes even triple check, his footnote citations. Later in Amsterdam, he told me that he systematically wrote for at least four hours a day—every day—seven days a week just to keep sharp; he even worked that New Year's Day morning when I was there. As well, he told me that he deliberately chose Greek mythological figures as his moniker, although my mother claimed that she suggested this idea to him.

Alvin W. Gouldner: Intellectual Contributions

Professor Gouldner's intellectual originality, craftsman-like discipline, and hard work made him a highly productive, path-breaking, stimulating, and often-controversial academic. He was to become sociology's iconoclastic gadfly who was both reviled and esteemed. Professor Chriss's first book on Gouldner (Chriss 1999c) is an extremely good typology that organizes and traces the evolution of Gouldner's intellectual development and career.

Although I am a political economist by background rather than a sociologist, the following are some *personal reactions* and *casual observations* to Gouldner's scholarly contributions. First, contrary to conventional wisdom, I found his work in industrial sociology to be his most interesting and seminal work. There are a number of reasons for this reaction. In the first instance, it was grounded in concrete reality and was devoid of "soc speak" and the impenetrable philosophic buzz words which characterized his later work. Studying the job-related problems of blue collar workers was still something fairly new in the mid-1950s, and represented a clear break with Mayo's earlier manipulative and employer-oriented human relations school. It was written at a time when industrial sociology and industrial relations were still in their infancy as academic disciplines and hadn't been co-opted by and subsumed into Human Resource Management in business and commerce schools.

Wildcat Strike (1954c) was, by any objective standard path-breaking, and in many ways remains so to this day. While there have been a number of studies dealing with labour disputes and work stoppages, his was the first to deal with a wildcat strike as such; in the intervening sixty years, to the best of my knowledge only two other monographs on the subject have been undertaken by academic sociologists or industrial relationists (Flood 1968; Lane and Roberts 1971; Scott and Homans 1947; Sayles 1954).

It can be argued that *Wildcat Strike* was, in its own way, an extension of Gouldner's left-wing worldview, which had been formed in the Young Communist League (YCL) and the Communist Party (CP). It is difficult to believe that his membership in the CP, with its emphasis and focus on the role of workers, wouldn't have influenced, at least to some extent, his scholarship and choice of research topics. The book is noteworthy, as well, because it was part of his industrial sociology trilogy, which was produced at the height of the McCarthy period. And unlike some sociologists, such as Lipset and Bell, he wouldn't spend the rest of his life and career recanting and repenting for his left-wing views. Indeed, he rarely repented for anything, either in his academic or his personal life.

Professor Gouldner produced a trilogy of books as his contribution to the then emerging field of industrial sociology. He was editor of the less well-known *Studies in Leadership: Leadership and Democratic Action* (Gouldner 1950), which compiled original selections from many who would become luminaries in sociology: Adorno, Feuer, Bell, Lipset, Bendix, Chinoy, Lazarsfeld, and Merton, his Columbia University doctoral thesis adviser.

Subsequently, in 1954, he published two books that flowed from his Columbia University doctoral thesis. *Patterns of Industrial Bureaucracy* (Gouldner 1954a) was the prequel to the much better known *Wildcat Strike*, noted above, although both relied on the same field work. On a personal note, *Patterns of Industrial Bureaucracy* is also special because it is dedicated to my brother and me. All the books in Professor Gouldner's industrial sociology trilogy were edited by his first wife, my late mother, Helen Sattler Deaton, a fact that is not ordinarily known.

Lastly, at a personal level, having spent over twenty years in the Canadian labour movement as assistant director of research for the Canadian Union of Public Employees (CUPE), the country's largest union, I came to have a special fondness for *Wildcat Strike* and the fascinating story it told. But in this regard I am unabashedly biased. I still have the original black and white film photos of the National Gypsum plant in Buffalo taken by Gouldner, but never used, for those two books. When I was an undergraduate at the University of Wisconsin-Madison, one of my industrial relations professors, Everett Kassalow, commented on National Gypsum's long history of anti-union practices and cited this book. But then, I don't honestly remember Gouldner ever being mentioned in any of my industrial sociology classes.

Interestingly, when I was in Amsterdam many years later and discussed *Wildcat Strike* with Gouldner, I got the distinct impression that it held a special place of affection for him. There was almost a moment of shared understanding or a bond between us regarding that book. Unfortunately, he never told me why or how he came to choose that topic for his doctoral dissertation in the first place. Only later when doing my own doctorate in Industrial Relations and Business Studies did I fully appreciate how much work went into that small volume.

My second major observation and reaction to Professor Gouldner's intellectual *oeuvre* concerns *The Coming Crisis of Western Sociology* (1970a), considered by many to be his *magnum opus* and a "monumental" contribution to contemporary sociological theory. Some consider it to be a "seminal" work in critical social theory, and this work, perhaps more than any other, has secured his place in the sociological canon. The tome is sweeping in scope and intellectually ambitious, but at times, in my opinion, it is pretentious and often unfocused and rambling. Indeed, it often reads like a Talmudic disputation.

There are contrarians, such as myself, who would suggest that with respect to radical sociology and critical social theory, Gouldner's reputation is far better served by his eclectic volume, *For Sociology: Renewal and Critique in Sociology Today* (1973a). This compiles a number of his most provocative essays such as "Anti-Minotaur," "The Sociologist as Partisan," "Sociology and Marxism," and his classic, "The Two Marxisms" which serve as an intellectual springboard to *The Coming Crisis* and in many ways form its thematic core in terms of undertaking an alleged "Marxist critique of Marxism."

Professor Gouldner evidently made his transition from industrial sociology to social theory when at the University of Illinois at Urbana (1955–59), resulting in his *Enter Plato: Classical Greece and the Origins of Social Theory* (1965).

How and why he went through this intellectual and professional metamorphosis I really don't know; that is an interesting subject for others to explore.

The leap from Hellenic to Marxist social theory is even more problematic and difficult to explain or understand. What was his reason or motive for this? Was it grounded in his own radical political past, including an early exposure to the Frankfurt School? (1979b:1, 3) Were there unacknowledged external political or academic influences? Was he trying to rescue Marxism from itself by reinventing or updating it by making it more relevant and flexible with respect to current conditions (like Browderism)? Did he use the radicalization of students and campus life during the 1960s as a way of promoting and legitimizing his views? Was he really concerned with or trying to promote progressive politics? Or, was it all a sophomoric, academic exercise?

In short, did Professor Gouldner view himself as the sorcerer's apprentice conjuring up a resurrected Marxism, or did he view himself as its pathologist and mortician? But why bother with such a lengthy and tortuous exegesis if the purpose was to merely exhume Marxism, like so many others, and then rebury it? He was certainly more than a disillusioned ex-radical turned Cold War warrior and hack like Hook, Howe, Burnham, Kristol, Barbash, Lipset and Bell (mostly Trotskyists).

By any standard, Gouldner's *The Coming Crisis* must be viewed as the penultimate intellectual effort and crowning achievement of a mature scholar at the peak of his career. Whatever else may be said about that work, it cannot be ignored. But what is the main theme of *The Coming Crisis*? As I read it, there is no one unifying or central theme; rather, there are a number of seemingly disparate topics loosely conjoined. But does the Emperor have any clothes; if so, are they new? Here I will briefly deal with six themes and issues raised in *The Coming Crisis*.

First, Gouldner's crisis of Western sociology is really the crisis of American sociology, and the two should not be confused. Thus, the title itself is something of a misnomer and is highly ethnocentric. European sociology has always had many competing intellectual schools and traditions within it. Marxist theory, in its various forms, is only one European sociological tradition. Soviet sociology would later crystallize Marxist theory and legitimize it.

What Gouldner argues, as I understand it, is that Parsonian structural functionalism is imploding ("entropy" is the term he uses), leaving an intellectual vacuum resulting in a "theoretical polycentricism" in American-styled sociology. But the crisis of Parsonian equilibrium theory was also historico-specific. The fact that it was becoming less relevant and explanatory at the time was no accident. This was self-evident to anyone who read a newspaper or watched television as the black ghettos burned, the campuses rioted, and the U.S. pursued a disastrous war in Vietnam. "The system" was hardly in equilibrium. Indeed, it was experiencing the most profound social and political unrest since the 1930s.

If reality was discrediting Parsonian functionalism and its legitimacy as the dominant theoretical school in American sociology, and Gouldner, in turn, set up Marxism as a straw man to similarly dismiss it, the real question becomes: What is going to replace them? And this issue, in my view, is never satisfactorily addressed or elaborated upon by Gouldner. Indeed, it is glossed over. This major flaw cannot be ignored.

Of related significance is that in the nearly thirty-five years since Gouldner's death we have gone from the crisis of American sociology to the decline of the American empire (Fergusson 2005) and the two issues are integrally interrelated. Structural functionalism in u.s. academic sociology closely parallels the consolidation and dominance of *Pax Americana*, especially in the post-World War II period, in the same way that Spencer, Kipling and Spengler are associated with the ascendency of the British Empire.

The converse is equally true. Given the mounting problems in the United States, and the advanced industrialized world more generally, ranging from pollution, unemployment, the debt crisis, economic instability, and military adventurism, to mention a few, suggests that we now live in an increasingly unstable world—one that is characterized by disequilibrium, not self-adjusting stability. Whether Parsonian structural functionalism has any remaining intellectual credibility or explanatory power is highly questionable. To paraphrase Yeats, "The center cannot hold," either geopolitically or intellectually.

Second, many commentators have mistakenly viewed *The Coming Crisis* as a critique of Marxism as an intellectual system, especially within the former Soviet bloc. In this regard they have misunderstood Gouldner's intention. As he himself clearly said, "A systematic analysis…of the crisis of Marxism…is… well beyond…the present study" (Gouldner 1970a: 455).

Gouldner focuses on the seeming convergence between structural functionalism in Western societies, especially the Parsonian equilibrium version, and Soviet Marxism. In particular, he examines the seeming contradiction between Marxism as a philosophy of social change and functionalism as a stabilizing force within a society. But this thesis is hardly new. Political scientists, historians and Kremlinologists, starting in the mid-1960s, all using their own theoretical frameworks and jargon, had already developed the so-called "convergence theory" with respect to the u.s. and the former Soviet Union.

Even the term "theoretical 'polycentricism'" used by Gouldner is not original and was borrowed from Italian Communist Party leader Palmiero Togliatti, who used it in 1956 in reference to the 1948 Tito-Stalin dispute, signalling the advent of what journalist-historian Richard Lowenthal referred to as "pluralistic communism"—that is, "polycentric communism" or "Eurocommunism." He makes no reference or citations to this literature (Lowenthal 1965).

Nevertheless, his exposition effectively outlines a lengthy analysis and critique of Marxism, albeit from a so-called "critical" perspective based on a purportedly Hegelian Marxist approach, rather than the economic determinism allegedly associated with the Second International or Stalinism. Whether Gouldner, in fact, successfully formulates a "Marxist critique of Marxism" is highly problematic given his decidedly muddled and metaphysical approach, which confounds Hegelian dialectics with Marxist dialectical materialism. This is compounded by his occasional flirtation with Maoist subjectivism.

Furthermore, it is certainly significant that Gouldner, as an alleged "radical" sociologist makes absolutely no reference in the book's index to "workers," "working class," "class," or "class analysis"; "social stratification" and "proletariat" merit fewer than a dozen citations. These topics are notable by their absence. To discuss or analyze Marxism without reference to the working class or the organization of work is an oxymoron.

Third, many reviewers of *The Coming Crisis* have suggested that one of its major contributions is to demonstrate that the social sciences and its various practitioners, including academic sociologists, are not neutral in their assumptions, constructs, research, or conclusions. In short, social scientists, regardless of discipline, incorporate a set of ideological values and biases into their work. But this surely turns the obvious into the profound.

The truths of the matter is that debates and discussions about a so-called "value free" social science had already been going on for decades, if not centuries, and are hardly new (Winch 1958; Blackburn 1972) Philosophers of history and science, for instance, had been dealing with this issue for more than two centuries. In the U.S., some disciplines such as economics had discussed, albeit from differing ideological perspectives, whether it is a "positive science," that is, "value free" or a "science" at all for at least 40 years.

And during the heady days of radical student politics in the 1960s and 1970s other disciplines such as political science, history, criminology, and anthropology, as well as sociology, initiated a fundamental re-examination of their respective discipline's hidden ideological biases. Many professional associations were forced to sponsor "alternative" caucus sessions challenging the dominant framework and theories of their disciplines in order to address the issues of the day.

A corollary issue dealt with in *The Coming Crisis* is the supposedly new insight that there is a "hegemonic" "paradigm" (to use Antonio Gramsci and Thomas Kuhn's terms, respectively), that is, a dominant school of thought or theory, and assumptions, within an academic discipline. But again, this is hardly new. Historical examples of intellectual blinders and unquestioned assumptions within academic disciplines and popular culture abound. So why should it shock any competent social scientist that various academic disciplines have hegemonic or dominant theories—liberal pluralism in political science, traditionally Freudianism in psychology, the neo-classical competitive model in economics, sociological positivism and Parsonian functionalism in sociology—and that all intellectual systems import their ideological values and biases into their respective disciplines, in turn, affecting their analyses, conclusions and policy prescriptions. Why should this surprise anyone?

What is uniquely, and quaintly, American about all these dominant schools in the social sciences is that they are based on an equilibrium model and the individual, unlike the Marxian conflict model based on social classes and collective behaviour. In short, *The Coming Crisis* with its emphasis on exposing the underlying ideological biases of the social sciences, including sociology and Marxism, is like a teenager discovering sex.

A fourth reaction to *The Coming Crisis* relates to its clarion call for what Gouldner termed "reflexive sociology." By this, as I understand it, he means social science practitioners—and their discipline collectively—should engage in self-examination, or introspection, and reassess the assumptions, biases and practices of their profession and its intellectual work. This would allow certain self-appointed sociologists, and presumably some from other fields, to arrive at a state of supposed "enlightenment" to form a "community of scholars," no doubt appealing to the vanity of some people. But nowhere does Gouldner address serious educational policy issues such as C.P. Snow's *The Two Cultures*—that is, the schism between the humanities and sciences, or affordable higher education in the U.S. It is difficult to take such self-serving musings seriously. Mills, some ten years earlier, put this idea more succinctly when he said, "The sociological imagination is the most fruitful form of this self-consciousness." (Mills 1959: 7)

By any other name "reflexive sociology" is academic or intellectual navel gazing. The problem is that at a certain point such navel gazing, as interesting or fruitful as it may be in some instances, becomes counter-productive and results in diminishing intellectual and political returns. In short, reflexive sociology does not necessarily lead to praxis—that is, political action. This shall be elaborated upon shortly.

Fifth, perhaps the most bald and surprising claim in *The Coming Crisis* is that the radicalized university students of the 1960s should be seen as the new revolutionaries or agents of social change (Gouldner 1970a: 400–401). That such a prominent sociologist could make such a flat assertion, without serious analysis or qualification, is more than troubling. Fortunately, Gouldner didn't go quite as far as some and suggest that youth are a "new class" (Rowntree 1968). Gouldner's claim, in retrospect, reads more like a New Left or SDS manifesto, rather than serious political sociology or political economy. Certainly his assertion has self-destructed under the weight of historical and political reality over the past forty years.

If Gouldner wanted to repeat the droll observation that the leadership of various left-wing revolutionary movements historically have tended to be young workers, intellectuals, or professionals such as Engels, Lenin, Stalin, Trotsky, Tito, Mao, Ho, Castro, Guevara, and many Third World leaders, he would have been on firmer ground. But students as revolutionaries, or as independent agents of social change? That is pure fantasy or wish fulfillment. Students are a stratum within their respective social class.

Contrary to his assertion that, "This [student] radicalism…seems to be a… new social movement" (Gouldner 1970a: 400), the brutal fact is that so-called student radicals, never a homogeneous group, lost their generational cohesiveness and shot their political bolt when they left the sinecure of their universities. Without a political organization to hold them together as a progressive force, they were atomized in the labour market and rendered impotent.

Surprisingly, Professor Gouldner seemed to have been unfamiliar with some areas of Marxist scholarship at the time in history, political science and economics. Thus, there are no references or citations to the work of Barrington Moore, Jr, Stanley Moore, Paul Sweezy, Paul Baran, James O'Connor, Ralph Miliband, Harry Braverman, E.P. Thompson, or the later work of Perry Anderson; nor is there any reference to the standard histories by Isaac Deutscher and E. H. Carr. Indeed, what is profoundly disturbing, if not alarming, is the pervasive un-and anti-historical nature of Gouldner's analysis—that is, its lack of historical context bordering on ahistoricism.

Sixth, and last, as Engels once said, "Marxism is a guide to action." If Marxism had not been revitalized by revolutionary activity in the early part of the twentieth century and bolstered by the success of the Russian Revolution, it would have died and been relegated to a short section or footnote in a philosophy textbook and would have been forgotten. Both Marx and Lenin spoke of the need to adapt political strategy, tactics, and presumably party organization, to historico-specific national conditions (Marx and Engels 1964: 93; Lenin 1925). Consequently, the creation of the Leninist party in response to specific Russian circumstances, transformed abstract political philosophy into concrete, programmatic, and successful praxis, that is, political action. Marx himself in the

Manifesto readily acknowledged that other models of transition may exist, including the electoral road, while Lenin railed against the "Russification" of revolutionary strategy and tactics in the west.

What seems to have vexed Gouldner the most is Marxism's claim that it is an "objective science." But why should this upset anybody? Any variety of neo-classical (i.e., mainstream) economists and supporters of the *status quo* such as F.A. Hayek, T.C. Koopmans, Paul Samuelson and Milton Friedman, amongst others, have claimed that economics is a "positive" or "objective science." So why shouldn't Marxian economics make a similar claim? The issue is not one of "biases," but, rather, what is epistemologically meant by "science." That is, can any social science discipline be considered a "science" with "objective laws"? But that, too, is old intellectual terrain.

What Gouldner has fundamentally done—personally and intellectually—is transform Marxism into Marxology. And this distinction is critical—intellectually and politically. That is, Marxism is no longer studied as a change-oriented political theory or philosophy leading to concrete political action, but is studied as just another abstract or esoteric subject within the history of ideas. In academia in the 1970s and 1980s, this became known as the "Marx(ism)-industry." Many prominent academic careers in various disciplines were built and thrived on this footnote-swapping blood sport. Gouldner, in fairness, was not the first or only person to engage in such a practice. He himself presciently and pre-emptively observed that, "Criticism is sometimes a way...men can draw...quick notice to themselves" (Gouldner 1970a:15); however, as someone else noted, "some people make the revolution, others live off it."

Gouldner's Marxology effectively emasculates and truncates Marxism by reducing it to nothing more than an abstruse and rarified philosophy, devoid of *realpolitik*. This is academic gamesmanship, not Marxism. The most fundamental tenet of Marxism, which has been obscured and forgotten by some, is that it is an ideology and method of socio-economic analysis intended to promote political action and social change. Those who do not understand this do not understand Marxism.

In terms of promoting political action and social change, Gouldner's critique of Marxism is a dead-end and leads nowhere except to perpetual navel gazing, footnote swapping, political paralysis, and another round of drinks at the faculty club. And that is the critical difference between rarified ideas in the world of academia and the politics of the street.

But we should ask, in the spirit of Socrates's dictum to critically examine one's life—that is, to be "reflexive" or engage in "auto-criticism," whether Marxism or left-wing political theory has led to changing a person's personal and political praxis and the way they live. Has that person become politically involved? What causes have they embraced? Most importantly, perhaps, is whether a person's lifetime intellectual work has left the world a better place. And that is the criterion—the standard—by which any person's intellectual efforts and contribution should, in my opinion, be judged.

What Professor Gouldner has eloquently proven, despite himself, notwithstanding his considerable erudite academic contribution to critical theory, is the veracity of Marx's oft-quoted statement, that "Philosophers have only interpreted the world in various ways; the point…is to change it."

Alvin W. Gouldner: Conclusion

In the final analysis, what assessment can be made of Professor Alvin W. Gouldner, the often abrasive and "difficult" man and critical sociologist? He is not here to defend or explain himself, which is certainly unfair and possibly results in bias, thus rendering any final judgment premature and prejudicial.

Alvin W. Gouldner is sociology's controversial iconoclast and gadfly, an intellectual street fighter and lone wolf. He was both feared and respected. Such people are rarely liked, regardless of their contribution. Whether he is allowed to enter the Pantheon of Sociology remains to be seen. Nevertheless, he still casts a long shadow over sociology and critical theory, as he does over the lives of many people.

This undutiful and rebellious son would have to conclude, based on the evidence, that Alvin Ward Gouldner, the man and the scholar, the complicated and tough outsider, was a brilliant son-of-a-bitch. But does one ever really know or understand their parents?

Richard Lee Deaton, Ph.D., LL.B.
Ottawa, Canada
Summer, 2014

Acknowledgments

Seven or eight years ago (maybe longer, I do not keep good track of these sort of things), I received an email from a young woman from Canada who informed me rather matter-of-factly, "I am Alvin Gouldner's granddaughter." Her name was Shoshanah Deaton, and she was a student at a university in Ottawa. She went on to explain that she didn't know much about her grandfather because the family didn't talk much about him, and that she was pleased to have come across my 1999 book *Alvin W. Gouldner: Sociologist and Outlaw Marxist*. She said that she would be giving the book to her father, Richard Deaton, after she finished reading it, and that he might be in touch with me in the future.

Perhaps several months later I received a very long and thoughtful "critique" of the book from Richard, and that was the beginning of a long correspondence—mainly by email, sometimes by phone—between us. At some point early on, after I had signed the contract for this book with Brill, it struck me that it would make a lot of sense to invite Richard to write the Foreword to the book, and thankfully he agreed. Although he was prompt in completing the foreword, I was still lagging badly after having missed a few deadlines and had to reassure him several times that at some point I would actually complete the book. The book is finally completed, and of course it is all the much better because of Deaton's foreword.

So obviously a very big thank you has to go out to Richard Deaton for contributing mightily to this project. His insights into Gouldner the man, the father, and the scholar are truly interesting and informational, providing a backdrop for the general discussion of Gouldner's thought that I tackled in the book. Richard was also a very important family contact for giving the okay for me to use various correspondences and unpublished works of Gouldner appearing in the book. On this point I also offer him a debt of gratitude.

I also thank my family—my wife Mandana, my daughter Ariana, and my son Johnny—for putting up all these years with my writing projects which sometimes take me away from them more than they (and I) would like. Yet love and understanding transcend all, and at the end of the day it's all good. I would also like to thank Stephen Turner at University of South Florida who dutifully read some of the chapters—I sent them sometimes unsolicited, but never heard a complaint or the standard "I'm too busy"—and really appreciate his friendship and collegiality throughout the course of writing this book.

And finally, I want to thank the editorial team at Brill. David Fasenfest was a pleasure to work with and was understanding about some of the things that emerged over the course of writing this book that led to delays.

List of Figures

5.1　First Page of Gouldner's FBI File　93
6.1　Cybernetic Ordering of the Human Condition　133
6.2　Cybernetic Ordering of the Telic System (G-Cell of Human Action System)　138
9.1　The Functions of the Sociology Subsystem (Burawoy's Categories)　199

CHAPTER 1

The Classics and Beyond

Introduction

Scientific disciplines are set up ostensibly as organized efforts to explain particular phenomena that are said to be pertinent to particular fields of study. In the social sciences, for example, economists study financial matters, political scientists study voting (among other things related to the polity), historians study the human past, psychologists specialize in the human person, and so forth. In each of these fields, individuals are trained and socialized into an understanding of prevailing concepts and principles relevant to their field or subfield. Along the way, individuals are also taught that a consensus exists about which authors are worthy of being read and which others have been relegated to the dustbin of history.

In my home discipline, sociology, there are rather clear cut guidelines reflecting a consensus about which thinkers are considered sociological classics, that is, old-timers who are still considered worth reading today, whose thought still presumably is pertinent to contemporary efforts at explaining sociological phenomena. Most sociologists are taught that there was a classical phase in which important contributions were made which helped established the field and gave those who call themselves sociologists the ability to make authoritative proclamations about all things social. This classical period was said to have extended over four decades, from 1880 to 1920. It coincides roughly with the publication in 1883 of Lester Ward's two-volume *Dynamic Sociology*, and ends with the death of Weber in 1920.[1]

Alvin Gouldner has his own take on periodization or eras within the development of sociology, and we will cover this shortly. However, here is the point I wish to make in talking about disciplinary consensus and the history of the field. In the end, a disciplinary consensus—in which thinkers are "in" or "out" at any given moment—is not very useful to the practicing sociologist. This is because sociologists have the liberty to read anybody they want, whether or not they are currently sanctioned as thinkers deserving of our attention. Most of us in academia are in the business of writing books and journal articles, and

---

1 With regard to the ending of the classical period signaled by the passing of Weber, I follow Poggi (1996: 41) in noting that Weber was "the last of the universally acknowledged sociology classics to die."

these remain available in libraries or, increasingly, online. It really doesn't matter how much dust has piled up on a book. You can do an author search, look for a title, and see if it's available. If it is available, you may discover that it has not been checked out for years, maybe decades. But so what? Just blow off the dust, tuck it under your arm, and read that book and learn from it. For the beauty of all this is that books don't just magically vanish from the shelves when their authors have fallen out of favor. They are there for the taking and for the reading. Really, the moral of this story is: To hell with disciplinary consensus. After you reach a certain point in your career—perhaps full professor with tenure—you can chart your own course, and read the authors you WANT to read. At this point in one's career, one need not kowtow to scientific peer pressure (Van Flandern 1993). Hopefully the choice of authors will coincide with the various courses you're required to teach, but often they do not. But this is not alarming: Almost all of us experience tensions between the topics that consume our time in the classroom and those of our research and writing.

Gouldner died in 1980 and his ideas have appeared only sporadically within the broader sociological enterprise since that time. Of course, Gouldner is the author of a citation classic, his 1960 paper "The Norm of Reciprocity," which as of 2015 is still one of the most-often cited articles written by a sociologist. Yet, as many have pointed out, the frequent citing of Norm of Reciprocity is often perfunctory and generally not central to the theoretical approach being used by the citing author. It is simply used as a famous and early statement on the nature of human cooperation, that is, the things people do to maintain exchange relations, usually in a work setting. (Indeed, the majority of cites to this paper are not being made by sociologists per se, but more often by psychologists and organization scholars.)

Making Sense of the Classics

It should come as no surprise, given the discussion thus far, that there are many ways of making sense of the classics in sociology. A sampling from a very large literature will have to do for now. Bryan Turner (2006) argued that there are three components to classical sociology, these being:

- A concern with the "social," broadly understood, as opposed to nature;
- A search or conceptualization of features or forces of society which transcend the individual in order to avoid the problem of methodological individualism or psychological reductionism; and

- A critical stance toward explanation, as sociological insights are by their design often counterpoised against mere commonsense.

Turner goes further and distinguishes classical sociology from classicality, the latter consisting of the three elements above regardless of whether or not the thinker was ever a sociologist (for example, Marx was clearly never an actual, working sociologist). Turner's approach is deeply problematic. For one, he seems to have no true sense of the periodization of classical sociology. An indication of this is his continual referral to Talcott Parsons as a "classic." Turner (2006:135) makes the absurd claim that "classical sociology came to an end with the publication of *Structure of Social Action* (Parsons 1937)." Actually, this book was published far after the closing of the classical era, which was 1920. Parsons was born in 1902, and in that year a true classical sociologist—indeed, the founder of American sociology—Lester Ward, was 61 years old! Parsons' earliest writings in sociology appeared in the 1930s, at least a decade after the end of the classical era. At best, Parsons may be referred to as a post-classical thinker whose writings represent a bridge between the earlier classical period and the later contemporary era of sociology.

A second problem with Turner's approach to the classics is the aforementioned distinction he makes between classical sociology and classicality. Let us consider again Turner's (2006: 135) definition of classicality, which is "the quest to understand and define the 'social' as a field of special intellectual endeavor, but also to grasp the social as a moral phenomenon distinct from egoistic individualism." Anyone who seeks to explain the social in ways described by Turner, especially the moral component, is said to be engaging in "classicality," and that project continues on into the contemporary era. But, why this extra term "classicality"? It seems strained and unnecessary. Turner is actually describing the sociological approach, which is circumscribed by the admonition that the moral dimension must be emphasized, which has the effect of defining out certain perspectives as non-sociological, for example, rational choice theory.

On another front, Connell (1997) rejects the idea of a classical canon representing fundamental insights into the social by a coterie of thinkers (mainly white and male) writing during the period 1880 to 1920. Connell rejects standard classical sociology because of its elitism, as women and persons of color were virtually invisible in the founding stories about who from the past are deserving of continuing recognition. Connell did note that, circa the 1990s, there was an attempt to correct some of the classist, sexist, and racist proclivities of sociology's origin story by engaging in a sort of "affirmative action" rethinking of the classical canon, opening it up to more women (e.g., Jane Addams) and persons of color (e.g., W.E.B. Du Bois) who had been unfairly neglected. Yet, Connell believes this is merely cosmetic, and does not speak to other more fundamental problems in the idea of the classics. For example, classical sociology was supposed to have been developed as a concerted effort to understand modernity, yet most of the sociologists writing in the late 1800s were not really interested in modernity (circa their time, in the late 1800s) at all. Instead of classical sociology, Connell suggests that we ought to do a better, more thorough job of studying the actual history of the societies within which sociology started appearing as a systematic intellectual effort, rather than referring to those texts that are considered canonical (Marx, Durkheim, Weber, etc.).

Franco Ferrarotti's (2003) take on the classics represents the broader, more inclusive idea of what counts as a sociological classic more typical of the European approach. For example, in his book *An Invitation to Classical Sociology*, Ferrarotti has chapters on Adam Ferguson, Pierre-Joseph Proudhon, and Richard Tawney, each clearly not sociologists. Certainly these three were important and influential philosophers, economists, or political scientists, but they were not sociologists. Ferrarotti also apes most other observers in defending the position that Marx is not only a sociological classic, but also even the premier one. He admits, however, that Marx's starting point is really political rather than sociological, but then defends this position by arguing also that Tocqueville, Comte, Spencer, and even Machiavelli are similarly operating from a political point of view. But there is a difference between all these thinkers on the basis of the historical and biographical evidence that can be gathered by anyone who wishes to do so. Marx never did any sociology, never referred to sociology in his own work, and never set out to solve sociological problems and identify them as such. He also was never interested in contributing to the development and advancement of sociology as a scientific discipline within the academy. The same holds for Machiavelli and Tocqueville. On the other hand, Comte and Spencer, although philosophers, did identify at least some of what they did as sociology and referred to it as such.

This issue of who should count as a sociological classic, or even backtracking a bit, thinking about what counts as a sociological classic in the first place, has been clarified somewhat in the work of Peter Baehr. Baehr (2002) argues that the idea of "founders" or "founding fathers" has at least four distinct meanings as it has been used in sociology. One type of founder is a "discursive founder," meaning that he or she came up with signal ideas or concepts which coalesced into paradigms within sociology over a number of years and led to a general consensus that this amounted to an enduring contribution to the discipline at large. An example of discursive founders are Comte's establishment of the positivist paradigm, or Weber's contribution to interpretive understanding

(*Verstehen*) as a viable method for sociology. These founders, so the sentiment goes, pioneered discourses which were shown to be efficacious over time and which are identified as essential frameworks for doing sociology.

A second type of founder is an "institutional founder," namely, a thinker who clearly worked in sociology and identified himself as such, helping in the early stages to administer ideas and resources toward the establishment of sociology as a scientific discipline. Notice that discursive founders need not be institutional founders, for clearly by no stretch of the imagination could Marx be considered an institutional founder—since he never worked or identified as a sociologist—yet many contemporary sociologists argue that he is a discursive founder.

Further, the ability to verify claims of institutional founding is more direct and palpable than the verification of claims of discursive founding, because the former is an empirical question that can readily be checked against the historical record. For example, I can scan through the fifty volumes of the collected works of Marx and Engels and find no use of the term sociology, and I can check what they did and note that they never held positions in any university setting, and certainly never had aspirations to further sociology as an academic field. On the other hand, there are no accepted criteria for accepting or verifying that thinker X is actually a discursive founder while thinker Y is not. The nature of arguing for a discursive founder is aporetic, that is, open-ended, hypothetical, and contestable (Baehr 2002: 9).

Within the interstices of these two types of founders, there are two more themes that have emerged in the sociological classics literature. That is, founders can be identified as either deliberative founders or appropriated founders. "Deliberative founders" are persons who are easily identified, according to the historical record and the evidence of their writings, as viewing their work in sociology as a primary effort to contribute to sociology as an intellectual enterprise. That is, they set out clearly, overtly, and with deliberation to put their conceptual stamp on what sociology should be and look like. In effect, this work was their prime intellectual vocation, perhaps even their master status. Simmel's concept of pure sociology, Durkheim's social facts, Ward's concepts of telesis, synergy, and the distinction between pure and applied sociology, and Weber's *Verstehen* approach, are all examples of the work of deliberative sociological founders.

Another way founders have been discussed and understood is by appropriation. These "appropriated founders" clearly did not work within sociology as either institutional or deliberative founders, but their ideas were picked up by later generations of sociologists and identified as canonical many years after the fact. Examples are numerous, including Gouldner's assertion that Plato was the founder of western social theory, Giddings' notion that Adam Smith was the true founder of sociology (although clearly working within economics and philosophy), and of course the claims that Marx was a sociological classic especially beginning in the 1960s, almost a century after most of his intellectual work had been completed.

Alan Sica's (1997) interesting take on this subject is launched with what he claims to be an unserious and superficial adoption by the sociological community of Merton's distinction between the history and systematics in the development of sociological theory. In short, the field wrongly interpreted Merton in believing the history of ideas should be abandoned in favor of the production of theoretical research programs tied to empirical content, such as is the case, for example, of status characteristics theory or network exchange theory. This has led to a wholesale diminution of the status of the classics in sociology, whereby many sociologists "remain unconcerned about the field's heritage" (Sica 1997: 283). This observation is doubly ironic, because many contemporary sociologists who claim to take the classics seriously, hence bucking the trend toward the neglect of the classics as described by Sica, actually do not have a firm grasp of sociology's heritage. The biggest and grandest error is, of course, the claim that Marx was a founding sociologist. He was not, of course.

But getting back briefly to the "old" way of understanding the classics, that is, that the classical era of sociology ran from roughly 1880 to 1920. It now seems, circa 2015, that there is a movement to do away entirely with this periodization, and it is occurring along two fronts. One of these currents, which have been in play probably since the mid-1990s, is to drop the term "sociological" entirely in favor of the more generic or diffuse "social" when referring to either theory or the classics. This has the advantage of allowing scholars in our field to claim that persons writing clearly outside of sociology or well before its institutionalization in the academy are, after all, sociologists. This means that sociologists can claim philosophers stretching back to the time of the ancient Greeks as their own. Under the rubric of "social," Rousseau becomes a sociological classic, and so do Tocqueville, Vico, Adam Smith, and even Ibn Khaldun from the 14th century. This allows the smuggling in of virtually anyone from any field and from any time in history, just as long as there is a glint, however faint, of a "sociological" orientation in her or his writings. They never have to utter the word "sociology," never have to identify themselves self-consciously as sociologists, never have to define what they were doing as contributing to the solving of sociological puzzles.

The use of "social theory" instead of "sociological theory" by sociologists could also be rising because of the claim that disciplinary boundaries are eroding and that that vaunted object of study specifically set aside for sociologists—society—cannot be left only to them. Now we have economists, anthropologists, philosophers, political scientists, historians, linguists, criminologists, social workers, psychologists, demographers, public health advocates, urban planners, and the newly evolving field of cultural studies—all of these and more are showing interest in society or its characteristics or components (structural, cultural, geographic, etc.), and they may be reading classical or contemporary sociologists to boot. Even more likely, though, is that sociologists are reading all these other persons and perspectives and gleaning from them ideas about how best to make sense of the social. Stephen Turner (1996) attempts to generalize the movement towards social theory (and away from a narrower sociological theory) by claiming theorizing about the social is a deeply human undertaking, which resists disciplinary capture. It is characterized by the ceaseless struggle between the head and heart, between the intellectualism of the systematics of theory on the one hand, and the lived experience of the history of theory, whereby solidarity is forged with thinkers whose biography and other noncognitive elements of the enterprise are judged compelling, on the other.

A second current in the reworking of the definition of "classical sociology" is to push the closing of the classical era beyond 1920. Many contemporary observers believe that limiting the era of classical sociology to coincide merely with its institutionalization in the academy is nostalgic or antiquarian. As Charles Turner (2010: 9) has described it, clinging to the traditional periodization of classical sociology is little more than a "quest for a glorious but unrecoverable past." It now appears that a number of writers are trying to defend the idea that the end of the classical era should be understood as the 1930s or even the 1940s. This move has the singular effect of absorbing Talcott Parsons into the classical canon, quite handy for those who argue that Parsons' work is no longer pertinent to concerns in contemporary sociology.

I believe that both of these current trends are misguided, and the only thing that one can do, while one still has the ability to write and get published, is to bring this "bad news" to the sociological community writ large and inform them why it is misguided. Some of these issues will crop up throughout the book, taking the form of an engagement with Gouldner over the classics and how to understand them. Gouldner developed his own four-period explanation of the development of sociology as an academic discipline, paralleling many of the historical events discussed above. After listing and briefly discussing the four periods, I will point out some problems in Gouldner's view of classical sociology.

Four Periods in the Development of Sociology

Gouldner's four-period development of sociology begins with what he refers to as "sociological positivism." This period runs roughly from 1824 with the advent of positivism within philosophy, which argues that in order truly to understand society we must divest ourselves of superstition, theology, and speculative or idealistic philosophy in favor of the tried and true methods of the natural sciences that emphasize precise measurement and observation of social phenomena. Gouldner argues that it was Henri Saint-Simon, rather than Auguste Comte, who was the more profound influence on the development of philosophical positivism. Gouldner (1970a: 89–91) believes that Saint-Simon predicted how this new science of society—sociology, which he (Saint-Simon) never named—would be needed in the face of social upheavals (such as the French Revolution beginning in 1789) and the ongoing expansion of the scientific revolution to the social realm. In this earliest phase of the development of positivism, in the hands of Saint-Simon sociology would act as a counterbalance to individualistic utilitarian culture. Saint-Simon was a socialist, and as such was concerned with rescuing society from the encroachment of a vulgar economism that emphasized individual utility, productivity, and consumerism. The radical sensibilities of Saint-Simon appealed more to Gouldner, a radical sociologist himself, than did Comte, whose conservatism appeared for example in his favoring a cognitive elite of entrepreneurs, financiers, and intellectuals over the lowly masses who could never comprehend or put into practice positivist principles. Indeed, following the model of the Catholic Church, Comte envisioned himself as the high priest of this new religion of humanity called positivism. Comte's earliest version of sociology, which he named in 1838, was based to a large extent on an unreflective acceptance of utilitarian notions from Bentham. According to standard utilitarianism, pleasure and pain are the basic engines of all life, and within human social life the assumption is that persons will gravitate toward activities that maximize their pleasure and minimize their pain.

Gouldner's second period in the establishment of sociology is Marxism. According to Gouldner, although Marxism held to a notion of social utility, it rejected Bentham's vulgar, economistic utilitarianism primary because of the way it smuggles in notions of profit—insofar as the hedonic calculus directs human beings to maximize pleasure while minimizing pain—as the central ontology of human social action. For Marx, the profit motive is not an enduring essence of all human beings; rather, it reflects a distortion or false consciousness within the capitalist system itself. Marx did not have much good to say about Bentham or Comte for that matter. Gouldner (1970a: 109) cites a biting criticism of Bentham by Marx, whom he referred to as that "...insipid, pedantic, leather-tongued oracle of the commonplace bourgeois intelligence of the nineteenth century." Marx was also critical of Bentham's lack of reflexivity, in that he assumed that what was good for the capitalists was good for everyone else. According to this critical stance toward Bentham, utility is not an eternal, universal feature of human nature which cuts across all classes, times, and levels of social development.

One of the glaring problems of Gouldner's second period is that all the developments attributable to the work of Marx and Engels happened outside sociology proper. In later writings, Gouldner did indeed indicate that the development of Marxism and sociology occurred independently of each other. For example, in Gouldner's (1980a: 374–375) response to Göran Therborn's description of him as belonging to the "American ideology" alongside other American sociologists such as Parsons, Mills, and Merton, he stated, "Therborn maintains a stony silence about the fact that Marxism and sociology thus have at least one ancestor in common, Henri Saint-Simon."

It is true that some—but only a handful—of sociological thinkers were influenced by the thought of Marx and Engels up through the 1920s. Several that readily come to mind are Albion Small (1912) and Werner Sombart (1902). In his *Contemporary Sociological Theories*, published in 1928, Pitirim Sorokin identified certain aspects of Marx and Engels' writings as "sociological," even while failing to point out that they never used the term "sociology" and were not interested in contributing to sociology as a scientific discipline. There were also later sociologists of the Frankfurt School who held to various aspects of Marxism as essential to conducting sociological analysis (for a summary, see Bottomore 1984 and Jay 1973). It was not until the 1960s that consensus solidified around the idea that Marx is a sociological classic. Yet during Marx's lifetime—he died in 1883—sociology was never on the radar as an active orientation in any of Marx's work, and very few people up to the time of his death ever spoke of him as a sociologist. Hence, Gouldner's notion that there was a second era of development in sociology that could be characterized as "Marxist" is a complete fantasy. This period of development did occur, but it was not of or for sociology. If anything, it was of philosophy, political economy, and political activism, which fell outside of the stream of intellectual development within sociology as a discipline or school of thought.

The label Gouldner applies to his third period is "classical sociology." He gets the periodization of the classical era right, which he describes as beginning in the last quarter of the nineteenth century and lasting until about World War I. This is consistent with the traditional understanding of the classical period as running from 1880 through 1920.[2] It is interesting to note that here Gouldner is acknowledging that Marx and Marxism had nothing to do with the era of classical sociology, since he treats these as two distinct eras. The error he makes, of course, is that he refers to his second sociological era as Marxism when in fact there were no meaningful connections between Marxism and the discipline of sociology prior to the classical era. It is also worth noting that contemporary sociologists, looking back on the sociological classics, are now lumping in Marx with the sociological classics, thereby denying the fact that Marx was appropriated later into the discipline as a backward-looking exercise beginning in the 1960s. Gouldner also gets right the decline of evolutionism during the classical era and how it was connected with the rise of functionalism, as well as his description of the continuities between positivism and functionalism.

Finally, Gouldner sees the fourth era of the development of sociology embodied in the emergence of Parsonian structural functionalism. Gouldner (1970a: 138) locates the beginning of this fourth period as "the late 1930s," with primary development in the United States. He argues that Parsons was reacting to two things simultaneously: the Great Depression and the rise of Marxism and communism in Russia and across Eurasia. Since Gouldner sees politics lying behind everything we do, Parsons was scrabbling together a voluntaristic theory of action—built upon German romanticism by way of Weber—as a way of sending the message that, in no uncertain terms, the capitalist system would survive the tensions it had been experiencing over the last several decades. This was a new optimistic and activist formulation of sociological romanticism; in effect, Parsons had "Americanized" German romanticism (Gouldner 1970a: 139). Parsons' emphasis on value-free and objective science—an emphasis he learned from Weber—meant that those students who came to study with him at Harvard could study the problems of the economy, the rise of communism, and the impending world war through a posture of detachment. As things to be studied objectively, Parsons and his students needed never question the existing order or the suffering many were experiencing all around them. These Harvard students could take solace that their ivory towers created a protective remoteness from the society which engineered these social problems in the first place (Gouldner 1970a: 175).

---

2 Gouldner's periodization of the sociological classics is also consistent with that of Schwendinger and Schwendinger (1974), who suggest that the founding of American sociology converged with a particular phase in the development of liberalism, specifically, corporate liberalism which gained ascendancy during the Progressive Era. This era ran from 1883 to 1922, bookended on each side by the publication of Ward's *Dynamic Sociology* in 1883 and Ogburn's *Social Change* in 1922.

Why is Gouldner taking so many potshots at Parsons and Harvard here? After all, Gouldner himself was an Ivy Leaguer, having studied with Merton at Columbia University. Was it simple competition, that is, between Harvard and Columbia, or between the master Parsons and his former student Merton? Perhaps both of these played a part in Gouldner's vitriol, but even more likely was the simple fact that as a self-identified radical sociologist, Gouldner was trying hard to write Marx into the sociological cannon while simultaneously jettisoning Parsons from the lofty perch he had attained by the 1950s and 1960s as the preeminent contemporary sociologist. Gouldner's elitism and lack of reflexivity is evident here. He believes that his Ivy League education is protected from the charge of elitism and detachment because of the way he came up through the ranks, from relatively humble beginnings as an immigrant Jew growing up in the Bronx. Parsons, on the other hand, was always around privilege of one sort or another, steeped in American Midwest parochialism and socialized into the values of religion and education from an early age. Gouldner was a Jew, but not a practicing Jew—as discussed by Richard Deaton in his foreword to the book—and his liberalism and secularism were compatible with the radical sensibilities which made Marxism a congenial system of thought. It went further than this, though. Gouldner and other radical sociologists of the fifties and sixties took it upon themselves to redefine Marx as a classical sociologist—indeed, the imminent classic—because they were desperate to import his radicalism into sociology and, indeed, to identify the evaluative paradigm as central to the sociological enterprise.

But, what of this business of the evaluative paradigm in sociology? In a 1963 paper, Helmut Wagner made the argument that there are three basic paradigms in sociology, namely, the positivist, the interpretive, and the evaluative. Summarizing Wagner (1963) briefly, the oldest of the sociological paradigms is the positivist, deriving of course from Comte. The characteristics of positivism include:

- Treats sociology as if it were a natural science;
- Concerned with explaining "what is" and believes in the possibility of value-free or objective knowledge;
- Emphasizes causal analysis, that is, deductive-nomothetic causation, by way of quantitative methods;
- Searches for universal covering laws;
- Deals with observable phenomena (of the five senses);
- No special methods are needed beyond those already established within the natural sciences;
- Examples of theories under the positivist rubric include behaviorism, functionalism, biological, ecological, mathematical, and some network approaches.

The main characteristics of the interpretive paradigm according to Wagner are:

- Sociology is a social science requiring different theories and methods than those of the natural sciences;
- Believes in explaining "what is" but has less faith than the positivists in the idea that by following the protocols of the scientific method biases, preferences, predilections, and values can be held at bay;
- Emphasizes interpretive understanding (*Verstehen*);
- Rather than the uncovering of universal truths, the goal is the more pragmatic or limited development of sensitizing concepts;
- Deals with both objective and subjective phenomena;
- Because sociology's objects of study are fundamentally different than those of the natural sciences, qualitative methods are preferred;
- Examples include symbolic interactionism, dramaturgy, phenomenology, and ethnomethodology.

Finally, the main characteristics of the evaluative paradigm are:

- The unity of theory and practice, with practice informed by an explicit normative, ideological, or non-scientific agenda;
- Concerned with "what ought to be" even more so than "what is";
- Most are versions of humanitarian reform theory;
- The identification and amelioration of oppressive social conditions, especially those that produce inequality;
- Rejection of value-free knowledge ("the personal is political");
- Examples include Marxism, feminist theory, critical race theory, and queer theory.

Notice that this was published in 1963, so by this time a consensus was appearing that sociology had an evaluative paradigm—ideological and political in nature rather than scientific, but nevertheless a paradigm—whose progenitor was Marx.

Gouldner, Durkheim, and Saint-Simon

To reiterate, in his 1963 paper Wagner notes the manifestation of an approach within sociology informed by Marx and Marxism even as it is identified as ideological and non-scientific. It is indeed the case that by the 1960s, many sociologists were eager to discuss Marx as a sociological classical, and that

Marxist-inspired critical or conflict theory was a major orientation within the discipline. After 1962 Gouldner himself climbed on the evaluative bandwagon, openly articulating a vision of science for sociology that was critical, hermeneutic, and post-positivist. From this frame of reference, there was really no longer a need to be tolerant of establishment sociology (read: positivism and functionalism), and Gouldner was thereby able to occupy the role of social critic. Indeed, this is what was demanded by the project of the unity of theory and practice.

Even so, there were indications even earlier than this that Gouldner's sensibilities were more in alignment with radical and socialist doctrine than with traditional sociological approaches. For example, Gouldner (1958a) edited a volume of Durkheim's writing on Saint-Simon and socialism, and his radical sensibilities are evident in the introductory essay. By the 1960s the meme in sociology was that Comte, the founder of both sociology and positivism, was "conservative" because of the emphasis he placed on objectivity, value-freedom, and modeling sociology after the natural sciences. Also, Comte was sanguine about the possibility of citizens-at-large working together to forge the just society. Rather than counting on the lowly masses, Comte set himself up as the bishop of his envisioned religion of humanity and entrusted financiers and other men of learning and reason to complete the Enlightenment project of the perfectibility of the human spirit. This came off as elitism (and worse) to Gouldner, so he was eager to find someone else to claim as the "true" founder of sociology.

Gouldner found that more agreeable founder in the guise of Henri Saint-Simon (1760–1825), an early French socialist with whom Comte worked in the early stages of his career. As editor of the volume on Durkheim's writings about Saint-Simon, Gouldner was generally unhappy with the negative tone Durkheim took toward Saint-Simon and his socialist doctrine. Nevertheless, Gouldner (1958a) was happy to point out, especially as discussed in a long footnote on pages ix and x of his introduction, that Durkheim himself acknowledged that Saint-Simon, rather than Comte, was the true founder of both positivism and sociology. In that footnote Gouldner explained that, although Durkheim had made a heroic attempt to dispel the myth that Comte founded sociology, the myth was holding firm even into the contemporary era, which to Gouldner meant that its persistence served some function for the discipline of sociology more broadly. According to Gouldner, the myth of Comte the father has persisted because Saint-Simon was also an early founder of socialist doctrine, and it would have been damaging to sociology's claim to scientific status had the truth been told that it was a socialist after all—Saint-Simon—who was its founder.

This little sidelight is an interesting reminder that sociology's origins are highly contested even to this day, even as a seeming consensus over the status of the "big three" classics—Marx, Durkheim, and Weber—for contemporary sociology has emerged since the 1960s. But it is interesting to note that Gouldner downplayed Saint-Simon's view that, in order to attain the perfectibility of mankind, his early formulation was that society would need strong central leaders—"priests" in Saint-Simon's terminology—forming a supreme council which would oversee the industrial arena and which, by necessity, would dominate all other areas of society. It was this implication of Saint-Simon's thought, that industrialism is the new priesthood as it rises above all other considerations in society, that Durkheim was opposed to (see, e.g., Humphreys 1999). In the end, it appears that the charge of elitism against Comte could have been applied to Saint-Simon and his school equally and as forcefully, yet Gouldner stood mute.

We should also briefly examine the evidence that Saint-Simon was the true founder of sociology, as claimed by Gouldner vis-à-vis Durkheim's writings on Saint-Simon. Durkheim titled Chapter VI of his study "The Doctrine of Saint-Simon: The Founder of Positivism." Durkheim is of course correct, and we could easily agree with him that the historical record confirms that Saint-Simon was the progenitor of positivism even as Comte's name became more famously associated with the doctrine after Saint-Simon's death in 1825. But alas, the historical record also shows that Saint-Simon never named sociology. He did, however, envision the emergence of a new social science based upon the positivist doctrine, which he usually referred to as "scientific politics." Durkheim takes the liberty of reading into the historical record that Saint-Simon innovated sociology within his philosophical work, but he really never did found it. How could he if he never named it? This was left to Comte, who named the discipline in 1838.

Saint-Simon believed that the new social science, which he never actually named "sociology," was beginning to emerge out of earlier Enlightenment efforts by various thinkers to achieve a systematic approach to realizing the perfectibility of humanity and human society. As later interpreters of his work explain (the so-called Saint-Simonians led by Enfantin and Bazard), Saint-Simon believed that the idea of perfectibility was "imperfectly" conceived by earlier thinkers such as Vico, Lessing, Turgot, Kant, Herder, and Condorcet to name a few of the most prominent. Saint-Simon suggested that even as these various thinkers produced works crackling with insights about the human condition, they never knew how to describe human progress fully or accurately. As the Saint-Simonians continue:

> All of them finally overlooked the fact that the only elements that have appeared repeatedly in the past and would interest the future were the Fine Arts, the Sciences, and Industry, and that the study of this triple manifestation of human activity was to constitute social science, because

it served to verify the moral, intellectual, and physical development of
the human race, its ceaseless progress towards the unity of affection, doctrine, and activity.

In IGGERS 1958: 32

But who understood better than Vico, who was actually the first to develop the
idea of a "new science" (in his *Nuova Scienza* from 1725)—predating of course
both Saint Simon and Comte by a century or so—that there are two kinds of
sciences, one dealing with the natural world and one dealing with the human
social world along with its culture and history? Where was Saint-Simon's great
stride forward, even past Vico, in the launching of the new idea of a "social science" or even a "sociology"? As it turns out, it was fictitious; every bit the myth
that Gouldner attributes to the "misguided" notion that Comte was the founder
of sociology.

Conclusion

Confronting Gouldner, as reflected in the title of the book, is an unfair fight. It
is unfair because one member of the argument is living (me) while the other is
dead (Gouldner). This means I can twist and distort Gouldner's words all I
want to suit whatever purposes are at hand. This may be reminiscent of how
some persons characterized Weber's ongoing debate with the ghost of Marx
over such things as materialism versus idealism, the nature of social class, or
the merits of communism (Giddens 1970). All I can say in my defense is that I
will attempt to be fair in my hermeneutic reading of Gouldner and other
authors brought into the discussion. A massive literature has built up over the
last 100 years of sociology's existence, and Gouldner's time in it as an active
participant—roughly from the early 1950s through the mid-1980s (he died in
1980 but an important work of his was published posthumously five years
later)—represents a relatively small trace in relation to the broader trend. In
publishing a second book on Gouldner I make no extravagant claims as to the
merits of Gouldner's thought. This will be left up to the reader to decide. It is
strange, though, that a thinker of Gouldner's stature has not received more
attention. But perhaps I am overestimating whatever stature Gouldner actually attained in the discipline. He never was named president of the ASA, but
very likely this was due to his combativeness and his penchant for stepping on
well-healed toes, rather than for any purely cognitive reasons.

As I documented in my first book (Chriss 1999c), and as attested to by his
son's foreword to this book, Gouldner was an extremely difficult person, and

his aggressiveness and pettiness turned a lot of people against him. Yet, there are glimpses of a sometimes caring and compassionate person away from the publishing world of academia. When Irving Horowitz died he left behind a vast trove of personal papers and correspondences, many of which were connected with his tenure at *Trans-Action* (later *Society*) magazine. Because he was a founding member of the magazine and its one-time editor, Gouldner of course gets heavy play in this material. (This material is contained in the Horowitz Transaction Publishers Archives, available at http://www.libraries.psu.edu/psul/digital/ilh.html.)[3]

For example, in a letter he wrote to Horowitz in the summer of 1964, Gouldner (1964a) tells of a car trip to the west coast. At the top of the letter the address is listed as 2805 Hilgard, Berkeley, California, and it is further stipulated in writing that this would be his temporary address through August 30 1964. As it turns out, this was Erving Goffman's address. Somehow, Gouldner got to stay in Goffman's house for the summer of 1964, presumably vacant because of the then tragic suicide of Goffman's wife. Perhaps Goffman was there, and invited Gouldner for company or whatever. In the letter Gouldner hints that he saw Goffman or at least was in touch with him, writing to Horowitz that "he was as well as you could expect considering his wife's suicide." Gouldner goes on to write that "It turns out that she did this by jumping off the San Rafael bridge," and that "Erving now says that she has so thoroughly upstaged him that no work that he could ever do in the future can command such reality." Although this could have been simply a business deal between two colleagues along the lines of, say, subletting a home for the summer, the tone of the letter implies that Gouldner and Goffman were friends, and that the former was offering support and consideration to the latter.

Another letter from Gouldner to Horowitz on July 6 1962 illustrates this softer or artistic side of Gouldner. Gouldner was writing on the news of the unexpected death of C. Wright Mills, and that he would be willing to contribute to a memorial issue of the magazine being planned for him. On page three, Gouldner offered a poem about Mills, which he sternly reminded Horowitz was for "his eyes only." He had presumably also shared the poem with "the literary critic around here, R.G. Langbaum," who opined that it was "not too bad." Gouldner (1962a) is somewhat proud of it, writing, "it is not a simple-minded eulogy, but a personal and fairly complex reaction." The poem is reprinted in its entirety below.

---

3 In occasionally referencing Gouldner's correspondence and other unpublished writings, I received permission to use this material from Richard Deaton, son of Alvin Gouldner and author of the Foreword to this book.

For Wright Mills

C. Wright Mills died the other day:
The big beefy Texan who use to
Ride motorcycles, build houses
Argue like Hell
And write Sociology
Is gone.

He was not liked by some
Who wear carefully composed faces,
Hold their cards close
To their buttoned-up chests,
And believe that a man should be
A good boy.

I myself never warmed to him
For his hate spattered
Yet he wasn't always that way
He became so, believing it was better
To be a monster
Than a worm.

But I was warmed by him:
For I loved the rasp of his claws
Sharpening on the soft wood.
And I shall remember him returning once,
Saying: Y'all listen here, you bastards,
I'm back.

Gouldner writes about Mills that he did not warm *up* to him because "his hate spattered," yet he goes on to write that he was warmed *by* what society made him into, namely, a tough son of a bitch who decided it was better to be a monster than a worm. This is where Gouldner ended up as well, yet as far as I know no one has written a poem about him. I considered including one here but decided against it because, well, it could be interpreted as a desperate ploy by me to appear more relevant or clever than I really am. No poems, then, but maybe a song or two down the road.

CHAPTER 2

Intellectuals and Radical Sociology

Introduction

Gouldner was trained in the hotbed of establishment sociology circa the 1950s, namely Columbia University. From Merton, Gouldner learned the ropes of conventional sociology and functionalism, even acknowledging that Merton also taught Gouldner to remain skeptical about unquestioned allegiance to certain master voices or proclamations. This is the program of "organized skepticism." Although Gouldner made a name for himself in the field of organizational sociology, his positivist roots were never firmly planted, and by the early 1960s was moving toward the role of social critic and taking a more evaluative stance toward his subject matter. Within this example of Gouldner's shifting allegiances is an interesting story to tell about the basic debate that has continued to plague sociology, and that is, is sociology akin to the natural sciences in which causal explanations are derived from careful, systematic empirical observations of the social world utilizing standard methodologies such as survey research, experiments, and statistical analysis? Or is sociology more of an art or humanities discipline, which seeks truth not through the quest for covering laws of the social universe, but rather through interpretive and evaluative approaches which aims more toward understanding? (Lepenies 1988) Within this discussion I will begin with a theme touched upon in Chapter 1, namely, Vico's conceptualization of a "new science" which emphasized moral, political, historical, and religious elements in opposition to the traditional sciences of the physical universe. I will go on to confront Gouldner on this issue, and I will also engage the two Gouldners (younger and older) in a dialogue with one another over the nature of science reflected in the time periods he (they) were writing.

Back to Vico[1]

In his writings on the new science, Vico (2002) notes that primitive social organization springs first from commonsense religious convictions (e.g., that

---

[1] Vico's writings on the New Science ranged over a period of years beginning in 1725. For this discussion I am using the 2002 edition of *Vico: The First New Science* edited by Leon Pompa.

there is [or are] a supreme beings [or beings] affecting our daily affairs, and that the dead should be buried), which reflected a common will of the people, thereby contributing to primitive social order. Over time, however, this original "vulgar wisdom" is converted into higher or loftier notions about the perfectibility of the race, leading to the formation of the sciences, disciplines, and arts. These newer sciences, disciplines, and arts were all "directed towards the direction and regulation of men's faculties," yet they were all deficient insofar as there had been no systematic study and research on the origins—that is, the history—of the civilizations within which these various undertakings emerged (Vico 2002: 11). These deficiencies of previous studies cited by Vico represent virtually the same argument St. Simon would make almost a century later concerning the failings of those who came before him (including of course Vico), the useful aspects of which could be built upon to erect a true "new science."

Reacting to Descartes who launched the idea that mathematical thinking and reasoning lead us to certitude about (at least) the physical universe, Vico argued that since human beings make the human social world, they should understand it better than nature, the laws of which are not available to experience but must be conjured through mathematical or logical axioms. As Cahnman (1981: 26) observes, "Vico especially objected to Descartes' disregard of history because it was lacking in mathematical certitude." Here Cahnman (1976, 1981) is correct to note that Vico's conceptualization of a new science of humanistic inquiry as a supplement to the (then) establishing natural sciences can certainly be pointed to as a key starting point for what would later be described and understood as the social sciences generally and sociology specifically. It is, according to Cahnman and other authors, an indication that Vico had already hit upon a sociology of knowledge, a historical sociology, and a hermeneutics insofar as the explanation of how people acquire status, property, and other social things must take into account the historical, cultural, and geographical contexts within which lives were configured.[2] Indeed, Marcuse and Neumann (1994: 119) go so far as to suggest that Vico was the first thinker to give a sociological account of social change. The object of study which gave rise to the institutionalization of sociology by the 1880s—this object being society in its totality—had already been articulated by Vico back in 1725, to the extent that the totality of material and non-material culture in its historical development was "the work of men."

---

2 Some additional authors who have made the case that Vico was either doing or had discovered sociology include O'Neill (1976), Stark (1976), and Swinny (1914).

Vico was also correct that the need to commemorate is what creates and sustains society. Versions of collective memory, whether battlefield tourism (think of holocaust museums or the site of the collapse of the World Trade Center), patriotism, nationalistic fervor, cinema, or religious rites and ceremonies, are omnipresent symbols of the self-understandings of large groups of people identifying with each other in shared histories. Commemoration is the self-exploration of a people, represented by the strivings of humanity the stories of which have been passed down from generation to generation (Runia 2007: 316). Here there is something like a fusion of memory with history—not the same thing—insofar as memory is done by living, breathing people in the moment while history is performed by scholars picking over the remains of a lost or forgotten past. Commemoration seeks to keep the past alive, even traumatic events, such as 9–11, that should never be forgotten. These things, the things of memory, contemplation, and shared visions, are what humanity can produce and understand by and for itself. Human beings cannot do the same with nature. It is cold and uncaring, doing what it will behind the backs of the human beings who happen to be alive at any particular moment. Hence, again, we see that Vico's new science champions human involvement in the making, remaking, and commemoration of these social worlds, and this triumphs over antiseptic attempts to explain a detached and uncaring natural world.

Commemoration is consistent with the human ability to externalize, that is, to represent internal experiences to larger circles and groups. And Vico noted that the fundamental human externalization is the practice of burying the dead. Burying the dead set the stage for tradition, for the solidarity of the religious congregation, for transcendence, for epiphany, and most importantly, for culture (Runia 2007: 324). Burying the dead "squares the circle" if you will, simultaneously creating closure and perpetuation: closure for a single life lived, and perpetuation of the memory of that individual in the hearts and minds of those who knew him or her or were told stories about his or her time on earth. Commemoration is the complement of burial, in that it shifts from individuals to events in the memory and retelling. The pilgrimages we make to commemorate events or remember the dead, in tight-knit congregations of like-minded individuals seeking truth and beauty and wisdom together, marks the highlight of the spiritual uplifting of that which goes beyond each of us. It is the shimmering house on the hill that we can see from a distance. We are attracted to it, and set off on sojourns to reach it—sometimes planned, other times spur of the moment—but we never can. It is a shadow, a chimera, yet every bit as vital to our everyday lives as rock, sand, and beaches.

All of this simply makes the point that the importance of something called a human science, distinct from the natural sciences, is something that Vico put on the map as well as anyone. Gouldner's criticisms of the failure of positivistic and establishment science to provide systematic insights into the human social world is consistent with the Vichian argument that human knowledge of history and culture is more secure than that of the natural world. Yet, interestingly enough, Vico was not necessarily comparing culture and history invidiously against nature. Vico's deeply religious sensibilities led him to attempt to understand human cognition and ingenuity as it emerges from the way human beings make their way through a physical world. In his *New Science*, Vico uses the biblical story of the flood to ascertain how politics would look if humans were in the state of nature and bereft of the social relations typical of human civilization. He believes that those who survived the flood—Noah's wayward sons and their descendants—would rapidly lose their humanizing imagination and decline into an animalism based upon the immediate needs of the moment, stuck as they were in the behaviorist hypothesis of stimulus–response. These isolated humans would lose both their civilization and their ability to make nature. As argued by Ephraim (2013: 725), Vico used the story of the flood to explain how men were "rescued from solitude by the intervention of a singular act of nature: a great thunderstorm, the first after centuries of floodwater evaporation."

To overcome such adversity, human beings had to learn to work together to achieve desired results. Vico's naturalism is not really the modern secular version of naturalism, however, because lying behind that great flood was the wrath of God. It was only through family relations, devotional religious practice, and the execution of noble wars (when needed) that the Hebrews and their gentile neighbors maintained sociability and were able to form adequate restraints against the passions (Robertson 2013).[3] These theistic sensibilities lying behind and animating Vico's conceptual arsenal were not palatable to secular humanists like Gouldner, who rarely had anything positive to say about religion (but see Chapters 7 and 8). Even though both St. Simon and Comte sought to construct a new religion of humanity based upon positivist principles, it was merely the attempt to adopt the successful form of organized religion, specifically that of the Catholic Church (Gouldner 1970a: 134), that led these thinkers toward a pseudo-theism.

The Vichian formulation is, as Habermas (1971: 148–149) has argued, the topos of the Scholastic tradition which includes the knowing subject in the

---

3 Indeed, in a letter he wrote to Filippo Maria Monti on November 18, 1724, Vico explained that he would draw the principles of his new science "from within those of sacred history" (Robertson 2013: 16, n. 56).

surrounding world which one either has a hand in creating (culture) or to which one must learn to adapt—preferably in groups—in order to survive and thrive. Actually, this articulation gets too close to a separation or perhaps a dialectical relationship between culture and nature, to the extent that more recent interpreters of Vico have insisted that his conceptual arsenal is shot through with hybridity, not one-sidedness (Ephraim 2013; Robertson 2013). Gouldner was a dialectical or dualistic thinker more than anything else, so he willingly went along with Dilthey's and even Weber's easy distinction between explanation and understanding represented in the chasm between *Naturwissenschaften* and *Geisteswissenschaften* (Ossewaarde 2010).

The Plight of Radical Sociology

Both St. Simon and Comte's ideas of a technocratic sensibility, which would emerge ostensibly as the new guiding force of the industrial era, intrigued Gouldner. For Gouldner, the technocrat is more or less the purveyor of applied science, while the intellectual represents the domain of pure science. It is quite strange that, even as Gouldner took "Ward" as his middle name not by birth but as a gesture of appreciation for the early American sociologist Lester F. Ward, there is no evidence from his earliest writings on the subject on through to his last days that he had ever read—because he never cited—Ward's work on pure versus applied sociology. Although most sociologists are unaware of it, Ward wrote two books on the subject, namely *Pure Sociology* (Ward 1903) and *Applied Sociology* (Ward 1906). This negligence was very likely due to Merton's relative neglect of American sociologists, a penchant he picked up from his teacher Talcott Parsons at Harvard, whose own eurocentrism was legendary.[4]

Gouldner (1957a) published an early paper on the theoretical requirements of the applied social sciences, and this will be the focus of the remainder of the section. Following Ward without citing him, Gouldner suggests that pure sociology is the quest to understand the first principles underlying and animating the phenomena that come to the attention of researchers. Sometimes this is pejoratively referred to as "knowledge for the sake of knowledge" insofar as any

---

4 In Merton's collected writings in *Social Theory and Social Structure*, Ward does appear in the index on three pages. The first two were rather perfunctory citations to the Ross-Ward correspondence as well as to Ward's six-volume mental autobiography *Glimpses of the Cosmos*. A bit later in the book Merton mentions Ward as one of the early cosmological thinkers in sociology who paved the way for later, specialized studies. As far as I know Parsons never cited Ward, although he was mentioned at least once in passing.

research conducted or concepts developed in the particular area of study has no immediate goals for accomplishing anything aside from expanding knowledge in the area under consideration. Applied sociology, on the other hand, speaks to a wider audience than the group of scientists seeking to expand understanding of the operating principles of the particular area under study. The applied social scientists must speak also to lay publics, for they aspire to intervene in their world to some extent according to guidelines developed within the pure stage. The rise of applied social science is the culmination of the unity of theory and practice, and this is why in this paper Gouldner refers to Marx as an applied social scientist par excellence, citing Marx's aphorism that the point is not only to know the world, but to *change* it.

In his discussion of not only Marx but also Durkheim and Freud as applied social scientists, Gouldner (1957a: 94) states "Marx is no Faustian, concerned solely with understanding society, but a Promethean who sought to understand it well enough to influence and to change it." Gouldner goes on to make the caveat that he is making no claim as to the veracity or correctness of the prediction or the soundness of the methodology Marx developed in moving forward towards implementation of the theory. The point is that enough information was included in the project to allow for real-world interventions to take place in the name of the theory (in this case, historical materialism). This is a monumental copout by Gouldner, who states he is here neither to praise nor bury Marxism, but merely to articulate the ways in which it meets the criteria of applied social science. Gouldner is sympathetic to the efforts toward applied social science because of the complexity of the project as it involves speaking to multiple audiences and overcoming obstacles toward implementation. This was written years before Gouldner (1976a) actually developed a more nuanced position on applied sociology, later arguing that any attempts such as these are public projects, or ideologies, which seek not only to put science into practice but also to use whatever rhetorical devices are available to win over a potentially ignorant, apathetic, or even hostile public, including persons in the corridors of power such as administrators and legislators. In some respects applied social scientists are like con men seeking to cool out the mark, the mark being the poor saps constituting a gullible public and those in positions of authority who are potential sources of funding. You must schmooze up to these funding sources, and tell them how wonderful they are, lest you run the risk of getting shut down even before getting a chance to show your mettle.

This is the hard lesson Gouldner learned only later, with the wholesale collapse of the Washington University, St. Louis department of sociology in the 1970s which, for a while anyway, was a department teeming with radical sociologists flush with funding even as they were railing against the very persons and institutions providing that funding. Etzkowitz (1988) has provided a useful summary of the trials and tribulations of radical sociology at Washington University. As chair of the department, Gouldner had by the mid-1960s assembled a collection of radical sociologists loosely united around Gouldner's (1962b) attack against value-free sociology. But by the early 1970s the department was in disarray, thanks in part to a nasty split between Gouldner and Horowitz over editorship of the journal *Transaction* (at the time housed at Washington University); to what was perceived as an injudicious attack against St. Louis funding sources for the department's Pruitt Igoe housing study (led by Lee Rainwater, Gouldner, and others); and for the hostilities that occurred within the department between Gouldner and one of his graduate students, Laud Humphreys. Humphreys' dissertation was later published as a book titled *Tearoom Trade* (Humphreys 1970). Gouldner confronted Humphreys to let him know he was not pleased with what he perceived as unethical research Humphreys was carrying out on men soliciting other men for oral sex ("quickies") in public restrooms. The two men got into a physical altercation with Humphreys being sent to the infirmary. Gouldner claimed he was acting in self-defense against Humphreys who was the initial aggressor, while Humphreys claimed Gouldner launched an unprovoked attack against him.

The schisms that developed within the department that led to its eventual demise were typical of any program of critical or evaluative theory, to the extent that true critical theory must at some point also seek to critically analyze its own assumptions or worldviews lest it be accused of merely kowtowing to the status quo (that is, the status quo of a sedimented or orthodox critical theory). Etzkowitz (1988, 1991) highlights two major cleavages in the department as those of (1) Academic Marxists vs. Activist Marxists, and (2) Revolution vs. Reform. By the early 1970s Gouldner was labeled as merely an Academic Marxist because he was not going into battle for particular oppressed groups, be they women, persons of color, sexual minorities, or "underdogs" of society more generally. Gouldner had already paid his dues to political activism in his youth stretching back to the 1940s, and by the 1950s with the execution of the Rosenbergs and the rise of McCarthyism, Gouldner and other left-leaning intellectuals (Jewish or otherwise) were scared off of political activism. Activist Marxists freshly emboldened by the feeling (circa the late 1960s) that Marxism was now respectable—indeed, sociologists were even calling Marx a founding father!—found fault in the older generation of Academic Marxists who were content to theorize from the sidelines rather than putting their convictions into practice.

There was also a disagreement over reform versus revolution, indicating differences of opinion on an acceptable timeline for meaningful change to transpire. In the quest to unify theory with practice for which all Marxist intellectuals strove, the question was, how rapidly could the transition from capitalism to communism occur? The reform option was the more conservative, as it directed sociologists to raise consciousness within the community about oppression and to speak to the atrocities of the capitalist system—including its racism, sexism, classism, violence (the Vietnam War being a focal point of concern), and homophobia—yet all the while working within the system (through university governance, through contact with stakeholders in the community, and through legislation) to seek desired reforms, incrementally if need be. The other option was revolution, and this was the belief that it could be accelerated with the help of radical intellectuals who would step in and play an active role in its attainment (Stark 1991).

The side with the revolutionary zeal was defeated, because by the early 1970s many of the activist Marxists in the department had been fired or reassigned. Gouldner himself was banished from the department in an arrangement where he was named Max Weber Research Professor of Social Theory in exchange for being physically vacated from the department (due to the Humphreys incident but also his own general bellicosity). As Etzkowitz (1988: 110) notes, "Washington University had assembled a group of radicals who could not agree on a strategy to act as a unified force within the department."

Today a similar thing is playing out within feminism. A recent cover story at *Nation* magazine carried the provocative headline "Feminism's Toxic Twitter Wars" (Goldberg 2014). This is a new type of academic dispute because it is carried across far-ranging social media, including Facebook, MySpace, email, academic listservs, chat rooms, blogs, and of course Twitter. It all started at a meeting at Barnard College held in 2012, where activist feminist bloggers recommended that resources go into funding online feminist bloggers and writers who otherwise were receiving no formal remuneration for their services.[5] This idea of remuneration for the unpaid work of feminists bloggers is similar to the second wave feminists of the 1960s who urged that, due to the patriarchal breadwinner-homemaker model of family life, the work women were doing as mothers, homemakers, and at schools and in the community, although essential, was seen as a "duty" and thereby should not be part of the paid labor force. In this light, it was especially important to find ways to fund the writings of feminist women of color as well as those within the transgender community in light of the fact that orthodox (and funded) feminists—including their publishing houses—were largely dominated by white women of privilege. The second-generation mainstream, white feminists, who received the brunt of the attack, were appalled that the younger, third-generation of feminists did not respect their elders for all they had done to make possible the ongoing critical

---

5 #FemFuture Online Revolution. Available at http://bcrw.barnard.edu/wp-content/nfs/reports/NFS8-FemFuture-Online-Revolution-Report-April-15-2013.pdf.

work of the current generation of feminists. This is the same "disrespect" that Activist Marxists had shown to Academic Marxists within the Washington University department of sociology forty years earlier.

But again, when we move from the younger Gouldner defending a Mertonian (rather than a Wardian) notion of applied sociology to the older Gouldner writing in 1976 about the dialectic of ideology and technology within the dark side of the dialectic, we see that the sort of ideological battles generated within sociology, Marxism, and feminism are part and parcel to science in its own right. For example, radical sociology could be explained away as merely part of the paradigm battles that occasionally crop up within any normal science. This harkens back to Kuhn (1962), and Gouldner used his ideas to good effect as early as 1970's *The Coming Crisis of Sociology*, although at that time he was stuck in departmental battles over radical sociology as discussed above. He was attempting to speak to broader audiences—indeed, to sociologists and to the academic community generally—and to an extent he was successful judging from the relatively high level of attention it received both inside and outside sociology. (The International Sociological Association lists Gouldner's *Coming Crisis of Western Sociology* as the 28th most influential book of the 20th century.) Gouldner's more nuanced view of science appears in the last few years of his life in the form of *Dialectic of Ideology and Technology* (Gouldner 1976a) and *Future of Intellectuals and the Rise of the New Class* (Gouldner 1979a).

Ideologues and Technologues

Gouldner, the radical sociologist who was not quite radical enough, shunned by Activist Marxists for being too much of an Academic Marxist, feels free to take some potshots at those very same leftist intellectuals for their lack of reflexivity and understanding concerning how much they could learn from mainstream or orthodox scholars like his teacher, Robert K. Merton. For Gouldner, although he was a mainstream sociologist—indeed, one of the most prestigious ever, rivaling Parsons for the top spot through the 1960s and perhaps into the 1970s—Merton escaped from being lumped into the pejorative "academic sociology" category because there was a tinge of Marxism in his functionalism. Gouldner sees in Merton a type of humanism that equates to the same concern with human suffering held by typical Marxists. In his 1938 paper "Social Structure and Anomie," Merton argues that in America much crime and deviance is produced not necessarily as a result of the pathological nature of individuals, but because of the American culture of materialism (reprinted in Merton 1968). The American Dream is the attainment of the good life through the accumulation of material rewards. Nearly everyone is socialized into valuing the acquisition of material goods, but the means to acquiring those goods are not distributed equally. Through no fault of their own, many persons who have been taught that there is an American meritocracy—if you work hard and play by the rules, you will be rewarded—find that even with their best efforts, they are thwarted from achieving the American Dream. Those who possess debilitating ascribed statuses whether race, gender, class, or otherwise, are more likely than their more privileged counterparts to experience anomie in this disjunction between effort and attainment. In the face of this sort of blocked opportunity, some will fashion illegitimate means toward the acquisition of socially valued goods. The most important thing for Gouldner, in interpreting the Marxist strand in Merton's thought, is that the capitalist system is largely to blame for its culture of materialism which promises rewards for hard work even as it does not distribute the means for their achievement equally.

Interestingly enough, Gouldner contents that intellectuals and technical intelligentsia suffer alienation and some forms of blocked aspirations, which he refers to specifically as the "blocked ascendancy" especially of intellectuals. Intellectuals, those bearers of high culture and advanced educational certification, often find themselves earning far less money than persons with far less prestigious degrees graduating in the fields of business, economics, commerce, finance, and so forth. Gouldner (1979a: 60) noted, for example, that by the 1970s there was a an oversupply of Ph.D.s in Western Europe and the United States, and even educated persons in colonial countries—even if they were of the technical intelligentsia rather than the intellectuals—were having trouble being remunerated at levels commensurate with their years of university training. One of the reasons nationalist movements against foreign imperialists swing into action is because native New Class intellectuals are desperate to take available positions requiring advanced education for themselves. One way this is done is through the taking over and creating of their own state apparatus, for example, through socialism, collectivizing the means of production and transferring them to state control—the newly created state apparatus of the native New Class—while simultaneously reducing or eliminating the ability of Old Class colonial authorities to influence local arrangements (Gouldner 1979a: 61). Intellectuals of the New Class who suffer blocked ascendancy tend to become politically active, not only because of perceptions that they are falling back financially but because their political influence is dwindling. Many intellectuals of the New Class, guided by secular humanist principles of amelioration with special emphasis on the eradication of oppression especially against vulnerable populations, seek to put into action their theories or ideologies, and this means either gaining political power or exerting influence on key political actors to do their bidding. This, again, is the effort to make good on the promise of the unification of theory and practice. This sort of world saving, engaging in the "good fight" against oppression in whatever form it may take, serves in large doses to buffet the alienation they may feel and the angst they suffer as intellectuals who, in the face of human misery all around them, may feel that they simply are not doing enough. There is a Promethean urgency to put their social positions as members of the educated class to good use, and getting their hands dirty pursuing goals within the profane sectors of economy and government is their calling, to borrow an idea from Weber.

Intellectuals and Gouldner's Sartre Talk

Less than a month before he died in Madrid, Spain on December 15, 1980—while on a speaking tour of Europe—Gouldner attended a colloquium held at Washington University, St. Louis. The colloquium was on the legacy of Jean-Paul Sartre, who had died earlier in the year, on April 15, 1980. Gouldner's (1980b) talk, titled "Sartre and the Intellectuals," ran about an hour, with the great bulk of the talk consisting of his reading from a text which was published posthumously in 1983 in *Theory and Society*, titled "Intellectuals and Artisans in the German Revolution of 1848" (Gouldner 1983). The first ten minutes of the talk, the transcript of which is provided below, consisted of Gouldner belittling and diminishing Sartre's thought on intellectuals, all along admitting that he knew very little of his work. He launched into his talk on the German Revolution, prefacing that the content would not deal with Sartre directly but would be, rather, in the "spirit" of Sartre.

After completing the talk Gouldner fielded questions from the audience. The first questioner asked whether it was intellectually honest to talk about the 1848 revolution instead of Sartre. Gouldner took incredible offense at the audacity of the questioner, responding "Shit! I'm not sure you even have the right to ask me the question. Who in hell are you to ask me that question?" Gouldner went on to chastise the questioner further, saying "If you learned nothing from what I've said, then that's your problem not mine. You got what you paid for."

The Washington University archives had a reel-to-reel recording of Gouldner's talk, and I asked them if it would be possible to transfer it to CD format. They were able to do this, and now the CD is available to check out from the library. Below, I provide a transcript of the first ten minutes or so of Gouldner's talk. After this, I will return with some further thoughts on Sartre.

INTELLECTUALS AND RADICAL SOCIOLOGY

Thank you very much. I'm startled to hear myself described as an expert in anything. I've studiously avoided that distinguished title, and have attempted to sort of pursue studies that have interested me, period. I was asked by Professor [inaudible] to speak about, not Sartre in general, about which I know and about whom I really know rather little—and I confess it right off—but most particularly about Sartre's views concerning intellectuals. That's what I was asked to speak about, that was my assignment, and that was what I turned my attention to.

Perhaps I had better immediately add that my comments are perhaps less to be thought of as an exposition of Sartre's views about intellectuals, which I find rather uninteresting, as being, let us say, in the spirit of Sartre. As you know, Sartre thought of intellectuals as being people of critique, thought of intellectuals as being people of contestation. And it was somehow evident, indeed I might say so self-evident to Sartre, that humanists, and especially humanistic intellectuals, were egalitarians. That, I must say, struck me as a surprise, and I wondered who had confided this to Sartre, and how he happened to know that, and what he would say in substantiation of that. And Sartre seems to believe that intellectuals, whom he spoke of in kind of a.... Basically Sartre's view of intellectuals was a Gramscian view. And in a way were one to speak about Sartre's views about intellectuals at all one should speak about Gramsci and forget about Sartre. Because I could find, for my part, very little in Sartre's discussion of intellectuals that had not been well and better said by Gramsci, and I rather think that though he frequently cites him, it often indicates a certain discomfort and uneasiness in his understanding of Gramsci, at least as I understand Gramsci. His conception, for example, of organic intellectuals (Sartre's) seems really to be substantially askew to and different from Gramsci's view on which he clearly relies.

Sartre apparently had the conviction that intellectuals' privileges presumably endow them with a bad conscience, perhaps especially and insofar as these privileges are at variance with their imputed values of egalitarianism. Again, I really know of rather little evidence—not to speak of systematic evidence—that would substantiate the fact that we intellectuals are persons of bad conscience concerning our privileges, or the ways in which our lives are at variance with our egalitarianism. Sartre, however, had no difficulty, considering whom he was, it was I suppose perfectly appropriate that he had no difficulty in speaking ex cathedra and simply making pronouncements as to what intellectuals felt or didn't feel, and what bad conscience or good conscience they had or didn't have. I confess that I only wish I had the knowledge and strength of insight that would have enabled me to speak with such confidence about what intellectuals are, or believe, or will become.

In very large part, or in very important part, it had seemed to me that Sartre's views on intellectuals were rather bleak, that he saw them greatly as living under the dominion of a system of hegemony that was not theirs, perhaps implying that they ought not, but they ought live under some other kind of dominion—the dominion of some mind perhaps. He's more specific than that; he conceives of intellectuals as living in a bourgeois economy essentially pursuing bourgeois goals, living bourgeois lives, and being rather unregenerate at this.

Now as I say this is a fairly bleak, and I find this at any rate, a fairly bleak unrelieved and conceivably misleading picture of intellectuals. I think that in some measure Sartre was speaking as a non-academic intellectual viewing his academic colleagues, i.e. us, with some distaste and alarm by reason of our somewhat mild-mannered, uncombative, meek behavior. And so, this as a form of domination or hegemony which he wanted, understandably, no part. So I'm trying to understand, what kind of consciousness could produce such a view? So, I think of this perhaps as a consciousness of a non-academic looking at academics, and I can only take my hat off to it, you know, and say yes I understand how that could be formulated as it was. For my part, however, in attempting to understand, as I say my remarks will be, hopefully, in the spirit of Sartre, not in the words of Sartre.

My view of the matter would be to address myself, and to encourage others to address themselves, to the question, under what conditions can intellectuals play a role on behalf of enlightenment? Under what specific kinds of historical conditions have they played such a role, or under what specific historical conditions do they find it difficult or less likely to play such a role on behalf of enlightenment? Now it is with that kind of historically delimited, modest, specific, non ex cathedra position that I wish to address myself to some of the recent researches that bear upon the question of, under what conditions could and do intellectuals play a role on behalf of enlightenment, play a role on behalf of reform, play a role on behalf of revolution?

Some of you may remember the interview that Sartre gave—he gave many, many interviews, I'm sure he regretted many interviews he gave, perhaps this one in particular—in which he said the wild and wooly thing, that if he had his life to live over again, he would have been a sociologist, or maybe even an anthropologist, conceivably an historian. Perhaps my comments about this question express a measure of sympathy with that erratic commentary on his part. Certainly a reading of his stuff on intellectuals leads me to such a view.

So I want to talk about now one specific historical setting which gives us something of a glimpse of the conditions under which intellectuals may play a kind of progressive historical role. In particular I want to talk about intellectuals in the revolution of 1848, and inspect more generally the question of intellectuals and their relationship to artisans. This was a matter of considerable importance to Sartre. He would not have phrased it in that manner, you see. He would have phrased the question as one of relationship of intellectuals to the working class, the relationship of intellectuals to the bourgeoisie conceivably. I think that there's a good deal of specific scholarly reason to reformulate the question somewhat and to raise the question here especially in connection with the revolution of 1848, a relationship between intellectuals and the artisans.

Now what is often referred to by Marxists such as Louis Althusser, and I might say my lecture tonight is dedicated to Madam Louis Althusser [in reference to Althusser's murder of his wife Helene on Nov. 16, 1980], as Marx's history-making encounter with the working class, is wrongly described, it seems to me, on several accounts. Of course his encounter was first neither with a class—if one can ever said to encounter a class as such—nor certainly was it primarily an encounter with workers in any Marxist sense of horny-handed factory proletarians.

Reflections on Sartre

The rest of the talk is simply Gouldner reading from his paper on artisans and intellectuals as mentioned above. Besides appearing posthumously in that 1983 *Theory and Society* article, this material also showed up as a chapter in *Against Fragmentation*, Gouldner's last book published posthumously in 1985. In the introduction to his talk, Gouldner talks about not knowing the work of Sartre very well, and shares a general disdain of his work on the grounds that, especially with regard to his work on intellectuals, Sartre's ideas were simply not original. On some level Gouldner may have felt that the public adulation Sartre had garnered during his life and afterward was out of proportion to its importance. Also, both men shared a relation to the issue of theory and practice, although experiencing these in reverse order. Whereas Gouldner was politically active earlier in his life and retreated from it in his later years, Sartre became politically active only later in life and became somewhat famous for it. Sartre was widely described as a public intellectual, and many have held him up as a model for putting his Marxist beliefs into practice. While Gouldner was working out the conceptual details of a reflexive sociology, Sartre was garnering more fame for his criticisms of European politics and occasionally running afoul of the law with his protest activities.

Probably the one thing that must have irked Gouldner the most about Sartre, though, was his contention later in life that literature was a "cop out," that it was a broadly bourgeois undertaking which was antithetical to truly making a difference in the world through political activism (Baert 2011b; Dimitriadis 2009). Also, Gouldner, a Jew, may have been puzzled by Sartre, a non-Jew, writing an acclaimed book on anti-Semitism (Sartre 1948) and using the Enlightenment and its liberal ethos of equality and democracy as setting the stage for the emergence of secular humanist intellectuals who sought to deny the particular aspects of identity which created both Jews and anti-Semites. Sartre even had the gall of making a distinction between authentic and inauthentic Jews. Recalling Gouldner's response to the questioner at the Sartre colloquium, one could hear Gouldner asking Sartre "Who in hell are you to make such an ex cathedra distinction about Jews?"[6]

Consistent with Gouldner's treatment of Sartre in his talk, whenever he did cite Sartre in his writing there was typically a negative tone. For example, in his *Two Marxisms*, Gouldner examines a wing of Marxist scholarship that holds Engels responsible for smuggling in positivism against the purer, more evaluative spirit of Marx's thought. This literature basically pits Engels against Marx, and by doing so Engels is made a convenient scapegoat for anything in the co-authored work of Marx and Engels that goes against the grain of the purported emancipatory philosophy of Marx. Gouldner (1980a: 251) holds up Sartre as one of the worst offenders in this vein, citing a passage in his book *Situations* where Sartre (1949: 213) makes a "reckless reference" to Marx's—quoting Sartre here—"destructive encounter with Engels." Gouldner's pointing out of this kind of parsing and splitting of the purity of Marxism versus the contaminations of Engels, whether at the hands of Sartre or other Marxist scholars, is consistent with Gouldner's argument that the writings of Marx, or Marx and Engels together, must be accepted warts and all and dealt with as a unity. This

---

6 Baert (2011a) argues that in this book Sartre positioned himself as a politically active Dreyfusard intellectual, thereby presumably heading off the kinds of criticisms that could have been made by Gouldner. The ironies continue, however, for by fashioning a dramaturgical or existential narrator taking the reader through the intricacies of Jewishness and ant-Semitism, Sartre becomes the kind of literati which he claimed to eschew. For Gouldner, this would be evidence of a lack of reflexivity on the part of Sartre and other such Marxist intellectuals.

splitting off of the co-authors from each other whenever convenient sets a precedent for the emergence of an entire cottage industry of Marx apologia, whereby whenever predictions of the theory do not find empirical support at the research front, or implementation of the theory runs off the rails—such as the recurring problem of the Marxist dictatorship—it can be blamed on Engels, or the improper operationalization of concepts by researchers, or misguided attempts by politicians (whether Lenin, Stalin, Mao, etc.) to implement revised versions of Marxism which essentially distorts the original or pure intent (i.e., the broad problem of revisionism). Gouldner's antagonism toward Sartre may also be at least indirectly traceable to his competition with Pierre Bourdieu, to the extent that both were working on the development of a reflexive sociology. Bourdieu always lauded his fellow Frenchman, applauding Sartre's work as a public intellectual and referring to him as a "total intellectual" (Swartz and Zolberg 2007: 215).

The ameliorative impulses of humanist intellectuals, which embolden belief in the inherent goodness of a theory because of its promise to alleviate suffering in ways described by that theory, can always go in the direction of allegiance to its prime directives at all costs. This zeal rises to the level of a secular religion that resists attempts to assess the veracity of its predictions using procedures of conventional science. Indeed, conventional or establishment science is rejected for being implicated in that selfsame social system which allowed whatever oppressive social conditions which are the focus of attention to arise in the first place. Radicalism finds a niche and a calling here, within the comforting infrastructure of theory which knows its adherents are right about what is ailing the world and how to fix it. Sartre's radicalism, showing up in the form of existential Marxism, appears later in his life after an early flirtation with conventional philosophy. Gouldner's radicalism shows up early in his real-world experiences as a member of the Communist Party, but having already experienced the "practice" side of the project of the unity of theory and practice, in later years he pursued the theory side more one-sidedly, leaving behind the practice side to others steeped in the righteousness of their mission.

Conclusion

There is one way, however, that Gouldner's radicalism showed up consistently, above and beyond any intellectual pursuits of realizing the unity of theory and practice, and that was in his interpersonal bellicosity. Even from his earliest days, upon his arrival in St. Louis as chair of the department of sociology and anthropology at Washington University in 1959, Gouldner had a penchant for rubbing people the wrong way. Although throughout the 1960s Gouldner remained a highly productive scholar, problems and tensions were brewing. A 1967 story from *Student Life*, the Washington University student newspaper, provided a glowing account of Gouldner receiving a university-wide post to pursue his research in social theory.[7] Under this arrangement, and responsible directly to the Provost, Gouldner was required to be in residency in the department only one semester a year, while being free the remainder of the year to do what he wanted. Now no longer officially connected with the department, Gouldner was given the official title of Max Weber Research Professor of Social Theory. Other points from the story noted that along with David J. Pittman, Gouldner was instrumental in bringing in a $750,000 National Institutes of Mental Health grant for studying aspects of life for tenants of the Pruitt-Igoe Housing Project. Additionally, the then current chair of the department, Robert L. Hamblin, praised Gouldner's scholarship as a key in sociology and anthropology's emergence as a first-rate and nationally recognized graduate program.

This of course was the public face of Gouldner's situation in the department. Just a year after this story ran in *Student Life*, members of the department were writing to Chancellor Thomas H. Eliot requesting that Gouldner be suspended from the University and placed on probation because of his physical attack against graduate student Laud Humphreys. The authors of the letter—Robert Hamblin, Joseph Kahl, Lee Rainwater, and Rodney Coe (1968)—referenced that accommodations had earlier been made to Gouldner to maintain the peace, and that what initiated these arrangements was the very ugly battle Gouldner had engaged in with other members of the department over control of the journal *Trans-action* (later *Society*). Gouldner was on leave for a European trip during 1965–1966, and he left the editorship of *Trans-action* in the hands of Irving Horowitz (Pittman and Boden 1989: 311–312). Upon his return, though, Horowitz refused to relinquish control back to Gouldner. Along the way, as he lost control of the editorship, Gouldner "engaged in insulting attacks, both on and off the campus, against his colleagues in the University" (Hamblin et al. 1968: 1). Gouldner could always fall back on his interpersonal bellicosity as consistent with radicalism, especially insofar as it was a requirement to challenge those in positions of power and authority for protecting oppressive social institutions (such as departments of sociology or higher

---

7   This is from the story "Gouldner Given University-Wide Post; Pursues Research in Social Theory", *Student Life*, Friday, April 14, 1967. I thank the Washington University library archives for making this material available to me.

education more generally) which provide a level of comfortable living for them while the masses suffered. Given such conditions, an angry visage is needed to shake people out of their complacency and work together to make the world right. In the pursuit of world saving you don't have to love or even like each other; you just need to be committed to the disassembling of social structures that maintain the status quo. But what happens when it all falls apart, when bellicosity or criticism run rampant and funding agencies disappear? Gouldner faced this conundrum throughout much of his academic career. The specific case of scholarship on crime and deviance, which we will turn to next chapter, continues this theme.

CHAPTER 3

Crime and Deviance

Introduction

It may seem odd that in this chapter I am applying the thought of Gouldner to issues of crime and deviance. Although he was a prominent organizational sociologist during the 1950s and 1960s, and later became a leading critical theorist analyzing problems in theoretical programs as diverse as functionalism, Marxism, labeling theory, and the welfare/warfare state, throughout most of his career Gouldner did not write specifically or directly about crime. Nevertheless, because Gouldner developed a systematic general theory touching upon most of the operations of the social system—especially its political or administrative structures and processes—there are avenues for illuminating the ways in which the administration of criminal justice operates in modern society. But since Gouldner also developed a social psychology, primarily by way of perhaps the key concept he ever developed, namely, the norm of reciprocity, it is also possible to ferret out explanations of the behavior of human actors. Although explanations of actors in diverse structural and cultural configurations certainly would be possible, for purposes of this chapter I am drawing out the implications of Gouldner's critical theory for a narrow range of actors, namely, lawmakers and lawbreakers.

Gouldner sought to achieve an elusive goal never fully realized by Marx and Engels, namely, the unity of theory and practice. By the end of his life in 1980, and on through works published posthumously as late as 1985, Gouldner came close to fulfilling this life project. The way Gouldner attempted to achieve this was actually articulated in a foreword he wrote for a book authored by Ian Taylor, Paul Walton, and Jock Young, titled *The New Criminology: For a Social Theory of Deviance*, published by Routledge and Kegan Paul in 1973. Gouldner noted that in this book the authors had broken free from the limitations of "practical" studies of particular substantive phenomena—in this case, the study of crime and deviance—to the extent that Taylor et al. linked their study of this specialized work in crime and deviance to more general social theories which are often merely silent partners in the enterprise. Rather than remaining at the infrastructural level, these authors showed the way to linking practice to theory by textualizing the theoretical aspects of their study, in this case, opting for a Marxist orientation. Yet, interestingly enough, the authors cite Gouldner early in their book as the scholar who showed how to employ a critical, reflexive social theory for purposes of "prying open" and illuminating understandings of any particular substantive phenomenon which comes to the attention of the theorist. In other words, Taylor et al. "successfully" applied Gouldner's model for unifying theory and practice, and it is in this spirit of further exploration and application that I discuss Gouldner's thoughts on crime and deviance which of course go beyond the particular aims of the new criminology theorists.[1]

The Funding of Criminological Research

I will get to Gouldner's writings as they relate specifically to the work of Taylor et al. and other criminologists shortly. First, though, let us consider Roland Chilton's 2000 Presidential Address at the annual conference of the American Society of Criminology (ASC). Chilton (2001) bemoans the fact that because much of the research conducted by criminologists is funded by government agencies, there is a strong expectation that such research will or should support existing government policies. He notes further that, with regard to the war on drugs specifically—a policy which Chilton and many other observers consider to be wrongheaded and a gross misuse of criminal justice resources—virtually no government-funded research has examined the problems created by our current drug laws and the tactics often used to enforce them.

Since so many criminologists are beholden to the state for their funding, they not only present research findings that appear merely to support existing drug policy, they also are likely to avoid some obvious subjects. For example,

---

1   I put the word "successfully" in scare quotes in this sentence because the argument is not quite as it appears. That is, this represents the polite and generous position Gouldner is taking as a scholar invited to write a foreword to a book. He provides adequate levels of praise for what Taylor et al. are up to here, but he pulls back somewhat intimating that at this point the model represents merely a promise toward the institutionalization of a system of helping which does not rely on tacit middle-class notions of propriety to set up the conditions or groundwork for the treatment or punishment of offenders. In some respects, this reluctance to launch an all-out embrace of the intellectual work of Taylor et al.'s "new criminology" is consistent with critical Marxism's distrust of intellectuals in general, insofar as they (whether intellectuals or technical intelligentsia) can use their privileged position to advance their own interests at the expense of the lowly masses. This is Gouldner's (1979a) thesis of intellectuals as a flawed universal class who even so must be tolerated to the extent that they typically are politically motivated to question the status quo and attempt to alleviate the suffering of the powerless, including criminals.

> There has been little if anything in the way of funding for studies of the corroding influence of the drug war on the system of justice. Given the money involved and the cases of corruption that occasionally surface, it is at least plausible to suggest that our state and national drug policies foster widespread corruption. This corrupting influence of a never-ending drug war may be formidable.
>
> CHILTON 2001: 3

Policy analysts and funding agencies generally want nothing to do with researchers whose policy recommendations are not considered politically viable, as, for example, the decriminalization or legalization of drugs to reduce demand of illicit substances.[2] Chilton recommends that criminologists develop independent research agendas and alternative sources of funding which could overcome the built-in limitations of federal research agendas for viable—meaning "politically expedient"—policy.

Chilton's admonition toward his fellow criminologists concerning their deepening dependence on the largess of the state covers virtually the same ground as Gouldner's plea to sociologists did many years ago. Although the target of Gouldner's original criticism was Howard Becker's (1967) and labeling theorists' partisanship for the underdogs—the "nuts, sluts, and preverts" (Liazos 1972)—of society, Gouldner's broader agenda was a criticism of the changing nature of social reform in industrialized capitalist nations.

In earlier times those who pushed for social reform were passionate and idealistic. They were the small businessmen, muckraking journalists, local political machines, and others with a stake in the fortunes of their local community. Today, with the rise of an ever-increasing technocratic social science eager to serve and administer the burgeoning welfare—now welfare-to-work (Schram 2000)—state as well as the criminal justice system, we now have a cadre of cosmopolitan social scientists who are highly mobile with dwindling localistic attachments. Like Becker, members of this New Class (Gouldner 1979a) profess they hold allegiance to the suffering of underdogs (such as crime victims; racial and ethnic minorities who are disproportionately targeted by criminal justice officials for harassment, arrest, criminal conviction, and incarceration; and those in poverty, especially single mothers of color), while also

---

2   Of course, this state of affairs has been changing more recently with the move toward the decriminalization or legalization of marijuana in places like Colorado and Washington. It is estimated that the legalization of medical marijuana in Colorado will bring in $70 million in tax revenue to the state in 2014. See http://www.huffingtonpost.com/2014/01/08/marijuana-sales-colorado_n_4552371.html.

maintaining a sentiment-free partisanship in order to meet the standards of scientific rigor and objectivity demanded by government welfare and criminal justice agencies (Chriss 1999c: 79). Gouldner (1968: 109–110) especially laments the fact that social reform has been transformed from a matter of moral zeal and heartfelt compassion to a kind of "engineering job," a technological task to be subject to bland "cost-benefit" or "system-analysis."

Old-fashioned liberals used to be prompted into social reform because of a twinge of consciousness or out of abiding personal interest; now, however, a growing legion of social scientists calibrate their liberalism "in terms of the government agency for which [they] will work, or whose money [they] will take" Gouldner (1968: 110). Personal liberalism becomes state liberalism, and social reform is no longer the avocation of dedicated amateurs but is increasingly the full-time career of paid bureaucrats.

Evaluation and Criticism

Chilton admires Gouldner's critique of any group of professionals who "sell out," that is, who put profit ahead of other considerations. From Gouldner's perspective, capitalism is distorting because of the way it elevates the profit motive about all else, even when it comes to servicing the poor and downtrodden in society. In essence, capitalism damages the link between theory and practice, to the extent that the profit motive "thingifies" one's thinking about the world, especially with regard to valuing quantity over quality. As caring human beings, we really should keep the health and welfare of others foremost in our thoughts irrespective of the cost and benefits of these commitments. Yet, just this impulse of critical theory has the potential of leading one down the path of the same sort of empty-headed partisanship which Gouldner railed against as practiced by Becker, labeling theorists, and the secular humanistic impulses of liberal criminology more generally.

This brings us back to the beginning of the chapter as it relates to Gouldner's (1973b) foreword to Taylor et al.'s *The New Criminology*. In essence, Taylor et al. adopted the *model* for unifying theory and practice developed by Gouldner. Although the authors share a few of Gouldner's theoretical commitments, they were of course not obligated to follow Gouldner conceptually lock, stock, and barrel. They used only a small subset of Gouldner's conceptual arsenal all the while adopting his model for setting up the framework for the study. Hence, a portion of my discussion will reflect and be consistent with a subset of Taylor et al.'s findings pertaining to issues of crime and deviance. But there is much more to explore regarding the implications of Gouldner's thought for illuminating the administration of justice and the social psychology of lawmaking and lawbreaking.

A primary orientation in critical or Marxist criminology is that the capitalist system itself is to blame because of the way it pushes people into acquiring worldly goods even if they have no means to acquire them legitimately. Ironically, this orientation also showed up in one of Gouldner's mentor's most famous papers, namely, Robert K. Merton's (1968, originally published in 1938) "Structural Strain and Anomie." Gouldner learned how a critical perspective could be embedded within a functionalist framework, yet in many ways Gouldner was satisfied with neither. As a ridge rider, Gouldner could never fully commit himself to a particular theory group or perspective because of the way consensual communities tend to ossify into vanguard parties protecting their own interests and claiming to be the champions of those they seek to liberate. Establishment or traditional approaches claim to have arrived at an Archimedean point where truth with a big T can be ascertained as long as fidelity is maintained to positivistic/scientific methods. These establishment or "big science" approaches had to contend with the embarrassment that their claims to universal truth and reason were produced on the back of deep gender, class, and race cleavages. That is to say, the great majority of the important public scientists emerging since the 1600s were white, European, heterosexual males.

Some of Gouldner's choicest critiques of sociology posing as the paragon of "big science" can be found in a review of *Sociology*, edited by Smelser and Davis published in 1969. Actually, as part of a review symposium published in *American Sociological Review*, Gouldner was supposed to have reviewed both this book and the Social Science Research Council's *The Behavioral and Social Sciences: Outlook and Needs*, which was published in 1970. To their consternation, the journal's book review editors, Marvin E. Olsen and Austin T. Turk, noted in a bracketed passage on the top page of the review "Professor Gouldner chose to limit his review to [Smelser's] *Sociology*." From this awkward start, Gouldner's review essay marks one of his most outlandish moments in print. Gouldner begins by noting the Smelser and Davis volume is nothing more than a cheap pitch for funds, and that the amount of space dedicated in the *American Sociological Review* for this review by four esteemed reviewers—including among them Gouldner himself—has "nothing whatsoever to do with its intellectual merits" (Gouldner 1970b: 332). Rather, it is little more than a well-managed promotional campaign. The evidence for this is that the editors, being in such a tizzy to get this book reviewed, required the reviewers to work off uncorrected page proofs rather than the completed, published version of the book. The book is primarily political, not intellectual, according to Gouldner. Indeed, the book provided official imprints of the pressing political concerns of the sociological establishment. For example, in the first chapter there is laudatory praise showered on the funding goldmine that awaits the discipline of sociology for those researchers committed to asking victims about their experience with crime, a new and "revolutionary" idea circa 1970. "What a classic of the sociological imagination!" Gouldner sneers with contempt. In effect, the report is directing true believers of the sociological faith to kneel and pray: "*Our masters who art in Washington, thou art not only rich and beautiful people, but also deep of mind as well; blessed be thy generosity*" (Gouldner 1970b: 332, italics in original). The next line is pure Gouldner gold: "The Report is not the work of ungrateful churls who play new games like 'hump the host' but the older game of butter-up-the-boss" (Gouldner 1970b: 332.).

The volume is unabashedly and shamelessly hitching its wagons to the expansion and bureaucratization of the welfare state, a new and pernicious form of bondage for sociologists and for growing legions of wards of the state. The framers of the report note that a freely developing sociology poses questions that authoritarian regimes do not want to hear, thus positioning sociology as high-minded defenders of liberalism and civic virtue. But what sort of embarrassing questions do sociologists pose to their own welfare-warfare state? Since it appears there are none to be found—indeed, even a conservative like Barry Goldwater finds little in sociology with which to take umbrage, and of course Ronald Reagan majored in sociology in college—perhaps American sociology is not freely developing, contrary to the report. This leads Gouldner to argue that for all its high-minded talk of ameliorating social pathologies and coming to the aid of victims of oppression, sociology exhibits a powerful conservative bias, all too eager to position itself as the handmaiden of the status quo. For example, the tradition of focusing on social problems— first put on the map in 1910 with Charles Ellwood's *Sociology and Social Problems*—really is a farce, insofar as whatever social change occurs is minor and incremental. The most important thing is to prop up the welfare state in order to ensure a steady stream of funded research.

Gouldner seethes with disgust at Smelser and Davis's report on the current state of sociology, to the extent that they provide pointers and directives for managing relations with the welfare state rather than helping those in need. Gouldner sees other ominous signs in the report as well, such as the editors recommending jettisoning the departmental system of sociology entirely in favor of the development of large, centralized research institutes. It is, for Gouldner (1970b: 334), the ideology of Institute Sociology, and not Department-based Sociology. Even further, the report champions old Chicago School ethnography, setting up sociologists as undercover detectives and informants to gather firsthand, up-close data about the growing legion of urban misfits. If they play their cards right, sociologists can then feed this information to police, social workers, and other authority figures, to help guide social policies which would further the cause of welfare statism, thereby assuring a continuing presence for sociologists in the corridors of power. This new alliance between Chicago School ethnographic methods, high science, and the authority structure would produce enough funds for all "responsible" groups willing to play by the rules of the game, including sociologists as servants to that power. In another classic jab, Gouldner (1970b: 334) writes, "Romulus and Remus may both find a teat to suck on the underbelly of the Welfare-Warfare Wolf; and, of course, those who are fed by the pack are expected to hunt with it."

At the end of the review the editors, Olsen and Turk, include yet another bracketed comment, an occurrence quite rare in the annals of scholarly journal reviewing. They had to set the record straight, stating that "Professor Gouldner is incorrect in saying that we were 'in a tizzy' to promote this volume and that the present symposium is 'an effort to publicize an official Report of... the Sociological Establishment'" (Gouldner 1970b: 334). Contrary to Gouldner, the editors state they were not concerned with publicizing or promoting the report, but instead, with getting the volume out to the larger sociological community whose members would likely find the material interesting and provocative. And they sent out pages proofs to the reviewers not because they were promoting the views expressed in the report, but to simply speed up the review process.

This was not Gouldner's first run in with James Davis (the co-editor with Smelser of the *Sociology* volume reviewed above). In 1962 Gouldner got a letter published in *American Journal of Sociology* where he took to task Davis's review of Gross' *Symposium on Sociological Theory*, an edited volume to which Gouldner contributed. (The chapter was "Reciprocity and Autonomy in Functional Theory.") Davis had the gall to refer to the papers in the Gross volume as largely "pretentious, windy, and pseudo-scientific," and that included Gouldner's piece. What is the problem here? Doesn't Gouldner also condemn positivists as espousing merely pseudo-science? On one level Gouldner likes Davis' manliness, that is, his ability to take a stand and pull no punches. However, in doing so Gouldner believes rather than rendering sound judgment, he is merely pronouncing sentence. His manliness was misguided and reckless insofar as he was willing to pass judgments on contributors with a wide assortment of backgrounds—philosophers, linguists, psychologists, logicians, and of course sociologists—without having the training to adequately judge papers outside of his field (such as Greenberg's chapter on descriptive phonology). It is, for Gouldner (1962c: 577), the same kind of courage "a tone-deaf man would need to publish a criticism of a symphony by Stravinsky."

Gouldner takes to task Davis' claim that, due to space restrictions placed on his review by the journal, he was not able to present the reasons behind his many judgments. But this is a copout by a literary vigilante who could have extended the word count had he requested to do so. Gouldner's (1962c: 577) final jab is: "Davis has acted as a judge in the best tradition of the Old West—a hanging judge. All one can learn from his review is that he is not afraid of the sight of blood."

Davis' (1962: 578) rejoinder was directed not only at Gouldner's negative letter, but also one written by Elliott Grosof.[3] He wrote, "Careful inspection of Mr. Grosof's epistemological thunderbolt and Mr. Gouldner's catty remarks reveals that my offense was to differ with them on some matters of opinion and taste. To this I plead guilty. I disagree with them on a number of matters of opinion and taste."

The Role of Social Critic in Criminology

As we saw above, as a self-avowed social critic Gouldner felt no pangs sparring with colleagues in the field, and sometimes even crossing the line of professional decorum in the process. Convinced that self-reflexivity was needed to overcome the positivist conceit that knowledge about crime or deviance can be objective and value-free, Gouldner was thereby emboldened to sneer venomously at those who thought otherwise. Indeed, critical or radical criminologists cite Gouldner (1970a) enthusiastically because of his stance that all knowledge is socially constructed and hence, there are tacit or openly avowed political commitments embedded in research and theory on crime, deviance, and the criminal justice system (see, e.g., Cullen et al. 2011).

It was not until the 1960s across America and Europe that the good old boys WASP club was challenged and somewhat dismantled with the rise of critical perspectives such as feminism, critical race studies, and later queer and identity theories. Now, the project of science is highly contested where newly struck interest and identity groups seek to create parallel sciences to rival those of traditional androcentric science. Gouldner could be all for this in theory, but he is also ready to note that these identity groups lead toward the blind alley of

---

3   In some ways Grosof's (1962: 577) criticism of Davis was even harsher than Gouldner's, writing in the first line of his review that "The appearance of James A. Davis' review of the *Symposium on Sociological Theory*, edited by Llewellyn Gross, marks a singular travesty of academic scholarship."

consensus politics where solidarity trumps reason and where culture is replaced by a Vanguard party—or a theory group—which cannot tolerate dissent or outsiders. As a ridge rider, always playing the insider/outsider game, Gouldner could not of good conscience join any of these new critical approaches for fear that he would be sucked into an uncritical and unreflexive acceptance of the party line.

Where does this role of the social critic—the ultimate social critic, one who can be critical even of his own critical theory and beyond—place Gouldner in relation to the explanation of crime and deviance? How will he traverse the minefields of hermetically sealed consensual communities ossifying into vanguard parties who have their own pet theories about how deviance and crime work and are ready to defend the veracity of their positions to the death? Indeed, how can we even come up with a "scientific" way of distinguishing between the normal and the pathological given the highly contested nature of social norms as they appear in particular configurations across time and place?

Gouldner notes, as he was always want to do, that technical discourses—such as those of crime and deviance—are always grounded in a larger or broader intellectual tradition. For example, since the rise of the Classical School of Criminology in the mid-1700s, the favored way of explaining why people deviate is because the benefits to be derived from the bad act outweighed the costs of being caught and punished. Bentham's utilitarianism, showing up explicitly as the deterrence theory, posits profit maximization as an eternal and enduring human characteristic, that is, as an ontological endowment of any species. This is analogous to the assumption of a pleasure/pain nexus which buffets about oftentimes unwitting organisms into behaviors which, at least over the short term, serve to maximize pleasure and minimize pain. Being more sympathetic early on to the critical approaches of Marxist theory, Gouldner may indeed have been sympathetic to Marx's distaste for Bentham, because Marx could never accept the way utilitarianism smuggled in profit as an enduring human trait. Indeed, Marx must reject this ontological assumption, to the extent that greediness and the desire to maximize profit at all costs—ascending to the ultimate position of profit for the sake of profit, leading to massive disparities between the haves and the have-nots—cannot work within the context of a critical theory which argues that such behaviors represent merely the pathologies and distortions of the capitalist system itself. Freed from the shackles of capitalism, human beings are by nature sharing and communitarian, a state of primitive egalitarianism that became increasingly eviscerated over the transitions from early society, to the stages of horticulture and agriculture, and then into the industrial age and beyond.

In tracing out this line of Marxist thinking, Gouldner noted that deviants are a kind of political low-life, more or less inconsequential in the big scheme of things in the struggle between bourgeoisie and proletariat. This extended into the perspective of the Chicago School, especially the second generation trained by Hughes, Blumer, and Becker. Deviants are hapless discards of the system residing in and on the streets of the urban metropolis: the hookers, drug users, mentally ill, con artists, homeless, and the dispossessed. Whereas Marxists saw the deviant as irrelevant from the perspective of the general theory, the Chicago School saw them in a needful way, to be studied and appreciated for their humanity and their fall from grace. They became champions for these underdogs, and they claimed that the fortunes of sociology rested on the concerted study of this vast class of urban deviants. This would position sociology as the first line beneficiaries of the expansion of the welfare state. Along the way, these Chicago School sociologists could beam with pride for taking the side of the underdog and identifying with the plight of the unfortunate and powerless.

Gouldner arrives at a point where the Marxist and Median approaches to deviance represents a kind of dualism, in which both sides are somewhat deficient for not being able to see or fill in the empty space between them. Dualisms are handy conceptual devices because they mark off that which is against that which is not. One side—for example, bad—resides in its own neat world, while the other side—say, good—resides in an opposite, neatly defined space. But on each side of any dualism is a ridgeline, where the two distinct sides almost meet and which represents something of a nether world. Gouldner seemed to always be seeking to identify and occupy these nether worlds. In the case of the topic of this chapter, this netherworld is that contained in the dualism of deviant and normal. We have to go beyond, so suggests Gouldner, either the mere acceptance of deviants as political lowlifes (the Marxist approach), or using deviants as the handmaiden of technicians acting as zoo-keepers for the burgeoning welfare state, thereby building sociology into a respectable, research-driven science. A useful study of deviance must be able to enter into the *Lebenswelt* of deviants without patronizing them or setting oneself up as champions to these underdogs.

The Organization of Attention

Although Gouldner never completed a formalized response to this question, aspects of what the answer may look like can be ferreted out from a combination of Gouldner's own writings along with some key secondary sources.

Gouldner's most useful writings for deriving a perspective on crime and deviance are his work on the secrets of organization (Gouldner 1963) and his theory of group tensions (Gouldner 1954a, 1954b, 1954c).[4]

Among the many factors leading to group tensions, one of the most prominent is the fact that in any concrete setting human beings are subject to prevailing organizational or institutional arrangements, the history and development of which may be only dimly perceived by them. This means that much of organized social life occurs behind the backs of human subjects, and indeed, furtive elements are often in play, which may affect all sides negatively. These furtive elements Gouldner (1963) refers to as "secrets of organizations," and they inhibit open and honest communication between organizational actors in much the same way that repression and suppression occur at the level of individual conscience. Gouldner analyses the specific case of the growing divergence between the helpers and the helped occurring within modern welfare agencies. Welfare agencies are set up ostensibly to attend to the "needs" of its clients, and according to professional (i.e., scientific) standards, the way needs are defined and responded to should be impervious to the whims of individual professionals and the clients to whom they attend. This is the public face of the organized helping professions. But the "dirty secret" is that "need" is a rhetorical not a scientific concept, and because of the bureaucratization of the helping professions only certain things and certain responses are defined as appropriate to the professional work being performed.

As Gouldner (1963: 171) argues, "The concept of need, in the context of the welfare establishment, serves to keep the secret that there is sometimes a conflict of interest among different groups in the community." In the real world, across the vast spectrum of human experience, persons find themselves in all sorts of situations which could lead them to seek professional help or to be mandated into it (for example, by functionaries of the criminal justice system). Gouldner's point is that in servicing client populations, meeting the needs of one group may lead to ignoring the needs of others, which leads in turn to frustration and resentment. How does the system deal with this inevitability, that not all needs can be met, and that when some needs are met it will produce frustration among those whose needs have been ignored? Especially when dealing with deviant and poor populations, the function of the welfare system is to spread gratifications around as broadly as possible, using cultural

---

4   It is interesting to note that during the 1953–1954 academic year at Antioch College in Ohio, Gouldner taught a course titled "Foundations of Clinical Sociology." A description in the course catalogue stressed that this was a counterpart to clinical psychology, its primary focus being on teaching students how to diagnose and treat group tensions (Fritz 2007).

inducements to remind those whose needs have not yet been met to work hard, stay in school, keep your nose to the grindstone, delay gratification, respect authority, and especially respect the system and do not lose faith in it. In other words, the dark secret of the helping professions is that all they really have to fall back on are middle-class values of propriety, hoping to instill prosocial adjustment by promising their charges that gratifications are forthcoming. To those with whom they cannot deal directly, they send out reassurances to burgeoning classes of deviants to sit tight and that "we are here for you" if only in spirit.

As we have seen, the importance of unfulfilled needs in the production of group tensions was first developed from Gouldner's study of a unique industrial conflict called a wildcat strike. The wildcat strike emerged, in somewhat serendipitous fashion, out of his ethnography of a gypsum plant in upstate New York (Gouldner 1954c). In that work Gouldner found that bureaucratization increases with management succession. Management succession often occurs when there is a perception that previous elements of management allowed things to become too "informal" or "indulgent" on the shop floor. Here, on the level of organizational analysis, there is a readymade Marxist assumption of how the owners or the bourgeoisie—here, the ownership and upper management of an industrial organization—dominate and oppress the lowly masses of workers at the level of the line staff. In many respects, within capitalism there is a ceaseless confrontation between groups holding different positions in society consistent with a different set of interests and identities. The goal of the owners is to smooth over feelings of resentment among those in the lower echelons so that they will remain happy, productive workers. In such classes of interests and positions, there are always available to the observer a set of symptoms marking the boundaries of group tensions. As Gouldner (1954c: 125) states, "Since men under stress verbalize their grievances, by examining them, the zones of disturbance may be tentatively identified."

Some of the most important symptoms to be studies are complaints, which are statements of frustrated expectations. The role of the sociologist is to take note of these accounts, and to see how sentiments mobilized on one side may be magnified to the point that identity (often class-based) solidarity could lead into open conflict against the other side. Gouldner originally struck upon this theory of group tensions within the context of his dissertation research at Columbia, but the kernel of the idea would show up years later in his more mature sociological work on intellectuals and the extent to which they could play the role of social critic of and for society. Here, for purposes of the criminal justice system, we see a massive dispute or conflict with those who are subjects of the system—namely, deviants and criminals and all those who defend them—and those who are guardians of the system, especially lawmakers but also everyday citizens who typically side with authority figures decrying the pain and suffering caused by these deviants. It is to this extent that, although the theory of group tensions was first developed within the context of organizational conflict, Gouldner could make the case that the theory could be generalized to other substantive phenomena beyond the industrial organization.

In 1965 Gouldner published the book *Enter Plato*, in which he traced out the historical development of philosophy and science from 700 BC onward. Although in this book he did not focus on this exclusively, he did nevertheless discuss early Greek philosophy's understanding of the rise of the city and how deviance was to be understood within this relatively new collective phenomenon (that is, the Greco-Roman city-state). This earliest notion saw crime and deviance as arising from ignorance and/or lack of virtue. This starting point can then be used to go forward in time to analyze later transitions in the understanding of deviance. Indeed, lack of virtue is for Gouldner a better starting point than what was later developed by the early Classical School of Criminology, that being utility. Yet, even here, Platonic notions of virtue can be assimilated to unreflexive assumptions of group consensus on what virtue means in the first place. In *Coming Crisis*, Gouldner spends some time on the convergence between Plato and Parsons' functionalism for their alleged "conservatism." Both posit a failure of morality, or the emergence of a state of anomie (Gouldner 1970a: 426). But how does Gouldner square this convergence on anomie between classical Greek philosophy and Parsons, which is alleged to be a deficient explanation of deviance, with Merton's own use of anomie, which in spirit at least he favors?

Gouldner argues that Greek philosophy, and later versions of morality informed by Christianity and Parsons' functionalism, both are intentions-oriented. That is, what is good or bad is based upon the intentions of the person looking out into the social system and deciding how to act. Christianity was supposed to inculcate a universal sense of the good based upon God's word, while the Greeks and Parsons talked about shared norms and a shame culture holding persons in place. But later versions of utilitarianism, which Parsons rejected at least in part, as well as wholly by Marx, replaced intentionality or the good with the useful. In essence, with the ascendancy of utilitarianism in bureaucratic capitalism men and women abandon intention-based morality—a universal vision of the good—and instead seek the most efficient means to accomplish goals. This modern emphasis on competitiveness and ends, rather than being directed toward appropriate means, is the modern version of anomie, which was central to Merton's Marxist-inspired version of middle-range functionalism (Gouldner 1970a: 67–68).

It is here that Gouldner develops a social psychology presumably lying behind all aspects of human social interaction, including consensual exchange relations but also those that are strained and which may lead to conflict, violence, or even worse. Gouldner (1954c) refers to this as the "organization of attention," meaning that persons operate with perceptions about the intentions and needs of others with whom they interact. This conceptual apparatus is from *Wildcat Strike*, one of the books produced from Gouldner's dissertation. As such, he sticks more closely to conventional scientific form, developing a series of hypotheses about the nature of the organization of attention and under what conditions it may lead interactants into conflict, deviance, or crime. For example, proposition five states "Tensions increase in the relationships between Ego and Alter if either, or both, does not perceive or is not aware of the expectations of the other" (Gouldner 1954c: 136). Parsons and other systems theorists were concerned with shoring up and making visible the systems of expectations which stabilize social relations and hence social order, and here at least Gouldner agrees, even going so far as adopting the clinical terminology of Parsons by way of Ego and Alter.

Human beings also desire approval from others, and when approval is not forthcoming, tensions between Ego and Alter will increase. Gouldner is able to link these observations to the theory of social structure and culture developed by Merton, insofar as persons who experience a disjunction between effort and attainment may come to see not only others with whom they are interacting as illegitimate, but also the system in its entirety. In other words, if agents of socialization and others within the orbit of the individual are not providing adequate levels of approval, this may indicate to the individual that the entire system is shot through with pathology or dysfunction, hence leading to anomie and possibly criminal or deviant activity. Gouldner is taking the cue that rather than direct internal motivation on the part of actors, those labeled deviant are more likely to be made bad by the system because of the deficient levels of positive reinforcement or feedback provided to these individuals in interaction. These conditions of failure in the exchange system—particular with regard to the delivery of gratifications to Ego vis-à-vis his or her dealings with numerous other Alters within a social system—may lead to hostility, distrust, the perception of a power deficit which must be corrected by the seeking of greater power, sometimes acquired through illicit means, and so forth.

For example, lack of power, real or perceived, may indicate to Alter that he or she cannot wait for satisfactions to be fulfilled, and so must cut corners or overtly violate normative proscriptions regarding the delay of gratification. The cultural conception of time is established by middle-class standards of propriety, and such constraints may tend to always cast those who cannot play by the rules of the game regarding waiting into the category of deviant or criminal. They will also tend to be isolated and thereby cut off from the solidarity of crosscutting group affiliations that is the lifeblood of the social order. At this point, there is a delinking from Parsons in favor of the subterranean critical elements of an evaluative paradigm found within Merton's conception of anomie and the structural arrangements within capitalism, which produce deviant adaptions among criminal innovators. This is especially evident in Merton's shifting blame from lawbreakers to the pathological aspects of the capitalist system, especially a materialist culture which prods virtually everyone into coveting valued resources even when they do not have the legitimate means to acquire them.

Loyalty and Group Tensions

Gouldner continued this analysis of strains and tensions conducing toward deviance within the social system in a paper published in 1954 in the journal *Social Problems*. In the beginning of the paper, Gouldner (1954b) lamented that the most important form of social tension sociologists should be dealing with, namely war, hardly attracted attention in the major introductory sociology texts during the period 1945–1954. In order to make a transition to his own work in industrial sociology, Gouldner suggested it may make sense to see whether or to what extent theories of group tensions at the interpersonal or organizational level could inform such tensions at the national or international level. Gouldner recommended one way of constructing this bridge, which is the observation that although no industrial organization could maintain itself if it disregarded economic aspects of its operation, it would be equally foolish to overlook the human aspect, specifically, the processes by which human workers remain loyal to their work organizations. Gouldner notes that although political groups work hard to maintain the loyalty of its citizens to their cause, industrial organizations had been less competent in this area, at least up until the time such deficiencies were uncovered in the Western Electric studies.

In Durkheimian mechanical solidarity, there was typically no serious problem with loyalty in the face of group tensions. In mechanical solidarity characterized by small, tight-knit groups bonded by blood, familiarity, and shared religious convictions, the tendency was for strong in-group solidarity and equally strong out-group hostility. For the most part members of each group would be loyal to their own groups. This would also be a point Parsons emphasized, namely, that primitive solidarity is assured to the extent that with regard to the self-collectivity pattern variable dilemma, actors would choose the group (Parsons, Shils, and Olds 1951: 219). But with the advent of modernity and organic solidarity, loyalty to the collectivity was less assured. Indeed, with the continuing economization of social life under capitalism combined with a new cultural emphasis placed on the individual, modern actors would be more likely to choose self over the group.

With the advent of modernity and organic solidarity, persons are cast adrift from the warm and nurturing bonds of primary groups, hence loyalties to these primary groups are imperiled. But also in modernity, there is supposed to be a parallel development of a public civil sphere where persons develop bonds and loyalties through their political associations as citizens. Legal socialization ideally inculcates in citizens a tolerance of (and hopefully even reverence for) anonymous others. This is the rise of the cult of the individual, namely, Durkheim's notion of healthy individualism as an antidote to the decline of tight-knit, primary group-based mechanical solidarity. Yet, in this transition from mechanical to organic solidarity whereby selves are turned into public citizens as opposed to the private, exclusive membership of tribes or clans, crime rates continue to rise and concerns over interpersonal aggression—especially the fear of being victimized by strangers whose numbers are growing—grow in proportion to state assurances that public spaces are maintained by a professional constabulary force.

Something for Nothing and Starting Mechanisms

Connected with this, the growing masses of the incompetent, the dispossessed, the downtrodden, the deviant, and the criminal populating the urban metropolis produce an acceleration of expert discourses which in turn produce seemingly definitive labels for the various conditions afflicting both victims and offenders. As a professional discourse, this labeling strategy filtered up from the everyday lifeworld, where persons had always labeled disreputable characters from the beginning. In primitive society, the original damning label was simply the other. With the move from mechanical to organic solidarity and the emergence of the human and social sciences, more labels emerged to compete with those labels emanating from the everyday lifeworld (Seidman 2013).

Before we go further with this line of discussion, it is important to note that labeling theory was a popular criminological theory during the 1960s, and as a good progressive liberal it would have seemed that Gouldner would have been sympathetic to the theory to the extent that it views those who are labeled as deviant as subject to the whims and caprice of the powerful ("lawmakers"), thereby leading to forms of oppression which must be critically analyzed. Yet, in several key journal articles Gouldner took to task a number of leaders of the theory, especially Howard Becker. It was here that Gouldner illustrated the strategy of "ridge rider," namely, the untethered critical theorist who must reject membership in any particular theory group or vanguard party in order to avoid blind allegiances and ideological and political acquiescence.

This outlaw or ridge-rider approach was also evident in Gouldner's most cited journal article, published in 1960, and was titled "The Norm of Reciprocity." This was a masterful analytical study, insofar as Gouldner illustrated how conventional sociological theories tacitly invoked the notion of reciprocity but rarely justified or explained how it worked within the context of face-to-face interaction. In the continuing quest to link grand, abstract theory to the practical realities of everyday life, Gouldner did a nice job laying the analytical groundwork for explaining in general how selves are developed through reciprocal exchange and how broader cultural and structural realities frame and nurture their development. It would have been easy for Gouldner to remain within the ambit of the traditional exchange explanation that assumes persons engage in such relationships because of the mutual benefits they provide to participants. But he did not, opting instead for a critical approach that does not rest on its laurels but instead must subject explanations to searing examination.

In 1973 Gouldner published a follow-up to "Norm of Reciprocity" which appeared in his collected volume *For Sociology*. In that chapter Gouldner noted the following pertaining to the limitations of the norm of reciprocity:

> Clearly, the norm of reciprocity cannot apply with full force in relations with children, old people, or with those who are mentally or physically handicapped, and it is theoretically inferable that other, fundamentally different kinds of normative orientations will develop in moral codes.
> GOULDNER 1973A: 260

This insight can easily be extended to "deviants" more generally, including of course criminals. In many respects, due to their location in the social structure and their experiences with blocked opportunity (Merton's and Durkheim's "anomie," which later criminological theorists refer to as "strain"), many of those labeled "deviant" cannot reciprocate benefits they may have earlier received. In an argument reminiscent of John Rawls, justice is not a sufficient condition for the stability of the social system. Especially with regard to deviants and criminals, a pure reliance on justice based upon reciprocity means that bad acts should be countered with painful punishments (the utilitarian position). Yet, the professionalization of punishment in the criminal justice system merely shifts vengeance and punitiveness out of the hands of the people and into the hands of police, courts, and corrections staff. This does not solve the vicious cycle of tit for tat vengeance. In other words, reciprocity fails, and in its wake emerges the norm of beneficence, or pretty much giving "something for nothing." Well before such criminological theories as restorative justice emerged, Gouldner's norm of beneficence had already seen the problem and worked out a solution.

Here Gouldner is giving considerable attention to starting mechanisms, that is, the things which in their infancy took hold as empirical realities within social systems and which developed traditions and ways of knowing about the area of concern. The idea of starting mechanisms was central to Gouldner's (1960) earlier paper on the norm of reciprocity, to the extent that Parsons and the functionalists tended to overlook them due to their ahistoricism, being for the most part uninterested in the etiology of social systems. Functionalists' "presentist" bias instead tended to direct their attention to the current operation of systems and the mechanisms and structures in place for its ongoing maintenance. The manifest use of the norm of reciprocity for functionalists is its importance in the stabilization of current and ongoing exchange relations within empirical social systems, directing interactants to provide things of value to those who provided valued resources to them at some earlier point. But where this facile employment of the norm of reciprocity breaks down in the hands of the functionalists is at the paleosymbolic or latent level of analysis, that is, the overlooked historical dimension of this norm as it emerged among presumably self-interested actors. In other words, the functionalists cannot account for how in the very earliest stages of the development of a social system actors escaped from a perpetual "You first!" stance. There would be a hesitancy to be the first to offer goods given no accumulated history that such acts were reciprocated later.

This ahistoricism of functionalists tended to impair their ability to think through in systematic fashion how starting mechanisms must work in order to explain the current operation of social systems, and that blindness toward etiology or determinate beginnings adversely affects a vast array of attempts to explain empirical social reality. Gouldner (1973a: 251) stated, for example, "Marriages are not made in heaven, and whether they end in divorce or continue in bliss, they have some identifiable origins." Modern thinking about marriage has evolved into the notion—now backed more and more by legal prescriptions—that persons of the same sex should be allowed to marry, and to not do so is discriminatory and an assault on the constitutional fabric of American society. If Gouldner had been around with regard to this contemporary turn of events, he would have had a field day throwing a wet blanket over the giddiness and self-assured smugness of those proclaiming that same sex marriage is consistent with the logic of the founding of the marriage institution from the very beginning. Gouldner would be there to remind us about the functional significance of marriage insofar as starting mechanisms are concerned. The question that needs to be asked is, "What is the starting mechanism for this idea, now sedimented into an institution, of marriage?" Clearly the only reasonable answer, based upon the historical record of humanity, is that marriage was a cultural invention made by human beings to tie adult males to their progeny, that is, to hold males accountable to the children they bring into the world. The original concept of marriage was a political and cultural innovation, used as an artifice to keep otherwise warring tribes or clans from engaging in hostilities by trading daughters for sons through dowries or other such systems of exchange. This was the invention of the "gift," and it ushered in the contemporary era of civility.

In the bigger picture, this means that procreation was at the heart of marriage as a social institution, that is, the social organization and regulation of procreative behavior. The starting mechanism for marriage, then, was procreation or its possibility. There is no record of a marriage system being developed anywhere throughout the course of human history absent this essential element. Granted, over time the link between procreation and marriage softened with the introduction of romantic love and the easing of restrictions (religious, legal, ethical, or otherwise) placed on marriages, which did not or could not lead to procreation (such as in the case of infertile heterosexual couples). But in the beginning, in the primordial establishment of a system of marriage, procreation was essential and pivotal. In ancient times, judgments about a woman's viability as a marriage partner were based not on charm or beauty, but on fruitfulness (Tannahill 1980: 62).

As the truest or purist critical theorist, much more radical than standard critical sociology because of his willingness to turn criticism back on itself, Gouldner would be there to bring the bad news about the starting mechanism concerning marriage. And once this starting mechanism is established, it leads to other uncomfortable questions, that is, uncomfortable for those who are concerned with such things as political correctness. (Gouldner never practiced political correctness and paid a price for it.[5]) One insight, for example, is that

---

5   Because of his willingness to challenge cherished ideas or dogmas of the political left and right, he was relegated to persistent outsider with regard to both camps. For example, on the mantra of the left's concern with inequality, Gouldner (1976a: 144) stated "No one calls for compulsory plastic surgery to make all equally beautiful, for compulsory surgery to make the smaller as big as the taller; for compulsory drug injections to make all equally great lovers or thinkers. And why should some, simply because they happened to be born earlier than others, be denied an equal prospect of future longevity? In fine: the inequalities condemned, and the equalities demanded, are always highly *selective*. But on what standards?"

if we carry out the logic of the constitutionality of same sex marriage, this means that we must define same sex couples as equivalent to infertile heterosexual couples. It is likely that such conceptual equivalences, however strained as such arguments may be, will likely continue to inform legal attempts to normalize gay marriage.

Yet with all this, it is also important to note another blind spot in the functionalist deployment of the norm of reciprocity, and this in turn has implications for thinking about wide classes of persons labeled deviant, defective, or disreputable. Perhaps the norm of reciprocity fundamentally is tied to traditional western societies and their penchant for economizing more and more areas of life, that is, the basic idea of exchange in which persons enter in relations for the mutual benefits accruing to them. In this state of affairs, perhaps there was no true ancient norm of reciprocity. Perhaps the true starting mechanism was something entirely different, and Gouldner suggests as much. Very likely, well before the institutionalization of capitalism and the taken for granted notion of exchange had taken hold, there was a norm of beneficence, namely, giving something of value to someone with no specific expectation of receiving anything in return. This is the idea of "something for nothing," and it was apparently a pervasive cultural element in a vast majority of pre-literate societies. However, with the development of a market economy and the taking root of a strong ethic of utilitarianism, those who give or receive something for nothing are viewed as deviant, that is, as non-normative. This of course cuts two ways: Givers are viewed in a positive light as "pure, unworldly idealists," while those who receive such gifts or want something for nothing are "commonly viewed as flawed, distorted, or incomplete people" (Gouldner 1973a: 267). Conservatives for the most part embrace this ethic of personal giving or charity, in that giving from the heart is spiritually uplifting and consistent with Christian brotherhood. On the other hand, those same conservatives likewise decry the development of poor relief and systems of welfare, in which those in need receive money and other essential resources through government programs, because the bureaucratization of charity hardens the heart of those who otherwise would have given freely but who now resent forced wealth redistribution (Spencer 1872 [1850]).

The norm of beneficence of course over time was subject to the distortions of the economistic redefinition and recasting of everything under the sway of emerging capitalism. That is, those who gave without an expectation of return could *afford* to give. This sleight of hand travels under the moniker of philanthropy, whereby the ultra-wealthy are able to make a public showing of their beneficence through the funding of schools, hospitals, or programs designed to help the poor or distressed. In reality, the tax systems of advanced capitalism are set up so that the wealthy can make a show of giving something for nothing, thus assuring public adoration for their good deeds and kind hearts. In reality, much of philanthropy is a cold calculation of the bottom line, for the super-wealthy actually help their financial positions through such philanthropy because they are able to move to lower tax brackets which effectively saves them more than whatever they ended up giving away. This is one way that capitalism perpetuates and even solidifies the public idea that economic elites and other persons in positions of power are by and large good. This is the cultural ethos that leads persons to believe that the good are powerful and vice versa.

Even further, this norm of beneficence—at least the public face of the norm—is that the lowly deserve our empathy and even admiration for the daily slings and arrows they endure. It is the idea that a society is only as good as the record of its treatment of the downtrodden, the powerless, and the dispossessed. It is consistent with the thesis of James Scott's (1985) *Weapons of the Weak*; or feminists who argue that those in positions of degradation, scorn, and systematic abuse—in this case, women as a class—possess keen and unfettered insights into the true dynamics of the relationship between the ruling and the ruled; or even animal rights activists who claim the innocence of animals and the various ways they are abused by human beings points toward a transcendent dignity which must be continuously protected and honored. The broad project is confronting the power of exclusion (Ryan 2009), and coming to the defense of all those who in one way or another are blocked from full participation in society, be they children, criminals, homosexuals, oddballs, nerds, immigrants, the slow-witted, the physically or emotionally disabled, the tattooed, sexual minorities, and whatever other currently labeled groups gain public attention.

Notice also that one of the key elements driving all this, that is, the compulsion to abide by the rules of reciprocity or beneficence and the condemnation of those who fail to live up to these ideals, is moral absolutism. Gouldner (1973a: 296) argues "Moral absolutism is the essence of the morality that has developed historically in Western civilization where it stands behind both reciprocity and beneficence." The failure to live up to such ideals entails social costs, and those who cause the suffering of others—especially the wealthy who do not give their fair share and hence give tacit, if not overt, consent to the perpetuation of systems which tolerate inequality and indignity—deserve punishment, perhaps in equal proportion to the deprivation, suffering, and pain of the lowly masses. For Gouldner (1973a: 296), moral absolutism "manifests an edge of punitiveness, a readiness to make others suffer," and "There is, in short, an edge of sadism in moral absolutism." Gouldner goes even further, in a position reminiscent of Nietzsche or even Adorno, to suggest that this trap of moral absolutism contributes to the increasing sense of meaninglessness experienced by persons in their everyday lives. In some ways also it is close to Weber's lament of the iron cage of bureaucracy to the extent that technological advancements have led persons into a pacified but stultified existence where their daily routines are more or less decided beforehand by forces only dimly perceived if at all. Part of this technology is of course the cultural patterns guiding decisions for action regard the norms of reciprocity and beneficence and how to react in cases of their violation.

Direct Brain Intervention with Deviants and Criminals: A Gouldnerian Reading

In his paper on sociologists as partisan for the underdog, Gouldner (1968) faulted Becker and labeling theorists for the way they attempted to set themselves up as managers or zookeepers of the exotic specimens that are the various types of human deviants. As a radical sociologist championing secular humanism, Gouldner was sympathetic to the plight of the suffering, especially when social structures and conditions created a steady supply of suffering, such as those reflected in Merton's typology of deviant adaptations. The labeling theorists, on the other hand, were concerned simply to manage those labeled as deviant—playing footsy with the power brokers of the welfare state as it were—rather than working to dismantle the broader system that was producing them. Management of social deviants has become a huge business conducted by for-profit and not-for-profit organizations alike. Techniques of behavior modification and control are particularly fertile areas for continuing development, study, and upgrading. For good or bad, technological innovations in the areas of medicine and elsewhere are making possible a range of interventions into human activities and behavior at an accelerating pace and widening spectrum. As the field of neuroscience continues to develop more exacting maps of the human brain and improve understanding of the neural pathways associated with various forms of behavior, there is increasing optimism that deviants and criminals can be "helped" through appropriate brain intervention techniques.

Behavior modification through drug treatment has been around for quite a while, as for example the diagnosis of attention deficit disorder (ADD) in children who receive doses of Ritalin to help them with their attention and/or reduce anxiety or hyperactivity (specifically in the case of ADHD). Additionally, men who are accused of sexual harassment may be put on an antidepressant such as Paxil, not because they are sad, but to tap into the benefits of the drug's side effects. In these particular cases, the antidepressant is prescribed because of the way it dampens appetites: sexual, gustatory, or what have you. Drugs may also be given to persons who do not understand or pick up well on social cues, and because of their clumsiness and awkwardness they may come to be defined by those with whom they interact as creeps or worse. Such persons are defined as having impairment in social interaction or communicative competence, and may be prescribed a range of medications including antidepressants or antianxiety drugs such as Guanfacine, Atomoxetine, or Fluoxetine (Wink et al. 2010). In effect, the creep, masher, or oddball is transformed into a clinical patient suffering from Asperger's or other disorders along the autism spectrum.

This brings us to an interesting question, this being, If a technology were available to enhance the morality or responsibility of persons deemed to have little or none of these valued traits, would it be in the best interests of society to deploy that technology? This is the question asked by Elizabeth Shaw (2014) in her paper on the potential for direct brain interventions of persons falling within various categories of deviant humanity. For millennia the instilling of appropriate societal values was left up to the informal process of socialization, whereby competent mothers and fathers impart the knowledge and values their children needed to adjust properly to their social world. Over time, however, there has grown a "family decline" thesis, which suggests that parents have abrogated responsibility for the upbringing of their children, and that now we must seek functional alternatives for carrying out this work (Chriss 1999b).

Interestingly enough, this problem touches upon a much older debate, that of nurture versus nature. Sociologists who favor the social construction of reality perspective would argue that everything under the sun is socially constructed, so that when persons go bad they do so because of bad parenting, criminogenic social conditions, or other factors related to the socialization process. The actual, physical development of the organism, that is, the developmental pathways, is constantly buffeted by real-world experiences of the organism. For example, Gottfredson and Hirschi (1990) argue that virtually all deviance and crime can be explained by low self-control, but where does self-control come from? It comes from adequate parental socialization of children during their development, especially insofar as parents are attentive to their norm-violating behavior and are willing to punish them when they step out of line. In many respects, the problem of low self-control is consistent with the concept of psychopathy or sociopathy, which refers to persons who have a callous disregard for the suffering of others, who are impulsive, and who seek short-term gratifications even at the expense of others.

Shaw (2014) reports that recent studies indicate that many persons who score high for psychopathy also score high on attention deficit, which may account for their antisocial behavior. We already use Ritalin to help young persons to improve their concentration, and this sort of neurological intervention is widely accepted for instilling prosocial adjustment in them. Wouldn't it make sense to engage in an even wider range of neurological interventions to instill proper values as well, not just in children but also in adults? Long ago Parsons (1951) shattered the distinction between deviance and illness, as he conceptualized illness as simply a type of deviance that could be responded to in like manner with other kinds. The main distinction, of course, was that illness would require treatment or therapy, as the sick person would be held blameless for their condition. In most other cases of deviance, especially criminal deviance, there would be held open the notion of free will and that the person did the bad deed with volition and full knowledge that it was bad (this being the legal requirement of *mens rea*). As a growing range of social deviance, including crime, is identified as some sort of brain irregularity, as indicated in neuroscience research, there is a tendency to view as moot the philosophical distinction between determinism and free will. The morality of dealing with social deviance gives way to a more or less technical/medical/legal/bureaucratic approach to growing legions of persons identified as "patients" or as "presenting" certain characteristics which can be understood within the context of a particular nosology (such as those specifying mental disorders in the *DSM*.). The specter of increasing reliance on medical technologies, drugs, and surgical interventions to control behavior, with the hopes of instilling pro-social adjustment in persons who did not receive adequate levels of socialization from their parents or other agents of control, is a set of circumstances consistent with Gouldner's lament concerning moral absolutism and the sadism underlying it.

The Thingification of Everyday Life

Gouldner's 1976 book *The Dialectic of Ideology and Technology* was subtitled "the origins, grammar, and future of ideology." This was during a phase in which Gouldner took the "linguistic turn," committed as he was to Chomsky, Labov, and other linguistics scholars. This was an attempt to shore up agency in the face of stultifying structural steering and control posited by the "grand theorists" (similar to Weber's "iron cage" or Habermas's "colonization of the life-world"). How, for example, did modernity usher in this new self, this newly emancipated and powerful person who has the freedom and disposition to get things done in this world? In a key passage Gouldner speaks for this new, powerful, emancipated, modern self:

> We have shown conclusively that Kings and Cardinals can be brought to justice. We no longer need to wait for the gods to resent their *hybris* and to bring them toppling down. We do it. By ourselves and for ourselves. The revolution, our revolution, is real and powerful and we are that revolution.... We are audacious. We exist without permission. Self-grounded, we now exist for ourselves. We can master the streets and we can master politics. We can achieve. We have one unified being... We are no longer parcelled-out beings that are given—like lands and castles—into the keeping of kings or clergy We are no longer isolated and restricted to a tiny, backward locality. We have friends and comrades everywhere. We expand out into and fill great nations and we citizens of the world now live in a larger universe. It is no longer our leaders who connect us to this world; we are part of it without mediation. No longer the small link in a large chain, we are the very center of it.
>
> 1976A: 69–70

In speaking for the modern, cosmopolitan individual seemingly teeming with agency and aplomb, Gouldner realizes also that this is a stance or ideology, and as such is limited by the ability of purveyors of that ideology to confront and overcome obstacles standing in their way. In other words, the idea of the modern emancipated self is an ideology, albeit a powerful one to be sure. It is a new form of romanticism where even deviants, criminals, and other misfits are gaining power and self-worth in this new and expanding era of human rights (Gouldner 1969b). They can demand things for and of themselves, since the old-fashioned notion of judging persons on the basis of current social status is broken and in hopeless disarray. (This is exhibited, for example, in the ongoing prisoners' rights movement and the move to abolish capital punishment. It is also evident in community corrections and the critique of total institutions in the vogue of a Goffman or Foucault, as well as in the project of normalizing previously deviant statuses such as homosexuality). Even in the face of stultifying routine exacerbated by increasing rationalization and bureaucratization, there are spaces for everyday persons to lay claim to freedom, emancipation, and recognition. For example, even as the modern regulatory society continues to expand with the aim of ensnaring more citizens—whether normal, pathological, or otherwise; it makes little difference—within incessant projects of surveillance, these same citizens are also becoming savvy about how the observers operate and are learning to avoid their gaze but also engaging in creative forms of countersurveillance (Brayne 2014; Chriss 2013).

Those in positions of power, especially those tasked with zookeeping the teeming urban masses, have always understood the perils associated with the everyday life. For the most part the informal realm of control, operating through informal agents of socialization (parents, friends, clergy, etc.) who work to ensure that their charges are properly attached to conventional others thereby maintaining adequate stakes in conformity, does a good enough job of keeping individual rogue cases to a minimum. From the perspective of the system and its zookeepers, the everyday life produces tolerable levels of alienation and anomie, which for the most part can be handled by the informal control system on a case-by-case basis (Gouldner 1975a). But in so doing, in gazing upon the world of the everyday life and studying it to understand better how to shore it up whenever and wherever deviant cases appear to be multiplying beyond tolerable levels, administrators and functionaries of the caretaker state—including of course sociologists—tend to objectify that everyday world and treat flesh-and-blood human beings as things. For Gouldner, this "thingification" of everyday life is due to poor reflexivity on the part of sociologists and other administrators who, after all, want only to make the lives of citizens "homey," that is, to ensure that their everyday life is cozy, predictable, and that order is maintained.

Gouldner (1975a: 432) states "The task is indeed to make men at home in the world. But it is only possible for *men* to be at home, not things. Things have a place, not a home." So truly to make a world a home, human beings must be allowed in it. This means peopling the everyday lifeworld, not thingifying it, as has often been the case for sociologists championing the goodness or the justness or the utility of the welfare/warfare state. One of the most pernicious ways that misguided sociologists attempt to make the everyday world homey for its residents is through pacification, namely, by withholding the bad news about the world and its major unsettling events—war, terrorism, stock market crashes, or what have you—because all these things are contrary to the establishment of a sense of certainty, familiarity, and order. This is one of the reasons Gouldner came to blows with his graduate student Laud Humphreys over his research on men having sex with men in public restrooms: He believed it was a total waste of time, a trivial pursuit, in light of bigger issues sociologists should be confronting such as war, economic inequality, political corruption, police brutality, and other structural issues.

Critical Criminology Then and Now

Gouldner's withering criticism of sociologists who seek to help underdogs but who fall short of truly emancipatory work because of their concern to sell their services to the highest bidder, is the basis upon which Taylor et al. (1973) built their project for a new criminology. Two years after the publication of their

New Criminology, Taylor et al. (1975) published an edited volume that brought together a variety of radical sociologists and criminologists to articulate a unified vision for this new criminology. Consistent with the fact that the authors had invited Gouldner to write the foreword to their 1973 volume, Taylor et al. (1975) gave Gouldner further voice in the introduction to their edited volume. Their main use of Gouldner here is in interpreting his broader criticism of utilitarianism as being consistent with criticisms made by left-leaning and radical intellectuals of their spinelessness and passivity in kowtowing to powerbrokers in Britain. In other words, the social-democratic tradition in Britain was never as radical as it needed to be, trapped as it was (and is) in a Fabianism which, although giving lip-service to the elimination of oppression and the expansion of opportunity for all, in effect merely replaced bourgeois rationalism with a socialist rationalism perverted by an unseen or unthematized infrastructure of utility (for example, pursuing policies aimed at "the greatest good for the greatest number of people" based upon conventional notions of utility).[6] Progressivism of the Fabian variety was willing to work within the system to construct a piecemeal socialism, the ends of which would be compatible with the vision of the good society emerging from the rubble of the proletarian revolution. This flaccid partisanship does not work, neither for liberal sociologists championing the plight of the underdog nor for Left intellectuals clinging to such Fabian myths as the belief that socialist ends could be attained even while leaving intact a meritocratic value system (Gouldner 1970a: 324).

This is the crux of the matter concerning Gouldner's railing against the welfare-warfare state, insofar as the helping professions—most importantly, sociology and social work but also psychiatry and counseling psychology—seek merely to instill prosocial adjustment in those deemed "deviant" rather than working to uncover the disreputable work that lawmakers, regulators, and powerbrokers are involved in seeking to maintain the system which produces and even needs a deviant class. However, even as Gouldner's anti-utilitarianism was consistent with a critique of Fabianism, which in turn represented a crucial element in the construction of Taylor et al.'s (1973) early version of critical criminology, at least one radical criminologist found fault with Taylor et al.'s embrace of Gouldner. On first blush, Pearson's (1975) concept of "misfit sociology" seems to align ideologically and philosophically with Gouldner's criticism of labeling theorists' concern with the management of a deviant class. Pearson (1975: 148) even seems to mirror Gouldner's position in characterizing misfit sociology as being an insider perspective which sides

---

6 For a useful discussion of the history of Fabian socialism in Britain, see Lasch (1991: 317–328).

with underdogs (misfits or deviants) and displays a theoretical tendency toward "de-reification." Pearson questions, however, Gouldner's unmasking of labeling theorists or misfit sociology's lack of radicalism, insofar as there is an aim simply to manage misfits through an enlightened and heartfelt zookeeping all the while attempting to endear sociology to funding agencies of the welfare state. Although Gouldner did indeed argue that the New Class of intellectuals is a potentially liberative force—and misfit sociologists such as the labeling theorists would be in the forefront of New Class intellectuals—their toadyism toward the powerful in the name of ameliorating the pathologies of the powerless and dispossessed would always work to circumvent the truly liberative work of fixing the pathologies of the system at its core. Pearson does not like Gouldner's sneering and dismissive attitude toward intellectuals as mere managers and zookeepers, or his disdain for the pseudo-radicalism of ethnomethodology that is actually little more than a fad or a sixties "happening." Pearson (1975: 153) notes, for example, Gouldner's description of the "know nothing New Left," but since he does not offer a precise citation to Gouldner here it is unclear where or under what circumstance Gouldner actually said or wrote this. Pearson goes on to argue:

> What is at issue for Gouldner is not "radical social science"—not matters of partisanship, objectivity, and scholarship—but politics, dressed as rationality. In his sometimes indiscriminate, but always passionate denunciation of Becker, Goffman and Garfinkel, there is always the impression that the conviction came first, and then, however Gouldner may attempt to present the matter as otherwise, argument followed after.
> 1975: 153

In other words, Gouldner shoots from the hip and proclaims by fiat that the labeling theorists—and misfit sociology as a whole—possess a politics at variance with his own, and because of this the entire project is tainted and requires withering criticism. This is ironic considering that Gouldner went out of his way arguing that a reflexive sociology would value rationality in seeking to bring to light how unseen domain assumptions shape and form the technical aspects of any theoretical undertaking. Pearson is making the point, what good is an unmasking when the person doing the unmasking refuses to take off his? Gouldner does not like Goffman's notion that we all wear masks and put on shows for the benefit of the audience—including labeling theorists who put on shows for funding elites regarding their expertise in understanding and ameliorating the plight of a deviant class, now soaring in numbers due to the multiple pathologies of a wretched urban capitalism—yet Gouldner never notices or, even worse, does not care, that his own mask is firmly in place while making proclamations to the contrary. This reflects some lingering concerns with the potential unending paradox of a reflexive sociology which must ultimately rely on critique for the sake of critique and hold to a correct politics as the necessary grounding for the various levels of critique and unmasking. That correct politics is historical materialism, and for all his railings against the failures and lack of reflexivity of Marxism, in the end this is Gouldner's fallback position, his core.

By extension, the rise of critical criminology in the form of the New Criminology of Taylor and colleagues around this time (mid-1970s) was based upon the attempt to extend Marx and Engels' writings into an area—crime and deviance—which they pretty much neglected. The principle focus of these early critical criminologists was class, insofar as the capitalist system could make easy scapegoats of those who lacked access to socially-valued rewards and who sometimes broke the law in pursuit of them, lacking as they did the legitimate means to acquire them (see, e.g., Chambliss 1975; Reiman 1989). This class-based explanation of crime and deviance remained intact through perhaps the 1990s, at which time new variants of Marxist-inspired criminology emerged, along the way shifting the focus from class to race, gender, and sexual orientation. Emblematic of this shift is Ngaire Naffine's (1996) book *Feminism and Criminology* where Gouldner's influence is direct and overt. One of her chapters is titled "The Criminologist as Partisan," a tribute to and reworking of Gouldner's paper "The Sociologist as Partisan." Naffine (1996: 41) cites approvingly Gouldner's characterization of Becker and the labeling theorists who, in their relation to deviants, are like "the Great White Hunter" who has "bravely risked the perils of the urban jungle to bring back an exotic specimen." Naffine (ibid.) picks up where Gouldner and earlier critical criminologists left off: "We might add, in feminist vein, that Becker was the great white *male* hunter whose romantic flirtation with deviant culture had much to do with his own style of masculinity." This appears in the form of paternalism where criminals and other deviants are made out to be victims, and in this victim status they are viewed as products of an oppressive system rather than as rebels against it.

Conclusion

I will have more to say on this in the last chapter, but suffice to say as we close this chapter that whenever Gouldner engages in this sort of moral anguish or righteous indignation it falls flat for the very reasons specified above. This is because Gouldner overshoots the target in his condemnation of mainstream sociologists and their purported lack of reflexivity. According to Gouldner's standard approach, all persons in positions of power or authority are condemnable because of the way they can stand over others, thereby thingifying or objectifying them and making them less than human. Even sociologists like Becker or the Chicago school theorists, who went out into the streets of Chicago and elsewhere to study the lives of those victimized by their conditions and surroundings with an eye toward ameliorating their plight: Even these people are condemnable! It appears, then, that no form of sociological practice or research method is safe from critical appraisal. This approach seems to close off entirely the much-vaunted attempt to unify theory and practice, which certainly seems to be so in the specific case of the sociology of crime and deviance. At the beginning of the chapter, for example, we saw that Gouldner lauded Taylor et al. (1973) for developing a critical criminology which went beyond traditional criminology's focus on practical problem-solving which was limited to the extent that it relied on the perspectives and assumptions of powerbrokers of officialdom. The problem is that criminal justice administrators and functionaries lack a critical perspective on criminal law as they, for example, hardly raise concerns or alarm that the system is set up ostensibly to crush those who lack resources to fight criminal charges. As a result, criminals and others labelled deviant are overwhelmingly those who the system has set up by definition as deserving our scorn, condemnation, and outrage. Certain classes of people lacking political power and/or cultural capital—racial minorities, homosexuals and other sexual offenders, and juveniles especially—are overrepresented in the crime statistics, and they serve as handy scapegoats for focusing and embodying societal concerns about crime. This is the general project of the critique of the status quo, a good representation of which is contained in the Sociology Liberation Movement's (SLM) "Knowledge for Whom?" declaration from 1968:

> Posing as disinterested scholars, we perform policy research for the powerful organizations...providing them with the knowledge they need...to control their "problems." We have placed our expertise at the disposal of the establishment, letting the development of our field be guided by the needs of those who can pay for our time... In the name of value-neutrality, we have failed (to help) the poor, the powerless or the unorganized.
> BROWN 1970: 29

This is the standard radical criminology line articulated by Taylor et al. and lauded by Gouldner in the foreword of their book, yet this also has the tendency to pass into unreflective partisanship among a group of like-minded believers—critical criminologists—who are convinced that their approach reflects not only the true but also the good. The Gouldner approach is, as I have stated previously, an ultra- or hypercritical approach that must remain aloof to traditional scientific notions positing the importance of a consensual community of researchers solving normal science puzzles. When a researcher identifies as belonging to theory group x or y, he or she tends also to gloss over the potentially discrepant aspects of the enterprise lying in wait within the infrastructure, including unstated or tacit assumptions of ontology, axiology, and epistemology. For Gouldner, theory groups make unwarranted claims about their ability to peer into the workings of the world. Even further, the traditional critical or even radical approaches—in the realm of crime and deviance or elsewhere—go one step further to claim that not only do they understand why people do bad things, they also know how to stop bad or hurtful things from happening in the first place. Usually this means changing the entire system from the ground up because it is shot through with multiple forms of oppression developed over a long period of time. What this means, then, is that revolution is the way forward.

Being sympathetic to revolutionary aspirations but reluctant to join others in their shared revolutionary zeal, Gouldner criticized all researchers whether traditional (conservative or liberal) or radical: The positivists feel that obedience to objective, naturalistic methods allows them to do what scientists are supposed to do, namely, explaining how things work and not really caring about the consequences of that knowledge or how it is be used and by whom. The traditional radical theorists hold to a particular theory that is unquestioned as to its veracity—for example, historical materialism of the Marxists—and armed with this unassailable knowledge, they seek to implement it so as to alleviate the real pain and suffering of the dispossessed or the powerless. Gouldner is not able to give allegiance to any of this, although as a self-identified radical sociologist he is more sympathetic to the latter.

Understandably, there is a tendency to lump Gouldner in with so-called radical criminology. In fact, some observers within the field of crime and deviance, such as Groves and Sampson (1987) go so far as to suggest that traditional criminology and radical criminology share more in common than is typically admitted to. Specifically, the authors claim that for all their alleged differences, traditional and radical criminology hold similar explanations of the causes of crime and deviance. Groves and Sampson (1987) point to three aspects of overlap or consistency in the causes of crime between traditional and radical criminology, insofar as both:

- posit the importance of social class as a key factor in criminality;
- employ social-structural models of crime causation which are consistently macrosociological in context;
- emphasize materialistic aspects of social structure and cultural orientations (for example, the value placed on the acquisition of material wealth) in the production of crime.

Here, Groves and Sampson (1987) are attempting to smuggle in to the model of conventional criminology a critical infrastructure consistent with Marxist assumptions of class conflict, materialism, and holism. Assuming the existence of such a critical infrastructure for conventional or academic criminology, Groves and Sampson can then argue for the bad faith of establishment criminologists who act as if they are blind to the critical assumptions undergirding their theoretical and methodological work. However, as Bohm (1987) has pointed out, the claim by radical criminologists that establishment sociologists and criminologists are crippled by a false consciousness concerning the nature of their work is merely indicative of the work that ideology does in guiding their (critical criminologists) view about the field. In some respects, then, Bohm's (1987) ability to see through the attempt by Groves and Sampson (1987) to rehabilitate establishment criminology by claiming for it its radical roots is consistent with some of the demystification work Gouldner has been doing all along in the name of increasing the reflexivity of sociological and criminological practitioners.

CHAPTER 4

Bourdieu and Reflexive Sociology

Introduction

Although Gouldner put reflexive sociology on the map beginning in the early 1970s, by the 1980s and beyond his version of reflexive sociology was displaced and largely relegated to the sidelines in favor of Pierre Bourdieu's version. Why did this happen, and what were the presumed benefits of Bourdieu's model over the one Gouldner proposed? The primary reason this happened was that Gouldner was overwhelmingly a *theorist* and rarely connected data or empirical observations to his analyses. In contradistinction, with publications like *Distinction*, Bourdieu provided models of how reflexive sociology provided benefits with regard to further empirical understanding of specific substantive areas. (Margaret Archer has been doing this sort of work as well.) The chapter will focus on this problem, the problem of the "armchair" sociologist spinning out elegant conceptual schemes and providing running critiques—a criticism that Gouldner ironically made of Parsons but which would apply equally to himself—but in the end being left with what many could argue are merely "empty" speculations about social life. I shall not make this harsh a judgment on Gouldner, but I will explain how and why Bourdieu triumphed with regard to the utility of reflexive sociology from the perspective of sociologists working at the research front.

Bourdieu's Reflexive Sociology

It is interesting to note that Bourdieu's sociology of science pushes a version of reflexivity that is quite similar to that of Gouldner, yet he rarely if ever cites him. However, both Gouldner and Bourdieu share certain commitments at the infrastructural level of their respective theories, namely, a Marxist ontology that takes for granted that subjectivity is forged through alienation, representing one aspect of the Hegelian dialectic. However, although Bourdieu tends to stay more within an orthodox Marxist framework—albeit sometimes critical of Marxism but still retaining tacit aspects of it within the infrastructure of the theory—Gouldner lets loose and applies a critical sensibility to all theories, including those of Marxism. In other words, Gouldner took critical theory more seriously than Bourdieu and everyone else for that matter, as he was willing to turn critical theorizing back onto the retaining principles and propositions of all evaluative theories themselves rather than glossing them over. This means that Gouldner's version of reflexivity was more robust and radical than Bourdieu's, even though both started out with concerns over how capitalism systematically alienates subjectivity.

For example, in his book *Distinction*, Bourdieu notes that as a critical theorist Gramsci articulated the concept of cultural hegemony or domination, whereby members of the lower class strive to present themselves and their values as being consistent with those of the middle and upper classes. But since they lack the social, cultural, or financial capital to copy all the trappings of a middle class lifestyle, the working and lower classes opt for cheap imitations or stand-ins for the pricier objects and symbols of the higher classes. This leads to the business of cultural mass production of these more affordable copies of the well-to-do, and as persons are in a race to keep up with the Joneses to show the outward appearance of having achieved the American Dream, along the way they become deeply alienated and prisoners of vulgar consumerism. This is why, for example, Adorno, Marcuse and other Frankfurt School critical theorists criticized not only the world of alienated labor, but also sneered at the masses' attempt to surround themselves with all the trapping of what amounted to, in Bourdieu's (1984: 386) phrase, "populist impeccability." The masses, then, lack reflexivity, in that they mistake the culture and symbolic objects of the powerful which they covet as naturally-occurring features of their everyday lifeworld, of their mundane and everyday existence. It is an example of the misrecognition afflicting the masses, and this misrecognition is built into the system of ruling that assures that their quest for pseudo-authenticity will always mark them as inferior to the true holders of power.

So for Bourdieu, one's life experiences and patterns of socialization and living amount to a living membrane, a habitus, within which such persons are immersed, constituting the taken-for-granted background of everything they do. It is akin to the fish, which possesses no knowledge of the concept "wetness." The goal of the critical theorist for Bourdieu, then, is to wake the masses out of their slumber of false consciousness by having experts map out all the details of the habitus within which they operate but of which they are unaware. This elitism, that is, of experts who possess the right theory and who also possess the tools by which to extricate the lowly masses from their alienated existence, is typical of Marxists like Bourdieu. From Gouldner's perspective, the reflexivity of Gramsci, Adorno, Marcuse, Fromm (see Cheliotis 2011), and by extension Bourdieu do not go far enough, for they culminate in a phalanx of experts, that is, the vanguard party. Gouldner tried desperately to avoid the problem of cognitive elitism in terms of how theorists come into contact with real flesh-and-blood human beings whom they hope to rescue. We will return to this issue shortly.

Later in his career Bourdieu turned his attention more and more to science, that is, to the philosophy of science or the sociology of science. Here instead of drawing upon critical theorists he was more apt to cite Woolgar, Latour, and Feyerabend. The reflexive project at this stage is simply the turning inward onto science itself with the aim of questioning the positivistic dictums of value-freedom and the favoring of objectivity over subjectivity. For example, Bourdieu titled a chapter of one of his books "Why the Social Sciences Must Take Themselves as Their Object" (Bourdieu 2004: 85–114). Yet, Bourdieu is not simply operating to uncover the conceit of positivistic sociologists that claim misguidedly that sociology is a science because it can aspire to objective knowledge just as do the natural sciences. Indeed, in an earlier book Bourdieu et al. (1991) argued that sociology WAS a science except for peculiarities that render it a science unlike those of the natural sciences. For the natural sciences really do have real objects to study which are separate from the hopes, thoughts, and aspirations of natural scientists. But sociologists and other social scientists take as their objects of study fellow human beings and the products of their organized activities. If fellow human beings were being studied merely as organisms that would be fine: that natural science was and is known as biology. But sociology is more than biology, because it takes into account the subjective realm of consciousness, thoughts, feelings, and interpersonal communications (leading to the assumption of intersubjectivity) along with the material and ideational products of their labor and activities (culture).[1]

Scientific Habitus

Like Gouldner, Bourdieu was concerned with developing a more robust social constructivism that took into account how explanations about all things, whether scientific or lay, were embedded in the social milieu or habitus within which human beings operate. Gouldner's solution was to move toward a linguistic approach, emphasizing the special speech variant—the culture of critical discourse—which intellectuals use to make their mark on the world. In this way, Gouldner could view all public projects as ideologies, thereby giving

---

1 Early American sociologists such as Lester Ward and Franklin Giddings embraced some version of Spencer's early attempt to solve this dilemma. Spencer's equation was roughly: Biology + Psychology = Sociology.

everyday folk equal footing with the privileged educated (Gouldner 1976a). Bourdieu (2004: 89) eschews the linguistics and semiotics of Gouldner in favor of as the Marxist-inspired habitus, and in the particular case of science, this would amount to identifying the particular aspects of the scientific habitus of scientists as they go about their work and research. Bourdieu is attempting to merge structural notions of habitus, or the phenomenological notion of the surrounding world, with a notion of subjectivity that affords levels of reflexive agency of actors who, because of this human endowment, are not totally at the mercy of their habitus. (Chandler [2013] argues for just this even as he overlooks the orthodox Marxist background within which Bourdieu operates.)

Taking into account the social construction of all things, including scientific knowledge, means that critically oriented sociologists of knowledge and science are able to bring into view how science really works, through the disposition of a reflexivity reflex. This simply means, the ceaselessness and restlessness concomitant to not allowing tacit, background assumptions of how the world works to infiltrate theoretical work. Or, stated differently, the reflexivity reflex guides those properly trained in the sociologies of science and knowledge to reject natural tendencies toward embracing *a priori* assumptions, while being alive—much like phenomenology—to the stream of events—cultural, historical, personal, psychological, sociological—leading up to that moment of discovery, insight, creativity, or what have you.

Even given the benefits of the reflexivity reflex, sociologists must also be on guard against narcissism, that is, looking back on one's own work and believing this act, in and of itself, is sufficient as a form of reflexivity informing deeper understandings of scientific work. Narcissism creeps in as part of the wisdom of taking into account the authorial voice, and conversely not acting as if data simply speaks for itself. But this sort of turning inward can become fetishistic, especially with regard to the aggrandizement of self. Bourdieu even takes a shot at ethnomethodologists, whom mistakenly claim that their radicality is embodied in the way they reject established ways of doing science, such as, for example, the deductive-nomothetic model for developing covering laws. The ethnomethodologists believe their radicalism is useful and consistent with the spirit of social constructivism via the principle of ethnomethodological indifference, as no particular method is favored over others, and that lay accounts must be studied on their own terms without overlaying *a priori* scientific principles over them in order to make sense of them.

Interestingly, on this point Bourdieu's critique of ethnomethodology converges on some levels with Gouldner's earlier critique. However, Gouldner's (1970a) critique was grounded in a nuanced position whereby, as outsider to the 1960s social movements which railed against the oppression of the establishment in general, he was positioned to see that ethnomethodology's critique of establishment science (and sociology in particular) was simply a cheap ploy—a parlor trick—to pull in a gullible group of young persons and their elder demigods (that is, students and professors) who were convinced that, because of Garfinkel's impenetrable prose style, this represented something really "new and big," perhaps even revolutionary. Being averse to joining bandwagons or vanguards, Gouldner was always positioned on the radical fringe to be the guy most likely to throw a wet blanket on any heady proclamations that this was an excellent way of "sticking it to the man." For Gouldner, showing up around the time of the radical ferment of the mid-1960s, ethnomethodology was really little more than a "happening" which promised, through its ethnomethodological demonstrations (such as the breaching experiment) to allow the relatively powerless to stick a finger in the collective eye of the stolid and staid establishment. The cries of pain and anguish from persons unwittingly exposed to the disruption of their daily routines makes ethnomethodologists little more than street artists like Jerry Rubin. Even so, their radicalism, however enfeebled or calculated it may be, is still an improvement over Parsons' unreflexive embrace of scientism and naturalism.

Gouldner thought that ethnomethodology was too gimmicky, too much part of the misplaced zeal of partisans who were hell-bent on overturning the establishment or, short of that, at least making their members uncomfortable. But it has no chance to succeed on the larger scale of really making a difference in the lives of people, especially with regard to the alleviation of misery and oppression. Bourdieu, too, sees ethnomethodology as missing the mark because of its fetish of technique and the discovery of the infinitely small—especially as embodied in one of its more successful empirical applications, conversation analysis—thereby losing sight of the reformist ethos which, for Bourdieu, is the *sine qua non* of any project of inquiry. Keeping this reformist endpoint in mind is supposed to keep scientists from becoming reckless and pursuing projects merely for their own sake. This position becomes circular, as it circles back on communist criticisms of the distinction between pure and applied science.

So Bourdieu, and to a lesser extend Gouldner, criticize any project which loses sight of the reformist goal of maximizing human emancipation and happiness. Should we really criticize ethnomethodology—or any sociological theory for that matter—because of its failure to heal the world? Why should it be an imperative to change the world instead of merely studying it? Is a program of pure sociology—knowledge for the sake of knowledge—totally useless? But what is utility? How should we judge effectiveness? Both Bourdieu and

Gouldner would have benefitted from reading Lester Ward's (1903, 1906) thoughts on the special place and role that applied and pure knowledge play in any systematic field of inquiry. But, more on this later.

Society as Both Objective and Subjective Reality

Although concerns over reflexivity turn scientists toward the study of how subjectivity gears into the social world, there is always lurking within this project the question of how social phenomena gear into the objective or natural world. In their widely acclaimed book *The Social Construction of Reality*, Peter Berger and Thomas Luckmann make a seemingly convincing claim that life as we know it is real in both an objective and a subjective sense. The idea that the world is an objective reality is very easy to accept. By way of our five senses and as a result of living with the things always all around us—rocks, trees, the sky, the birds and bees, other people—we come to accept the notion of an obdurate reality "out there" that we have to take into account whenever we do anything. It is the idea that the world is the way it is regardless of how we think about or perceive it. It just *is*. It is a stubborn, incessant reality.

But there is also a subjective reality: the notion that thoughts, feelings, attitudes, desires, motivations, dreams, aspirations, and the like reside in our heads—in our minds and our memory—and that these internal depictions or representations of whatever is out there in the "real world" are every bit as real as the objective reality that exists outside of us. Society, then, exists as both objective and subjective reality (Berger and Luckmann 1966: 129). Indeed, in an attempt to do away entirely with what is contended to be an artificial divide between the world "out there" and the representations or images of the world that we carry around in our heads, some authors speak not of objectivity versus subjectivity. Rather, they speak in terms of "internal" objectivity (subjective states and mindful activity) and "external" objectivity (the real world "out there"; see, e.g. Hanna 2004; Zizek 1999). Among other things, this move attempts to repudiate the idea of a Cartesian subject thinking about and reacting to an objective world "out there," as if there were a clear line separating the inner from the outer (Elliott 2003).

For purposes of this discussion, however, this move will be avoided. Merely changing the name of something—for example, internal objectivity instead of subjectivity—changes only the way we speak of the thing, but not the thing itself. It is one thing to take for granted lay or commonsense notions about the subjective reality of our inner lives, but it is quite another to try to open up this area for scientific investigation. Early American sociologists like Lester Ward,

Franklin Giddings, and Charles Ellwood (among others) have been criticized for accepting far too uncritically the claims everyday human beings make about their own subjectivity. These sociologists were also taken to task for conceding to psychologists that the mind and all its products are amenable to scientific analysis, and that such psychic elements are indeed real and must be taken account of in order to build sociology as the legitimate science of society. This uncritical, nonreflexive acceptance of the so-called psychic or subjective dimension of reality led the early American sociologists to create a sort of "psychological sociology" which was the forerunner to the modern social psychology emerging from the writings of Dewey, Mead, and the philosophical pragmatists.

Richard Wollheim devoted a good part of his career in philosophy to examining the methodological and epistemological difficulties involved in the scientific quest for subjectivity. One part of his discussion is particularly well suited for our purposes:

> An initial difficulty with subjectivity that has far-reaching consequences is that by and large subjectivity cannot be described in any direct fashion. We get nowhere when we try to say either what subjectivity is in itself or what it is in the case of a given mental state—unless we do this obliquely.
> WOLLHEIM 1984: 38

Wollheim argues that we can arrive at subjectivity only obliquely because it is merely one aspect of mental phenomena, and the various other parts—intentionality, psychic force and psychic function, quality of consciousness, and significance—simply cannot be artificially separated from one another (see also Watier 2003). One thing is clear however: any attempt to marshal external evidence concerning the "realness" of a mental phenomenon, including its subjective aspects, must always show up in the form of a communication (verbal or otherwise) about the mental state that the subject is alleged to be experiencing. Subjectivity, then, is reported by human subjects, either verbally through talk or through other forms of display, such as the routine presentation of self in everyday life (Goffman 1959; Habermas 1984).

From the scientific perspective, the holism, or the joining together, of the otherwise distinct worlds of inside and outside, of subject and object, must eventuate in a methodology or tradition of study which favors the study of speech, in conjunction with an assumption concerning the reflective ability of human beings as they situate themselves in relation to strips of activity which they are experiencing or have experienced in the objective physical world. It is instructive to note, for example, that the earliest attempt to develop a science of collective or group psychology—the *Volkerpsychologie* of Wundt—went hand in hand with the study of speech, or linguistics (*Sprachwissenschaft*). Since the subjectivity of a mental state is not directly observable, it must be gotten at indirectly, through subjects' self-reflection and behavior (verbal or otherwise).

Hence, from the perspective of a science of subjectivity, there are two aspects, one internal and one external. Rather than internal and external objectivity (as mentioned above), in this domain we may speak of internal and external *subjectivity*. The external aspect of subjectivity is subject's reports about what they are experiencing in their head, which may be gleaned by a researcher either directly through talk or indirectly through nonverbal behavior. Giddings and Durkheim, who developed the notions of "consciousness of kind" and "collective conscience" respectively, understood how memory links the individual to the social collectivity, and how in turn memory itself is the "common currency" of the language we all speak (Sayer 2004: 85). The internal aspect of subjectivity is subject's capacity for self-reflection, or *reflexivity*. It is this second, internal aspect of subjectivity that is the primary focus of this chapter.

Symbolic Interaction, Reflexivity, and Social Justice

From Mead and later as codified by Blumer, the symbolic interactionist perspective posits reflexivity as an essential human capacity, one that is vitally important to the development of the self and the sustenance of everyday social interaction. Further, within the context of the lifeworld, reflexive awareness is not a special ability that only a few gifted or special persons possess; rather, all persons naturally and unproblematically are able to look back upon themselves by taking on the attitude of the other, so much so that they are typically not even aware that they are acting reflexively in developing a sense of self.

Assuming that reflexivity is an inalienable human capacity, Holland (1999: 472) argues that social theorists must engage in some modicum of reflexive practice as well. Hence, according to Holland, the claims made by Gouldner (1970a, 1980a) that certain theorists or certain species of theory (especially functionalism and Marxism, but also symbolic interactionism, dramaturgy, and even ethnomethodology) lack reflexivity, simply do not comport with the reality of natural reflexivity that all humans, including of course social theorists, possess. As Holland (1999: 473) continues, "It is misleading to assert that some [theoretical] positions are reflexive and others not, falling into the same trap as the demarcationist philosophies of science. If reflexivity defines human being, we postulate subhuman or nonhuman creatures if we say that others are not reflexive."

Is this true? Do we really postulate that persons are "subhuman" or "nonhuman" if we say they are not reflexive? Let us investigate this issue further by considering a similar suggestion made by Vaughan and Sjoberg (1986) that the capacity for social reflectivity is the most essential characteristic of our humanity. They argue that the human ability to reflect on ourselves and our social location and situation gives us all, potentially, the power to shape social reality even as we are being shaped by it. This is in essence our humanness: the ability, through a mindful and reflective consciousness, to transcend particular settings.

A moral principle following from this is that persons have a basic *right* to the social conditions of reflectivity. As Vaughan and Sjoberg explain,

> Since reflective consciousness is a potential only realizable in social contexts, every person and group rightfully should have access to the necessary social structures for developing and sustaining reflective consciousness whereby one achieves human status.
> 1986: 139

Indeed, the right to human status—which can only be achieved if social arrangements that facilitate social reflectivity are present in the first place—is *fundamental*. Social conditions that deny one's human status, such as genocide, slavery, or apartheid, in effect reduce persons to mere "objects."

Clearly, here, Vaughan and Sjoberg are valuing subjectivity as a moral good. Conversely, oppressive social conditions that treat persons as objects reduce them to "subhuman" or "nonhuman" status, as suggested by Holland above. This is in keeping with the *Verstehend* or hermeneutic tradition within social and political thought—of which symbolic interactionism is a part—that emphasizes interpretation or "thick" description over causal explanation (Geertz 1973; for a summary see Habermas 1984: 102–141). In essence, the value-free and objectivating impulses within positivistic social science, which in effect render research subjects faceless or as mere data points to be manipulated by the researcher, can be seen as perpetuating similar sorts of violence against reflexivity and subjectivity as discussed above (Agger 1989).

It is interesting to note, however, that from another theoretical perspective, under specifiable conditions it is actually necessary to render persons as objects *before* they can become subjects. I am of course referring to the Hegelian dialectic, which Marx appropriated famously from Hegel to fashion his own dialectical materialism. This is dialectical or interactional objectivity.

Marshalling a form of "soft" structuralism (as described by Mayhew n.d.), Gouldner (1974a) suggests that residing within the deepest structures of Marxism is a "metaphoricality" concerning the nature of the proletariat and its emancipation (Chriss 1999c: 143–147). In effect, the proletariat is a metaphor for a variety of oppressed or disadvantaged groups. Although Marx originally envisioned the British working class as the concrete historical agent of socialist revolution, later generations of Marxists and neoMarxists easily substituted other historical agents as bearers of the revolution. As Gouldner explains,

> It is because of this metaphoricality of the proletariat in Marxism that it has been capable of dropping the proletariat and searching out other historical agents to replace that tired "heart" of the revolution. Again, this also makes it understandable how Marxists can concretize "socialism" in such a surprising variety of forms, for example, as a "people's democratic dictatorship," presumably (perhaps only) capable of emerging even in societies with scarcely a proletariat.
> 1974A: 32

The most profound basis of Marxism's metaphoricality is concretized in the paleosymbol of "enslavement." Indeed, Marxism's metaphor of enslavement evokes images of bodily confinement that inflict gross indignities on the person (Gouldner 1974b: 392). For Marx, the revolution must struggle to make manifest this brutal essence of capitalist enslavement. The choice of socialism, then, is ultimately a repudiation of the barbarism inherent in class or caste systems whereby one group of persons rules over another, and only through socialism can the ultimate goal of universal emancipation be realized.

Further, Gouldner suggests that the metaphor of enslavement is the central "switching house" whereby rebellions of all kinds—not just proletarian rebellions—fall under the rubric of Marx's general explanatory scheme. This "labeled" metaphor of enslavement is traceable to an even more deeply buried "unlabeled" metaphor of enslavement assimilated from German philosophical idealism, particularly from Hegel's notion of the dialectic of "masterbondsman" (Gouldner 1974b: 402).

The proletariat's transformation from object to subject, from false consciousness to class consciousness, delivers not only a new self-awareness to the proletariat as a class, but also provides a liberating transformation of the entire society. Now neither object nor subject, the proletariat transcends the earlier material conditions that enslaved it, and through the revolt produces a new thesis, namely socialism. This parallels on a much grander scale Marx's view of the unfolding of the *Geist* in materialist terms with the historical transition from feudalism (thesis) to capitalism (antithesis) to socialism (new thesis or synthesis).

It seems here we have a fundamental contradiction between the hermeneutic approach, which suggests that self and self-consciousness arise only under liberative social conditions in which reflexivity is assured, and the Hegelian or dialectic approach, which suggests that the self and subjectivity arise just as readily out of oppressive conditions whereby for a period of time at least selves are treated as objects. On its face, this contradiction or disagreement is traceable to the split between Kant and Hegel over transcendental reason, or the ultimate grounding of understanding and interpretation.

Hegel was opposed to Kant's distinction between noumena and phenomena. For Kant, the universality of judgments acts as the transcendental ground of reason (Hacking 1983: 98–99). In making this move, Kant limited knowing to the objects of possible experience, shared collectively, and declared that noumenon, the thing-in-itself, behind appearances was unknowable. In order to understand why this is a problem for Hegel, we shall turn to an illuminating discussion provided by Hans-Georg Gadamer.

According to Gadamer (2000), Hegel's main objection is that by separating the appearance from the thing-in-itself, Kant was in effect imbuing reason with too much power. In essence, reason has no limit, because it is reason and reason alone that is able to discern the presumed distinction between appearances and things-in-themselves. But what makes a limit a limit always includes knowledge of what is on both sides of it. As Gadamer (2000: 343) explains, "It is the dialectic of the limit to exist only by being superceded." Like the dialectic of master-bondsman, subjectivity arises out of the limits imposed by objectification; it does not emerge necessarily in and for itself. Kant's separation between appearance and the thing-in-itself makes transcendental reason the arbiter of reality. But rather than absolute reason, self-consciousness for Hegel arises only out of the difficult battle to be recognized by the other.

The Problem of Recognition

This issue of recognition has come to the fore especially within political and social theory over the conceptualization of social justice or the "good life" more generally (see Furedi 2004: 162–174). Indeed, over the years across modern western society and increasingly among the so-called developing and less-developed nations, social movements have arisen based upon group demands for recognition of the unique identity or cultural attributes such groups are claiming for themselves. Further, these demands for recognition are grounded in the claim that the dominant culture and major social institutions of society (especially the polity and economy) have systematically ignored and injured members of these groups through their failure to provide mechanisms for assuring members' full participation in society.

Although the demand for recognition is sometimes—indeed often—coupled to a demand for economic reparations to offset the historical damage done to these groups, the central issue is nevertheless always about group identity and the demand for recognition and acknowledgement of this identity claim. From this perspective, social movements such as feminism, civil rights, gay rights, multiculturalism, anti-colonialism, and reparations for African-Americans as a corrective to the injustices of slavery, are all to some degree movements for recognition. Such movements for recognition and identity are appearing more frequently and in sometimes unexpected places and circumstances. For example, the sans-papiers, a group of activists in France consisting of unregistered immigrants, are trying to make visible their identity as modern migrant workers while asserting their right to full societal participation (Ruggiero 2000). These and other kinds of groups that historically have sought to remain invisible are now seeking recognition from state governments and fellow citizens, attempting in so doing to reject their deviant or marginalized labels.

Charles Taylor (1994) argues that groups that perceive that they are being misrecognized or not recognized at all are suffering real damage insofar as persons in the wider society are routinely mirroring back to members of these groups confining, demeaning, or contemptible images of themselves (Taylor 1994: 25). This distorted image of the self leads to a host of problems in the living conditions and life chances of members of misrecognized or unrecognized groups. For example, feminists claim that patriarchal societies operate is such a way as to socialize women into internalizing a depreciatory image of themselves (see, e.g., England and Browne 1992). Likewise, for centuries whites have projected a negative image onto blacks, and these powerful cultural scripts and practices have made it virtually impossible for blacks to resist adopting a deleterious self-image.

There are at least two types of explanation for the continuing growth of claims for recognition as well as claims for monetary reparations or redistribution of societal assets. First, Weber's notion of rationalization could be marshaled to suggest that as persons adopt more of a strategic or instrumentally rational approach to everyday life, and as more formalized mechanisms (such as law) are made available to settle disputes or conflicts between the citizenry, citizens are apt to translate their suffering as underprivileged groups into monetary terms (Habermas 1999: 203–205). Indeed, this represents a leading pathology of modernity, namely the consumerist redefinition of everyday life.

Connected with this, a second broad approach is to note the historical sweep of emancipation through juridification, leading to the development of modern constitutional democracies and the later welfare state. In earlier times, when the social order was held together by informal group consensus, government—whatever there was of it—represented a collective conscience that acted on behalf of the people, often punitively and harshly, against those who dared violate the moral order. Preindustrial governments or societies by no means could be characterized as compassionate in their treatment of, and attitude toward citizens. In fact, such governments often acted oppressively, wielding their coercive powers arbitrarily against the citizenry to stifle dissent and ensure social order (Chriss 1999a: 9).

It was not until the late 1700s that the modern democratic state first came into view. Social movements such as the French Revolution of 1789 and the American democratic revolution against the British sovereign marked a mass repudiation of the concentration of power in the hands of a few government elites. As Habermas (1987: 360) argues, this wave of juridification, which ushered in the democratic constitutional state, sees the idea of freedom already incipient in the concept of law given constitutional force. Here, constitutionalized state power was democratized, and citizens, as citizens of the state, were provided rights of political participation.

In essence, the ideas of the monarchy and the "divine right of kings" were overthrown and rendered illegitimate. Citizens' rights are no longer defined only on the basis of property rights and economic status. Now, laws come into force only when there is a democratically backed presumption that they express a general interest (the "general will") to which all those affected could agree. Also the lifeworld—the realm of everyday life—is incorporated more meaningfully into the operation of the polity that once dominated the lifeworld through generalized, delinguistified media such as power (seated in the polity) and money (seated in the economy). Power is more structurally dispersed away from the sovereign by way of the creation of differential governmental institutions, for example, the legislature, the executive branch, and the judiciary.

Although the polity acts more compassionately toward its citizens in the democratic constitution state, there still exists a high degree of unreflexivity with regard to the issue of recognition per se. It is not until the emergence of the democratic welfare state, beginning in the 1920s, that we see the fuller institutionalization of policies and social roles dedicated to enacting and carrying out the work of amelioration and recognition. The modern welfare state, illustrated by the struggles of the European workers' movement and especially by the emergence in the United States of President Roosevelt's New Deal program in the 1930s, represents another in the line of freedom-guaranteeing juridifications occurring across western society. As Habermas (1987: 361–373) argues, this can be understood as the institutionalization in legal form of a social power relation anchored in the lifeworld and in class structure. Here, constitutionally guaranteed protections are being made explicit with regard not only to one's occupational status or citizenship status, but also to virtually all other statuses comprising a person's status set.

Originally, the movements that gave rise to the early welfare state were aimed at ameliorating problems besetting the economic institution, illustrated by policies such as placing limitations on working hours, improving working conditions, ensuring the freedom to organize unions and bargain for wages, social security, and protection from layoffs. In effect, these movements represented efforts by the citizenry to create protection from economic harm accruing from the unequal distribution of valued resources in capitalist society (Fraser 1989). Initially, then, welfare state guarantees were meant to cushion the external effects of a production process based on wage labor that, although creating prosperity for some and a higher standard of living for the citizenry as a whole, also produced in some pockets of society levels of poverty, disadvantage, and despair previously unseen or unimagined.

Eventually, of course, the idea of freedom-guaranteeing juridification burst out of the confines of the economic realm (in terms of one's status as a worker) or claims against the sovereign, into virtually all areas of social life. In other words, the force of law as a guarantor of rights is now being used as a wedge to provide relief to citizens within the contexts of informal lifeworlds, in that claims of damage are being made on the basis of debilitating identity or nonrecognition connected to an expanding list of statuses. Now, above and beyond claims being made on the basis of "citizen" or "worker," within constitutional welfare states persons are making identity- or recognition-related claims on the basis of gender, race, ethnicity, age, disability, sexual orientation, marital status, and so forth.

This progression in the change of western polities could be interpreted as a slow but inexorable move toward incorporating greater reflexivity into law and policy. Many things "taken for granted" in earlier times are being looked at in different ways and subject to reflective critique or appraisal pertaining to the treatment of persons, objects, other living entities, and the environments within which they are situated. For example, "green politics" reflects heightened awareness of the damage being done by humans to their environment and ecology, with environmentalists pressing for changes in law and government policy to stop the unthinking use and misuse of natural resources (see, e.g., Luke 1997). Connected with this, more and more persons are questioning the traditional way human beings have thought about and used animals ostensibly for their own purposes. The "animal rights" movement has fundamentally challenged the "unreflective" nature of long-standing policies, attitudes, and behaviors toward animals, and animal rights advocates are demanding that new laws be passed to protect animals from abuse at the hands of humans. Ever since the publication in 1976 of Donald Griffin's book *The Question of Animal Awareness*, a paradigm shift of sorts has taken place in ethology, the science of animal behavior. Earlier ethological views assumed that animal behavior was a stimulus–response biological event, simply the result of causal or functional laws. Now, however, ethology is moving toward explaining animal behavior as an expression of their *subjective* experiences. And as this shift progresses, ethology is brought closer into alignment with our daily views on animals (Lijmbach 1999: 199).

The Issue of Reflexivity within Recognition Discourse

The idea that the development of the welfare state, as well as more recent claims for recognition by a growing number of persons, is spurred on by a growth in reflexivity and heightened awareness about the plight of the other, is made explicit in John Rawls' (1971) theory of justice. According to Rawls's concept of *reflective equilibrium*, justice consists in considering society from an impartial standpoint, a so-called *original position* in which people reach agreement about their talents and attributes deprived of additional information (such as a person's race or job or education)—the so-called *veil of ignorance*—that constrains persons to act impartially in conceptualizing the good or just society. Constrained to impartiality in this way, Rawls suggests that people would choose to maximize the wellbeing of the least advantaged members of society as a hedge in the eventuality that they themselves might fall into this group (Doppelt 1988). Through the process of reflective equilibrium, that is, by reflecting on their own situation and placing themselves in the shoes of the less fortunate in society, persons come to an understanding of the justness or goodness of welfare as institutionalized and enacted within government policy.

We must be cautious, however, in equating too easily the notions of rightness or goodness on the one hand, and justice on the other. I earlier discussed the split between Hegelian and Kantian orientations toward subjectivity and consciousness, and I now want to illustrate how this shows up explicitly in the discourse on recognition couched within the broader framework of social justice. Nancy Fraser, for example, claims that:

> It is now standard practice in moral philosophy to distinguish questions of justice from questions of the good life. Construing the first as a matter

of "the right" and the second as a matter of "the good," most philosophers align distributive justice with Kantian *Moralität* (morality) and recognition with Hegelian *Sittlichkeit* (ethics).

2001: 22

Fraser is arguing that norms of justice are thought to be universally binding, thus consistent with Kant's categorical imperative, while claims for recognition of difference involve qualitative assessments of the relative worth of various cultural practices which cannot be universalized, thereby maintaining consistency with Hegel's dialectic.[2] Fraser attempts to bring these two divergent impulses together in a more comprehensive theory of justice that incorporates both redistribution and recognition. Specifically, she suggests that recognition ought to be treated as a question of *social status*. Here, what is required is not recognition of group-specific identity—which tends to cause difficulty insofar as such claims of identity get entangled in ethical considerations of the various claims made by various groups—but rather the status of group members as full participants in social life. Hence, misrecognition or nonrecognition is no longer seen as distorting group identity, but rather is seen as causing the social subordination of group members to the extent that they do not enjoy full participation in ongoing group relations, as peers alongside those not similarly misrecognized. Fraser's (2001: 24) "status model" aims, then, to overcome subordination "by establishing the misrecognized party as a full member of society, capable of participating on a par with other members." This is reflective of a "pragmatic" turn in critical theory, one which posits not merely the problem of misrecognition but looks at the real world consequences of persons being disvalued because of certain traits, characteristics, or identities (ethnic or otherwise; see Decker 2012).

From the perspective of the status model, misrecognition arises wherever social structures or cultural norms or practices distort interaction so as to impede parity of participation. In many ways this is similar to the position of Vaughan and Sjoberg (1986), which was summarized earlier. To reiterate, Vaughan and Sjoberg assert that the right to human status is fundamental, and that to achieve human status social conditions must be present that facilitate social reflectivity. Lacking such social conditions, persons would be cut off from self-actualization or their own subjectivity, in essence being treated merely as subhuman "objects" within the social system.

---

2 This is essentially in agreement with Habermas (1973: 150), who stated "Because Hegel conceives self-consciousness in terms of the interactional structure of complementary action, as the result of a struggle for recognition, he sees through the concept of autonomous will that appears to constitute the essential value of Kant's moral philosophy."

Noting these similarities, however, Fraser's and Vaughan and Sjoberg's models diverge on the issue of reflexivity. Because Fraser emphasizes status and participation, she is much less concerned with articulating whether or to what extent reflexivity operates to generate or sustain selves, much less claims of identity or recognition. However, rather than suggesting that Fraser's status model is somehow deficient as a result of her silence on the issue of reflexivity, I want to use this tension instead as a springboard for developing explicit linkages between reflexivity and recognition.

Bringing Reflexivity Back in

To reiterate, there is seemingly good evidence of a growth in claims for recognition among various groups in society, and these recognition claims go beyond the more longstanding strategy of seeking economic reparations for the historical harm done to these groups (whether because of slavery, colonialism, internment, racism, classism, heterosexism, sexism, and so forth). The ongoing waves of juridification culminating in the modern welfare state and beyond (see O'Neill 1999), as outlined by Habermas (1987, 1996, 1999), seem to point to an opening up of reflexive awareness on the part of legislators and citizens about past and current mistreatment of certain groups and persons. With regard to recognition claims per se, the recognition or acknowledgement of this mistreatment amounts to a new view that persons deserve respect and should be assured full participation in society as fellow human beings (Honneth 2001; Walby 2001).

Perhaps what we are witness to presently is the ultimate realization of what Durkheim (1984 [1893]) referred to as the "cult of the individual" (Chriss 1993). The cult of the individual arises under organic solidarity, as modern societies become more heterogeneous as a result of immigration, displacement by war, ongoing industrialization, mobile capital, flexible markets and labor, the decline of the nation-state, and of course globalization (Castells 1997). With so much cultural diversity, and as persons hold fewer and fewer things in common, the last remaining thing shared by all is the notion that "we are all human." Men and women now worship each other's quality of "otherness." As Durkheim explains,

> As societies become greater in volume and density, they increase in complexity, work is divided, individual differences multiply, and the moment approaches when the only remaining bond among the members of a single human group will be that they are men. Under such conditions the body of collective sentiments inevitably attaches itself with all its

> strength to its single remaining object, communicating to this object an incomparable value by so doing. Since human personality is the only thing that appeals unanimously to all hearts, since its enhancement is the only aim that can be collectively pursued, it inevitably acquires exceptional value in the eyes of all. It thus rises far above all human aims, assuming a religious nature.
>
> 1951 [1897]: 336

If this were indeed the case, that is, if the modern condition is typified by a growing concern with respecting and providing ritual attention to persons because of their humanity, because this is the last thing we hold collectively, why would persons struggle for satisfaction of a single desire, that of recognition (Fukuyama 1992)? Why would a continuing and inexorable move toward the realization of the emancipatory ideals contained within western civil law and the democratic constitutional state, which presumably now satisfies human wants at levels never before achieved, generate so much overt attention on the problem of recognition?

What I would like to suggest is that, although humans are endowed with natural abilities of reflexivity in the production of selves and subjectivity, modern social systems have in effect overburdened the reflexive process insofar as pressures toward associationism and expanding cross-cutting group affiliations (Simmel 1950) are producing more selves, or more possible versions of self, than we can realistically handle. Both Durkheim and Simmel argued that one of the benefits of modern societies was that the individual is liberated from the constraints of the primary group and is free to form associations with a variety of different persons and groups. In traditional societies characterized by mechanical solidarity, individuals mechanically acquiesced to the will of the group, and because everyone was pretty much like everyone else, the sense of self that persons developed was limited insofar as it was merely a reflection of the unitary collective conscience. In this sense, within earlier traditional or conventional society, subjectivity was somewhat impoverished, and it is not until the emergence of liberalism and modernity, that is, the post-conventional society, that human personality fully blossoms.

In essence, the modern (or postmodern if you prefer) subject has become "decentered." This derives from James' (1890) notion that persons possess as many selves as there are distinct individuals or groups with whom such persons interact.[3] This implies that the modern decentered subject moves

---

3 The actual quote from James is "A man has as many social selves as there are individuals who recognize him and carry an image of him in their mind." Baumeister (1998) claims, perhaps

through its varied personae, contemplating which roles to take, which identities to affirm, and which selves to present as situations dictate (Goffman 1959; Schrag 1989: 155).

Conclusion

With the advent of the language of reflexivity, the concepts of objectivity and subjectivity have been thrown into disarray across the human sciences. Both Bourdieu and Gouldner have staked out their own claims on how such concepts should best be understood. Bourdieu has embraced, more explicitly than Gouldner, a Marxian notion of the habitus to overcome perceived weaknesses in how scientists had used or engaged with these terms in the past. Bourdieu admits that he is following the program Marx suggested in his *Theses on Feuerbach* in attempting to avoid the fallacy of a materialism which views knowledge as merely a passive recording by a Cartesian subject of real things in the real world. Instead, what is emphasized is that there are important "active" elements of knowledge that should not be relegated to idealism (Bourdieu 1984: 467). In essence, Bourdieu wants to escape from the philosophy of the subject without doing away with agents. The way around this impasse is the invocation of habitus (Wacquant 1996: 215).

Gouldner uses some aspects of the Marxist tradition even while rejecting entreaties to join the theory group, for joining may eventuate in the ossification into a vanguard that kills theory. About as close as he comes to an orthodox Marxist position is viewing all talk of objectivity as a form of alienation. Gouldner states:

> For some sociologists the claim to objectivity serves as a façade for their own alienation from and resentment toward a society whose elites, even today, basically treat them as the Romans treated their Greek slaves: as skilled servants, useful but lower beings.
> 1970A: 439

---

correctly, that this quote often has been taken out of context and taken too literally. James backed off his assertion shortly after it appeared in print, suggesting that it is more correct "to propose that there are as many social selves as *groups* of individuals who know him, and that changes in behavior with different audiences resulted in 'practically' a division into different selves. The multiplicity of selfhood is a metaphor. The unity of selfhood is its defining act" (Baumeister 1998: 682).

The claim of objectivity is useful to the sociologist because he or she can use it to claim expertise about how badly the underdogs of society—hippies, drug addicts, prostitutes, homosexuals, criminals, and the like—are being treated. But these scientistic proclamations about the condition of the downtrodden amount to little more than a "...bitchy and carping, tacit and partial unmasking of society's failures" (Gouldner 1970a: 439). Here, Gouldner joins with Bourdieu to denounce social scientists for their failure to make good on the Enlightenment promise of the production of the good society. The search for the good society is ceaseless and part of the tragedy of human existence because it can never be attained, at least not insofar as the highest aspirations of our humanity are concerned (Chriss 2002).

Yet, even so, Bourdieu (1988) separates himself from Gouldner without mentioning him, as when he wrote in the pages of Gouldner's own journal, *Theory and Society*—eight years after Gouldner's death—that he (Bourdieu) rejects the language of crisis. The title of his paper, "Vive la Crise! For Heterodoxy in Social Science," was purposely ironic, as he argued that there is currently and never was a crisis, although the theoretical interregnum that Gouldner predicted was on its way has always been here even though a few well-placed sociologists tried to argue that conceptual unity characterized our discipline. Conceptual unity also means that we really don't need to borrow from other disciplines, and indeed as the queen of the sciences, it is the other social sciences that must come to us to shore up their own shaky foundations. Bourdieu argued that we (sociologists) are on the cusp of discovering that some of our old self-understandings were misguided (an essential lack of reflexivity as argued by Gouldner), such as for example the assumed opposition of disciplines that is destructive and must be overcome. Other antimonies sociologists must overcome include: divisions into theoretical schools and the distinction between objectivism and subjectivism. And it is quite handy that Bourdieu's own concept of the habitus is offered as the way out of the morass of the subject/object divide. As Lemert and Piccone (1982) noted, Gouldner had developed such insights about reflexivity, or lack thereof, and the disciplinary difficulties emerging from it at least a decade before Bourdieu. But Gouldner, lacking the churlishness that characterized much of his work and life, was typically gracious toward Bourdieu, such as naming him to the Editorial Board of *Theory and Society* and occasionally citing him in his own work.[4]

---

4 An example from Gouldner's (1979a: 100) later work is his statement that one of the most important French contributions to the literature on the New Class was Bourdieu and Passeron's (1977) *Reproduction in Education, Society and Culture*.

Even with the competition between Gouldner and Bourdieu, and even with Bourdieu garnering more acclaim in sociology and beyond up until his death in 2002, these two scholars were fellow travelers who favored European-style social theory over stodgy and parochial American sociology which, as Mills and others had suggested (see Gill 2013), had lost its way long ago. Both also fostered radical sensibilities, including an interest in Marxism albeit for different reasons and in different intensity. The next chapter explores some of the history of Gouldner's early venture into radical politics as well as later attempts by Gouldner and others to make sense of Soviet sociology after Stalin.

CHAPTER 5

Radical Politics and Soviet Sociology

Communism in the United States

Before Israeli statehood and before Auschwitz, some American Jews maintained an interest in, and even supported, communism. As Alexander argues,

> ...it is impossible to deny that a full-blown romance between American Jews and leftist political-economics did indeed exist. Even the slightest perusal of the historical record of the first half of the twentieth century reveals that socialism and related ideas once stood as a foundation of American Jewish identity. Perhaps for a while it was even *the* foundation.[1]
> 2010: VII

Some of this early history has been repressed, for example, in Irving Howe's (1976) reflections on his own activities among the "New York intellectuals" beginning in the 1930s (Horwitz 1995). Although in that 1976 retrospective Howe was more inclined to deal with socialist intellectuals rather than Jewish involvement in American communism, in an earlier book co-authored with Lewis Coser he did indeed cover some of this ground. Summarizing from Howe and Coser (1962), the Communist Party of the United States (CPUSA) was first formed in 1919. An earlier Socialist Party was formed in 1901, with original membership of approximately 10,000. By 1912 Socialist party membership had reached 150,000, an astonishingly rapid increase. This was the era of muckraking, its major goal being to expose the greed, avarice, and barbarism of the business class. In many ways it was consistent with the criticisms of the business and industrial classes made by Saint-Simon in the 1820s (Gouldner 1958a).

Differences of opinions and factionalism within the Socialist party became apparent by 1912. One of the more critical fissures was that which developed between defenders of compensation versus confiscation, representing a

---

1 This observation is corroborated by Srebrnik (2010: 1), who stated "For much of the 20th century, Jews comprised a disproportionate component of the American left. Before World War I, the Jewish Socialist Federation, claiming 14,000 members, was a significant segment of the Socialist Party."

left-right ideological split (e.g., Debs vs. Steffens). A new, distinctively Marxist left appeared by 1915, and it went international with the pending outbreak of World War I. At this point American Marxists were very much anti-war and anti-imperialist above and beyond any factionalist disagreements.

The Bolshevik uprising in Russia gave rise to more strident and confident movements within the left wing of the CPUSA, as its members believed such a proletarian revolt could happen in the United States. This coincided as well with more rabblerousing and labor strikes. By the early 1930s the Great Depression ushered in an era of ultra-leftism (Buhle 1980). A pressing concern among the far-left was marshalling organizational energies to confront the spread of European fascism, and Stalin in Russia served this purpose well.

Intellectuals started turning leftward as well during this period. A brief but deeply committed turn to Stalinism ensued between 1930 and 1936. As much as anything this movement documented the hardships and struggles of the people as a lived conviction. Misery and injustice in any form were the points of focus and contention for these intellectuals. The zeitgeist of the Great Depression and left-ideological reactions to it led to the formation in 1932 of the League of Professional Groups for William Z. Foster (as president). Luminaries such as Dos Passos, Sidney Hook, Granville Hicks, Langston Hughes, and Leonie Adams were among its members. Left-wing politics and ideology were dominant among literary magazines, theater groups, dance troupes, and other parts of the American cultural apparatus (Howe and Coser 1962: 282).

Indeed, it was here that the fusing of literary criticism with Marxism began, and it has continued pretty much to this day (Gouldner 1976a). But as Stalinism turned more into totalitarianism, literary critics had to confront this stain in the otherwise lofty ideals of expanding human emancipation under communism. It was not an easy thing to pretend to overlook. This got even more complicated when the pact between Hitler and Stalin was announced in 1939. Hitler's invasion of Russia in 1941 threw the commitments of intellectuals to communism into further disarray. Some sided with Trotsky's critique of Stalinism, fascism, and totalitarianism, while others remained loyal to Stalin.

The Decline of American Communism

By the end of World War II in 1945, the membership of the American Communist Party stood at between 75,000 and 85,000 members. It had gained some measure of respectability since the 1930s, and indeed upwards of one-fourth of American labor union workers were members of the Communist party. But in a mere fourteen years, by 1959, it had been left in shambles. The decline after 1945 was startling, as documented by David Shannon (1959).

Earl Browder was expelled from the party in 1946, and Foster once again rose to prominence in the CPUSA. Browder was considered too right leaning and too conciliatory towards capitalism (Ryan 1997). The Communist party line was now that there were no redeeming qualities to American capitalism, that it was inherently reactionary and imperialistic. Browder went to Russia in 1946 and agreed to take over a publishing business providing Russian-language books to the American market. However, he soon lost all of his investment in the enterprise. By 1948 Browder was asking to be reinstated in the Communist Party.

Communists saw Henry Wallace, vice president under Roosevelt during the War, and later Secretary of Commerce under Truman, as someone within the American political structure who could be counted on (primarily because he was viewed as being not as bourgeois as Browder). Truman asked Wallace to resign his post, and he did so in 1946. The American Communists wanted Wallace to run as an independent candidate for the 1948 presidential election. But Wallace was more dedicated to a Keynesian "progressive capitalism" than he was to full-blown communism. Nevertheless, the communists thought he might still be useful to them because of his connection to traditional American politics as an insider. Wallace thereby was "a relatively easy mark for the Communists," and easily manipulated, as he did not see that the Communists were using him because of his ties to the establishment.

Wallace's growing popularity among Communists was in direct proportion to the growing unpopularity of Truman. Although Wallace was not really a communist and did not know much about left politics, he publicly denounced red baiting, and typically had kind words to say about communists because of their efforts to end oppression and subjugation in whatever forms they took. Wallace was saying publicly he intended to continue working for causes within the Democratic Party, but kept feeling the tug of communists insisting on a third party run. Truman was betraying the Roosevelt tradition, and the pacifist wing within the Communist Party started grudgingly seeing Wallace as a possible alternative to continuing American imperialism.

Wallace ran on the Progressive Party as an independent. The Party got on the ballot in 45 states, and won considerable labor support although was opposed by the top A.F. of L. and C.I.O. leaders. Even so, most of the C.I.O. rank and file supported Wallace. Foster and others within the leadership of the CP never really trusted Wallace, describing him as a "petty bourgeoisie" (Foster 1952: 472). His relatively small vote count had a lot to do with liberals and progressives worrying that votes for Wallace would harm Truman's chances of winning the presidency for the Democrats. Wallace was supported only as a "lesser evil" candidate. In the 1948 election Wallace received 1,156,103 votes, a far cry from the 20 million votes he publicly stated he expected to win in April 1948 (Shannon 1959: 180; Truman won the presidency). Half of Wallace's votes came from New York City and California. He carried two electoral districts in the East Bronx, Gouldner's own stomping grounds. Gouldner's connection to radical politics will be further elaborated in the next section.

Gouldner's FBI Files

For many years the Federal Bureau of Investigation has conducted surveillance on sociologists who were perceived to hold subversive political beliefs or involved with radical groups and activities. Mike Keen (2003) has documented pervasive FBI surveillance of a number of sociologists beginning in the 1940s under the auspices of FBI director J. Edgar Hoover. Keen (2003) notes, for example, that between 1936 and 1952 appropriations for FBI surveillance operations against domestic targets increased 1800 percent, with the number of personnel increasing during this period from 609 to 6,451 agents. Most of this attention was directed at prominent members of the academy who were members of the Communist Party or otherwise sympathetic to left-leaning political causes. Keen filed Freedom of Information Act (FOIA) requests to gain access to the FBI files of a number of sociologists including W.E.B. Du Bois, Ernest Burgess, William Ogburn, Robert and Helen Lynd, E. Franklin Frazier, Pitirim Sorokin, C. Wright Mills, and even Talcott Parsons. The period of the 1930s through the 1950s, with Hoover at the helm, led the FBI into questionable practices including "loyalty checks" whereby particular scholars under surveillance would be visited by agents, sometimes on multiple occasions.[2] This produced a chilling effect, as many targeted scholars refrained from community and political activities while confining themselves to sanctioned university activities (in teaching, research, and administration).

As Gouldner was a self-professed "radical sociologist" operating during roughly this same period, it made sense to file my own FOIA request seeking access to Gouldner's FBI files (see Figure 5.1). I filed these in late 2011, and in February 2012, I received 42 pages of records on Gouldner responsive to my request. The reports

---

2 This information is from a study cited by Keen in the introduction to the later *Transaction* edition of his *Stalking Sociologists*. This cited study is Lazarsfeld and Thielens (1958).

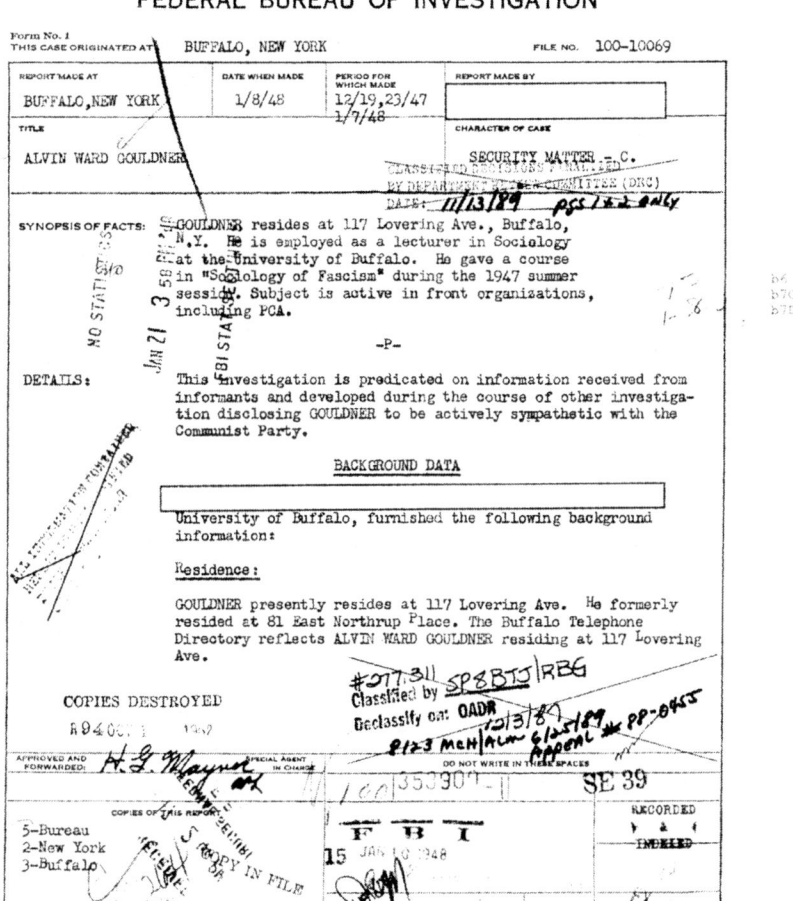

FIGURE 5.1 *First Page of Gouldner's FBI File (from Federal Bureau of Investigation, now in public domain because of author's Freedom of Information Act request responded to on February 1, 2012; FOIPA Request No. 1181369–000).*

cover the period roughly 1943 to 1953. I was told I would have to submit a special FOIA request for records after 1953. I did this, and in late 2012 I received a response from the US Department of Justice that there are no further records responsive to my request after 1953 concerning the FBI files of Gouldner. In the summary of Gouldner's FBI files, initiated below, I will sometimes refer to Gouldner as AWG.

1. AWG was a member of the Communist Party (CP) beginning in 1943 and had disagreements with the "faction system."
2. While in Buffalo AWG was head of the local chapter of the Progressive Citizens of America (PCA), pushing for housing rent control and working to defeat anti-labor bills. PCA was, according to the FBI, a known CP front group.
3. AWG joined the Sacco-Vanzetti Club in 1944, another CP-affiliated group.
4. Later, in 1948 while at the University of Buffalo, AWG resigned from the CP, verbally attacking CP members for their bad leadership and lack of qualifications. According to narratives in the FBI files, AWG was pro-Tito and was sympathetic to the Trotsky wing and an anti-Stalinist. On this point, AWG suggested that Tito in Yugoslavia had every right to pursue socialism the way he wanted to without Russia's interference. AWG became more vocally hostile towards Soviet communism. In my personal correspondence with him, Richard Deaton claims most of this information is wrong. It wasn't that AWG and his first wife, Helen Ruth Sattler, resigned from the CP. Rather, they were expelled from the CPUSA for Browderism, which was the project of Americanizing Marxism and making the Soviet experience relevant to the conditions in the United States. Deaton also suggests that AWG favored no particular sides in the factionalism dispute. In reality Gouldner was an independent Marxist, an observation that is consistent with the role he played as a ridge-riding Marxist outlaw.
5. Both AWG and wife Helen went to Washington, DC after Gouldner's graduation from CCNY to work for the Quartermasters Corps. Actually, while AWG was at Quartermasters Helen, who did graduate work in economics at Oberlin, worked as an economist for the National Labor Relations Board in DC. The FBI file also states that a year later AWG served in the US Army at Fort Lee, Virginia for about a year before starting work at Columbia. This is the first known confirmation of Gouldner having served in the US military, although the circumstances of his early discharge remain unclear.
6. The FBI was very interested in AWG's interest in Marx. AWG stated in a University of Buffalo publication, the *Argus*, in 1950, that "Marx made a man out of me and [redacted] (Columbia U.) made a scientist of me." Obviously the redacted name is Robert K. Merton.
7. Beginning in 1947 AWG campaigned heavily for Henry Wallace for President. Indeed, he was vice chairman of the Erie County Wallace for President Committee. A year later he had Wallace as a guest to coincide with hosting in his home a meeting of the American Labor Party and the

PCA, yet when it came time to elect officers AWG put all suggestions by CP members "off the record" with regard to canvassing for and supporting Wallace. No CP members were elected to office. In personal correspondence, Deaton again points out that the FBI information is wrong. As Deaton stated in personal correspondence, "My parents put Henry Wallace up for the night when he was to address a campaign rally in Buffalo. My mother told me that Wallace showed up at their home stinking drunk and they desperately had to sober him up before he was supposed to speak that evening. Wallace was always smeared as being close to the SU and the CPUSA, which may explain why AWG wanted to [keep] CPers at arm's length in Buffalo."

These snippets from the FBI files confirm Gouldner's early involvement in radical politics, although the errors in information-gathering and documentation by the FBI in Gouldner's case lead reasonable persons to wonder how far off the mark law enforcement surveillance of communist activities was in general, especially during the 1950s.

Communism and Jewish Intellectuals

After the 1948 election, concerns over communism escalated. In 1950 FBI director J. Edgar Hoover testified before Congress that there were (at the time) 54,174 active members of the Community Party. By 1953 this figure had declined to 24,796 (Shannon 1959: 218). The Rosenbergs were found guilty of espionage in 1951 and executed two years later. McCarthyism was in full swing. William Foster, a central figure in the Communist Party in America during the 1930s and 1940s, stated that:

> The history of the Communist Party of the United States is the history of the vanguard party of the American working class. It is the story and analysis of the origin, the growth, and development of a working class political party of a new type, called into existence by the epoch of imperialism, the last stage of capitalism, and by the emergence of a new social system—Socialism.
> FOSTER 1952: 15

By the end of his book on the history of the communist party in America, the author still valiantly carried the mantle of the CPUSA, stating

> The Communist Party of the United States works and grows in the spirit of these [international] Communist parties. It knows that, living up to the principles of Marxism-Leninism, it will one day lead the American working class and the nation, even as it is now the best representative of their interests. Nor can all the powers of arrogant capitalist reaction balk the C.P.U.S.A. from fulfilling this historic role.
> FOSTER 1952: 572

One of the key elements of the factionalism within the CPUSA was the emergence, beginning in 1928 and culminating in 1938 with the formation of the Socialists Workers Party, of a decade of development of alternative visions and approaches to socialism and communism embodied in the writings and work of Trotsky (Cannon 1972). For followers of the faction, Trotskyism created the possibility of an anti-Stalin left, as opposed to the conservative or right-oriented general critique of socialism and communism already evident in American culture, ranging from official government censure (e.g., Hoover and McCarthy) all the way to the anti-communist sentiments of the masses (Fenyo 1977).

Sidney Hook was a good example of an intellectual who took this route over his career, even though near the end Hook endorsed Ronald Reagan for president in 1980. In other words, once anti-Stalinism begins, even located on the political left, it can easily migrate over to a general critique of socialism from the right. Much of this movement of the anti-Stalinist left was contained within a coterie of Jewish intellectuals living in the northeastern United States, and specifically in New York City. They were referred to as the "New York Intellectuals." As Wald notes:

> Seeking to forge a liberal Jewish cultural movement under the aegis of 'cultural pluralism' in the 1920s, they found themselves propelled first toward Communism and then toward Trotskyism during the 1930s. Their experience produced several of the earliest pioneers of the anti-Stalinist left who later achieved national prominence as New York intellectuals.
> 1987: 27

These Jewish intellectuals were close in spirit to Isaac Deutscher's (1968) idea of the Non-Jewish Jew, who being expelled from their homeland lived in the interstices of host countries, getting along as best they could in the face of rampant anti-Semitism. These intellectuals had to simultaneously battle ambivalence concerning their ethnic background while embracing a universalistic internationalism (Wald 1987: 28). Jewishness receded into the background in the attempt to attain this universalistic standard (of emancipation and the elimination of human misery) even as many wrote for Jewish magazines and about Jewish issues. One always had to guard against a vulgar Jewish-centric orientation instead of embracing loftier universal, humanitarian goals. The problem of Zionism and the recognition of Israel as a legitimate state amidst the turmoil of Middle Eastern politics—not the least of which involves the ongoing Israeli-Palestinian conflict—is emblematic of this tension between Jewish localism and cosmopolitanism (Avineri 1981).

Rather than assimilation, the goal was cultural pluralism, which became apparent during the second great wave of immigration to the United States coinciding with the Progressive Era (1890 through 1910 or so). The pluralist doctrine was merged with American pragmatism in the hands of John Dewey, who actually presided over the Trotsky trial in Mexico in 1937. This was the Dewey Commission of Inquiry, seeking findings as to the veracity of the Moscow Trials in which Trotsky was found guilty of sedition. It came as no great surprise that the Dewey Commission "found" that Trotsky had been framed in that trial.

Gouldner was raised in this milieu of the New York Jewish intellectual scene, and he came to early radical politics through it. It may also make sense that Gouldner's FBI file goes cold in 1953, as that was the year that the Rosenbergs were executed by the United States government, convicted of espionage and treason. The execution of the Rosenbergs left many American Jews—those who were actively involved in the communist party, left-leaning intellectuals, or simply fellow travelers—to ask the question, "Is this good for the Jews?" Most Jews ran for cover, including presumably Gouldner, after 1953 (Horwitz 1995). During the radical ferment of the 1960s, Gouldner had moved away from political activism and was scolded by some in the New Left for it. But there was an untold story of sorts, that Gouldner had already paid his dues to leftist politics—as documented in Gouldner's FBI files—had experienced as a lived conviction the execution of the Rosenbergs and the aftermath of McCarthyism, and chose to lay low and settle into the role of Marxist outlaw and social critic thereafter (Chriss 1999c).

A sociology of knowledge approach would seek to connect Gouldner's Jewishness, more directly than I have done here, to his scholarly work. It is clear that, whatever impact his ethnicity had on his theoretical work, Gouldner attempted to mute it in his writings, that is, at the level of the textual or as a public avowal. Playing the role of the non-Jewish Jew in earnest, many Jewish sociologists of Gouldner's day did likewise, including Erving Goffman, Robert Merton, Irving Horowitz, and Harold Garfinkel to name only a few. In his remembrance of a long career as a sociologist engaged in overt studies of Jewish life, Marshall Sklare (1993: 7) noted that when he was at the University of Chicago (where he received a master's degree in sociology in 1948), Louis Werth was the only Jewish member of the sociology department who identified as a Jew. This was ironic insofar as Werth was also an opponent of Zionism and proud of the fact that he married a Gentile woman. And later, when Sklare (1993: 8–9) went to Columbia University to work on his Ph.D. in sociology (which he completed in 1953 under the supervision of Seymour Martin Lipset), he noted that even though the two leaders of the department were Jewish (Merton and Lazarsfeld), their self-identification as Jews was so muted that they were minimally Jewish, by ancestry only. Indeed, at age fourteen Merton abandoned his given name of Meyer R. Schkolnick (Gieryn 1994).

Speaking of Goffman, Dmitri Shalin (2014) has more recently actually attempted to connect overtly Goffman's Jewishness to the production of his dramaturgical theory of action. Shalin calls this project "biocritical hermeneutics," whereby the researcher goes even beyond Mills and Gouldner to show the reciprocal effects that biography, theory, and history have on any particular intellectual's work. In particular, Shalin argues that

> ...Goffman's theoretical commitments fed on his experience as a son of Jewish immigrants struggling to lift himself from the anonymity of Manitoba and that his continuously evolving theoretical agenda shadowed his personal transformation and self-discovery.
> 2014: 3

I simply have neither the ability nor desire to apply Shalin's biocritical hermeneutics to a deep analysis of the connection between Gouldner's Jewishness and the record of his scholarly and personal activities, above and beyond what I have already done in noting the beginning of, and then the abrupt end to, Gouldner's involvement in radical politics in 1953. But it is worthwhile to note that such an analytical strategy is out there and has been utilized in the case of Goffman. It will be up to readers to decide the extent to which such an approach provides useful new insights into Goffman's intellectual work.

There is another speculation that could be applied to Gouldner's reticence to refer to his Jewishness in his own work. For Gouldner, playing the role of non-Jewish Jew may have had as much to do with his role as a man's man—call it machismo or chauvinism or whatever you like here—and one of the dangers of openly announcing one's ethnicity within the new multiculturalism is that it could be construed as laying claim to victim status (Seidman 1998). Gouldner may have viewed any talk of his Jewishness as a sign of weakness, as a play for sympathy as a member of an historically oppressed group. Perhaps it was this stance, this commitment, which fueled his interpersonal belligerence and hostility. This is the transition from the merely non-Jewish Jew to the Tough Jew (Breines 1990).

Yet such insights need not remain at the level of one person (Gouldner) struggling with how or to what extent personal biography—here specifically, Jewish ethnicity—influences professional work. There is a larger story to tell about the study of Judaism within sociology, including Gouldner's brief participation in Jewish studies (Chriss 2001; Wrong 1982). After completing his master's degree at Columbia University in 1945—studying under Robert McIver, *not* Robert K. Merton as I had previously reported elsewhere[3]—Gouldner worked as a research sociologist under Marie Jahoda, working on the "Studies in Prejudice" series directed by members of the Frankfurt School in exile and funded largely by the American Jewish Committee (AJC). The AJC was a voluntary organization established in 1906 ostensibly for the defense of Jewish interests, specifically to study issues of anti-Semitism. By the mid-1940s and fresh on the heels of the end of World War II and the defeat of the Nazis, Frankfurt School exile Max Horkheimer's Department of Scientific Research and Program Evaluation at Columbia University was developing an active research agenda concerned with authoritarianism and prejudice especially as it related to the sort of virulent anti-Semitism culminating in the Holocaust. The leading consulting sociologist for the AJC was Paul Lazarsfeld, and he sometimes recommended staff members from his own Bureau of Applied Social Research to work on behalf of the various research projects connected with AJC (Platt 1996: 149). Gouldner was one of the young sociologists recommended by Lazarsfeld to work at the AJC.

Gouldner's immersion in activist politics during this time was congenial with the scholarly work he was pursuing at Columbia University particularly as it related to his connection with the American Jewish Committee. The AJC was explicitly established to study questions of the lives of American Jews and Jewish continuity in the Diaspora more generally. This provided Gouldner a living, breathing example of the project of the unity of theory and practice.

---

3   I was made aware of this error only after receiving a copy of Gouldner's vita (dated June 1979) from the Washington University library. On the first page Gouldner writes "Gouldner received his Masters from Columbia University under Robert McIver for a study of trade union leadership."

Toward the Unity of Theory and Practice

By the time of the publication of his *Coming Crisis of Western Sociology*, Gouldner had parlayed his earlier experiences with radical politics into a discussion in chapter 12 of that book focusing on the development and institutionalization of sociology in the U.S.S.R. In this section I reflect upon these writings as well as consider implications for contemporary Eastern European sociology.

Gouldner used the emergence of academic sociology within the Soviet Union as an illustration of his broader thesis concerning the crisis within Marxism generally. Gouldner based many of the points he developed in the chapter from time spent in Russia, Yugoslavia, and Poland during 1965 and 1966.[4] In a section titled "Functionalism Goes East," Gouldner argued that Soviet societies circa the mid- to late-1960s had experienced a take-off point of industrialization, and rather than being concerned with social change, for example, the transition from capitalism under the sway of proletarian revolt, they are now as much or more concerned with stability, that is, with understanding how a system is self-sustaining after a proper equilibrium point has been reached. As Gouldner (1970a: 455) explains, "…as Eastern European nations today begin to achieve heightened industrialization, they too seem to manifest a need for a theory that focuses on the spontaneous mechanisms conducive to social stability and order."

For Gouldner, the theory of order and stability par excellence is functionalism, arguing that in seeking to establish a basis upon which the Soviet system could maintain a self-sustained social order, Soviet intellectuals would find Parsonian functionalism congenial to these aims. Parsonian functionalism is, according to Gouldner, conservative because the primary focus of the theory is concerned with how a social system becomes stabilized over time, yet this "conservatism" is useful to Soviet bloc nations as well struggling to maintain new systems already achieved. They seek, for example, to guard against the reappearance of Stalinism by being attentive to the moral components of any ordered system, something that Parsons (by way of Adam Smith) had always argued is crucial to the explanation of social order. In speaking with Soviet

---

4 Gouldner traveled extensively abroad during these years. In a letter to Mary Strong at *Trans-Action* magazine writing from Cortivallo, Switzerland on Jun 15, 1966, Gouldner (1966) stated by that time the cities he had so far visited were London, Stockholm, Frankfurt, West Berlin, Korcula (Yugoslavia), Munich, Bologna, Milano, Venice, Padova, Warsaw, Leningrad, Moscow, and Paris. This letter is held in the Irving Horowitz Transaction Publishers Archives, available at http://www.libraries.psu.edu/psul/digital/ilh.html.

scholars, Gouldner reports that they had newly discovered a concern with self-control and developing the "spiritual life" of their countries. This is not neo-Marxism, but rather standard or traditional academic sociology transplanted in the Soviet bloc. It turns its back on the tradition of Marxism-Leninism and seeks to translate the writings of leading Western sociologists, particularly Merton and Parsons, but even the mathematical sociology of Harrison White and James Coleman. These writers are crucial for establishing research traditions mirroring the advances made in western sociology through the 1960s.

Indeed, this concern with methodology seemed to Gouldner to also be symptomatic of a general eschewing of theory among the Soviet intellectuals with whom he spoke. Theory often is formulated within distinct traditions or schools of thoughts, sedimenting into competing paradigms or work groups which become harder and harder to reconcile over time. At this early stage of development in Soviet sociology (circa the 1960s), there is a need, so argues Gouldner, to close ranks around the best methods for doing empirical or concrete studies of pressing issues of the day, because it will be easier to forge a consensus over the contributions sociological research can make to explain current conditions.

Although Gouldner developed these positions from his personal observations of sociology in the communist bloc, he was also influenced by whatever publications from western authors were available concerning the development of sociology in these countries. One of the earliest was a 1962 paper by Robert K. Merton and Henry W. Reicken titled "Notes on Sociology in the U.S.S.R." Merton and Reicken were part of an American delegation that was given permission to study the behavioral sciences in Moscow, Leningrad, Tashkent, Tbilisi, and Kiev in 1961 (Engerman 2009: 199). As Merton and Reicken explain,

> The broad purposes of the tour were to establish or reinforce intellectual relations with Soviet colleagues and to identify major trends in the behavioral sciences, especially emerging developments not yet reflected in Soviet publication.
> 1962: 7

The authors noted that the Russian Academy of Sciences held to a guiding motif for all scientific research being conducted in the country, the aim of which was to "participate actively in the building of a communistic society in the U.S.S.R., to help defend the socialist victories of the workers, and to strengthen world peace" (Merton and Reicken 1962: 8). At this time, there were no research institutes specifically designated as "sociological." Rather, for the most part sociological research took place under the auspices of the Institute of Philosophy at the Academy of Sciences, with very little independent research being conducted elsewhere in scholarly departments at universities. The key question driving specifically sociological inquiries was, is it possible to distinguish between historical materialism and empirical sociology, or are they one and the same? Soviet sociologists by this time had come to the conclusion that grand theories developed by Marx, Engels, and later by Lenin could not possibly have predicted all the empirical elements transpiring in the transition to communism. This meant that sound sociological research would need to take a more pragmatic orientation, guided obviously by the general philosophy of historical materialism while remaining alive to any empirical evidence that would either bolster or bring into question the guiding philosophy.

By the end of their report, Merton and Reicken (1962: 14) were unclear what sorts of advances sociology could make within the U.S.S.R., to the extent that "sociological research is conceived as primarily the handmaiden of programmed social action." In earlier times, especially under Lenin, Stalin, and (then) currently under Mao, there was little tolerance for questioning or testing the major theoretical propositions of Marxism. Mao had a convoluted answer to the question, "Can Marxism be criticized?" His answer was basically, certainly it can, but the questioning itself is meaningless, for Marxism represents an eternal truth as solid and as infallible as, say, the theory of gravity. Mao gave lip service to the idea of intellectual debate and contention, and under his reign presumably a hundred schools of thought would be able to contend. But this can occur only insofar as, in the end, only one school of thought, Marxism, is positively confirmed (Gupta 2000: 109).

From the Marxist perspective on science, the distinction made between pure and applied science is indicative of a false consciousness on the part of bourgeois scientists who do not see that their interests are shaped by the broader economic system within which their work is embedded. Bernal (1939) made this Marxist position clear, a position which is impatient merely with knowledge for its own sake and that application of science in the name of expanding plenitude, enlightenment, and health for all is the only legitimate goal. In his examination of this issue, Polanyi (1975) reports on a discussion with Bucharin which took place in 1935, wherein Bucharin took the standard Marxist line that wherever the distinction is made between pure and applied science, scientists are deprived of the consciousness of their social functions, that is, they suffer from false consciousness within the capitalist system. In this case, science is merely ideology, which develops guiding principles such as objectivity and value-freedom which blind bourgeois scientists to their true goals, which is the emancipation of the human spirit and the equalization of life chances to guarantee full participation for all in social life.

But if science exists to fulfill basic human needs, and if it is judged on the basis of a preexisting philosophy (Marxism) concerning how well it is doing or not doing in attaining those needs, where is the autonomy of science? Polanyi (1975: 18) asks, "How can science, if it is to submit to adjustment of its social function at the hands of society, maintain its essence, the spirit of free inquiry?"

Interestingly enough, in his discussion of Soviet sociology Gouldner did not mention a report on the profession published in *American Sociological Review* in 1965. (Perhaps this was because Gouldner was on his European tour and simply missed the issue.) In this report Allen Kassof (1965) delivered a blistering report against American sociology as seen from the Soviet perspective. He first points out that sociology had been the beneficiary of the political thaw in the Soviet Union since Stalin's death. Indeed, from the mid-1930s through the mid-1950s sociology as an independent area of study in the Soviet Union had virtually disappeared (Fischer 1966; Fitzpatrick 1979; Osipov and Yokchuk 1966; Pankhurst 1982; Shalin 1978; Shlapnetokh 1987; Weinberg 1974). Kassof's second major point is that the pinnacle of bourgeois sociology was reached with the rise of functionalism, which is viewed as little more than political reaction servicing the needs of the capitalist system. Kassof summarizes various Soviet critics, such as Osipov and Zamoshkin, who view the chief "ideological offenders" of bourgeois sociology to be Marion Levy, Robert Merton, Talcott Parsons, and Ely Chinoy. Kassof also cites Novikov's blistering attack of Parsons, including such missives as the theory of action is merely an apologia for entrepreneurship within state-monopoly capitalism; that the concept of the social system fetishizes the personal elements within social relations to conduce toward productive activity as normative; and that bureaucratization is indicative of a broader trend of development occurring naturally in the social world, insofar as the human spirit seeks greater predictability and organization of all things. In other words, functionalism appropriates naturalism in the defense of the legal-bureaucratic elements of capitalism operating in the realms of both business and of everyday life.

To summarize, Kassof sees functionalism as certainly neither scientific nor value-neutral, but instead as shot through with pro-capitalist assumptions about how the social world "really works," making it nothing more than state propaganda. It is ironic that such a critique is made, for it is very much the same thing Merton reported on after his visit to the Soviet Union, namely, that Soviet sociology was nothing more than a handmaiden to state planning under the sway of Marxism and historical materialism. Even further, Kassof views industrial sociology as a tool of monopoly capitalism, as simply a form of "managerialism" which seeks to quell worker resentment in the face of the oppressive aspects of the capitalist work setting. It should be noted that in the

1940s Merton led a thriving program of industrial sociology at Columbia University, and one of his star students was of course Gouldner. In fact, rather than saving capitalism, the narrow empirical studies of industrial sociology "provide the Marxist observer with further evidence of the crisis of capitalism" (Kassof 1965: 117). It is a futile quest for the secrets of rational organization and the management of the capitalist economy (and everyday life for that matter), but it is self-defeating because it only serves further to exploit workers while benefiting the profit-maximization activities of the industrialists.

It is also interesting to note that Kassof cites one prominent American sociologist as a "tragic hero" who escapes the charge of bourgeois propagandist. Kassof cites Grishiani, who argues that C. Wright Mills is that tragic figure, for he had the courage to confront the American ruling elite for their militarism, imperialism, and their misguided notions about science (especially the problems besetting both grand theory as well as dustbowl empiricism). Mills was a tragic figure because although he did see the problems of capitalism, he could never completely free himself from "fruitless, scholastic, and anti-historical bourgeois sociology," and wrongly looked for a convergence between capitalism and socialism even while also viewing Marxism as outdated and utopian (Kassof 1965: 118). Mills' opting for Weber over Marx reflects the same sort of false consciousness which plagued his sociological colleagues such as Merton and Gouldner, who saw Weber as a safe or pragmatic alternative to a Marxism which was, circa the 1940s and 1950s in America, viewed as ideological, unscientific, and actually quite dangerous (especially in light of McCarthyism).

Hence, in the earliest stages of the development of sociology in the Soviet Union immediately after the death of Stalin, sociology was viewed as a capitalist "pseudo-science" which feigned scientific status through the fetishism of conceptual schemes, a criticism both Mills and Gouldner leveled against Parsons' penchant for grand theorizing. At least initially, these Soviet sociologists rejected Merton's, Gouldner's, and even Parsons' theory of the convergence of socialism and capitalism as merely a symptom of false consciousness (Vucinich 1974). Of course, Gouldner was aghast at this convergence while Parsons believed sociology in the Soviet Union would throw off the shackles of Stalinist ideology and move closer to the American model of scientific professionalism (Engerman 2009: 204). In his 1965 paper "An American Impression of Sociology in the Soviet Union," Parsons was optimistic about the slow but inexorable movement of Soviet sociology away from rank ideology and toward science. For Parsons, a true science is universal because it transcends national, religious, or ideological boundaries, and he welcomed this development of sociology within the Soviet Union (Parsons 1965). Over time Soviet sociology did indeed move closer to the scientific ideal Parsons had hoped for a decade earlier, especially as embodied in a report on the progress of Soviet sociology by Jiri Kolaja. In that report Kolaja (1978) stated, "A modern society, if it is to develop, cannot do without science," and because sociology has slowly been admitted into the Soviet Union since the death of Stalin, this portends well for the future. Nevertheless, Irving Horowitz observed that "In a free society one expects a critical literature," yet there was no indications in Kolaja's report that such a critical literature had truly emerged in the Soviet Union. Indeed, critical sociology was still relatively muted in the Soviet Union, and what there was of it was perfunctory and ritualistic, certainly not yet creating the condition for "fundamental revisions in orthodox Soviet Marxism-Leninism" (Horowitz 1978: 376).

Around this same time, John Fraser (1975) published a paper in the journal *Studies in Comparative Communism* that took umbrage at Gouldner's insistence that Soviet sociology was converging toward American functionalism because it needed a theory that would be able to explain stability and order. In arguing that Soviet sociology is now coming around to viewing functionalism in a more positive light, Gouldner also argued that this harms the growth of critical or dialectically negating theory. Fraser (1975: 371) goes on to argue that "Gouldner misunderstands the relationship between science and ideology" and that "in the case of a non- or pre-science like American functionalism, he confuses a system of concepts with ideology." In essence, Gouldner's critical theory is idealistic and does not belong in or to Marxism. Even Gouldner's notion of reflexive theory is deeply ideational. It is not "of" Marxism because it is closer in spirit to German idealism than it is to political economy. As Fraser (1976: 378) argues, "The very principle of reflexive sociology, its rejection and negation of the positive, makes his condemnation of Soviet sociology as revisionism or neo-Machism appear to emerge from a position of 'orthodoxy.'" Yet Gouldner is also opposed to orthodoxy in the form of Parsonian functionalism and establishment sociology. His rejection of a new conservatism within Soviet sociology, as it cozies up to American functionalism, which poses as a radical sociology, is actually only an empty shell of critical analysis because it is not consistent with the ontology and epistemology of Marxism. (The same sort of criticisms were made by Soviet sociologists against the "tragic hero" Mills who did not fully embrace Marxism in favor of the "safer" or more pragmatic critical theory of Weber.)

The editor of the journal invited Gouldner to respond to Fraser's criticisms, but he declined. In his place, though, Washington University colleague Paul Piccone stepped into the fray. Piccone took the position that communism was already in deep decline (circa the mid-1970s) and that attempts to shore it up by writers like Fraser were simply the last gasp of desperate radical intellectuals hoping to fulfill the promise of the overthrow of capitalism at the hands of the proletariat or other appropriate historical agents. The first point of Piccone's criticism is that Fraser misquoted Gramsci with regard to his argument that Gouldner held a flawed understanding of the relationship between science and ideology. When Fraser stated "Gramsci argues that it is possible for one social group to absorb the science of another without ingesting its ideology," he fundamentally misunderstood what Gramsci was referring to. Piccone argues that if you look a few more sentences beyond that quote, you will find Gramsci say "in reality, even science is a superstructure, an ideology," and hence Gramsci realized that all sciences or scientific perspectives—functionalism, Marxism, or what have you—are unavoidably ideological by their very nature (Piccone 1976b: 294). Fraser was attempting to hold to the standard line of Stalin-era sociology and science that historical materialism did indeed represent an objective or determinative law, and that it was not simply ideology subject to being subsumed or watered down in the evolutionary movement toward scientific objectivity which both Parsons and Gouldner theorized was happening. The second point of Piccone's criticism is connected with the first: Fraser's attempt to defend a materialist version of science (which would apply to Soviet Marxism regarding its unassailable assumption of historical materialism) is precisely the kind of reification for which "bourgeois" philosophers and sociologists have been condemned by critical Marxists from Lukács to Marcuse. Fraser's defense of Soviet sociology, then, is merely a form of objectivistic idealism that "degrades science to scientism and reification" and, if Fraser's is an accurate portrayal of Soviet sociology, it attests to its total bankruptcy (which of course it shares with its Western counterparts; Piccone 1976b: 295). In his rejoinder, Fraser (1976: 297) makes the claim that Piccone's "protestant fundamentalism places him, incongruously, alongside those in the U.S.S.R. who would dismiss sociology out of hand as 'non-Marxist.'"

Piccone and Gouldner

Here we must draw back briefly, and consider the career of Paul Piccone in somewhat more detail, as his career has important parallels, intersections, but also tensions with that of Gouldner. Piccone was born in L'Aquila, Italy in 1940, and he and his family immigrated to the United States, in 1954, with their eventual destination being Rochester, New York (Luke 2005). He received his Ph.D. in philosophy at SUNY-Buffalo in 1970. Shortly thereafter Piccone secured a tenure-track position in the department of sociology at Washington University, where Gouldner had been since 1959. In 1968 he founded the journal *Telos*, which initially was dedicated to exploring (and sometimes translating) European social theory, particular that of phenomenology and the Frankfurt School. Later, the journal became even more eclectic, moving away from concerns over western Marxism and taking a decidedly right turn in its politics toward Carl Schmitt, a thinker whom Piccone and fellow *Telos* travelers viewed as having crafted an indispensable critique of liberalism and its failures (Jacoby 2009).

In 1977 Piccone was denied tenure at Washington University even as many prominent scholars came to his defense including Gouldner, Daniel Bell, and Jürgen Habermas (Agger 2007). After a few years of battling the administration over the tenure denial to no avail, by the early 1980s Piccone resettled in New York's East Village as the journal continued to thrive.

Interpersonally Piccone was much like Gouldner: brusque, brash, demanding, aggressive, and assertive. In an extended remembrance shortly after his death in 2004, Tim Luke (2005) aptly described Piccone as brash, bombastic, brusque, cantankerous, cranky, and difficult, with a booming voice whose unique cadence still echoes among those who knew him and worked with him. Yet those who worked with him at *Telos* also knew him as generous and giving of his time, even as his editorial and intellectual standards were exhausting for those who worked on multiple drafts of the manuscripts which would eventually make their way into the pages of the journal (as attested to by Antonio 2011).

Telos was influential among many left-leaning intellectuals within philosophy, sociology, political science, and literary criticism, and following a meeting in 1976 between Piccone and Bob Antonio, there were plans to establish a *Telos* group at the University of Kansas (Dickens 2011). This occurred at the Midwest Sociological Society meeting held in St. Louis of that year. Although always loosely organized, the group hung together over the next several years by a core including Antonio, Susan LoBello, Bob Rucker, Mike Lacey, David Dickens, and Alan Sica. Several Kansas *Telos* conferences were held, the first at Antioch College in Ohio in 1977, the second in 1978 on the campus of Washington University in St. Louis. Piccone dutifully showed up for the festivities and always provided biting commentary in response to presenters whenever the opportunity arose. During the time that *Telos* was headquartered at Washington University, even though Gouldner's office was right next door to the *Telos* administrative office, he was never part of any *Telos* group, Kansas, St. Louis, or otherwise. This is consistent with Gouldner's always opting for the outsider or ridge-rider position in relation to any organized activities or school of thought.

Nevertheless, Gouldner did attend that 1978 *Telos* conference, and some memorable pyrotechnics ensued owing to the highly volatile personalities of both Piccone and Gouldner. Here is a description of the conference from a report published in *Telos* by the St. Louis *Telos* Group:

> Given the rate of disintegration of the Left politically as well as theoretically, those who still keep alive an interest in emancipatory activities have a need to convene periodically to share ideas and positions and to consider new political and theoretical projects. For this reason, a conference titled "The Totally Administered Society" was seen as a good opportunity to bring together many of the people around *Telos*. The Adornian title, of course, was not taken literally: such a society is certainly impossible.[5]
>
> 1978: 169

The members of the conference's first panel, on the topic of "Theories of Bureaucracy," were Gouldner, Jean Cohen, and Dick Howard. (Franco Ferrarotti was supposed to be on the panel as well but was a late cancellation.) It fell upon Gouldner to open up the proceedings, and he launched into material combining his earlier work on bureaucracy with his yet to be published book on intellectuals and the New Class. In his Columbia University dissertation work supervised by Merton, Gouldner conducted an ethnography of a gypsum plant in upstate New York—he was in Buffalo serving as an assistant professor at University of Buffalo from 1947 to 1951—and set about to test some theories of bureaucracy, primarily those of Weber. Weber (1978 [1922]) had emphasized that the bureaucracy was paradigmatic of the rise of Occidental rationalism, and this rationalization swept up everything in its path in the name of greater efficiency and predictability. Merton had warned not to accept uncritically proclamations about social reality from the masters in the field, such as Weber's iconic writings on bureaucracy, but to always be alive to the actual empirical realities of real flesh-and-blood human beings doing things together in the real world. There was, of course, the Weberian lament of the iron cage of bureaucracy, that the quest for greater predictability and efficiency also has the negative side effect of trapping the human beings working in the formal organization into a dull, lifeless routine where punching the clock and abiding by the rules became more important than pursuing the goals for which the organization was set up in the first place. This is the organizational pathology of "goal displacement" (Merton 1968: 249–260).

---

5   In the issue of *Telos* in which it appeared, the summary of the conference is listed only as being authored by the St. Louis *Telos* Group, and that is how it is cited here. Just to be clear, however, Dickens (2011) reports that the summary was authored by Paul Piccone.

In his ethnographic study of the gypsum plant, however, Gouldner found an indulgency pattern, that is, that even within the trappings of the rule system of the formal organization there were informal systems of understanding between supervisors and line staff allowing quite a bit of "off the books" behavior to take place, such as allowing workers to take tools home from work or to smoke in areas designated as non-smoking (Chriss 2001). The day-to-day work environment, in other words, was not all that oppressive or degrading of the human spirit. Indeed, it appeared to Gouldner that supervisors, especially those who came up through the ranks as former line staff, genuinely cared about their shop personnel and bent over backwards to assist them in any way they could. This finding was a basic repudiation of the popular view, since Weber, of bureaucracy as oppressive and deadening of the human spirit, and Gouldner went further to specify that the more oppressive and coercive aspects of bureaucracy were associated with management succession. That is, all things being equal, levels of bureaucratization and close supervision increase with changes in management (Gouldner 1964b).

So what we have here, then, is Gouldner opening a conference on the Totally Administered Society with a salvo, arguing that bureaucratization does not necessarily equate to oppression and enfeeblement, although it *may* go in that direction with management succession. Gouldner had to hedge his bets here, on the oppressive nature of bureaucracy, because he was going to argue further that it would be intellectuals—in the universities and elsewhere—who would constitute modern bureaucracies and whose radical potential represented the last best chance of attaining the good society. This meant that Gouldner argued that intellectuals and technical intelligentsia represented a New Class. But this would not be the old bureaucrats who typically were uncritically obedient to top management. The bureaucrats of the New Class would be armed with higher levels of training, education, autonomy, and cultural capital than their predecessors which served not only to increase their mobility but also their ability to persuade through rhetoric. This meant that managers of the New Class would have a lesser need for the punitive, coercive measures of "ordering and forbidding," instead placing more emphasis on human relations, the mastery of soft skills, and the realization of productivity through creativity (Gouldner 1979a: 51).

Those assembled at the conference were not happy with Gouldner's remarks. Those in attendance thought that Gouldner had simply abstracted out the bureaucracy from the society in which it is embedded, thereby failing to acknowledge the deleterious political and economic consequences of the broader capitalist system itself. One of the speakers on the panel, Jean Cohen, went further and argued that Gouldner was operating with a flawed one-dimensional concept of rationality, one which saw intellectuals and technical intelligentsia—not the same—unified into a single class position based upon their possession of higher education and cultural capital. Cohen rejected Gouldner's position, arguing instead that intellectuals do not constitute a unified class, neither in the sense of a class "in itself" nor "for itself." In essence, Gouldner is "reinforcing the principle of domination legitimated by knowledge" while "seeking to obscure all counter-rationalities in lieu of the claims of scientific rationality" (St. Louis *Telos* Group 1978: 171–172).

Later, near the end of the conference, Paul Piccone presented a paper on "The Changing Functions of the Left," charging that all the presenters so far—including of course Gouldner—were stuck in the past and unable to transcend the framework of the old or the new left. Too many self-identified radical intellectuals were all too willing to argue that even within the Totally Administered Society, the contradictions of the capitalist system itself would still, at some unspecified point in the future, produce historical agents who (or which) would help usher in the hoped for socialist or communist revolution. For example, the idea of the existence of a "proletarian" public sphere, argued in an earlier presentation by Oskar Negt, was preposterous. Piccone went on to illustrate the bankruptcy of both the old and new Left to the extent that many radical intellectuals were still apologizing for the travesties of statism and bureaucratic collectivism in Russia and China. Although by this time (1978) Gouldner had already moved to a position critical of Stalinism, he was still holding out hopes that Maoism or Castroism represented emancipatory versions of Marxism that should not be summarily discarded by the Left. After Piccone's talk Gouldner took the floor, and as Dickens reports,

> ...Alvin Gouldner took the microphone under the guise that he was going to ask a question, then proceeded to launch a wholesale attack on *Telos* and its editors, especially Piccone, for their alleged lack of any positive theory of politics. When Piccone finally cut him off after about twenty minutes, Gouldner began yelling "Scandal! Scandal!" as if he were the victim in a Stalinist show trial.
> 2011: 66

This infighting between left-leaning intellectuals was a recurrent feature not only during Gouldner's career, but throughout the development and ascendancy of critical theory itself since the 1920s. Piccone (1976a: 131–132) noted, for example, that even while seeking solutions to the social, political, and economic disruptions of World War I, the leading Hegelian Marxists of the 1920s—Korsch, Gramsci, and Lukács, all of whom were intimately involved in council movements of the time—were likely to direct their harshest criticisms toward fellow social-democrats for vulgarizing critical theory into a set of slogans which did not contribute to the emancipation of the downtrodden and distressed. But unlike Gouldner, who always held out hope that human emancipation could be maximized through a concerted project of critical, reflexive theory, Piccone lost faith in the left-liberal agenda, exhibited in the pages of *Telos* and elsewhere by the late 1970s, becoming increasingly intolerant of "sloganeering" and "empty-headed" radical theory. In this sense, Piccone moved quite close to Adorno's late lament that Marxist scholars had lost their way in championing political activism as the end all and be all of critical theory. Indeed, Piccone's (1978) artificial negativity, culminating in conservative populism while embracing Schmitt, is essentially the lived conviction of Adorno's thoughts on "resignation." As Adorno (1978) argued, activist critical theorists from the Frankfurt School onward tended to view suspiciously those who talked a good game, who knew their Marx or Engels or Gramsci, but who were reluctant to translate these ideas into political action. In other words, the standard approach of critical theory is that there should be a ceaseless effort to unite theory and praxis (especially in the sense of Korsch). But with so much emphasis placed on the action dimension, this can lead to a generalized prohibition of thinking. As Adorno (1978: 166) noted, "Repressive intolerance toward a thought not immediately accompanied by instructions for action is founded in fear." It is capitulation to the mob or collectivity. But true creative, enlightened thought must stand apart from the rush into activism for the sake of an alleged "true" theory, for ceding oneself to activist solutions without proper contemplation of its ramifications—that is, without an understanding of the relationship of parts to the whole—leads into dogma, or worse, totalitarianism. Indeed, for Adorno (1978: 168), the one who truly fights the good fight, who does not give up, is "the uncompromisingly critical thinker, who neither superscribes his conscience nor permits himself to be terrorized into action." Even further, in a missive aimed at Korsch among others, Adorno argued that

> The call for unity of theory and practice has irresistibly degraded theory to a servant's role, removing the very traits it should have brought to that unity. The visa stamp of practice that we demand of all theory became a sensor's placate. Yet whereas theory succumbed in the vaunted mixture, practice became nonconceptual, a piece of the politics it was supposed to lead out of; it became the prey of power.[6]
> 1973: 143

---

6 Adorno (1973) saw no way of linking his theory to the politics of the proletariat, and he was unwilling to cede ground to any of the parties claiming to speak for the oppressed. As Martin Jay

Following Adorno, the repudiation of empty-headed partisanship for left-liberalism, and its requirement for activism, is on display in Piccone's (1994) demolition of David Ost's (1994) defense of liberalism. Aghast at Piccone's and *Telos*' Schmittian turn, Ost suggested that there is no more Left in *Telos*, and he went on to describe five features of the Left, these being:

- A critique of capitalism
- Antagonism toward social hierarchies
- Sensitivity to the plight of the marginalized and oppressed
- Skepticism toward state power
- A commitment to full participation in public life for all citizens (Ost 1994: 138).

Contrary to Ost's optimism concerning the ability to clearly delineate between liberalism and conservatism, Piccone (1994) argues that since the demise of the Cold War any meaningful distinction between them has been lost. On the critique of capitalism, Piccone argues that this is no longer the province of the political Left, as many on the Right, including in both the United States and Europe (referred to by Piccone as "paleoconservatives"), have articulated various critiques of capitalism, primarily as a result of the destruction of traditional communities and the undermining of the informal systems of control (based in primary groups and family life) creating the social conditions for self-help.

Piccone rebukes Ost's second point as well, namely, the Left's antagonism toward social hierarchies. Ost's position is only partial at best, because it is not hierarchies per se that the Left detests, but *illegitimate* hierarchies. The orthodox socialist and Marxist Left never accepted this; indeed, the idea of a critical Marxism in which correct ideas if properly implemented will lead to the good life, always begs the question, who embodies these great ideas? Which strata of society could help along the proletarian revolt? The lowly masses? No, not really. There is a requirement, at least on some level, that enlightened intellectuals committed to the goals of social reconstruction informed by the tenets of historical materialism would have to do the bulk of the work. Even in natural or organic communities, natural hierarchies emerge, with the two earliest being those of sex and age.

How about Ost's third point, sensitivity to the plight of marginalized people? Again, the Left does not hold a monopoly here. Rather, the religious Right has always been concerned with the downtrodden, the dispossessed, the weak and infirm. Most of the teachings from Christianity to Buddhism, to Hinduism

---

(1984: 16) has observed, Adorno "stubbornly defended the virtues of what he called '*nicht mitmachen*', not playing along or compromising in the name of practical expediency."

and beyond, emphasize the notion of *charitas*, whereby true believers of the faith are instructed to develop direct personal relations with those less fortunate in the community. Indeed, the Right's version of charity and care are better than the Left's, according to Piccone, because the former provide charity directly, out of the goodness of their own heart as informed by religious teachings, while the Left's charity is administrative and bureaucratic, overseen by a new class of professionals making handsome livings off the largess of the welfare state.

On Ost's fourth point, the Left's skepticism toward state power, Piccone has a field day. The most organized "skepticism" toward the centralized power of the state is found among so-called "right-wing extremists" such as militia groups. Indeed, big government liberals love centralized federal control because of the way state-funded pork barrel projects are distributed to constituents who curry favor with the government through their donations, voting records, volunteer work, and so forth. The fifth point, a broad participation in public life, amounts more or less to redistributive policies which place more persons on the public dole who are stricken with debilitating and disreputable identities (Blacks, women, Jews, homosexuals, etc.). This attempt by the state to extend recognition to such disvalued groups to offset historical inequities in access and opportunity to socially valued goods incentivizes the further monetarization of private life and identity by defining their plight in economic terms, and it is in economic terms—through approaches such as social justice, public interest litigation, or reparations—where presumably their access to full participation in public life is assured. But in reality, this is merely an involution, which points to the validity of Piccone's artificial negativity thesis in the first place. For in this instance, rationalization means the consumerist redefinition of everyday life. Where the free market has failed to instill pro-social behavior and the adoption of middle-class values, the government through its redistributive efforts will seek full inclusion of the citizenry in all aspects of social life, whether in housing, employment, education, relationships and marriage, or civility more generally.

However icy, strained, or combative the relationship between Gouldner and Piccone may have been, between the years 1975 and 1977 the two men traded favors, as Piccone (1975, 1976c) published two papers in Gouldner's journal, *Theory and Society*, while Gouldner published two papers in Piccone's journal, *Telos*. The first appeared in 1975 under the title "Prologue to a Theory of Revolutionary Intellectuals" (Gouldner 1975b), while the second was published in 1977 with the title "Stalinism: A Study of Internal Colonialism" (Gouldner 1977). These two papers were an extension of the continuing work Gouldner was doing on Marxism and intellectuals especially beginning with the first book in his "dark side of the dialectic" series, namely *Dialectic of Ideology and Technology* (Gouldner 1976a). We will examine these two papers below, and then we will be in a position to examine why it was that Piccone took a decidedly right turn in his politics toward the "new populism," while Gouldner remained firmly ensconced in the tradition of radical sociology even as he was joining the critique of Stalinism emerging from both the left and right political spectrums.

Prologue to a Theory of Revolutionary Intellectuals

What was Gouldner up to in this paper, and how does it connect with the broader framework of studies on Marxism and intellectuals that consumed the last decade or so of his life?[7] It should be noted that a few years before the publication of this paper in *Telos*, Gouldner published a sympathetic piece about Maoism in *Partisan Review* (Gouldner 1973c).[8] He begins that paper with a theme from *Coming Crisis of Western Sociology*, namely, that in order to fashion a truly critical theory which aims toward the emancipation of the human spirit and the demolition of oppressive social structures and arrangements, this critical theory must be reflexive, otherwise theory is merely dogma which is blind to the contradictions which may lie deeply buried in its infrastructure. Hence, in the first few lines of the Mao paper Gouldner states that his aim is to develop a Marxist critique of Marxism, realizing that such an auto-critique is only possible with a healthy dose of reflexivity guiding the effort. This lack of reflexivity has characterized most versions of critical and Marxist theory up to Gouldner's time, and partially explains the horrendous violations of human rights under such communist leaders as Lenin and Stalin even as they were championing the liberation of the oppressed. However, in this paper Gouldner (1973c: 244–245) makes the case that Maoism "has achieved a reflexivity superior to that of Western Marxisms," to the extent that it has squarely faced the "bad news" about its own internal contradictions. Gouldner traces some of this reflexive advantage of Maoism to the fact that unlike other Marxisms which emerged within Christian cultures shot through with millenarian religious fantasies about an ideal end time (which could, for example, be represented by

---

7 Gouldner originally presented this paper as a talk at the Amsterdam Festival of the Social Sciences on April 10, 1975. Around the same time he presented other versions of the paper at the British Sociological Conference in Canterbury, the meetings of the Transnational Institute in Amsterdam, and at the University of Rome.
8 Portions of this paper, titled "Marxism and Mao," can be found in the chapter on "The Two Marxisms" from Gouldner's 1974 collection *For Sociology*.

the final resting point of the unfolding of the dialectic under communism), Maoism was devoid of such concepts of salvation or the afterlife, and as it was nurtured within a crumbling edifice of Confucian culture it also was more realistic and less prone to transcendentalism. Indeed, unlike the other major world religions, Confucianism places a premium on humanism (Chung et al. 1989).

Part of Mao's Cultural Revolution was the elimination of the academic intelligentsia. Interestingly, here Gouldner (1973c: 246) cites Sartre's view of the moribund future of the intellectual, arguing that "his privileged status is over," and that he must be absorbed in the struggle of the masses (i.e., the working class) rather than being concerned with his own petty interests. This is interesting because a few years later, in a talk he gave at Washington University, Gouldner gave Sartre short shrift, arguing that everything Sartre had to say about intellectuals was said better and more profoundly by Gramsci, even as he titled the talk "Sartre and the Intellectuals." Hence, here he argues that Sartre expresses an essentially Maoist view of the intellectual.

Mao is more realistic and more reflexive than all other Marxisms because it lives in the moment, among the unwashed masses, and does not kowtow to some highfalutin theoretical scheme pushed by an out of touch intellectual elite. Mao made this part of his cultural revolution a reality with the closing of Chinese universities between 1966 and 1970. Mao wanted nothing to do with any of the remnants of Mandarin culture, especially as embodied in the ethos of the Western university. Maoism, then, represents a massive critique and dismissal of Western bourgeois intellectuals, an effort in essence to overthrow all forms of elitism, including the cognitive elite of the universities. It is also an attempt to create a deep rupture with the past, a great leap forward. Gouldner's (1973c: 251–252) apologia for Mao's anti-intellectualism is striking: "Mao's antiintellectualism, then, is a way of destroying the links with the past and the limits of the past itself; it is not an expression of a contempt for mind or learning."

Hence, Maoism understands contradictions and negations, understands that Marxism, too, has a false consciousness. Mao opposes the Old Regime and seeks to destroy all links with the Chinese past because they carry potentially fatal seeds of its own destruction in the march to fashion a communist society. Maoism wants no part of the old order to live inside the one that is currently being built. Indeed, there is no way forward with the revolution except through the death of Western Marxism (Gouldner 1973c: 253). These remarks form a backdrop for the Prologue paper, generalizing from the special case of Mao and China to a general understanding of the role of intellectuals in revolutionary transformations.[9]

---

9 We will return to issues of Mao and communism in Chapter 9.

Everywhere socialist revolutions have appeared the middle-class intelligentsia spearheaded them, whether in Russia circa 1917, in China beginning in 1921 (through the efforts of Ch'en Tu-hsiu, Li Ta-chao, and Mao Zedong), or with Ho Chi Minh in Vietnam. Some of this prodding of intellectuals into revolution struggle occurred through world-historic changes, including the spread of colonialism, imperialism, and industrialism. Indeed, it was these new realities, perceived as depredations against the homeland, which were especially likely to motivate Third World intellectuals into action. They act on behalf of a demeaned national identity, working to organizing peasant (rather than proletariat) resistance however they can manage.

In impoverished Third World countries, with no stable working class from which to develop a proletarian revolutionary force, it would be the intellectuals that would create the impetus for social resistance against the system. Many of these intellectuals were schooled in Western societies, and were in a position to bring back the cosmopolitan outlook, some of which is in the form of critical perspectives such as Marxism, to apply to the locals and their situation. Rather than acting in their own interests, these Third World revolutionary intellectuals claim to be acting on behalf of oppressed and downtrodden countrymen who have suffered the slings and arrows of colonialism and other associated depredations. Along the way these transplanted intellectuals pick up new speech variants and styles, and are able to speak the language of revolution as informed by Western Marxism. As Gouldner (1975b: 15) argues, quite apart from the formal systems of education they were exposed to while studying overseas, Third World intellectuals also are imprinted with "a special grammar of reflexive discourse that, in various other ways, estranges them from their *local* culture." The old ways of understanding society are discarded, and new technical approaches to organizing it are implemented, in the image of a new, enlightened society freed from the trappings of both localistic symbols and cultures (such as a prevailing religious belief system) and alien features which have served to colonize it over the years. The intellectual, in other words, understands and seeks to implement a revolutionary organization built in accordance with the guidelines of a vanguard party committed to the tenets of historical materialism.

For Gouldner, then, a prologue to the full-blown development of revolutionary intellectuals is the exposure to the new speech variant of the culture of critical discourse (CCD), which is the backdrop for the system of solidarity, scrabbled together in the formation of the permanent revolution. CCD opens the way for radical intellectuals to develop political sensibilities oriented toward a grinding critique and rejection of the status quo in their own country. The template provided by Marxist doctrine, nurtured within the solidarity-making enterprise of the vanguard party, delivers to the intellectual a handy way of comparing and contrasting the reality of a fractured homeland versus what is possible if revolutionary principles are properly implemented. But unlike technical intelligentsia, who favor production and professionalism as builders and preservers, for intellectuals what is prized is "creativity" which by necessity breaks with the traditions of the past (Gouldner 1975b: 25). Much of the creativity is represented by the tenets of historical materialism which are made accessible through the culture of critical discourse and which can be put into practice in the real world within the supportive infrastructure of the vanguard.

Yet, there is a conundrum here, in that original or pure Marxist thought grounded liberation in the strivings of a working class who comes into class consciousness as a result of the depredations of the capitalist system spurring them into action. There is really no need for revolutionary intellectuals from the vanguard taking them by the hand and showing them how to throw off the shackles of the capitalist system, or be taught how to make the transition from false consciousness to true or class consciousness. Indeed, in the original Marxist formulation, if we are to take seriously the concept of base-superstructure, social location determines thoughts and ideas. How could Third World intellectuals, most of whom have privileged backgrounds and schooled in the best Western universities, adopt the consciousness of the downtrodden and the oppressed? There is no historical role for intellectuals qua intellectuals in the revolutionary struggle, at least according to scientific Marxism, and this represents one its most fitful nightmares.

As we move to a discussion of Gouldner's 1977 *Telos* paper on Stalinism, we see that Gouldner continues his concern with how reflective social theorists, tutored in the best schools and who come to champion the plight of the oppressed, believe as a result of the acquisition of this most extraordinary speech variant—the culture of critical discourse—that they have the truth on their side, and that whatever must be done—politically, culturally, economically—will be done in order to liberate the oppressed. This setting up of themselves as the champions of the oppressed can lead to not only elitism, but to terror and totalitarianism in the name of the "good." The move from scientific Marxism to humanistic or critical Marxism, as in the case of Lenin, Mao, and Stalin to name a few, reflects the fact that the Marxist project of emancipation can lead to the "disguised will of some intellectuals to *dominate*, to impose their own values and their own form of life on others" (Gouldner 1975b: 36).

From the 1930s until his death in 1953, Stalin oversaw the rapid industrialization of the Soviet Union, seeking to perfect communism while presumably learning from the mistakes and false starts of previous leaders such as Lenin. For example, although early on Lenin invited intellectuals into the corridors of power in the Communist Party of the Soviet Union (CPSU), by the early 1930s under Stalin admission of intellectuals into the CPSU was made more difficult (Gouldner 1985: 45). The cultural approach that Mao took in China was already well understood by Stalin with regard to the project of "socialist realism." As Hollander (1966: 353) explains, socialist realism was the "theoretical framework for the complete subordination of the arts to the political objectives upheld by the Soviet regime." The appropriation of the arts and other culture-making apparatus of society was a concerted attempt to alter Soviet citizens' perceptions of reality. In essence, Stalin set up an intricate system of indoctrination, attempting to make heroes of Stalin and members of the Soviet government while making enemies of all those who questioned the legitimacy of the program.

The most important trait of a good Soviet citizen was "party-mindedness," that is, unwavering loyalty to and complete identification with the Party. This characterization of the model citizen, dedicated to the Party above all else, was emblazoned in popular literature underwritten by the Stalin regime. Other traits that were central to the good citizen, carefully orchestrated by the propaganda machine of Stalin, were patriotism, collectivism, a propensity to hate, vigilance—that is, letting citizens know that the rest of the (capitalist) world was hostile to the aims and ambitions of the Soviet state and warning them to be alive to how such challenges to its legitimacy may appear. With regard to the propensity to hate, the good Soviet citizen would be expected to hate the enemy in equal proportions to his or her love of the Party (Hollander 1966: 356). By the same token, the indoctrination program carefully crafted the view of the enemy as unscrupulous, ugly, cowardly, duplicitous, hateful, and sexually depraved. This negative characterization of enemies was malleable over the years as internal and world historical events led to shifting alliances between the Soviet Union and other countries, and the indoctrination literature followed these trends. For example, the Stalin Constitution of 1936 declared that, thanks to the great purges, all antagonistic social classes within Soviet society had been eradicated (Hollander 1966: 362). Indeed, Stalin and his henchmen engaged in extreme forms of political repression against citizens and their families who were labeled enemies of the state (Alexopoulos 2008).

Gouldner asks, "What is the essence of Stalinism?" Attempting to stay true, at least partially, to a social construction of reality approach, Gouldner argues that Stalinism cannot be understood merely as a unique historical event. It must also and necessarily be understood in relation to the goals and aspirations of any analyst who poses the question, what is the essence of Stalinism? Reflexive sociology must always be alive to the lived convictions of the analyst, even to some degree incorporating these reflexive insights into the project at hand. This brings up an interesting issue, which I shall turn to briefly before getting back to Gouldner's analysis of Stalinism as internal colonialism. Stephen Savage wrote a book in the early 1980s that served as a defense against some of the brutal attacks Talcott Parsons received from the like of Mills, Gouldner, Dahrendorf, and other beginning in the 1960s. At the heart of Gouldner's reflexive sociology—indeed, lying at the heart of his broader sociology of sociology project (see, e.g., Friedrichs 1971)—is that in any work of analysis there is a silent infrastructure always in play informing the technical level in the production of the theory or conceptual scheme. Although positivistic sociological theorists went about their work oblivious to the tacit or infrastructural dimension of theory (Fuhrman 1984), Gouldner argued that the tacit system of domain assumptions—in the areas of epistemology, ontology, and axiology—is central to sociological work. But Savage (1981) argues that Gouldner conflates two distinct spheres, namely, the instruments with which sociologists produce their everyday work, and the human subjects who operate these tools of the trade. Gouldner's mistake, according to Savage, is that he reduces sociology to sociologists. It is analogous to the attempt to analyze "a lump of coal or a pick-axe in terms of the social and personal experiences of the coal miner" (Savage 1981: 7).

Savage's critique is a rejection of Gouldner's instrumentalist position, namely, that one's tacit set of domain assumptions represent a set of commitments that give shape and form to the theory. In other words, for Gouldner, the silent infrastructural level of theory, including the theorist's sentiments, values, aspirations, political beliefs, and ideology determine many important aspects of scientific productivity, including theorists' concepts and theories. Jeffrey Alexander, although applauding Gouldner's postpositivism, also finds fault along with Savage that, in his critique of Parsons, Gouldner has conflated dimensions of theoretical logic that must be kept distinct. In claiming that positivistic notions that science can be value-neutral are misguided and mythical, which Alexander favors in the spirit of the dawning of postpositivism in sociology, Gouldner has made an error in claiming that this infrastructural dimension is inherently political or ideological. Gouldner's conflation is the error of positing that one dimension along the multidimensional continuum of theoretical logic, namely, one's political presuppositions, is instrumental in determining another dimension, namely, our models, theories, concepts, or classifications (Alexander 1982: 43–44). Alexander is correct to the extent that Gouldner's strategy unnecessarily politicizes sociology: everything under the sun reflects political positions and posturing. Indeed, 1970s sociology was mired in tired political debate over whether theorist x was conservative, and what that meant for the sociological enterprise.

There was no greater disservice done to anyone in our discipline—ever—than Gouldner's incessant wailing over the alleged conservatism of Parsons. As a matter of fact, Parsons was a registered Democrat, and a big-government one at that. Indeed, Parsons was attempting to set up sociology as the leading social science that would be first in line to receive the largess of a burgeoning American welfare state. He was even a proponent of nationalizing the social sciences, and of strengthening the ties between education and government, including funding of their research by the National Science Foundation and other government agencies (Klausner 1986). So Parsons was a big-government liberal, although admittedly he was not a radical, and this drew Gouldner's ire. Indeed, Gouldner railed against the Welfare-Warfare state, arguing that in their quest to secure government funding to study "nuts, sluts, and preverts" (Liazos 1972), sociology is not coming to the aid of the oppressed at all. Instead, they are using them for their own aggrandizement and benefit. Agreeing with Liazos, Gouldner (1968) sees the quest for funding by big-government liberals such as Parsons as empty-headed partisanship that is devoid of critical and emancipatory aims. Well, yes, this may very well be the case, that some sociologists are living *for* sociology instead of living *for* the people who are in distress. Anyone who has aspirations of treating sociology as a science, rather than as a massive effort at societal betterment and restoration, may be prone to receiving this sort of judgment. Treating sociology as a science may mean, for example, that real flesh and blood human beings are simply data points that can be mined for whatever purposes suit the researcher, all the while benefiting the scientific status of sociology just so long as the methodological protocols are rigorous and stand up to scholarly scrutiny. This opens up positivism and traditional science to criticisms that their proponents treat persons merely as objects rather than honoring their subjectivity, that is, their humanity.

Gouldner typically fell on the side of critics of positivistic "big" science, but he was not Pollyannaish about rescuing the dignity and humanity of those poor saps being victimized by an uncaring and callous, well-funded research machine. Indeed, placing overweening emphasis on subjectivity, feelings, and emotions effectively treats everyday persons as fragile therapy clients, thereby pandering to the psychologization of the human person and badly deforming a specifically sociological approach to our subject matter.

Conclusion

I spent some time this chapter covering the history of Jewish involvement in American communism beginning in the 1930s. This was done not to cast aspersions on Jewish intellectuals, but simply to create a backdrop of the historical and cultural circumstances implicated in Gouldner's involvement in radical politics from 1943 to 1953. By 1953, coinciding with the execution of the Rosenbergs, Gouldner's commitment to public politics came to an end, although he continued to champion the role of social critic and (for the most part) wrote sympathetically about radical sociology until his death in 1980. Gouldner's decision to retreat from activist politics seemed perfectly reasonable given this set of cultural, historical, and biographical circumstances, yet many on the Left or radical side of the political aisle continued to wring their hands over this failure of political will, over this tragic "cop out." Gouldner understands this dynamic all too well, as he lived through it as a younger, idealistic political activist who sneered with disdain at elders in the academy or elsewhere who lacked the gumption to put their convictions into action. Gouldner (1970a: 11) stated, for example, "It is undoubtedly correct that sociology often attracts young men and women of reformist inclination and prior radical outlook, and some of their subsequent criticism of sociology may indeed derive from their frustrated expectations." Even though Gouldner railed against sociology (circa the 1970s) for its conservatism and its kowtowing to the status quo, being the good left Hegelian he was, he also realized that sociology's internal contradictions allow for the radicalization of sociologists given the right set of circumstances (biographical, institutional, psychological, economic, historical, and so forth).

Eight years after Gouldner's death a special issue of *Theory and Society* was published which was dedicated to examining the effects of sixties politics on contemporary (circa 1988) social theory. Co-editor David Swartz (1988: 616) explained "In recognition of the twentieth anniversary of 1968, this special issue of *Theory and Society* assembles seven articles that explore various developments in social theory and sociology since the sixties." Co-editor Charles Lemert (1988) was given the privilege of commenting on the seven articles preceding his (written by Theda Skocpol; Ivan Szelenyi and Bill Martin; Randall Collins; Charles Tilly; Peter Evans and John D. Stephens; Raymond Boudon; and Pierre Bourdieu), and he spent much of his time apologizing profusely for not being able to secure a contribution from a feminist scholar. Lemert (1988: 799) was actually *embarrassed* at this turn of events, that feminist theory and the movement that gave rise to it, described by him as "perhaps the single most enduring achievements of sixties politics," was absent from the special issue. To make up for this gaffe, Lemert fell all over himself piling up sweet talk about the greatness of feminist theory, how it has contributed to the breaking down of the provincialism, stuffiness, and stodginess of something called "sociology" as a distinct discipline, along the way ushering in an amorphous "social theory" era which transcends the old, outdated discipline system of traditional science. He also joins with feminists such as Judith Stacey and Barrie Thorne in lamenting that sociology has yet to experience a feminist revolution. Where radical sociologists criticize non-reflexive sociologists for kowtowing to the status quo and clinging to now outdated notions of value-free knowledge and positivist methods, "enlightened" radical sociologists like Lemert kowtow to feminists and other evaluative theorists. It's all a matter of picking your poison: Who's kowtowing to whom?[10]

For example, why should there be a feminist revolution in sociology? Why is this needed? In fact, there is a contradiction in thinkers like Lemert on the one hand lauding the coming age of polycentrism within sociology while on the other pining for feminism to become the central orienting perspective for the discipline. Of course, this would be analogous to the Marxist notion of the necessity of the temporary way station of state socialism on the way toward full-blown communism once the state finally withers away and dies. Rather than "Workers of the world unite!" radical sociologists who are sympathetic to the demise of the disciplinary system of conventional science are urging, "Social theorists of the world unite!" For now, feminism will have to be content with making inroads into particular stand alone disciplines such as sociology, and as the new gynocentric or standpoint perspectives proliferate across the discipline more broadly the old, androcentric perspectives upon which it was built will disappear, and with it, the effective disappearance of what once was known as sociology. This was Lemert's dream back in 1988, but he gave indications back then that by now, in our present time some 25 years later, the triumph of gynocentrism over androcentrism would have transpired. It has not, of course, and those who keep pushing for either the demise of sociology as a distinct discipline or the realization of a feminist revolution continue to be disappointed.

Lemert goes on to argue that feminism—especially Sandra Harding's version which seeks to find epistemological solutions for overcoming conventional dichotomous thinking—addresses the question of the relation between knowledge and power in a unique and powerful way. Connected with this, Lemert (1988: 803) asks, "How can knowledge be power? How can one be both a successful academic and political? How can one be, academically, both in the disciplines and beyond them?" Even approaching a point in time in which such questions are asked reflects a growth in consciousness

---

10   In fact, what Lemert is up to here is very close to a description provided by Franklin Giddings (1908: 797) of "those authoritative persons who are but too glad to seize upon the opportunity thus afforded them to become the confessors and demigods of a worshipful sex" (see also Chriss 2006a, 2006b).

through which persons experience the realities of oppression or strength and are able to ascertain the conditions of others in shared power relations. It is not good enough merely to reflect on one's own experiences as an oppressed person, or to theorize about collective experiences of shared oppression on the basis of race or gender or sexual orientation, say. A more sophisticated approach to the problem of oppression and how to overcome it must be able to understand how firsthand experiences with oppression act as a starting mechanism launching questions—perhaps even scientific ones—about the nature of that lived experience. The experience of being excluded, of being treated as the other, of feeling powerless, of being barred from full participation in society—all of these insights, according to the feminist perspective and all those who champion it, are born within the crucible of personal experience. But one must also learn to extrapolate from the one to the many, not by way of a simplistic additive theory of oppression, but by conceptualizing how power relations work irrespective of any particular set of empirical circumstances giving rise to initial glimmers of realization about those relations.

This idea that Lemert illustrates, flowing from the questions he raised above, concerning the insights feminists contribute to the new and expanding program of social theory, which transcends the stifling suffocation of disciplinary parochialism, is little more than chimera. For example, the question "How can one be both a successful academic and political?" begs another question: What if someone chooses not to be political within the context of his or her academic work? Or even better, What if someone rejects the idea that everything is political, including the personal? What then? If this strikes radical sociologists as bizarre or unacceptable, then they indeed have a very weak and tenuous handle on the project of explaining the social. If all one has to fall back on is the Marxist chimera—or, perhaps phrased more generously, the Marxist trope—that false consciousness is to blame for intellectuals opting out of political activism, then perhaps the greatest of all reflexive sociologists, Alvin Gouldner, would have to be characterized as suffering from a deep paralysis of false consciousness for merely writing about political activism rather than living it and giving it his all. Of course, radical critics of Gouldner's lack of political activism during the 1960s were unaware of his earlier activities in the Communist Party, and Gouldner never felt obliged to tell anyone about it. He felt no need to wear his radical credentials on his sleeve.

Gouldner of course is to blame for much of this mess. After all, it was he whose own agency and volition set him on a course of investigating the philosophical foundations of knowledge claims in sociology. As a defender of

Enlightenment reason but also as a secular humanist and outlaw Marxist, Gouldner would be oriented toward this work from a critical perspective that tended to look skeptically at the irrational and the mystical. His penchant for dialectical thinking tended to go in the same direction as Marx's inversion of Hegelian idealism, and the form of idealism most likely to be rebuffed and repudiated was religion. The next chapter picks up the story from there.

CHAPTER 6

Religion and Critical Theory

Introduction

In *Coming Crisis of Western Sociology* Gouldner wrote a section titled "The Piety of Functionalism." Gouldner argues that functionalism in general and Talcott Parsons in particular possess a distinctively religious ethos. The argument hinges on how Comte, in his formulation of both positivism and sociology, was seeking desperately to shore up the social group's hold over the individual in the wake of cultural trends, which suggested the rise of atomistic individualism. With ongoing secularization, there was a concern that the morality of the group, originally assured through the solidarity of the religious congregation, could no longer be assured. Comte tried to figure out some way of maintaining the morality of the group through consensus building and the shoring up of attachments between like-minded individuals, but stripped of the religious ideas which had effectively kept humanity in the dark. The solution was to build a new secular religion of humanity, utilizing the methods and approaches of the natural sciences to better understand the human condition. Since the mass public was ignorant or apathetic about gaining better knowledge about the social world, it would be up to a new cadre of technocrats who had the wherewithal to understand the positive principles and put them into practice to attain the good society.

For Gouldner, Parsons and functionalism were the immediate heirs to this religion of humanity envisioned by Comte. Comte and the immediate generation following did not successfully implement the formal structures for this new religion of humanity, and secularization—that is, the waning of religious affect—was moving forward unabated. This was not bad in and of itself, but the side effect was that the old morality of the fire and brimstone of the church pulpit was eroding as well, and in the modern world there were more social problems even as economic well-being was improving for the majority. Functionalism in Parsons' hands was dedicated to finding and resuscitating the value basis for the alleviation of human suffering as men and women are enveloped in a supportive infrastructure, namely, the humanity of the group. Following Durkheim, who theorized that the old mechanical solidarity of tight-knit groups and the development of an overarching collective conscience was fragmented and likely gone forever, there nevertheless was a quest for functional alternatives, in essence seeking a modern social solidarity, namely organic solidarity. In the place of the cozy arenas of primary groups and socialization—families, friends, the village, and cultural homogeneity—there would now be the requirement for a new professional class of experts to provide wrap-around services to persons who were not properly bonded to conventional society. Parsons was sympathetic to the rise of a welfare state where deviance was seen as illness and where therapeutic practitioners—including sociologists leading the charge of providing information to government administrators about how to handle the hordes of the urban dispossessed—would be called on to use their expertise in the betterment of society.

This attempt by Parsons and the functionalists to seek and revivify morality in the new era of organic solidarity characterized by unhealthy individualism is, for Gouldner, a functionalism shot through with religious convictions. Gouldner reads Parsons as seeking a functional alternative for the long lost mechanical solidarity of old, and on this basis any morality would do. The paramount concern for Parsons is the shoring up of a tenuous social order, and this work contains at its root a religious zeal, with Parsons serving as functionalism's priest in much the same way that Comte envisioned himself the archbishop of the new religion of humanity. But Gouldner takes no pleasure in unmasking the religious roots of Parsonian functionalism. He states "Although I am not 'religiously musical'—to borrow Max Weber's term—I do experience this exercise in righteousness as somewhat repellent. …If I disapprove of Functionalism, it is not because it has a religious dimension [for Marxism has one, too], but because of the *kind* it has, and most especially because of the *kind* of morality it seems to embody" (Gouldner 1970a: 264).[1] Gouldner, like most self-respecting left-leaning to radical intellectuals, must always be on guard against the invocation of spirituality in the classroom or in their writings because, to be blunt, spirituality taints a person as "unintelligent," and this is the last thing any person of learning wants to be tagged with (Lindholm 2014: 136).

Parsons and the functionalists see society as godlike, much like Durkheim's notion that society is God in his study of primitive religion among the Arunta tribe. This informs Parsons' deeply pious conception of society, and the norms and values providing whatever solidarity is left in a fracturing modernity are sacred. For Goffman, with the rise of organic solidarity the individual and his subjectivity become a new object of worship. But for Parsons, he and his

---

1 While Gouldner hints at a religious dimension of Marxism, Parsons (1968: 331–332) is more explicit, stating "Religion here is interpreted as a functional universal of societies, so I should not hesitate to call Marxism-Leninism, as it is institutionalized in communist societies, a 'secular-political religion'."

followers must continue to argue that it is society and the group that is the fount of sacrality. Even further, this pious notion of the sacredness of the collectivity informs Parsons' vision of science: Science is not merely useful as a worldly activity; it is the highest calling, set apart from the profane world as dedicated men and women go about their work dutifully, somberly, and with great austerity and asceticism to achieve the good society (the Garden of Eden). This is even why Parsons and the functionalists have often refrained from applied science, because it would bring them closer to an engagement with the profanations of a tainted world.

Here, Gouldner is railing against that part of Weber he hated most, namely, his enrapture in the Protestant work ethic. Parsons used much of Weber's work in a direct and unreconstructed manner, rarely parting ways with him on crucial conceptual and methodological points. Although not a religious zealot, Parsons was likely more "religiously musical" than Gouldner, who kept his Jewishness in the background of much of his work. Although, it is interesting to note that in November 1962, Gouldner served as keynote speaker before some 400 Jewish women at the "Tell-It-Straight" Institute for the Women's Division of the Jewish Federation. The conference was held at Temple Israel in Creve Coeur, Missouri, the same suburb of St. Louis in which Gouldner lived with his wife, Helen. There is no record of his talk, but the blurb in the St. Louis paper (the *Post*) reports that the speakers would be discussing "problems and values of contemporary living from the standpoint of religion and morals."[2]

Parsons (1978: 233) stated that "First, I am not a Roman Catholic, but a somewhat backsliding Protestant of Congregationalist background." Parsons takes the Protestant ethic thesis even further than Weber, attributing to religion in general and Protestantism in particular many of the benefits and advances of the modern world. Parsons' functionalism emphasizes first the *potency* of Protestantism, as it has given rise to many of the key economic, technological, and scientific advances of the western world. Parsons argues as much, suggesting that the ethos of the Puritans of seventeenth century England is the background for Anglo-Saxon achievements in economic productivity, science and philosophy, in rational analysis of the normative order (including of course the continuing reliance on law for matters civil, criminal, and administrative), and of heightened individualism (Parsons 1977).

This individualism is the healthy individualism of Durkheim rather than the unhealthy individualism of the modern era leading into the disasters of

---

2 This is taken from a packet of information about Gouldner I received from the library archives at Washington University-St. Louis in 2013.

anomie and egoism (Chriss 1993). This healthy individualism would culminate in the cult of the individual, made possible by the successful implementation of institutionalized individualism across society. According to Parsons, sociology is the social science discipline most concerned with integration, focusing as it does upon the institutional aspects of social action. Although no system is in perfect equilibrium, the goal of the social system nonetheless is the harmonic balancing between the needs of the collectivity against the needs of the individual. The science of sociology should be able to figure out how to strive toward approaching and maintaining this balance, for example, through understanding the optimization of the internalization of the normative expectations of the group, thereby creating a template of need-dispositions (in the personality) which would correspond with the institutionalized value patterns residing at the collective level (Parsons 1968).

The second way Parsons conceptualizes the importance of Protestantism is in its *goodness*. Unlike other religions, which emphasized otherworldly asceticism, monasticism, and retreat from the world, Protestants threw themselves into the world and would be known by their good works, not by how much they prayed. Gouldner (1970a: 255) views Parsons as being almost giddy about the great strides in humanitarianism that Christian brotherhood and salvation have brought to the world, stating that "There is no other single institution to which Parsons attributes such potency and goodness: the Church has been the rock and the light of modern civilization." This has the added advantage of equating the powerful with the good.

The Powerful and the Good: Evangelical Protestantism

Gouldner was an activist in Communist politics early in his life but gave it up after 1953 with the execution of the Rosenbergs and the rise of McCarthyism. He therefore had good reason to abandon political activism when he did, and this need not be pursued further here. On the other hand, Gouldner would be loath to accept forms of political activism that did not meet with his ideological sensibilities. For example, what about Christian fundamentalism that takes the position that homosexuality is a sin, that out-of-wedlock pregnancies constitute a social problem, or that supports the traditional patriarchal family of fathers as breadwinners and mothers as homemakers and caregivers? Would Gouldner favor this nexus of values to become connected to a set of concerted political activities? Of course he would not. Most Marxists—Activist and Academic alike—would sneer at this sort of populist sentiment put into action, for it violates the creative and emancipatory aspects of the life of mind which should seek critical engagement with texts and received wisdom. As Paolucci describes it, both

> Religious fundamentalism and right-wing political outlooks...adopt a strict reading and adherence to the official institutional discourse of the system that contains them. Religious fundamentalists believe in the inerrant word of holy texts and, in the United States, original legal theory similarly purports to interpret the Constitution through its written word as stated on the page, both thus eschewing interpretive and/or reformist approaches.
> 2011: 130

Actually, what I said above about Gouldner is not quite accurate. He would be loathsome not only of doctrinal orientations to religious texts; he would be—and was—loathsome to ALL doctrinal orientations, including those of presumably emancipatory programs such as Marxism or communism. For doctrine which is treated as holy and the interpretations of which cannot be easily negotiated have the penchant for turning into dogma guarded by a vanguard party. Paolucci is a Marxist who seems to be unaware or unconcerned about this problem, for he spends much of his time explaining away the real-world horrors that have occurred in the name of Marx and Marxism (see, e.g., Paolucci 2004, 2011). In contradistinction to Paolucci's attempts to absolve Marx of the occasional horrors emanating from the application of Marxism in the political realm, Pellicani (2014) argues that historical materialism and the dialectic method at their roots contain the religious zeal of the pursuit of utopia, but this is not attained through good works, proper living, or devout faith in an almighty beneficent spirit. Instead, a communist utopia is achieved through the absolute destruction of capitalist society because of its spoilage by bourgeois culture, social structure, organization, and personality. This policy of the smashing of the capitalist system, along with the ruthless purging of all enemies of the state, is not an aberration brought about by misunderstanding or misapplication of pure Marxism by Lenin, Stalin, Mao, or the Khmer Rouge in Cambodia, but is a logical derivative of it.

For Gouldner (1976a), theories are ideologies that attempt to make a mark on the world in ways specified by the theory. They are public projects. As public projects they come into conflict within the public spaces of other ideological or theoretical projects. The rise of political activism among American evangelical Protestants is a type of public project—or ideology or theory—that will be the focus of this section. The evangelicals are attempting to secure their own understanding of the world, as received through the teachings of an inerrant Bible, against the encroachment of secular humanism. As another public project competing against and alongside others, secular humanism may be seen as a subset of that process which Weber (1958, 1963) described as rationalization. Although rationalization and its cognates bureaucratization, specialization, and textualization lead to greater efficiency and predictability in modern life, they may also usher in a variety of pathologies. The incursion of Christian fundamentalism into secular spheres such as the political or the scientific (e.g., the intelligent design debate; see Fuller 2006) is inevitable and promises to continue unabated. In this regard, it may be helpful to consider Parsons' (1978) argument that even with the increased emphasis placed on cognitive rationality, the problem of ultimate meaning—specifically the problem of salvation—is the single most salient factor underlying and informing human social action.

Wuthnow (1991) has provided a discussion of three major theories of religion and politics, namely modernization theory, world-system theory, and critical theory. For purposes of this chapter, critical theory will receive the bulk of attention since it is Gouldner's home base. However, because we will be explaining questions of ultimate meaning or nonempirical reality from a Parsonian perspective, there is a ready-made but unexplored connection to modernization theory. The strand of critical theory pursued early on will be that of Habermas, although even here, because he has taken seriously some aspects of Parsons' systems theory, he is not a pure representative of the critical or evaluative paradigm. Indeed, Agger (1992) observed that Habermas's ongoing effort to forge a theory of communicative action represents the "Parsonianization of Marxism." To the extent that Habermas indeed represents something of a synthesis between Parsons and Marx, it would bring to fruition one of Gouldner's (1970a) major predictions, that being the eventual convergence of Parsonianism and Marxism.

Habermas and the Pathologies of Modernity

Wuthnow's discussion of critical theoretical approaches to the problem of religion and politics focuses on Habermas's (1984, 1987) development of a theory of communicative action. Habermas's effort is a variant of one particular axis, namely the soteriological, in the construction of domains of knowledge (Eisenstadt 1988). To summarize briefly, Habermas's (1984, 1987) theory of communicative action follows a long tradition whose guiding concern has been to identify and, ultimately, to propose ameliorative solutions for the variety of social pathologies which has plagued humanity during the period which has come to be known as the "modern."

Combining Weber's concern with the process of rationalization and Marx's theory of alienation, Habermas is primarily concerned with what he calls the "sheering off of system from the lifeworld" or the "colonization of the lifeworld" (Chriss 1995). Stated differently, Habermas is concerned with the deleterious effect of the growth of instrumental rationality on the everyday lifeworld. For Habermas, then, the overriding social pathology of modernity equates to the problem of how the societal steering media (Baum 1976), which ostensibly guide "functional integration" at the systems level, have grown to outstrip and hence have made less relevant the "societal integration" arising from actual human communicative conduct. Habermas borrows the idea of generalized media of interchange directly from Parsons. Within the context of Parsons' AGIL schema, the steering media stand as analytical constructs that serve to establish "relations between and among diverse and variant phenomena" (Parsons 1978: 395) contained within each of the four groupings of the social system. These media circulate at the highest level of generality within each of their respective functional subsystems (power in the polity, influence in the societal community, value-commitments in the fiduciary system, and money in the economy). The ultimate purpose of the steering media is functional integration, through the ordering and intertwining of the consequences of action.

Wolfe's (1989: 20) quote illustrates what Habermas is up to here: "...as modern societies come to rely ever more thoroughly on either the market or the state to organize their codes of moral obligation, living with the paradoxes of modernity will become increasingly difficult." As we move further and further away from primitive mechanical solidarity based on likeness and familiarity, we now have to balance our obligations not only to our primary group associates, but also to an expanding array of secondary (or even more distant) associates. This likely will lead to greater confusion as we struggle to juggle the "inward" moral rules geared toward dealings with the primary groups of civil society and the "outward" rules of nonintimate and distant social relations.

One indicator of this modern frustration arising from the juggling of a new set of moral obligations is the disenchantment with the modern world documented by many thinkers over time, including Marx, Weber, Durkheim, Gouldner, and Habermas. This is driven largely by the belief that distant and anonymous forces control our lives and collective destinies, and in turn this has produced a variety of social movements and rebellions over time. As Wuthnow explains,

> ...many of the religious movements we see emerging in various parts of the world—especially those in advanced industrial societies—can be understood as protests against the growing bureaucratization and monetization of the lifeworld. Environmentalism, home schooling, certain

variants of feminist theory, and even Christian or Islamic fundamentalism may be understood as examples of such protest.

1991: 10

Parsons' Telic System and the Problem of Salvation

As modern societies continue to organize themselves around the growth of knowledge and emphasize the ethic of cognitive rationality (Parsons and Platt 1973), there has arisen as well a heightened sense that certain matters of ultimate concern (Tillich 1952)—which, as stated earlier, we understand to be the soteriological problem or the "problem of salvation" (Parsons 1978: 390)—have yet to be adequately addressed through the more conventional secular channels, especially that of science. The implications of one of Parsons' last major theoretical efforts—namely, the paradigm of the human condition—is that a key concern of persons situated in particular lifeworld arrangements is the problem of salvation.

This only makes sense in terms of Parsons' explication of the "action frame of reference" as an analytical strategy for explaining how and upon what grounds human beings decide to carry out their life tasks. In his latter period, Parsons applied ideas of cybernetics to his four-function scheme. The cybernetic principle is that "things high in information control things high in energy." Within the action frame of reference, the human condition paradigm becomes the highest or general analytical level possible insofar as one is now able to incorporate meaningful explanations of the religious realm, of ultimate values or what Persons terms the "transempirical" or, similarly, "nonempirical reality." As illustrated in Figure 6.1, in terms of the human condition paradigm the cybernetic hierarchy of control designates the physico-chemical system (the A-cell) at the lowest level of control (and the highest energy), then on through in ascending order to the human organic system (G), the action system (I), and finally to the pinnacle of the cybernetic hierarchy, the telic system (L).

At this highest level of generality the telic system (L) "controls" the human organic system (G) insofar as questions of ultimate meaning—questions such as What is the meaning of life? What is our purpose? How was the universe created? Why am I here?—may be seen as the crucial element underlying the motivations and orientations to action of individual human beings. This is consistent with Harry Johnson's (1979: 313) description of religion as providing to its believers "...a kind of code, model, or paradigm that shapes or patterns a more or less total way of life: inner experience, action, and judgment." Such ultimately unanswerable questions may be resolved through faith, and in this sense we see that religion serves a tension management or pattern maintenance function, as

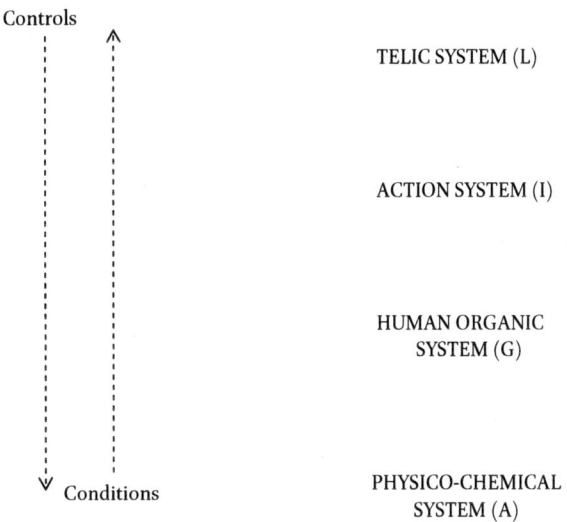

FIGURE 6.1 *Cybernetic ordering of the human condition*

is readily evident in the variety of prescriptions for salvation offered up by the world's religions (see Weber 1963). As Parsons (1978: 363) states, "The telic system may also be said to be relevant to problems of orientation in relation to telic considerations that arouse strong emotions in human beings. The problems of suffering and of evil as Weber deals with them are examples."

Weber, Rationalization, and Standardization

In his *Protestant Ethic and the Spirit of Capitalism*, Max Weber (1958) explains how certain religions evolve from the more primitive or traditional (e.g., those based on magic or mysticism such as Confucianism or Buddhism) to the more modern or rational (e.g., those based on prophecy which carry the potential to upgrade through the marshaling of charismatic authority—a social change embodied in the idea of "breakthrough"—as in Protestantism). Rationalization involves above all else intellectual clarification, or the systemization of ideas. This may be seen in the increasing normative control of action that Weber illustrates is brought to bear through the institutionalization of formal, as opposed to merely substantive, law. Formal law is more rational than substantive law insofar as the former is guided by broad principles which in turn lead individuals to adopt a total way of life, which is itself based upon a set of sociological behavioral norms implied by these general principles, not by specific events. In contrast, the implication of substantive or equity law, based as it is on doing justice merely on a case-by-case basis, is that individuals' actions are guided by a set of ideal norms that can only be explained on the basis of individual psychology.

Following Weber's discussion of the progression of civilization or, more specifically, of the rationalization of religious systems and the implications for behavior contained therein, we may recast our own concern with modernity in terms of the problem of standardization. That is, within modern western society pressures toward standardization of norms of conduct persist and continue to proliferate in all facets of social life. We witness, for example the imbroglio that has erupted around the problem of hate speech. Traditionalists want to leave decisions regarding how to react to offensive speech to actors in their everyday lifeworlds, to act informally and to use interpersonal or group pressures to bear to sanction offenders appropriately. But this reflects a slapdash of individual notions of offense, and the multitude of ways actors acting in their capacity as fellow human beings could react to such slights signals the messiness and unpredictability of everyday life. Questions of standardization—through law primarily, but also through attempts to change norms through recourse to experts in medicine and other professions—arise when there is a sense that the variability of responses to certain stimuli can no longer be tolerated. Any system of social control—legal, medical, or the informal realm of everyday life—seeks to derandomize conduct.

On another front, we may witness the ongoing debate over standardization of concepts within sociology. As has been the case with many social science disciplines, sociology's history has been typified by slow and painful efforts to legitimize its own knowledge claims toward the ultimate goal of institutionalizing sociology as a scientific discipline within the academy. Many within the discipline now believe that the legitimation and eventual institutionalization of sociological knowledge will occur only when sociologists are able to illustrate to the rest of the world that they can agree upon a relatively small group of concepts and terminology which presumably constitutes the core of what is knowable or even known about the social world.

Although talk of standardization of concepts has died down somewhat since the early 1990s, the idea of a "central concept" is still very much alive. For example, feminists claim that gender is or should be sociology's central concept, while for years Jack Gibbs (1989) has claimed that it is control. Marxists are likely to pick alienation as their central concept, while symbolic interactions might choose the self. And of course, criminologists would push for crime as being the central organizing concept for the discipline writ large. It should be obvious at this point that claims for a central concept—or a small handful of related concepts—is an ontological move in that, because sociological phenomena are shot through with a massive plurality of factors, multiple central concept candidates vie for attention in the cognitive space of the discipline. Indeed, this is where the sociology of knowledge steps in: It is worth studying in its own right how theory group A hit upon concept y as their central concept while theory group B hit upon concept z. This brings to bear, in very big terms, the importance of history over systematics in the study of sociological theory. It is this slapdash and happenstance that motivates talk of order, stability, and standardization of concepts for purposes of establishing sociology as a true science.

Evangelical Protest and the Problem of Salvation
Within the religious realm standardization operates primarily through the work of doctrine. As Charry (1992: 31) has noted, "Doctrine summarizes what Christian intellectuals believed and confessed to be the truth about who God is and what God has done and why, as a way of standardizing Christian belief and practice." Explanation of specific doctrines is one way of separating truth from error about those theological matters central to Protestant belief and practice.

This general quest to conquer uncertainty (Fox 1959) is the driving force behind standardization. Processes of modernization, especially the forces of rationalization as described by Weber (1958), continue to affect the relationship between religion and politics, especially as this concerns the origins of the rise of the New Christian Right and of evangelicalism more generally. Indeed, the process of secularization itself—certainly a type of rationalization—has heightened the sense of urgency among evangelicals that the certainty of their own teachings and beliefs, now under siege like never before, need to be reaffirmed in the public arena.

David Watt (1991) has traced the history of the evangelical movement in the United States during the twentieth century, and notes that in the early 1960s evangelicals began commenting more frequently, from the pulpit as well as through the secular mass media, about what they perceived as several disturbing trends. The trend of expanding reach beyond the local congregation has been facilitated into the twenty-first century through the growth of megachurches, televangelism, and use of social media. Joel Osteen, pastor of Lakewood Church in Houston, Texas, is currently the biggest and most successful of the televangelists, with a current estimated net worth of $40 million. Evangelists in the public eye tell a tale of becoming motivated into action and proselytizing their faith against the backdrop of the tumultuous 1960s including race riots, campus disturbances, experimentation with drugs and sexual lifestyles, failed military operations, and the perception of a general decline in morality, epitomized by the elimination of prayer in many public schools. This morality decline is traceable to three closely related problems: the decline of the American family, America's rejection of family values, and the country's drift away from its Christian moorings (Watt 1991: 67).

Distress or perceived crisis is a necessary but not a sufficient condition for motivating those perceiving such crises into concerted political activity. What, then, was the sufficient condition or conditions that led large numbers of evangelicals into political activism during the 1960s and 1970s? The master trend of modernization, namely rationalization, certainly can be seen as a major contributory factor. The process of secularization, a subset of the more general rationalization phenomenon, involves among other things an ongoing and vigorous campaign toward the separation of church and state, between religion and politics. This ethic had served, up until perhaps the early 1960s, to instill within many worshippers the idea that, because of the visibility and seeming indefeasibility of this church/state separation, they were doomed to political impotence.[3]

Although he never wrote about it specifically, Gouldner would not be surprised by the rise of political activism and the public proselytization of the faith conducted by Protestant evangelicals. He stated that, as much as anything, religion was and has been a successful public project, an ideology, which sought the unity of theory and practice through the efforts, both public and private, of true believers. For Gouldner (1976a: 28), Protestant-grounded modern ideology "unleashed a vast political force in the modern world," and "sedimented with Protestantism on the level of character structure, ideology was the Gospel of Labor in Politics."

This political mobilization among evangelicals reached its zenith with the election of Ronald Reagan as president in 1980 and his reelection in 1984. Pat Robertson, a successful TV evangelist, was a viable Republican candidate for president for a short while in 1988. By the early 1990s, a string of embarrassing scandals, sexual and otherwise, were connected with a number of prominent evangelists (including Jim Bakker, Jimmy Swaggart, Terry Smith, Robert Tilton, and more recently Robert Schuller; see Swanson 2012 for a summary). Nevertheless, it is important to carry through with the analysis of the rise of Protestant evangelicalism through this period, to the extent that Parsons

---

3   There have of course been spurts of concerted political activity among American Protestants in the past, such as the millenarian-based movement known as the Second Great Awakening which reached its crescendo during the late eighteenth and early nineteenth centuries. As Rogers (1992) has suggested, however, this movement may be viewed merely as a precursor to today's more fully established religio-political organizations, such as the Moral Majority and the New Christian Right, these latter of course becoming institutionalized, somewhat ironically, as a result of the processes of rationalization and standardization.

developed a conceptual scheme, based largely on Weber's work on bureaucracy and religion, which helps shed light on how and why it happened the way it did. Once carried through to its conclusion, we will then be in a position to compare the efficacy of the conceptual scheme to the more critical or evaluative approaches to these issues as represented by Gouldner, Habermas, and others.

The Evangelical Doctrines: Salvation and Atonement

For Parsons, "ultimate fulfillment," which is located in the G-cell of the telic system, represents the goal-directed behavior that is itself informed by the doctrinal ideas of salvation and atonement. (See Figure 6.2) As both Weber and Habermas (among others) have suggested, Protestantism is a religion organized along the axes of asceticism and inner-worldliness. The inner-worldliness of Protestantism, and hence evangelicalism, directs its followers toward the ethic of building the kingdom of God on earth.

This ethic is reflected in the three general principles of American evangelicalism, stated as follows:

- The formal principle which recognizes the critical priority of the Bible for all Christians;
- The material principle which confesses that Jesus of Nazareth is God's sign of reconciliation with the world;
- The pluralism principle constituting evangelicalism transdenominationally, emphasizing the personal experience of being "reborn" and of salvation in Jesus (Trembath 1987).

Because they gather their knowledge of the world through the teachings of an inerrant Bible, evangelicals' sense of religious certainty far exceeds any certainties they may have regarding claims to secularly-derived knowledge (Ellingsen 1988; Wilcox and Jelen 1990). Among those evangelicals who profess to have their everyday social actions guided by the word of God, the received notions of sin and its resolution are key. To close the gap between actual practices in the world and staying true to the word of God (which is the problem of the unity of theory and practice with which Gouldner and the Marxists have been concerned), there must be a certainty of belief about salvation (Trembath 1987). The disjunction between the divine intention in scripture and the human reception of scripture can be overcome by faith. This is also analogous to Goffman's (1979) distinction between the "mythic text" and the "performance text" regarding the ways persons manage impressions in the everyday lifeworld.

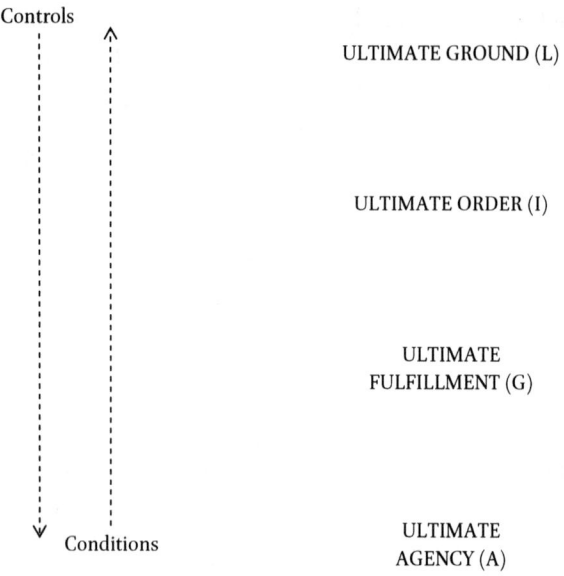

FIGURE 6.2 *Cybernetic ordering of the Telic System (G-cell of Human Action System)*

The battle that evangelicals have waged in the public sphere is a battle over what they perceive to be the ideal society, as informed by the word of God, which has not been attained because of the sinfulness of modern life and the wrong path down which secular humanism has taken us. The struggle to forge a society more in tune with God's word is in keeping with the ascetic impulse of building God's kingdom on earth for His glory.

Secular humanism represents the amoral ideology of a society turned away from the teachings of the Bible, and this moral decline, brought about through an increasing reliance on science and other nonbiblical sources, became the focus of the entire evangelical movement (Hunter 1987; Jelen 1991). Furthermore it should be noted that the successful political activities of evangelicals in the United States (at least through the early 1990s) is traceable to the doctrine of atonement (Jacobs 1990). The atonement doctrine may be viewed as a "satisfaction" theory as implied by its idea of a substitutionary death, namely Jesus giving his life for the sins of humanity. This ethic is in keeping with the American sociocultural context within which the hegemony of capitalism and the ideology of bourgeois liberalism, suffused as it is with the notion of atomized individuals struggling for survival in an open free market, reign supreme (Cladis 1992; Collins 1992). The satisfaction doctrine of atonement is attractive particularly to American evangelical Protestants because, since it is impossible for ordinary human beings to satisfy God, the currently sinful state of the world provides justifications—the idea of a "calling" surely comes to mind—for them to pursue whatever secular political work is necessary, all the while reinforcing the belief that God Himself offers satisfaction for human beings in the form of a perfect man (Jesus).

Back to Parsons: Rationalization and Atonement

For evangelicals questions of ultimate meaning superordinate all facets of social life, and these inform the actual social practices of human beings, even as we recognize that slippages do indeed exist between the mythic and performance texts. Parsons' paradigm of the human condition posits the telic system as the pinnacle of the cybernetic hierarchy of control, that is, humanity's quest to reach out to the cosmos to satisfy questions of ultimate meaning—sin, atonement, and salvation—which must be placed into a systematic ideology of faith which itself mimics the organized knowledge bases of science and other secular systems of understanding. Rationalization has had a dual force impelling evangelicals into proselytizing their faith in the public arena of politics. The first involves the triumph of secular humanism, which takes humanity further and further away from its Christian heritage, thus providing the object of their collective focus. The second is a bit more complicated, but it is this: In order to compete with the cognitive rationality of science, law, medicine, business, and other triumphal secular forms, religious must also play the game of rationalization in the public square, meaning it, too, will become politically active and vigorously oppose the threat of secularization wherever it is found: in the courts, in the mass media, and at the ballot box (whether the debates are over abortion, prayer in schools, same-sex marriage, hate speech, and so forth).

Since evangelicals hold to the impossibility of human beings' satisfying God, the doctrinal prescriptions, which serve to designate the exemplary life, are, in themselves, insufficient to merit the ultimate heavenly reward, namely salvation. Following from the three major tenets of Protestantism, evangelicals believe in the necessity of maintaining a personal relationship with Jesus Christ for one's salvation. This personal relationship supports as well the necessity of the proselytization of all humankind (Hunter 1983: 47). This urge to proselytize the word of God has over the years encroached further and further into the secular realm, including that of political activism.

As the process of rationalization continues and as pressures toward standardization of knowledge expand into all areas of life—government, business, the family, education, law, and even religion—battles over knowledge claims, especially between those of science and religion, will continue to intensify. With one foot in the secular and the other in the religious realm, evangelicals hope to one day return to the forefront they occupied in the early 1990s with regard to the establishment of ground rules for the direction of future confrontations. This is seen, for example, in Joel Edwards' (2008) set of guidelines for a reenergized and activist public evangelicalism for the twenty-first century. Wherever these may lead, it is safe to say that intellectual questions of modernity and postmodernity will continually refer back to the two master trends of rationalization and salvation for their resolution.

It should also be noted that, since the collapse of politically active, conservative evangelicalism in the early 1990s, there has appeared a "new evangelicalism" whose members hold more moderate economic, social, and religious beliefs. Rather than focusing on political activism, these new evangelicals are concerned with poverty, the status of immigrants in the United States and in Europe, and a greater concern with pacifism especially in light of the unpopular war in Iraq precipitated by the threat of international terrorism (Pally 2011). This progressive version of evangelicalism is almost unrecognizable in relation to that which came to prominence earlier among the religious right. Had Gouldner been alive to witness this transition, he may have suggested that those who call themselves evangelicals came to a more profound collective self-reflexivity about their domain assumptions, perhaps being jostled into realization of this with the election of President Bill Clinton in 1992. Gouldner would also be likely to view this as evidence that assumptions about clear differences between Democrats and Republicans are erroneous and need to be rethought (as, for example, in the argument of Pabst 2013).

Ethics and the Religious Question

Although he admits to not being "religiously musical," is there a significant religious component at the core of the thought of Gouldner, Habermas, and other secular humanist intellectuals generally? Gouldner reads and cites primarily scholarly treatises in sociology, philosophy, politics, and other areas of related study. With the triumph of secular humanism within intellectual discourse, there are few reasons for Gouldner to bring in or confront overtly religious writings in his own work. On the other hand, the triumphal form that cognitive rationality takes with regard to the secular humanism of science, law, and politics, means that religious scholars often find themselves venturing out of their base in liturgical studies and into the fields of science, philosophy, and so forth as suits their needs.

When evangelicals proselytize their faith through concerted political actions, they are guided by an explicit set of writings represented by (what they believe to be) inerrant scripture. Intellectuals, too, describe themselves as being guided by public texts and discourses available to all according to the ethical tenets of science (e.g., transparency, peer review, the culture of critical discourse, and so forth). But as a critic of traditional or mainstream science, Gouldner has argued that there is always a silent subtext—the infrastructural level of any theory, ideology, or public project—which accompanies and impinges on publicly ratified or certified texts. Here, we must spend some time covering Gouldner's structuralism, that is, his positing of latent meanings residing at the paleosymbolic level of any public project. Perhaps we will find religious or theological elements at this deep, paleosymbolic level of theory, even among those who avoid citing religious or religiously oriented texts.

The ethic of public communication in science is a farce, so suggests Gouldner. Paradigms—evaluative, interpretive, or positivist (Wagner 1963)—not only aver publicly how sociologists should approach their subject matter, they also contain guidelines that restrict communications at the paleosymbolic level. This level reflects the shared but tacit domain assumptions that theory group members hold, which in effect are the sources of informal solidarity adding value to the explicitly avowed paradigmatic elements on public display. As Gouldner (1976a: 224) states, "The paleosymbolic tends to be spoken in private settings, among those previously known to one another, and who, for this reason alone, as well as others, share interests." Through a concerted effort toward reflexivity, scientists can attempt to come to grips with some of these hidden or unstated assumptions residing at the level of the paleosymbolic, so that they may understand the sorts of extrarational elements holding their belief systems together. Indeed, through a diligent program of reflexivity, they may even discover contradictions between the stated and the unstated (that is, infrastructural) levels of theory, that is, between the textual and the paleosymbolic.

Gouldner's study of the infrastructure of Marxism concerns us here. In his paper on "The Metaphoricality of Marxism and the context-Freeing Grammar of Socialism," Gouldner (1974b) asks, "Why is Marxism agreeable to the project of revolutionary politics?" Gouldner pointed out that the theory predicted that revolutions would be led by the proletariat (working) class in capitalist and advanced industrial societies. Yet there is a glaring problem: The successful political revolutions to date were carried out in countries with no proletariat to speak of, and which were only marginally capitalist. At the surface or textual level, then, Marxism was wrong, yet it was still successfully implemented in other types of societies utilizing different historical revolutionary agents than what the theory called for. The surface variability of Marxism may have something to do with a deeper, more profound element residing at the infrastructural or paleosymbolic level that acts as the switching house allowing for flexibility in seeking revolutionary agents. Here, it is clearly evident that Gouldner is employing methods from structural linguistics, being heavily indebted to Saussure and later thinkers such Bernstein, Bateson, Chomsky, and Vygotsky (Jay 1982).

Gouldner believes he has located the paleosymbol residing at the deepest level of Marxism, which makes possible the application of the theory to many societal conditions not technically specified by it. This deep or latent structure, this underlying metaphor that provides a fundamental grammar uniting all those disparate projects which speak "Marxism" or which can recognize the conditions for socialism or communism, is *enslavement*. In the original theory of Marx and Engels, the proletariat stands as a metaphor for enslavement, for a class of human beings unduly debased, treated as objects, and held in chains by a callous and uncaring master class (the bourgeois). Yet, because the paleosymbol of enslavement is located deep within the infrastructure of the theory, any oppressed group can be identified as the appropriate historical change agents given the right conditions. In effect, the paleosymbol of enslavement produces the context-freeing grammar of socialism, whereby adherents to the theory can understand, identify, and act upon the theory in accordance with the deep meaning of the paleosymbol. This is similar to standard structural linguistics, and reflects the impact of the "linguistic turn" that became fashionable from the 1960s forward across the social sciences. This is simply the idea that with regard to language, it is the deep rules (syntax, structure, and grammar) that can give rise to sometimes great variability at the surface level, that is, in the ways in which it is actually spoken (e.g., idioms, dialects, and other speech variants; Saussure 1966).

Following Chomsky, Gouldner suggests that Marxists comprise a community of speakers who understand the symbols of the language system. The deep or latent paleosymbol of enslavement serves to derandomize conduct, thereby directing actors to do things in accordance with the latent grammar. There are three generative grammars of socialism, according to Gouldner (1974b: 398):

- **Socialist critique** – members of the theory group are aware of the plight of the oppressed group (proletariat or otherwise) and motivated to change it;
- **Vanguard party** – a set of rules for organizing across society to join the have-nots in their liberation struggle;
- **Society** – the knowledge about what a socialist society looks like, so that changes are directed toward a known, finished product.

This is in essence a system of morality and directives for correcting the real damage done to a group of oppressed people. It is here that Gouldner (1974b) engages in some clever comparisons of Hegel to Marx and Engels. Hegel appropriated the idea of the dialectic (thesis, antithesis, synthesis) from the ancient Greeks, who sought the conditions for rational discourse within society where only the weight of the better argument would prevail (Gouldner 1965). Speaker A is assured freedom to speak in a protected public space, and he or she speaks to those assembled to inform them that he will explain something, that is, present a thesis. After he finishes, Speaker B will get a turn to offer a rebuttal or an antithesis, explaining how speaker A is wrong and how his thesis is an improvement. Speaker A and Speaker B then have a back and forth (a debate), defending the best points of each of their positions as best they can. Eventually, when the dust has settled, they will arrive at a new thesis (synthesis) reflecting the best points that survive from the debate. This new synthesis represents truth with a small t, and as it becomes accepted as good knowledge over time it will become a thesis in its own right. But all theses are subject to challenge, so eventually someone will come along to offer an antithesis to the received wisdom. And so the dialectic continues to unfold into the future, until eventually truth with a big T emerges, at which time debates over the nature of empirical reality and our place within it will cease.

Hegel appropriated the project of Plato (and later Aristotle), who was seeking to construct the conditions for a stable polis in which reasoned discourse (philosophy) could be assured, and converted it to the grand, cosmological level, framing it within the tradition of German idealism as the unfolding of the *Geist*. For Hegel, the unfolding of the spirit does not eventuate merely in the creation of civil society, as the Greeks were hoping: it ends in God. As Gouldner notes, in his *Philosophy of History* Hegel celebrates Christ as the "pivot of the world" and affirms the metaphoricality of man's (or humanity's) reason as springing from the divine. Gouldner (1974b: 400) cites approvingly Nikolaus Lobkowicz (1967: 181), who argued that Hegelianism "…is the ultimate expansion and fruit of Christian faith; it is faith transfigured into rational thought."

In seeking to ground critical theory in the real world, specifically in the realm of economics and labor, Marx "turned Hegel on his head," in effect borrowing Hegel's dialectical method but converting it into a material philosophy. But perhaps Marx simply wanting to rid Hegel of the paleosymbol of God better explains this inversion, which is widely proclaimed as occurring because of Marx's rejection of German idealism in favor of a new historical materialism. So by turning Hegel on his head, Marx attempts to restore the power of reason to humanity, and with this gains purchase on explaining the worldly (that is, economic and social) conditions under which it either flourishes or is stunted, deformed, or blocked.

Whether Marx was successful in eliminating God from his theory is not the point here. Rather, the point is that a self-avowed radical sociologist like Gouldner could apply Saussurian structural linguistics to identify the deep or latent elements which often lay hidden or dormant in a theory, and which when discovered sometimes act as an embarrassment (or worse). At one point Gouldner (1974b: 409) does suggests that the paleosymbol of enslavement, which directs members of the theory group to close the gap between the real (oppression) and the ideal (its elimination) according to three grammars of socialism, "…is the very deepest structure of Marxism, grounded as it is in Western society's Judaic-Christian asceticism and transcendental ethic." But Gouldner gives Marx an out, arguing that one way of retaining a Godless version of an inverted Hegel is simply to shift to Kant's categorical imperative, namely, the moral precept that "ought implies can" when confronted with human suffering. Here, the religious question is sublimated to the historical trend of Western society, namely, the growth of rationalization and secularization, favoring Kant's rationalism over Hegel's mysticism.

More on Religion and Critique

It may be the case that Gouldner's use of structuralism is ironic, for it can be traced at least as far back as Durkheim's (1965 [1915]) work in the *Elementary Forms of the Religious Life*. Durkheim argued that the totemic emblem was a symbol of the social solidarity of the group, organized into a church tightly bonded together around members' shared orientation toward the sacred. It is essentially the experience of the awesome power of the group over the individual that ushers in civilization, for in the primitive state of the savage horde there were no structures in place to compel individuals into normative or moral behavior. In essence, society is God, or rather, the paleosymbol of the totemic emblem represents a value-added dimension for compelling persons to abide by societal proclamations of the good according to teachings of the belief system. In this, society is God, there is really no way to tease it out like Marx later tried to do by inverting Hegel's dialectic to a materialism which would presumably eradicate that apotheosis of idealism, namely, the belief in God or the gods guiding worldly affairs.

What of the invocation of Kant to move toward a rationalized or secularized notion of the good or the just or the moral, thereby attempting to elide the religious or theological as guide to the good life? The debates still rage about the source of the good, that is, whether or not it is essentially an innovation of the religious impulse or one that can be attributed to secular humanistic notions of brotherly love that need never reach back to Christian charity. For example, Rodney Stark (2003) has argued that all manner of social phenomena have originated with, or been heavily influenced in their development by, belief in God. Specifically, Stark (2001, 2003) makes the case that monotheism—the belief in one supreme God—has given rise to such things as the Reformation, science, witch hunts, and even the end of slavery. In opposition to the Marxist explanation that slavery comes to an end only when it is no longer economically profitable (a materialist explanation), Stark suggests that slavery ended because it violated religious beliefs concerning Christian charity, morality, and the "good life" more generally (an idealist explanation). This form of idealism, which argues that beliefs and ideas have a distinct causal impact on the material conditions of our existence, is similar to the famous "Protestant ethic" thesis of Max Weber (1930).

It is noteworthy that nowhere does Stark (2001, 2003) cite the work of William Graham Sumner (1906), who devoted a number of pages of his *Folkways* to the issue of slavery. Perhaps it is because Sumner cited authors who claimed that Christianity formally recognized slavery before later repudiating it. Sumner (1910: 591) argued elsewhere that the later impulse of secular humanism had effectively "colored" and "warped" Christianity, stating further "Humanitarianism led to opposition to slavery, and to the emancipation of women. These are not doctrines of the Bible or of Middle-Age Christianity." To the contrary, Stark argues that humanitarianism evolved out of, or at least was the secular equivalent of, religious—and specifically Christian—morality. On this issue, Stark's position is consistent with that of Charles Ellwood (1925: 388), who stated:

> Christianity, especially, has insisted upon the brotherhood, that is, the essential kinship, of all mankind. It has endeavored to make the sympathies and sentiments natural to the family group the standard for all moral and social practice. It has declared that the bonds of sympathy, altruism, and love, which are naturally characteristic of the family, should be the bonds that should unite all humanity. The great expansion of sympathy and altruism in Western civilization has been very largely due to these idealistic teachings of Christianity. Christianity has thus been one of the most powerful forces in the development of modern humanitarianism.

As Stark continues his argument, well before Europeans instituted slavery in the New World, Pope Paul III had decreed in 1537 that "Indians and all other peoples...should not be deprived of their liberty or of their possessions...and are not to be reduced to slavery, and whatever happens to the contrary is to be considered null and void" (quoted in Stark 2003: 291). Once it was instituted in Europe and the United States, slavery met the continuing strong opposition of the Vatican, and its eventual abolition in the United States was initiated and achieved by Christian activists. The American abolition movement began in Philadelphia with the publication in 1746 of *Some Considerations on the Keeping of Negroes*, a pamphlet written by John Woolman, a Quaker. Throughout the pamphlet he referred to the "sin of slavery." Influenced by Woolman, by 1770 the Quakers had moved to a position that prohibited their members from owning slaves under penalty of exclusion from the church. As Stark (2003: 341) argues, "Thus was launched the American abolition movement."

After 1770 other groups joined the Quakers in condemning slavery, some of which were not affiliated with a specific denomination. Most abolitionists, however, were Christian. Together these Christian abolitionists formed the Anti-Slavery Society in 1833. Just five years later, in 1838, there were 1,000 chapters. Overwhelmingly during this time, it was church organizations—not secular clubs and organizations—that issued formal statements arguing for the abolition of slavery. Where anti-slavery pronouncements were made largely by religious organizations, pro-slavery rhetoric was largely secular, making reference to such things as economic and business interests, "liberty," "states' rights," and so forth (Stark 2003: 344). As the abolitionist movement made more headway in the North it started pulling in powerful secular interests, culminating of course in the election of Abraham Lincoln in 1860. Rather than a war fought over economics, the Civil War was as much or more about moral visions (Stark 2003: 346). As Stark summarizes:

> (1) abolitionism spread through the Christian churches in the North, sustained by moral indignation, (2) inflamed not only by the existence of slavery in the nearby South but by the testimony of ex-slaves and the predations of agents who captured and, often, kidnapped runaway slaves all across the North. Finally, (3) very few people in the North profited directly from slaves. Thus the abolitionists were well situated to confront slavery from a close, but *external vantage point.*
>
> 2003: 347

To reiterate, Stark's thesis is situated within the classical idealist tradition, which states simply that ideas are an autonomous force in their own right that can give rise to material reality. The subjectivity of the position is obvious: Belief in "one true God" prompted the formation of social institutions such as science and social movements such as abolition, which culminated eventually in the end of slavery. This is opposed to the materialist argument that says the good must spring only from the real, life circumstances within which people find themselves, in comportment with the generalized thrust of Western culture toward secularization and cognitive rationality.[4]

Back to Habermas

Gouldner is best described as a Marxist outlaw, for although sympathetic to the aims of human emancipation focusing on the material realm of labor and economics (now construed as the program of social justice, to be discussed more fully next chapter), he was also not a blind devotee of standard left-liberal intellectual positions. Indeed, he developed forceful critiques of empty-headed progressivism that are sometimes closer in spirit to Carl Schmitt than to anyone on the left side of the political spectrum. For example, although he never cites Schmitt (1985), Gouldner acknowledges that liberalism—especially the far-left version that moves toward socialism and communism—tends toward totalitarianism insofar as the requirement to liberate the oppressed—embodied in the paleosymbol of enslavement—pushes forward even against popular sentiment or constitutional restrictions placed upon the redistribution of resources to right historical wrongs. For Gouldner, modern-day liberalism (circa the 1970s) has become a technocratic liberalism that sees the appropriation of power in the polity as the central mechanisms through which to attain the good life. The sociologists of the left intellectual vanguard hold up the power of proper technique in the service of a burgeoning welfare state, to the extent that it would be the sociologists in charge of determining how resources would be redistributed in the name of not simply economic or criminal justice, but social justice. Liberalism develops a one-sided determinism hell-bent on seeing through the reconstruction of society as guided by the tenets of the evaluative (that is, Marxist) paradigm, and in so doing develops blind spots part and parcel to the dogmatism of any vanguard party. As Gouldner argued,

> ...the Democratic Party has been, par excellence, the unifying agent forging both the welfare and the warfare sides into a single coin. It has been

---

4 Actually, there is a further irony here, and that is Stark's argument that monotheism stands behind and informs secular notions of the good. For Weber argued that rationalization affects everything, even religion. To wit, the transition from polytheism to monotheism is itself indicative of the work of rationalization within the theological realm. Although interesting, the implications of this cannot be pursued here.

> the party of active imperialistic adventures abroad, on the one side, and of welfare legislation, on the other. The alliance of the liberal technologue with the Welfare State through the Democratic Party, therefore, cannot help but be an alliance with the Warfare State.
>
> 1970A: 502

This is similar to the loss of faith in leftist politics that occasionally cropped up in the writings of intellectuals from the Frankfurt School of critical theory, such as the concern articulated by Horkheimer and Adorno of the emergence of a "totally administered society" whether in the hands primarily of the Republicans or the Democrats. It reflects, as much as anything, the disenchantment of the bureaucratization of the world raised by Weber and others. Weber (by way of Nietzsche) was even concerned with how the rise of legal-bureaucratic thought was squeezing the creative elements of modern society—led by the demise of the charismatic figure—out of the picture entirely. In the first issue of his journal *Theory and Society*, Gouldner published an interview with Jürgen Habermas—the most prominent of the second generation of Frankfurt School theorists—and in the introduction to the piece interviewer Boris Frankel tells about Habermas's tribulations with the German Left. Many in the camp of German Left activists called Habermas a "cop-out" for allegedly calling in the police to deal with a student-administration confrontation on the campus of Frankfurt University in the early 1970s. In his defense, Frankel (1974: 37) writes that Habermas in fact *did not* call the police (implying that Adorno actually did), but that Habermas "...did criticize various student tactics as being short-sighted and counter-productive which earned him abundant criticism from many students." This is the same icy relationship that developed between the New Left and Gouldner because of his reluctance to engage in activist politics during the 1960s.

Yet behind the scenes, somewhat shut out from open acceptance by the leaders of far left politics, Habermas kept plugging away developing a theoretical program for the emancipation of the human spirit in the best Marxian tradition. This was of course the sanitized, secularized version of world saving, which Marx tried to accomplish via the inversion of Hegel and the eradication of idealism and theology. In brief, rather than Marxist class-based oppression, Habermas (1984, 1987) believes that the greatest source of oppression in modernity is systematically distorted communication (as discussed earlier in the chapter). Following both the ancient Greeks and Hegel—but also, like Marx, maintaining the form of the dialectic while discarding its idealism—Habermas is seeking to assure reasoned communication, embodied in the ideal speech situation, whereby only the weight of the better argument prevails.

Taking the linguistic turn at about the same time as Gouldner, Habermas draws on speech act theory—but also Parsons (systems) and Weber and Mead (lifeworld)—to argue that the conditions for establishing such an ideal speech situation are retrievable within the structure of actual, lived talk. Not only do speakers present theses and antitheses through their talk, connected to these utterances and gearing into the world in meaningful ways are tacit validity claims residing at the infrastructural or paleosymbolic level. Through their talk, speakers raise validity claims pertaining to normative rightness (the social world), subjective truthfulness (the subjective world), and propositional truth (the objective world), and hearers may respond in yes/no fashion to those claims. If conducted within a protected environment where indeed only the weight of the better argument prevails, you have the ideal speech situation and the realization of the good.

In seeking to connect practice to theory, Habermas (1996) later developed a discourse principle that would give teeth to the moral project embedded in the theory of communicative action. This proceduralist theory of democracy hopes to avoid the extremes of leftist (conflict) and rightist (consensus) politics, by grounding it in the unthematized institutionalization of procedures and conditions of communication (the validity claims) that ultimately lead to the thematized or overt conditions arising from democratic opinion- and will-formation (Chriss 1998). The discourse principle states, "Just those action norms are valid to which all possibly affected persons could agree as participants in rational discourse" (Habermas 1996: 107). It is concerned with the distribution of resources equitably across society—including the assurance of free and open communication—but never lapsing into the condition of either free and unencumbered atomistic individuals (the fallout from the philosophy of the subject) or citizens held in check by coercive state power (as in the pathologies of the welfare-warfare state in agreement with Gouldner). Here, Habermas veers away from Hegel and toward an embrace of Kant.

Predictably enough, nowhere in this lofty intellectual project of Habermas is there even a hint at a religious solution to the problem of curtailed communication or the achievement of the good and just society.[5] And of course, as

---

5 More recently, though, Habermas has shown a willingness to engage with religious thought in ways recommended by Ahn in this chapter's discussion. This change of heart seems to be associated with the return of religious fundamentalism in light of the 9/11 terrorist attacks against the United States. The thesis of an unbridled, unidirectional secularism must be rethought, now within the context of a postsecularism in which religious elements return to play a crucial role in conceptions of the good life. For a summary of these more recent writings of Habermas, see Swindal (2012).

stated earlier, there is no requirement for secular intellectuals to dip into the theological literature, or even to bring to bear their own religious beliefs or experiences, as they go about their theory work. Indeed, one of the traditional notions of good science is that the authorial voice should be muted. Of course, this stems most directly from positivism and its admonition that scientists should avoid use of the first person pronoun in their writings. The other sociological paradigms—the evaluative and the interpretive—soften up this requirement, and sometimes even champion the inclusion of biography and social background (especially as it pertains to race, class, gender, and sexual orientation) in scholarly work. However, being also for the most part highly committed to secular humanism, these "softer," more critical and more hermeneutic perspectives would rarely venture into the realm of personal spirituality, even as warrant for public confessionals has expanded with the ascendancy of the therapeutic ethos (Chriss 2013).

Coming from an overtly theological perspective, Ilsup Ahn (2009) examines Habermas's (now Kantian rather than Hegelian) project of human emancipation and points out that the secularized approach to eradicating oppression appears to have its limits. Habermas has indeed developed a proceduralist moral theory in an effort to attain the good life, but the project of decolonizing the lifeworld will continue to be thwarted, according to Ahn, because Habermas and other secularists have not come to grips with the fact that the substantive ethical vision guiding their work is Christian realism. Drawing primarily from Reinhold Niebuhr, Ahn argues that Habermas's (and by extension Gouldner's linguistic solution) focus on the system as pathological, that is, as illegitimately penetrating into the lifeworld and distorting the everyday practices of social actors, conveniently overlooks the class of colonizers who carry out this illegitimate colonization. In other words, in the hands of secular theorists there is no envisioning a moral self. Ahn, by way of Niebuhr, argues that the inability of Gouldner and Habermas to actually identify the class of real, flesh-and-blood colonizers distorting the everyday lifeworld is the result of a secular discourse which must avoid at all costs the realization that amoral selves—the colonizers—lack Christian virtue.

Similar to the political activism of the Protestant evangelicals, or to Weber's lament over the stripping away of Calvinist inner-worldly asceticism in the expansion of latter-day industrial capitalism, Ahn seeks to reaffirm the role that religion could play in reconstructing the system for the better. In seeking to articulate the importance of identifying and dealing with persons as colonizers, Ahn incorporates Niebuhr's critique of the greed and avarice of financiers that contributed to the beginnings of the Great Depression. In 1929, for example, Niebuhr was in his first year of study at the Union Theological

Seminary (Ebel 2012). This critique was not derived from Marx or any other secularists, but from biblical teachings concerning brotherly love and Christian charity.

Conclusion

Gouldner sees this kind of project as sheer folly, an attempt to return to a golden age where Christianity guided moral understandings of the world. Indeed, religion is useful insofar as it sets the world into fixed categories which are antithetical to each other: sacred and profane, good and evil, friends and enemies, Heaven and Hell, saved and damned, and so forth. A religious sensibility provides a foundational approach to life that sees things in the stark contrast of black and white. The more secular, more liberal, more humanist approach discards black and white explanations in favor of shades of grey. The secular humanist orientation argues that reality is complex, and that in order to explain social phenomena, one should take care to work through the nuances and intricacies of any social fact or phenomenon which becomes an object of study for the scientist.

This move away from the foundational certainties of religious teachings means that now, in the postmodern condition, a polymorphous perversity is in ascendancy in which meaning is endlessly deferred. Cozy understandings of the world handed down across generations and grounded in Christian ethics must now give way to more enlightened, secular explanations which take into account the true complexity of the world and the social construction of reality based upon the interplay of multiple variables. (This is why we need an ever-burgeoning class of technocrats to operate increasingly sophisticated inferential statistics software.) In an otherwise critical appraisal of Goffman's dramaturgical theory, Gouldner does concede that Goffman was right about the middle class's declining faith in traditional religious moralities. In a passage worth quoting at length, Gouldner states:

> Once sacred symbols, such as the flag, are mingled defiantly with the sensual and become, as in some recent art forms, a draping for the "great American nude." "Pop art" declares an end to the distinction between fine art and advertising, in much the same manner that dramaturgy obliterates the distinction between "real life" and the theater. The "Mafia" become businessmen; the police are sometimes difficult to distinguish from the rioters except by their uniforms; heterosexuality and homosexuality come to be viewed by some as akin to the difference between righthandedness

and lefthandedness; the television program becomes the definition of reality. The antihero becomes the hero. Once established hierarchies of value and worth are shaken, and the sacred and profane are now mingled in grotesque juxtapositions.

1970A: 390

In order to deal with this new chaos of blurred genres and boundaries, the new middle class places greater and greater importance on appearance, as if this is somehow more grounded in a stable, collective reality than all the other things mentioned above. Whereas in premodernity the group reigned supreme, and in modernity the individual rose to prominence in opposition to dominance by the group, in postmodernity the image reigns supreme, with all its attendant pathologies (including the inflation of the image; see Baudrillard 1981; Klapp 1991). The linguistic turn under Gouldner and Habermas has given way to the aesthetic turn, perhaps first launched by Benjamin or Adorno. In any event, wherever the symbol plays a prominent role, the religious icon always has an opportunity to battle for public recognition alongside the secular ones (whether political, artistic, marketing, and so forth).

This could be something akin to the idea of the "resurrection of the image" advanced by Jackson (2009) and others, whereby meanings previously submerged at the deepest levels of the paleosymbolic now burst into the open, operating on the front stage and out in the open for all to see. This could be a good thing, for latent structures and their deep meaning could work behind the backs of a hapless mass public, thereby foiling various public projects of hope and amelioration. What role religion could play in either solving or deepening such dilemmas remains to be seen.

CHAPTER 7

Social Justice, Politics, and Religion

Introduction

Critical theory in contemporary sociology owes much to Karl Marx's program of eradicating oppressive social conditions, in particular, the unequal distribution of resources in capitalist society and the class conflict that ensues. Gouldner's particular brand of critical theory stresses the importance of social theorists confronting their tacit, hidden "domain" assumptions—axiology, ontology, and epistemology—in order to bridge the gap between personal sentiments and public avowals. That is to say, visions of the good life embedded in the infrastructure of theory by way of the assumptions theorists make about values, about reality, and about knowledge are inexorably intertwined with the technical dimension of the theoretical system itself. Only by overtly acknowledging these otherwise hidden domain assumptions can sociologists hope to construct theories of society that are consistent with social justice outcomes.

As discussed in Chapter 4, this is the project of reflexive sociology. However, the process of critically evaluating one's assumptions in this way often leads to a fetish of critical contemplation that is actually inimical to the creation of the just society. In other words, reflexive sociology tends toward "navel-gazing" where theorists turn inward on their own thoughts and ideas to such an extent that they become paralyzed because any choices they make concerning how to accomplish or implement social justice are subject to endless rounds of critical self-reflection (Howard 1994).

It should also be noted that the emphasis Gouldner places on reflecting upon one's and other's tacit or hidden assumptions about the world, about knowledge, and about values converges somewhat with John Rawls' (1971) concept of reflective equilibrium and the veil of ignorance, whereby adequately reflexive members can envision themselves in socially undesirable circumstances. Under such conditions, rational human beings would seek whatever help is available, and rather than rely on happenstance the just society institutionalizes help as a matter of routine operation to cover such contingencies. Rawls hence strongly supports the notion of the modern welfare state, a position about which Gouldner (1968) is much more ambivalent. What this illustrates is that although the notion of careful or critical reflection about self and society is a common strategy among theorists of justice, the ultimate conceptions of justice that emerge from it vary widely.

This apparent dead-end of reflexive sociology also marks the analytical difficulties in conceptualizing and implementing social justice itself. In this chapter I locate the points of difficulty shared by both reflexive sociology and social justice in informing policy and critical pedagogy towards the ultimate goal of assuring just outcomes. This will be accomplished through an analysis of Guillermina Jasso's unabashedly positivistic work on social justice. Before analyzing Gouldner's reflexive sociology in more detail, however, we must first briefly survey the way social justice has been conceptualized within sociology and the social sciences, and particularly those themes of social justice, implicit or overtly stated, appearing in the writings of Karl Marx.

Social Justice in Sociology

Within sociology, issues and themes of social justice overwhelmingly appear in the form of distributive justice, namely, the problem of the unequal distribution of resources in society based upon gender, class, race or ethnicity, or any number of additional ascribed statuses. For the most part, then, social justice and distributive justice in sociology come down to an examination of the forms and nature of inequality (stratification) in society, a description of the classes or people systematically receiving fewer economic, cultural, or political resources, and the development of theories of inequality, the ultimate purpose of which to establish an equitable and fair redistribution of such resources (Rytina 1986).

The inclination toward distributive justice issues and research within sociology follows from certain historical realities associated with the rise of sociology as a scientific discipline. As Habermas (1984: 1–7) has argued, sociology arose as an academic discipline out of the great social changes occurring across the west beginning in the late 1700s. Three social phenomena in particular—industrialization, migration, and democratic revolutions—created the sense that society was changing so profoundly that old ways of knowing—whether rooted in philosophy, theology, ideology, mysticism, tradition, superstition, etc.—no longer provided adequate explanations of society and social order.

Much of the attention of students of society beginning in the early 1800s focused especially on the "crisis" brought about by the emergence of industrial capitalism, particularly with regard to the unequal distribution of resources in society. As Habermas (1984: 4) argues, sociology's "theme was the changes in social integration brought about within the structure of old-European societies by the rise of the modern system of national states and by the differentiation of a market-regulated economy. Sociology became the science of crisis par excellence; it concerned itself above all with the anomic aspects of the dissolution of traditional social systems and the development of modern ones."

Although it certainly increased productivity and brought a higher standard of living to the citizenry as a whole, industrialization also created even greater social class divisions, as those who owned the means of production (the capitalists or *bourgeoisie*) were far better off in terms of power, prestige, property, and life chances than those who did not (the workers or *proletariat*). Under feudalism and other earlier economic systems, although men and women may have been dominated in the sense of not having full autonomy or personal freedom in relation to others (for example, as members of slave or peasant classes; see Scott 1990), they still nonetheless maintained immediate and direct connections to the products of their labor, whether it was working the fields, forging hardware as a blacksmith, or producing or selling small arts or crafts. But with the rise of the factory and the large-scale production of goods under industrial capitalism, men began leaving their homes and farms for the workplace. For Marx, it is the workplace that becomes the site of a new and deeply troubling form of alienation experienced by members of the proletariat. As Gouldner explains,

> The decisive form of alienation is now not that of man but the worker's alienation from objects he produces and from the means of production with which he produces. This alienation, Marx came to hold, was a result of property institutions essential to capitalism, centering on that division of labor in which some—capitalists—own and direct the means of production and purchase the labor power of others—the proletariat—who are subject to their domination. For by reason of their ownership of the means of production, the capitalist can direct their use and also own the products they produce.
> 1980A: 181

Gouldner goes on to argue that although alienation is not a new concept, Marx's unique contribution was the way he transformed the problem of human suffering. Where once alienation and other forms of human misery had been viewed as timeless, eternal, and tragic dilemmas of the human condition, especially as represented in the tradition of idealism running from the ancient Greeks through Hegel and Nietzsche, Marx concretized the problem of alienation under industrial capitalism, arguing that it was the product of an historical and special division of labor that arose at a particular place and time under capitalism. Where once it had been viewed as insoluble and beyond the scope of human intervention, under Marx alienation was placed in the historically newer discourses of ideology and politics, thus making it amenable to human intervention (Gouldner 1980a: 181).

Evil and Goodness

Marx's refocalization of the problem of alienation follows the path of much of the work of the social and human sciences, insofar as efforts are made to bring into relief an aspect of everyday life that heretofore has been taken-for-granted or hardly noticed. In this particular case, Marx took a commonly understood part of everyday life under capitalism, namely "economics" or the economic realm, and cast it in a new, problematic way. Although many come to see money and economic interests as "good" in the sense of the power, prestige, and property it bestows on individuals (thereby tending to equate the "good" with the "powerful"), this sentiment is characteristic only of the relatively unreflective masses who are socialized into accepting the values of individualistic materialism. Notice, however, that materialism is viewed somewhat more ambivalently from the perspective of certain nonsecular systems of belief. For example, Christianity promulgates a view of economics and economic interests as selfish and inimical to Christian charity and brotherhood. Christian doctrine thus acknowledges the economic realm as a potent and powerful force in the world, while at the same time displaying much less conviction that it is a morally "good thing," thereby reversing the lay tendency to equate the good with the powerful.

It would appear, then, that Christian doctrine has been sufficiently self-reflexive in "seeing through" the façade of the modern industrial juggernaut of capitalism and its this-worldly orientation that emphasizes individual calculation of benefit at the expense of others. But Marx goes Christianity even one step better, according to Gouldner, by demystifying the economic system which under Christianity tended to be viewed as a debasement of "human nature" or as representative of any number of sins, whether greed, avarice, egotism, or uncharitability. Marx attempted to completely jettison normative views of capitalism, that is, the issue of the "goodness" of the economic, by arguing for the historical *necessity* of certain economic conditions at certain times in the history of civilization. As Gouldner (1985: 254) states, "Marxism instead stresses that the economic is the realm of necessity, that the evil it does is also necessary, until the conditions requisite for the elimination of present suffering have matured."

In viewing capitalism as an historical force, Scientific Marxism[1] promulgates a theory of dialectic laws and destiny, positing that the structures of

---

1 As Gouldner (1980a) argues, there exists two distinct strands or orientations within Marxism, namely, *Scientific Marxism* and *Critical* (or *Humanistic*) *Marxism*. Critical Marxism places emphasis on voluntaristic action rather than on unfolding laws of historical materialism. In this sense it may be seen as a theory of violent revolution, of a call to mobilize the workers of the world out from their slumber of false consciousness toward the overthrow of their bourgeois oppressors.

advanced capitalism would, because of the internal contradictions of that system, eventually collapse, thereby leading inexorably to the emergence of socialism and, ultimately, communism (Chriss 1999c: 144). It is the force of the laws of social evolution (or economic determinism) that will lead ultimately to the expropriators becoming the expropriated with the advent of the revolt of the proletariat. In this sense, we may see Marxism as a passion play in which justice is ultimately served, culminating in its most vivid act, namely the expropriation of the bourgeoisie. Interestingly enough, however, this act of justice is an act of retribution, not restitution, insofar as the aim of the proletarian revolt is to take property from the bourgeoisie rather than to give property to the dispossessed (the workers).

The suffering the proletariat endures at the hands of the bourgeoisie is a necessary evil, then, according to Marx, a necessary (but transient) stage in their ultimate emancipation. Indeed, Marx's guarantee to the proletariat that their suffering is necessary for their eventual emancipation is close to the sort of religious asceticism that promises salvation or grace to true believers in the afterlife who practice self-discipline and self-denial in this life. All socioeconomic systems inflict costs, pain, and suffering against some of its citizens, even during a so-called "progressive phase." We have seen for example that the advent of industrialization led to the expansion of productivity and a higher standard of living of the citizenry as a whole, even while widening the economic gap between social classes and creating a burgeoning class of "have-nots," namely, the underclass (Rytina 1986; Wilson 1987). Yet, according to the laws of economic evolution under Scientific Marxism, human suffering cannot be surmounted at any time one wishes; certain conditions must obtain before the situation can improve or change. Marxism sees all around it the suffering and oppression of the working class at the hands of the capitalists, but Marxism emphasizes above all the biding of time, the suffering of blows, and using this hardening to suffering as a lever of social change. Indeed, one must so harden oneself to suffering "as even to be capable of inflicting it on behalf of historical necessity, expecting that 'history will absolve' us" (Gouldner 1985: 255). (This problem of violence and aggression within Marxism will be returned to in the final chapter.)

The Two Marxisms: A Lack of Reflexivity

Although Gouldner suggests that Marxism's level of self-reflexivity is superior to religious doctrine in that the former attempts to trace the historical evolution of capitalism from earlier economic forms (seeing things in the world for "what they are" rather than as mystical or divine creations, thereby assuring closer affinities between real flesh-and-blood human beings, their objects of inquiry, and the assumptions they make about the world around them), Marxism itself suffers from fatally high levels of unreflexivity.

How could this be? Gouldner makes the point that Scientific Marxism, positing universal laws of economic development that ensure that the transition from capitalism to socialism will eventually occur, is optimistic in that it predicts a future state of affairs will come to pass in ways prescribed by the theory. This is, however, optimistic from the vantage point of the theory and its theorists only, for the heavily deterministic nature of the theory renders it oblivious to the real human suffering that will take place among the proletariat, who are the disposable—though indispensable—raw material fueling the workers' revolution. Indeed, as a theory of science and high modernism, Scientific Marxism is "objective" in its not taking into account the subjective states of participants in the unfolding chain of events. It is an unfeeling, value-neutral scientific theory of revolution (Chriss 1999c: 167).[2]

Seen from this vantage point, Scientific Marxism's claim that the temporary suffering of the proletariat is necessary for the greater good, namely the emergence of communist society, is dubious. The price paid in human suffering and agony in the transition from capitalism to communism appears far greater than the benefits likely to accrue to citizens of the communist state. The aims of social justice cannot be accomplished, according to Gouldner, through the positing of universal laws of economic evolution or material determinism. This is because such theories lack reflexivity in not being sufficiently mindful or aware of the potential nightmare versions of the theory that await if and when the attempt is made to put them into practice.

There is, however, another strand within Marxist thought that might plausibly assure greater, more profound social justice outcomes than those of Scientific Marxism. This is of course Critical (or Humanistic) Marxism. Whereas Scientific Marxism is optimistic from the perspective of the theory and its theorists,

---

2   Like many Enlightenment thinkers, Marx and Engels were not unique in emphasizing a split between "mere" philosophy on the one hand, and positivistic science on the other. Gouldner (1980a: 73) quotes Engels (1941: 15), who stated that "There is an end of all philosophy in the hitherto accepted sense of the word, ... instead, one pursues attainable, relative truth along the path of the positive sciences, and the summation of their results by means of dialectical philosophy. At any rate, with Hegel philosophy comes to an end; ... he showed us the way out of the labyrinth of 'systems' to real positive knowledge of the world." This tendency by Marx and Engels to make such a sharp distinction between philosophy and science is a symptom of the false consciousness and lack of reflexivity of Enlightenment intellectuals in general, according to Gouldner.

Critical Marxism is pessimistic insofar as it posits that certain conditions in capitalist society are oppressive, as felt and experienced as a lived conviction by real flesh-and-blood human beings. Critical Marxism thus defines the social situation of persons in such a way as to maximize their importance as "subjects," that is, as "actors," who by their actions attempt to ameliorate a desperate situation (namely, their exploitation and subjugation at the hands of the bourgeoisie, and the economic injustices that ensue). Critical Marxism thus imbues its actors with a sense of agency, which of course is lacking in Scientific Marxism. It is pessimistic only to the extent that the future is uncertain rather than assured.

Critical Marxism arose through the efforts of Europeanized intellectuals who realized that one important prediction of Scientific Marxism, namely, that proletarian revolts would occur in advanced industrial capitalist societies whenever conditions were favorable, simply was wrong. That is, modern economic revolutions have largely been an affair of industrially backward societies, of the peasantry, and of their agrarian revolution under the tutelage of radicalized intellectuals. As Gouldner (1980a) argues, Critical Marxism arose out of this essential paradox, that underdeveloped Third World economies were spawning worker revolts, while the expected proletarian revolts against industrial capitalism never came to pass.

From the perspective of assuring social justice outcomes, it would appear then that Critical Marxism has more to offer than Scientific Marxism, insofar as the former emphasizes the subjective states of actors and is sensitive to their suffering at the hands of a dominant class. Indeed, because Scientific Marxism had laws of historical determinism at hand, it never felt it necessary to win over the hearts and minds of the proletariat through direct appeals or demonstrations. With destiny on their side, Scientific Marxists were less apt to take into consideration the feelings or emotions of the masses who would join them in revolutionary struggle by any means regardless.

Critical Marxists, on the other hand, with no firm assurances about the future, had to rely on the good graces and support of the masses in order to see the revolution through. Critical Marxists had to be concerned, then, with establishing their hegemonic authority before they could win over the proletariat. And this is where the great hope for social justice under Critical Marxism breaks down and collapses. Because Critical Marxism cannot assure a future state of affairs (because it lacks the deterministic laws of Scientific Marxism), coercion or brute force might need to be employed against the masses if appeals and persuasion (propaganda) fail to win them over. Marxism's lack of reflexivity becomes abundantly clear here, as an insidious nightmare version of the theory takes over in the form of regimes of terror.[3] This is what has happened for example in China and Cuba, according to Gouldner, and the tendency for Critical Marxism generally is to lapse into such regimes of terror when things don't go as planned. (But terror could even be part of the plan, as discussed in Chapter 9.) We see, then, a very dark, nightmarish version of Critical Marxism submerged beneath its public avowals of humanism, social justice, and liberation from oppression.

Reflexive Sociology in Action

Gouldner's (1970a) program of reflexive sociology is as much as anything a critique of the blind allegiance to certain doctrines (such as positivism or value-freedom in science) or cultural codes (such as meritocracy or individualism in capitalism) that persons are apt to accept or defend simply because of tradition. This notion, that "that's just the way things are," is deeply inimical to the development of critical insights into current social arrangements and to understanding how we arrived there in the first place. Indeed, Gouldner offered reflexive sociology as a program for helping persons maintain critical insights into "legitimate" knowledge, that is, prevailing notions of "what is," rather than accepting such claims passively. Gouldner warned that acquiescence to legitimate knowledge might serve merely to reaffirm and accept the status quo. There have been many forms of oppression justified on the basis of the status quo, of "what is," and Gouldner tried to create a program of inquiry that was alive and sensitive to this reality.

As we have seen, through his deconstruction of Marxism Gouldner was able to excavate the nightmarish and even oppressive aspects of a system of thought whose noble aims were the elimination of oppression and subjugation by one class at the hands of another. Because of its lack of reflexivity, because it did not properly understand the relationship between the infrastructural and technical levels of theory, even a program of liberation as widely heralded as Marxism was shown by Gouldner to have a dark side.[4]

---

3   Gouldner (1977) provided a case study of one particular regime of terror, Stalinism, describing all such regimes as a form of internal colonialism.
4   The *infrastructural* level of theory refers to the background or domain assumptions (about the world, about knowledge, and about values), as well as the ideological presuppositions theorists hold but which often are not explicitly stated or avowed in the theoretical system itself. The *technical* level of a theory refers to the actual theoretical system, that is, to its form and content (e.g., utilization and construction of concepts, methodologies and analytical techniques, formal versus discursive format, etc.). Gouldner (1970a: 29–51) argues that oftentimes theorists are blind to the ways in which the infrastructural level of theory impacts and shapes the decisions made at the technical level, that is, with regard to the construction of the theory itself.

What this means is that theorists of social justice must be vigilant in seeing and drawing connections between the social contexts of theorists (whether themselves or others) and the theories they produce. Only when theorists make explicit their tacit domain assumptions and ideological predilections can they understand how commitments made at this silent, infrastructural level impact the overt, technical level of a theory, that is, the actual theoretical system itself. Gouldner's important insight is that all theories tend to become self-enclosed systems that have trouble admitting to—indeed are often blind to—the repressed or hidden potentialities of the system. In effect, by systematically blocking off access to the tacit assumptions of a theory out of ignorance or out of fear of what lies waiting there, theorists will continue to produce theories that are doomed to cycles of failure and intermittent fits and starts. Only by being true to oneself, that is, by having an understanding of one's and others' assumptions about the world and one's place in it, can a theory survive the dynamic flux of the social system within which it and its author are embedded. Only then can theorists maintain fidelity with the empirical social world.

It is important here to be clear that the aim of reflexive social theory is not in the first instance to produce better or more perfect theories (in the sense of, say, a theory's predictive power or its parsimoniousness). Although this certainly could be a subsidiary benefit of the program, the major goal of reflexive sociology is to make theorists aware of their nightmares, of the bad news as well as the good news. Gouldner's invocation of the terms *bad news* and *good news* relates to his idea that social theories are like ideologies in that they attempt to mobilize publics on behalf of projects (Gouldner 1976a, 1978). In other words, theory has an ideological function insofar as it is designed as a vehicle for disseminating certain types of news that support theorists' public projects. Gouldner's program of reflexive sociology aims, then, to make theorists aware of the tensions that often exist within their own theories, especially of the less desirable implications of their theories. By practicing reflexivity, theorists can increase their openness to bad news as well as good news.

Indeed, Gouldner (1976b) argues that it is the task of the reflexive social theorist to help people remain critical and skeptical of *good* news, and correspondingly, to *remember* it. Expert discourses purporting to speak the truth often mask their own desires and interests behind a veil of objectivity and value neutrality. Reflexive social theorists can help persons see and understand the connection between interests, desires, social location, and material groundedness (the infrastructural) on the one hand, and information, claims, reports and news (the technical) on the other. As Gouldner (1976b: 7) states, "An emancipatory and Socratic social theory is centrally concerned with maintaining an openness between technical discourse and everyday life, between extraordinary and ordinary languages, between pure reason and practical reason." Hence, it is the special task of the reflexive social theorist to focalize the significance of persons' everyday lives as a grounding of theory (Gouldner 1975a: 424), thereby illustrating the immense importance of theorists' personal realities to what is proclaimed publicly in their theories (Gouldner 1969a).

An Application to Social Justice

No matter how technical, objective, or analytically rigorous a theory of social justice may be, it is constructed within a social milieu or context by an individual who has acquired certain conceptions of the good life as a result of his or her immersion in that selfsame social world. The positivistic conceit of science, namely that one can separate oneself (one's values, aspirations, and ideological predilections) from the products of one's labor (in this case, theories), must be abandoned in favor of a more contextualist account of the creation of knowledge and theory (Fuller 1998; Gouldner 1968, 1969a, 1970a). As we have seen, Gouldner's program of reflexive sociology is one such account of theorizing that may be of benefit in elucidating the contours of the broader class of social justice theories. However, the range of issues and approaches falling under the social justice rubric is enormous (see Jasso 1999: 134; Marshall 1994; Rytina 1986; Wallerstein 1997). In order to keep the application of Gouldner's program to a more concrete level, I shall examine Guillermina Jasso's attempt to develop a positivistic theory of social justice.

Jasso (1999) begins by suggesting that there is a widespread taken-for-granted notion that injustice is pervasive. But how much injustice is there really? And compared to what? Jasso's intent is to assess individuals' notions of the kinds of injustice that exist in the world, as she makes the case that the way people *think* about justice and injustice is implicated in their *behavior*, whether personal distress, divorce, revolution, or international conflict (Jasso 1999: 133).

Jasso constructs two justice indexes that are limited to matters of distributive and retributive justice. One justice index is termed J_{I1}, and deals with unjust underreward and unjust overreward, while the other index, termed J_{I2}, collapses underreward and overreward onto a single justice continuum. Jasso employs mathematical models to construct and assess the indexes, and her data are taken from the International Social Justice Project.[5]

---

5 This project involved the administration of a survey to a random sample of citizens of 13 countries in 1991 and 1992. Five of the societies are Western-style democracies (West Germany, Great Britain, Japan, Netherlands, and United States), while eight are in the post-Communist transition (Bulgaria, Czechoslovakia, Estonia, East Germany, Hungary, Poland, Russia, and Slovenia).

Jasso measures various dimensions of justice. For example, persons are asked about the amount of justice or injustice they perceive are associated with taxes, wages, wealth disparities in their society, fines, academic grades, beauty, and so forth. Each of these areas may represent a *good* or *bad* depending on whether or not the person feels the burden is too great to shoulder, or, for example, whether or not the person is positively or adversely affected (helped or hurt) in any of these areas. Since members of society are both rewardees (receivers of goods or bads) on a personal level as well as observers of others' plight or situation across society more broadly, there are two additional types of justice measures: the first kind concerns one's own holding, termed the *reflexive* justice evaluation, while the second concerns another's holdings, termed the *nonreflexive* justice evaluation (Jasso 1999: 135).

With regard to justice perceptions of income, respondents were asked (1) whether they thought they were underpaid, overpaid, or fairly paid; (2) what they were actually paid; and (3) what they considered their just job income. This particular component of Jasso's justice index was created by computing the natural logarithm of the ratio of the actual job income (number 2 above) to the reflexive just job income (number 3). An overall measure of perceived injustice about job income can thus be created in this manner, and the 13 countries can be compared to assess which ones have a greater portion of their citizens who believe that theirs (or others) income is just (the reflexive justice index concerning just income). Surprisingly, in all countries respondents perceived a condition of underreward, namely, that they believed they weren't being paid what they were worth. However, when Jasso examined the rank order of the 13 countries on the just income reflexive justice scale, she found across the board that citizens of the eight post-Communism transition societies reported higher levels of perceived (reflexive) job injustice than did citizens of the five Western-style democracies.

Let us now examine several elements of Jasso's argument from the perspective of Gouldnerian reflexivity. The one most striking feature of her analysis is the utilization of sophisticated mathematical models to construct and assess her theory of social justice (Jasso 1999: 136–156). The analytical strategy of examining human social processes by way of mathematical models reflects a range of hidden, tacit assumptions residing at the infrastructural level of her theory. In this case, Jasso shares with other like-minded colleagues the assumption that sociology is indeed a science (in the positivistic, nomothetical-deductive sense), and that any and all social and psychological phenomena of interest can be meaningfully operationalized, that is, measured. It further reflects the positivistic assumption that social processes possess a lawlike orderliness, and that by following the rules of the scientific method these laws of the social universe can be "discovered" (Hacking 1983; Hempel 1965; Nagel 1979; Turner 1985).

Furthermore, Jasso's use of survey research to gather data on social justice reflects the taken-for-granted assumption that human beings are rational insofar as what they say about what they do and think can be reasonably equated to what they *actually* do and think. There is also an implicit theory of cognition and interpretation at work here, insofar as survey research assumes that different individuals interpret and respond to the set of questionnaire items in exactly the same way. This is an especially important assumption when dealing with cross-cultural analysis where it is necessary to translate questionnaire items into multiple languages.

Jasso's use of mathematical models and survey research in constructing and assessing her theory of social justice reflects a commitment to the ideological notion that objective, quantitative social science is best equipped to explain issues of social and distributive justice. It reflects the positivistic notion of the "arithmetic ideal," namely, that explanations of the social world that employ quantitative methods and that are analytically rigorous (in terms of following the protocol of the scientific method) provide a degree of precision and accuracy that surpass the more speculative "explanations" of lay knowledge, superstition, religion, tradition, or even social philosophy.

Religion and the Enlightenment

This is all well and good, but we must further analyze the possible nightmare versions of Jasso's theory that can be inferred from her infrastructural commitments. An examination of the history of ideas shows that social science came into existence as a direct challenge to competing systems of belief about the social world that were considered to be deficient in some manner. For example, Auguste Comte, the founder of positivism, vehemently opposed religion because he felt that it was the source of much of the human misery and suffering that he was witness to during his lifetime. His *System of Positive Philosophy* (Comte 1830–1842: 5–6) introduced positivism as a new "religion of humanity" that would overcome the superstition, dogma, metaphysics, and mysticism of religion.[6]

---

[6] *Positivism* in sociology suggests that social phenomena are amenable to systematic analysis via the implementation of the scientific methods of the natural sciences, and through such analysis the laws of the social universe could eventually be ascertained. As Dilworth (1990) reports, the type of empiricism espoused by the early positivists (such as Saint-Simon and Comte) restricted scientific investigation to phenomena and their regularities only. It was felt, then, that the search for the deep causes of such phenomena was fruitless because human understanding is incompetent to decide such things. So Comte and the early positivists argued that anything beyond the immediately observable is necessarily inaccessible by human perception, and that hypotheses that attempt to uncover such hidden or metaphysical aspects of phenomena are doomed to failure or, at the very least, merely wild speculation.

Indeed, the rise of Enlightenment rationalism and science ushered in a massive repudiation of god and religion, and in this form of morality (namely, secular humanism) it would be human beings who would make their own destiny and perfect society in their own image (Nietzsche 1954, 1956). As a sociological positivist, Jasso is an inheritor of not only the technical aspects of the methodologies of quantitative analysis, but also the ideological dimensions of this heritage of thought, especially the belief in the betterment of society through science. Where religion tended to view God as the source of human agency in the world, providing the unseen faculty of "will" to human beings, by the late eighteenth century such theological explanations of society and social justice became increasingly discredited in favor of explanations based in Enlightenment-inspired rationalism and positivism.

In essence, theodicy underwent secularization. As Fuller (1998: 98–105) argues, an early example of this was Scottish Enlightenment philosophical histories of civil society in which omniscient divine agency was replaced by the notion of fallible human agents who are unaware of the consequences of their actions. Indeed, the secular/scientific notion of "unintended consequences" is the equivalent of the religious notion of "divine agency" or the philosophical notion of "will." Later, Darwin's theory of evolution, positing "laws" of natural selection and the survival of the fittest, completely secularized justice as simply the battle of the "natural" survival instincts of all species, including of course human beings.

In like fashion, Jasso's "discovery" of the nature of social justice through the employment of objective and value-free positivistic methods could be seen, from the perspective of Gouldnerian reflexivity, as simply a way of sneaking in theological notions of divine intervention, but packaged in a form more acceptable to modern-day social scientists. The nightmare for Jasso and other positivists is that their quantitative and objective methods are simply a screen for hiding the fact that they, too, must rely on metaphysical notions of will or divine intervention to explain such things as the reflective sense of job income justice, for example. This is because the explanations Jasso provides for the logic of the mathematical models underlying her analysis are so arcane and esoteric that most of us—including the great majority of social scientists— must simply take her word for it. Where once the imponderability of God's word ruled the day, now the imponderability and inaccessibility of highly technical mathematical formulae serve to explain justice.

Likewise, Jasso's belief in the perfectibility of society through science is akin to the spirit of Christian charity, beneficence, and altruism. Although positivist social scientists claim that their research merely reflects "what is" through a sober and dispassionate collection and analysis of data, their unstated agenda is the liberal ideology of secular humanism, namely, the perfectibility of humankind through the workings of human agency untainted by the invocation of divine or metaphysical agents. The nightmare here is that often what "ought" to be, that is, our personal or collective visions of the good life, informs what "is," that is, research reports that claim to reflect objective data or simply the "facts." But no scientist can ever completely escape the dialectic between content and context, between her reports about society and the impact of that selfsame society on her reports about society (this is the program of the sociology of knowledge, of which Gouldner's reflexive sociology is a part; see Mannheim 1936).

The Problems of Reflexive Sociology

We have now seen an example of how Gouldner's program of reflexive sociology may be used to analyze the nightmares or paradoxes associated with one particular theory of social justice. Although I have argued that there are benefits to be derived from an examination of the tacit, hidden dimensions of any public avowal or project, there are also limitations and problems within reflexive sociology itself that must be addressed.

Above all else, reflexive sociologists champion the role of social critic. From the perspective of reflexive sociology, the social critic must always be alive to the connections between the social contexts of theorists and their public avowals, that is, their theories. This is what was done in examining the social contexts and silent subtexts of Jasso's theory of justice. But if indeed social scientists should embrace the role of social critic in the way Gouldner espouses, how far can or should this critical, self-reflexive method be taken? Isn't it surely the case that somewhere along the way such a reflexive program of critical theory will reach a point of diminishing returns? Can the line easily be drawn between criticism for the sake of clarifying one's philosophical commitments, thereby setting the stage for the creation of a distortion-free, liberating vision of society on the one hand, and criticism merely for the sake of criticism on the other?

Gouldner seemed to have arrived at the horns of this dilemma near the end of his life, and was leaning toward the position that indeed the program of critical self-reflexivity becomes a "runaway norm" that, by folding back upon itself and bringing into doubt the very foundation of its own assumptions and cognitive framework through endless cycles of self-reflexive critique, ultimately disestablishes everything in its path, including itself.

Indeed, Jasso shares with most other contemporary social scientists and intellectuals a particular speech variant Gouldner (1979a) refers to as the "culture of critical discourse."[7] The culture of critical discourse (CCD) is the form of public rationality distinctive to intellectuals. It is a form of speech and writing that emphasizes that all assertions are open to challenge. That is to say, intellectuals are supposed to marshal empirical evidence to support whatever claims they make about the world, and these claims are to be adjudicated within a public forum of fellow scholars or intellectuals who supposedly possess the expertise necessary to assess such claims. Since CCD forbids reliance on the speaker's person, authority, or status in judging knowledge claims, the speech of the New Class of intellectuals is characterized as impersonal, disembodied, decontextualized, and self-grounded (not in individual speakers, but in a consensual community).[8]

Although most intellectuals share and abide by the norms of CCD, most do not take it to the extreme espoused by Gouldner. For example, even among speakers of CCD, most hold certain questions or issues to be off limits or not worthy of challenge or even discussion. For example, Jasso and other quantitative social scientists spend little time examining or challenging the taken-for-granted assumptions underlying the utility or efficaciousness of quantitative methods. This reflects a range of taken-for-granted working assumptions about the world, about knowledge, and about values that all consensual communities share more or less unproblematically.

Gouldner takes the logic of CCD one step further and opens to question and examination this range of tacit assumptions about the world, which reside of course in the infrastructure of theory. But by extending criticism and reflexivity in this way, Gouldner also seems to have signaled the internal limitations that CCD imposes on itself. Since all assertions are open to challenge, the culture of critical discourse, taken to the Gouldnerian extreme, must also engage in auto-critique, and critique of that auto-critique, and so on. In essence, CCD puts its hands around its own throat to see how long it can squeeze. As Gouldner explains,

> There is an unending regress in it, a potential revolution in permanence; it embodies that unceasing restlessness and "lawlessness" that the ancient Greeks first called *anomos* and that Hegel called the "bad infinity".
> 1979A: 60

---

7 Gouldner (1979a: 28) describes the culture of critical discourse as "an historically evolved set of rules, a grammar of discourse, which (1) is concerned to *justify* its assertions, but (2) whose *mode* of justification does not proceed by invoking authorities, and (3) prefers to elicit the *voluntary* consent of those addressed solely on the basis of arguments adduced."
8 This is reflected in the strong tendency toward "we-talk" evident in most positivistically-oriented scientific journals which admonish authors to avoid the use of the personal pronoun "I" in their writings (see Spiegelberg 1973).

The lessons learned about reflexive sociology as applied to issues of social justice are worthwhile, namely, that theories of social justice must reflect the personal aspirations and values of the particular theorist or theory group. There is no way around this; the social context and location of theorists inexorably impact the nature, form, and content of theories. This puts us on guard to be wary of claims made by certain justice theorists that because of the "objective" nature of the methods employed in the particular study, that their justice findings somehow are an advance over more "speculative" approaches found in religion, philosophy, or everyday life. This indeed might be the case, but not necessarily because of the particular *methods* employed. In order to adequately assess the perspicaciousness or accuracy of any theory, both the technical *and* infrastructural levels of the theory must be examined in their totality.

Having said this, however, we must also guard against allowing critique to run rampant. Acknowledging that theories of social justice reflect the personal aspirations, hopes, and values of a particular theorist's or theory group's vision of the good life should in no way automatically diminish their findings or suggestions. Rather, a systematic analysis of the way our otherwise hidden assumptions about knowledge, about values, and about society affect our theories should only strengthen the public discourse about social justice and about the good life more generally.

Conclusion: Social Justice and the New Pope

The unexpected resignation of Pope Benedict XVI in early 2013 led to the convening of a papal conclave to select a new pope. That new pope was named on March 13, 2013, and his name is Pope Francis (born Jorge Mario Bergoglio in Buenos Aires, Argentina in 1936). Among his early official duties was the release of his apostolic exhortation, a summary of positions the Pope holds about matters of the Catholic Church, but which also contains reflections on and recommendations about the state of the world. This exhortation, the *Evangelii Guadium* (or "The Joy of The Gospel"), was first made available in December 2013.

Pope Francis chose to highlight in the second chapter ("Amid the Crisis of Communal Commitment") the problem of the continuing redefinition of life in monetary terms. Francis makes the case that the rise of economic prosperity around the world under global capitalism has not benefitted everyone equally, and that too much of what passes for economics today is merely an "economics of exclusion." He goes on to lambast the idolatry of money, and that the true Christian calling should be a repudiation of the "god of money" in favor of the original mystical relationship between the true God and His people held together in a community of mutual respect and dignity. This theme was reaffirmed in May 2014, whereby Pope Francis called on the United Nations to pursue more vigorously the "legitimate" redistribution of wealth so as to ensure that those who are suffering—financially, emotionally, or spiritually—are not left behind. For Francis, the benefits of democratic and capitalist progress have been uneven, and in some measure have done damage overall because of the callousness of spirit which afflicts those who have made it financially. The ultimate work of the Catholic Church, in staying true to its mandate of help and charity in serving all God's children, is the encouragement of economic and social systems that allows for the distribution and apportionment of all those goods that "God's providence has placed in our hands."[9]

American news media instantly fell in love with this more "liberal" or "progressive" pope, and *Time* magazine named Pope Francis their "person of the year" for 2013. What was especially emphasized in the *Time* article was that Francis was the first non-European pope in 1200 years, and that this is a pope that the masses can embrace after many years of aversion to the Catholic Church. Criticisms of the Church were based primarily on priest sexual abuse scandals, but also its previously hardline stance on hot button political issues such as homosexuality and abortion, although Francis has reaffirmed the traditional stance of the Catholic Church with regard to the latter.

Interestingly enough, in some of her later work Jasso (2007) takes the positivistic attitude toward the unity of science to heart and attempts to find continuities between the various types of justice social and behavioral researchers have been studying for the last century. In her mature unification project, Jasso finds that there are three primordial sociobehavioral forces, namely comparison (or justice), status, and power. Some of this converges with recent proclamations by the new pope and movements of thought within philosophy and the social sciences toward finding a way of repairing the split that occurred years ago between religion and science. To reiterate, the Enlightenment was based on human beings' faculties toward reason, and that all things being equal the attainment of the good life would be based on "facts" as ascertainable within the scientific method emphasizing objectivity and value-neutrality. Comte and others realized that in order to create this new science of humanity irrational belief systems would need to be tamed and eventually jettisoned, at least from the public arena of the competition of ideas. The first casualty of this "cleaning up" was the repudiation of organized religion because of its irrationality, mysticism, and exaltation of metaphysics over physics.

---

9   This is quoted from a story from the *Russian Times* published on May 10, 2014, located at http://rt.com/news/158088-pope-francis-un-redistribution.

Even with the rise of science and the attempt to force religion to retreat from the public realm of ideas and instead speak to their members within the safe confines of private sanctuaries, whether in churches, synagogues, temples, or residential abodes, there was an ongoing cleavage in public politics and ideology regarding left/right stances. All things being equal, the religious ethos tended to be imbued with a right-leaning politics or ideology, while secular activities were left-leaning. Granted, public politics still tolerates, for example, a largely left-leaning Democratic party and a right-leaning Republican party, but the ethos of participation in the public square over time has conduced more and more to a triumph of left to radical secular humanism and a squeezing out of tolerance for right-leaning ideas informed by religious sensibilities. This is seen, for example, in the battles waged over the exclusion or criticism of homosexuality on religious grounds, or new mandates within Obamacare that requires organizations to provide certain types of contraceptive drugs to their employees even if employers are opposed to them on faith grounds.[10]

These same cleavages are playing out on the global level with regard to the battle of localism (more conservative and traditional) versus cosmopolitanism (more progressive and open to change and experimentation), issues Gouldner grappled with both early and later in his career. The next chapter will take up these issues in some detail.

---

10   In 2014 the Supreme Court ruled in a 5–4 vote that the Affordable Care Act's mandate for employers to cover certain types of fertility drugs for their employees violates the Religious Freedom Restoration Act for certain businesses whose owners hold religious beliefs which are opposed to the provision of such drugs. The key to the ruling was that the business in question, Hobby Lobby, can be treated as a person for purposes of judging the "substantial burden" criterion regarding a "person's" religious belief. The dissenting view led by Justice Ginsburg averred the majority erred in making the judgment that a business can hold religious beliefs, but there was also a split by gender, as the five majority judges were male pitted against the four dissenting judges in the minority who were female. The Supreme Court ruling plus the dissent can be accessed at http://www.google.com/url?sa=t&rct=j&q=&esrc=s&source=web&cd=2&sqi=2&ved=0CC8QFjAB&url=http%3A%2F%2Fwww.supremecourt.gov%2Fopinions%2F13pdf%2F13-354_olp1.pdf&ei=nUfQU475E8uuyASDooH4DA&usg=AFQjCNF9W6vopXaVmot25Wj38oDDE6dofw&bvm=bv.71667212,d.aWw.

CHAPTER 8

Locals, Cosmopolitans, and the Politics of a Global Humanity

Gouldner on Loyalty vs. Expertise

In his earlier research in industrial sociology, Gouldner (1957b, 1958b) found that two general role orientations could be found within organizations. These are local and cosmopolitan, both of which are latent roles or identities to the extent that they are not captured within manifest or textualized pronouncements or role expectations within the organizations, such as those found in employee manuals or standard operating procedures. The local orientation or role can be found within the guise of the "company man," that is, workers who display loyalty to the organization. They are committed to the local rules, procedures, and cultures of their workplace above and beyond the official proclamations of the requirements of the office.

The cosmopolitan orientation or role, on the other hand, is one in which the organizational actor is committed more to concerns or ideas existing beyond the confines of the organization. An example given by Gouldner (1957b) is the cosmopolitanism of the "expert," whose deep knowledge of a particular area of expertise often takes him or her beyond the local concerns of solidarity and organizational commitment. As Gouldner (1957b: 288) explains, "For these reasons the [cosmopolitan] expert is more likely than others to esteem the good opinion of professional peers elsewhere; he is disposed to seek recognition and acceptance from 'outsiders.'" Gouldner summarizes the key distinction between these two latent identities as follows:

- *Cosmopolitans*—those low on loyalty to the employing organization, high on commitment to specialized role skills, and likely to use an outer reference group orientation;
- *Locals*—those high on loyalty to the employing organization, low on commitment to specialized role skills, and likely to use an inner reference group orientation. (1957b: 290)

Gouldner (1958b) examined one particular kind of formal organization—the university—and used factor analysis to tease out more specifics about the nature of locals and cosmopolitans in these types of organizations. He discovered four distinct local and two distinct cosmopolitan types. Among the locals, the first type is the *dedicated*, or the true believer. Their deep commitment to the local organizational culture shows up especially strongly in affirming the distinctive educational philosophy of the college. A second type is the *true bureaucrat*, a person totally committed to the rules and procedures of the organization. Indeed, the true bureaucrat has read every word of the professor's employee manual and is often available to provide guidance on all manner of administrative issues that the other professors are oblivious to. The third type of local is the *homeguard*, but rather than being committed to their local organization or community, they are more focused on departmental matters. This means that the homeguard tends to be a lower-level administrator committed to issues of the operation of the department rather than to professional activities such as publishing or attending scholarly conferences. The homeguard tended overwhelmingly to be female, and this reflected the fact that, circa the 1950s, females were badly underrepresented among university faculty. This of course began to change in the 1960s with the emergence of the second wave of feminism. The fourth local type is the *elder*, representing the oldest faculty members who had been with the organization the longest. They have intimate knowledge of the informal networks of the organization, as they are likely to know more of its members in comparison to others. The elders are the carriers of the history and activities of the organization, and in that sense possess a wealth of knowledge about local university matters that is useful to others located at various levels in the institution.

There are also two types of cosmopolitans. One is the *outsider*, persons who are "in" the organization rather than "of" it. They see their position in the organization as temporary and are willing to leave if the price or circumstances are right. They have little knowledge of either the formal or informal networks of the organization, directing more of their time and energies to outside matters such as scholarly conferences, national and international organizations, and scholarly publishing. They are committed to their specialized skills and training and resist trends toward interdisciplinary education. The other cosmopolitan role is the *empire builder*, who sees his or her role as building the reputation of the faculty of his or her home department and increasing its prestige and autonomy. This means that the empire builder often comes to loggerheads with university administrators regarding the running of the department, seeking outside experts from his or her own field to fashion an ideal, cutting-edge department that could attain national if not world distinction.

Gouldner noted that the expertise of cosmopolitans often comes into conflict with the loyalty of locals. For example, a department that is hopeful of increasing its prestige may recruit a nationally renowned scholar. However, it is unclear how long they would be able to keep this scholar, as his or her expertise represents a cosmopolitanism which likely would lead him or her to seek greener pastures beyond the confines of the local department and university. Further, Gouldner believed his findings to be generalizable beyond the university setting, stating that "It may be that the study of relations between cosmopolitans and locals in modern organizations can provide clues for the analysis of conflict within educational, governmental, hospital, and other bureaucracies" (Gouldner 1958b: 467).

Kantian Issues

The distinctions Gouldner found with regard to latent roles in organizations pertaining to localism vs. cosmopolitanism can be extended beyond the organizational level, as Gouldner recommended, to broader issues in philosophy, politics, and sociological theory. This transition in levels must first take into account the thought of Kant and how cosmopolitanism and localism have been configured across the development of human history. As Stade (2014) has argued, Kant's starting point for his own cosmopolitanism was the self's place in nature, where at least initially everything was available to everyone on the basis of natural right. But in the transition from a nomadic to a sedentary existence and the invention of property, natural urges toward taking all that was available was subdued by moral and legal guides regarding the acknowledgment of the rights of others to their property. This is reflective of the growth of reason acting cybernetically to guide and direct the great energy of the passions that held sway under original cosmopolitanism. Pojman (2005: 62) has articulated this Kantian stress on the triumph of rationalism in human development insofar as morality is reason internalized while law is reason externalized.

Hence, the primordial cosmopolitanism of free access to all that was within reach gave way to ideas of hospitality, mutual respect, and community, all of which are necessarily local projects of social control. Under this form of localism, generated by the understanding of the place of property in mediating relations between self and other, the social was conflated with privilege, that is, the privilege to claim private property hence overturning primitive collectivism (even while acknowledging the latter's impoverishment in the condition of nomadism). By the time of the rise of the bourgeoisie and the emergence of free markets with the demise of feudalism, all aspired toward the accumulation of property, again always a project of localistic activities and enforcement. In this scenario, cosmopolitanism is transformed again, this time into the stranger (Simmel; see Pels [1998]) or the free-floating or public intellectual (Gouldner, Bourdieu, and later proponents of public sociology; see Chapter 9).

The idea of cosmopolitanism also coincides with recent articulations of globalization, although as a concept in the hands of Beck (2012) and others there is a tendency to assume such a new world assemblage is already upon us, thereby tending to neglect the empirical indicators that such has actually taken place.[1] In her study of how persons use reflexivity to make their way through the world, Archer (2007) conducted in-depth interviews with twelve persons from a larger group of subjects who had taken a thirteen-question survey on their occupational concerns and patterns of social mobility. Archer found a cosmopolitan bundle of attributes among the persons she interviewed, some of which converge with Gouldner's findings in the context of industrial organization. Her cosmopolitan subjects shared these five characteristics:

- Their primary group socialization played a negligible role in the courses of action they chose later in life (most of the subjects were in their thirties), indicating a *rejection of traditionalism*;
- The subjects mixed and matched some aspects of their early lives with new aspects which emerged within the rather turbulent and contingent environment of opportunity; this represented a level of contextual discontinuity from their localistic experiences and upbringing, with subjects actively choosing along the way the condition of *disembeddedness*;
- Subjects engaged in high levels of reflexivity and self-monitoring to posit to themselves (the internal conversation) various *projects*, and these took distinctive shape in the empirical world as particular activities which were open to modification through subjects taking into account thinking about those activities (and thinking about thinking about those activities et cetera);
- Subjects had to take into account the various *constraints and enablements*—both cultural and structural—confronting them in the early stages of their cosmopolitan or nontraditional journey; if these were not sustainable, they could return to the traditional path, similar in ways to Gouldner's homeguard;
- All this work of forging a new place in the world and leaving the nest bouncing between reflexivity through self-monitoring and experiencing activities in the real world resists capture in such static concepts as habitus (Bourdieu)

---

1 Beck (2012) seeks to get away from the old notion of cosmopolitanism associated with early European philosophy (e.g., Kant) and toward the new term "cosmopolitization." This new term captures certain essential elements overlooked by philosophers and sociologists, including the corporeal level (the body) which sociology has historically been antagonistic toward because of its conflation with biology leading to the problem of biological reductionism.

or globalization (Beck). However, Archer did not take into account Beck's later notion of *cosmopolitization*, which because it includes corporeality might also provide analytical space for sufficient levels of reflexivity as well. (Archer 2007: 60–61).

Further Analytics

We have reviewed empirical work on locals and cosmopolitans (Gouldner and Archer) and the more philosophically grounded approaches that posit broad historical changes giving rise to new conditions such as globalization (Kant and Beck among others). I want to now move toward an analysis of the convergence of thought among two European theorists, Gabriel Tarde and Carl Schmitt, who settled on the importance of localism in opposition to the master trend of cosmopolitanism posited by many other European and American thinkers as an aspect of modernity, rationality, and globalization. Tarde was selected because he was (along with Durkheim) the most important figure in the development of sociology in France, although many observers (including Gouldner) ignored him for reasons to be delineated below. We have touched upon Schmitt briefly earlier, particularly in relation to Paul Piccone's work as editor of *Telos* and the documentation of the rightward turn toward Schmitt by followers of that journal by the mid-1970s. This convergence on localism represents a nightmare of liberal thought, consistent with the nightmare versions of various undertakings analyzed by Gouldner, including those of industrial sociology, functionalism, labeling theory, social work and other helping professions, and Marxism (e.g., Gouldner 1980a). This also represents an analytical extension of critical theory which otherwise does not and cannot come into view by those theorists who hold to traditional (that is, unreflexive) views informed by Marxism or neoMarxism.

The Problem

Gabriel Tarde (1843–1904) was an eminent French criminologist and sociologist who attempted to establish sociology as a scientific discipline on the basis of the universal principle of repetition. In the social realm, this principle was imitation. But how does imitation work, and where does it start? In his quest for a starting mechanism for imitation, Tarde admitted that much of the work of society emerges through individual and social duels, that is, antagonisms and oppositions over decisions concerning whether or not to adapt any particular innovation, invention, or form of life. In many respects, this discovery of Tarde's converges sharply with the political theory of Carl Schmitt (1888–1985), who argued that the essence of social life, including the establishment of the state and even politics itself, is the friend-enemy distinction. Implications for contemporary theorizing by way of analyzing the logic of the duel in Schmitt and Tarde will be discussed.

For Tarde, repetition is the universal and unifying principle observable across all phenomena whether inorganic (physical objects), organic (the hereditary or vital, i.e. living organisms), or, following Spencer (1897), superorganic (the massing of individual organisms into swarms, hordes, herds, or societies). The repetition principle in the physical world is *vibration*. Vibrations of light, sound, electricity, and so forth propagate waves of their effects onto receiving objects, piling up resemblances in their wake. With regard to the organic world, all resemblances of vital origin result from *heredity*, specifically, from hereditary transmission. After fertilization, cells divide and multiply in rapid succession, as offspring carry many of the traits and characteristics of their parents' bloodlines. This is Haeckel's (1866) motto of "ontogeny recapitulates phylogeny" writ large. Finally, social resemblances are propagated across societies by *imitation*. But imitation is not simply hard-wired in us as instincts; otherwise it would not get us much past simple reproductivity. For imitation to find its true and full social force, particular organisms that take the initiative to create a novel innovation or invention, which in turn leads to other like organisms following along, must initiate it. Indeed, as a social force imitation represents an important modification of instinct (Tarde 1903: 4).

Here, Tarde easily opens himself up to the charge that he embraces a vulgar "great man" theory of invention and innovation. It is this individualistic or psychologistic bias, presumably, which brought Tarde to loggerheads with Emile Durkheim as both were battling for supremacy in late 19th century French sociology (Clark 1973). Durkheim (1938 [1895]) instead favored a "social facts" paradigm that viewed social phenomena as a *sui generis* reality that could not be reduced to the elements comprising them.[2] Yet such innovations as

---

2 In pursuing this social facts paradigm, Durkheim was also desperately attempting to show how the social is distinct from the merely biological or psychological. But Tarde did not really care about social facts per se, and in this sense was able to assimilate the social into the non-social through the cosmological notion of universal repetition. This disagreement represented a vast chasm between Durkheim and Tarde, as discussed further by Karsenti (2012), Schillmeier (2009), and Toews (2012).

described by Tarde need not at all be the product of advanced cognitive or intellectual endowment. It could be accomplished equally well by chance or happenstance, such as a horse breaking from the pack and creating a stampede. Hence, we see that Tarde is closed in on both sides, for the idea of the importance of a single perhaps unwitting instigator of group actions brings him close to the crowd or mob psychology of Le Bon (1896; see also Borch 2006, 2009; Brighenti 2010).

Dueling Innovations

Nevertheless, Tarde was never shaken in his belief that all resemblance is due to repetition, whether imitative, reproductive, or vibratory. All repetition flows from some innovation whether physical (e.g., light emanating from some central point), mechanical, hereditary, or social. But how do some innovations or discoveries win out, for surely there would be waiting in the wings a plurality of other candidates creating the conditions for imitation or reproduction or propagation? Tarde assumes that by nature human beings are inquisitive and creative, and will seek to use whatever resources in the environment are available for the greater or more efficient satisfaction of ends. The desire to invent is part of the logical need for unification of a people living together and striving towards shared ends. Even though temporary equilibrium may be reached as to agreements on how current resources are to be used for satisfying ends, there is yet ceaselessness and restlessness concerning finding something new or better presumably waiting just over the horizon. In other words, alternatives appear or are made available, and the people spend time debating how the new item or innovation on the scene may improve upon the old ways of doing things. At least in the beginning when new innovations are introduced, quarrels among the people are routine over the efficiency or cost of one option compared to another. Examples of these in Tarde's day included disagreements over cane sugar versus beet sugar, the stagecoach versus the locomotive, and the sailboat versus the steamboat (Tarde 1903: 158). In hindsight, we know which of these alternatives eventually won the day. Yet Tarde's point is to state the general principles of how alternative choices for organizing ways of living appear in the real world.

Most essentially, what happens is that human society operates upon the logic of the duel. For example, in a society where two languages are spoken, enough of a rivalry between speakers of the languages will arise that eventually one of the languages will be favored by more of the people and will eventually become dominant. As Tarde explains,

> Linguistic progress is effected first by imitation and then by rivalry between two languages or dialects which quarrel over the same country and one of which is crowded back by the other, or between two terms or idioms which correspond to the same idea.
>
> 1903: 154–155

It is the role of the sociologist to gather data on each concrete duel to ascertain why one alternative was favored over the other. Even though in the beginning it may appear that an area of life reflects a multitude of options for ordering it, in reality through the process of logical simplification opposing aims or judgments are always two in number. For example, a military skirmish may have a number of discreet armies fighting, yet they are not all fighting against each other. They all are aligned on one side opposing a legion of forces on the other. Such issues may "always be summed up in a *yes* opposed to a *no*" (Tarde 1903: 155). Collective life amounts to a continuous dialogue, whether taking place informally in the everyday lifeworld or in more formalized settings, of questions followed by proposed solutions. Each discreet end-goal nexus must be, according to Tarde, approached on the basis of an affirmation or a negation.

Tarde goes on to assert that inventions certainly satisfy desires, but also may further provoke them. Indeed, the desire to invent or discover grows with its satisfaction (Tarde 1903: 43). If the innovation is judged to be beneficial to the particular social end for which it was designed, that judgment is likely to be multiplied in the minds of many through diffusion and imitation. This is consistent with Durkheim's (1984 [1893]) notion of the insatiability of human appetites, an ontological assumption traceable to Schopenhauer's concept of the will (see Mestrovic 1988). The will spurs humans—indeed, all living things—to pursue gratifications, and these life plans will not always be coordinated with the desires of others. Imitation was, for Tarde, the primary way that conflicts between persons pursuing their desires would be limited or at least held in check. But like light waves emanating from a single source, they are refracted into numerous colors or rays by various receiving media (Giddings 1896: 111).[3] These receiving media are extremely varied in the empirical social world, represented not only by the individual minds or personalities receiving the stimuli, but also on a mass scale by great variations across races or nations regarding tastes, customs, fashion, language, and politics. Again, the diffusion of innovations in the social world does not always lead to perfect imitation,

---

3   Tarde argues that both conflict and invention arise from imitation. As Ellwood (1901: 723) explains, for Tarde conflict is the interference of two dissimilar waves of imitation, while invention is the union of two harmonious imitations.

especially when several alternatives are vying for attention. This conflict may, as we have seen, eventuate in a duel where one of the alternatives wins the day (as we saw in the case of competition between two languages).

But it is also important to note that in these duels the vanquished usually do not simply disappear, but instead fill other roles still considered socially useful. When steamboats came on the scene, sailboats and oars did not magically cease to exist, but shifted over into recreational and sports-related activities. Indeed, sometimes alternatives to the status quo are created or proposed because change in that area of life is deemed desirable *in and for itself*. As Tarde notes,

> In the case of industry and fine arts, it is for the pleasure of change, of *not doing* the usual thing, that that part of the public that is influenced by fashion adopts a new product to the neglect of some old one.
> 1903: 164

Individual and Collective Duels

Tarde is here struggling with the empirical complexities arising from his own seemingly parsimonious concept of resemblances arising either from vibration (the inorganic world), reproduction (the organic world), or imitation and invention (the social world). Eventually, Tarde had to acknowledge that duels taking place in any of these areas—but especially in the organic and social worlds—could logically occur at either the individual or collective level.

Tarde (1903: 165) initiates this work of clarification by stating "The social duel commences only after the individual one has ceased." What does this mean? On one level, it is indicative of the social psychology Tarde was attempting to work out simultaneous to the cosmological project of explaining how the universal principle operates across all space and time. Actually, from the perspective of adherents of Durkheim's social facts paradigm, what Tarde is doing here is not really a "social psychology" at all but a pure or vulgar psychology derived from Bagehot's (1872) own "suggestion-imitation" psychology (see Ellwood 1921: 231; Leys 1993). Tarde needed this individual level mechanism to explain how concrete individuals are influenced by others in shared social environments. Tarde's (1899) conceptual system required that he take seriously the individual, and that indeed, society is what it is because of the sorts of imitative behaviors engaged in by its inhabitants.

Returning to the issue of the duel or conflict, it is Tarde's position that any individual confronted with a new stimulus will hesitate before accepting that new innovation. This simply means that human beings must by necessity weigh ingrained habits, customs, and traditions in the decision whether or not to imitate some new cultural or social element. Here, at this level, it is an individual duel. If hesitation wins the day, the person refrains from imitating, and nothing new arises. The social fabric is not appreciably altered, meaning that any possible social duels are stifled. It is only with the decision to imitate, at the individual level, that social duels eventually emerge.

At this point Tarde engages in a thought experiment. What if, in some nation, all its members were suspended in a state of indecision? Virtually all conflicts would end, for indecision takes people away from the activities that make society what it is. The clearest type of the social duel, namely war, would come to an end because of the hesitation to declare war by key government officials (Tarde 1903: 165–166). Likewise there would be no elections, because no one would run for office. There would also be an end to religious and scientific schisms and disputes. There would be an end to litigation as well, because there would be no plaintiffs and hence no defendants. There would even be an end to linguistic disputes because there would be no one willing to come forward to argue for the advantages of one language or dialect over another.

If or when inaction or irresolution among all people of a nation reaches this absolute stage, there is perfect unanimity and the elusive utopia is reached. Of course, Tarde sets this up merely to point out the fiction of ever achieving perfect unanimity through indecision and inaction. Here, tradition and the current status quo would reign indefinitely, and culture would cease to exist. This means that social duels are necessary to sustain the life of society. It is a corollary of the utilitarianism of Hobbes, that life is an individualistic, brutish struggle for existence. Here, many conflicts—but not all, such as war perhaps—are functional, in that they lead to innovations, social upgrading, and resiliency thereby avoiding the deadening ossification of dogma and unquestioned tradition (Coser 1956).

The Rise of the State

If human nature is as Hobbes depicted, individuals would pursue their own gratifications even at the expense of others, and a war of all against all would ensue. But in the transition from the primitive horde to later advanced stages of civilization, the potential war of all against all was subdued. It was, as Locke pointed out, subdued because of the greater cognitive endowment of human beings in comparison to other animals. The main project of social evolution has been the slow and inexorable triumph of head over heart, or the intellect over the passions. With their greater cognitive endowment, human beings learned how to take dominion over all other creatures and to direct nature's energies and resources toward desired human ends (Bentham 1843; Ward 1883). But even as they attained this lofty status, humans realized that what they required most was protection from their own kind (Spencer 1897). Human beings struck upon the social contract, namely, the agreement that individuals will refrain from unbridled pursuit of their own interests in exchange for the reassurance that some external force—the state or the Leviathan in Hobbes' terms—will use coercion or its threat to keep everyone else from pursuing theirs. Tarde's (1903: 174) position is consistent with this utilitarian and contractarian tradition of thought, as he states: "The very first form of government was in answer to a demand for security which had until then received no satisfaction, and this circumstance was favourable to its establishment."

Enter Weber
By the beginning of the 20th century, as Durkheim had already eclipsed Tarde as the leader of French sociology, Max Weber was gaining notice in Germany and elsewhere for his writings on economics, jurisprudence, comparative religion, and later sociology. Interestingly enough, Weber shared Durkheim's misgivings about the viability of Tarde's vision for sociology, but for somewhat different reasons. Following the German *Verstehen* tradition, Weber argued that sociology is a science that concerns itself with the interpretive understanding of the actions of human beings. For Weber (1964), human behavior counts as "action" only to the extent that actors attach a subjective meaning to their behavior. And further, action is "social" insofar as its subjective meaning takes into account the behavior of others. By couching theory and research at the level of the subjective meaning that actors have about their own actions and the actions of others, sociologists may thereby aspire to develop causal explanations about social life. In essence, Weber argued that sociologists should strive to "interpret action by understanding the motives of the actor from the 'subjective' point of view, i.e., the investigator attempting to put himself in the actor's place" (Parsons 1964: xxiii).

Weber took pains to make a distinction between, on the one hand, human processes and phenomena that are sociological, that is, that have cultural meaning from the perspective of observers of and participants in such social action, and, on the other hand, other human phenomena which are devoid of subjective meaning. For example, Weber did not count as social action the simultaneous opening of umbrellas among a number of people reacting to an approaching rainstorm. This is because the opening of umbrellas is in reaction to a physical event, the rainstorm, and hence lacks *Verstehen* or subjective meaning. Here we have a case of mere imitation among human beings, but it is purely reactive and hence "there is no meaningful orientation to the actor imitated" (Weber 1964: 114). This is consistent with Mead's (1934) repudiation of imitation as a pre-social, instinctual, or mimetic process, in that it typically does not require the mindful activity necessary for the development of the human self (Latour 2002; Leys 1993; Toews 2003). However, this is not a complete repudiation of Tarde's position, for Weber admits that certainly *some* types of imitation do meet the criteria of social action, especially those backed with cultural or normative expectations such as in the areas of fashion, art, music, law, language, social relationships, and politics.

Weber's position on the rise of the state was also consistent with that of Tarde (as seen earlier), even while the esteem granted to Weber's writings on the subject far surpassed that granted to Tarde throughout the twentieth and into the twenty-first century. It is important to briefly review Weber's theory of the state, as it will set the stage for the discussion of German political scientist Carl Schmitt, whose writings on the subject contrast sharply with Weber. In doing so, it will also be shown that in at least one important sense Schmitt is consistent with Tarde, and that is the emphasis Schmitt places on the logic of the social duel, specifically, the distinction of friend and enemy.

In the transition from early to modern times, there is a qualitative shift in human social organization and culture, variously described as the transition from mechanical to organic solidarity (Durkheim 1984 [1893]), from ascription to achievement (Maine 2002 [1861]), or from traditional to legal-bureaucratic authority (Weber 1968 [1925]). Beginning in the 18th century, the projects of social control and security were systematically taken out of the hands of everyday citizens and placed into the hands of government functionaries. As Weber put it, social relations moved from primarily communal to increasingly associative (Gane 2005). The rise of the state, which seeks a monopoly of the use of force over a particular jurisdiction, represents the pinnacle of imperatively coordinated associations emerging in modernity.

Tarde assumes that there is a universal need among human beings to be directed and guided. What starts out in early childhood socialization in the infant-mother bond has its corollary in the rights, responsibilities, and protection of citizens by the state (Barnes 1919: 256). The origin of political parties is the logical duel occurring first at the level of individuals, in consideration over visions of the good life. The preeminent social duel emerges when critical masses of citizens are motivated to defend particular visions of the good life, seeking to win over legislators to their perspective. Weber placed great emphasis on the rise of legal-bureaucratic rationality in the formation of the state, even as he doubted that instrumental rationality would actually lead us to the good life. He felt nonrational elements, especially those embodied in the charismatic leader, were needed as a buffer against the iron cage of legal-bureaucratic rationality which stultifies innovation and leads to a deadened ossification of rules for the sake of rules. It is here, with the holding out of the importance of nonrational elements in social life, that Weber and Tarde converge, especially for those who argue that the crowd or the mob, fueled by blind, emotionally-charged or unconscious imitation, is the ultimate endpoint of Tarde's social psychology (see, e.g., Barry and Thrift 2007; Lindholm 1992; Toscano 2007).

Schmitt on Friends vs. Enemies

Indeed, Weber's notion of the rise of rational-bureaucratic and legal thinking leading to the disenchantment of the modern world leads in turn to Carl Schmitt's formulation of the "state of exception," namely, the modern state's tendency to suspend rules in times of uncertainty. For Schmitt, the very reality of the existence of this state of exception points to weaknesses in the entire liberal political edifice because of the way it overplays the calculability and rule-drivenness of everyday life (Yelle 2010). This decisionism on the part of Schmitt was derived largely from Kierkegaard's (1964) notion of repetition in which politics is a repetition or copy of religion. For Schmitt (1985), liberal governance is a metaphysical construct amounting to little more than political theology (Espejo 2012). It is analogous to the ancient Greek idea of recollection (Gould 2013). Tarde, too, relies heavily on repetition and recollection, but receives these notions more directly from Antoine Cournot's (1956) probabilism rather than from Kierkegaard, whom Tarde rarely (if ever) cites (see Clark 1969). However, both Cournot's probabilism and Kierkegaard's decisionism are derived from Leibniz's monadology. Hence, Leibniz provides the primordial connective tissue between Schmitt and Tarde, propagated through Kierkegaard (in the case of Schmitt) and Cournot (in the case of Tarde).

It is in this sense that Schmitt accepts most of Weber's ideas concerning the rise of the state and its essential characteristics, especially as this relates to political control over a sovereign jurisdiction or territory.[4] However, Schmitt goes one step further than Weber by attempting to distill the essential elements comprising politics in general and the state specifically, that is, as a specific type of political authoritarian association. Schmitt suggests that ultimate

---

4 I note here briefly that Schmitt is a conservative and was for a short while during the 1930s a member of the Nazi party in his native Germany. Nevertheless, Schmitt today is read by a number of radical and far left thinkers, primarily because they find his critique of liberalism and his views on the formation of the state appealing. For more on this seemingly odd state of affairs, see Dyrberg (2009) and Turner (2011).

distinctions can be ascertained in various spheres of life. For example, in the realm of aesthetics the essential distinction is between beautiful and ugly. In morality, it is good versus evil. And in economics, the main distinction is between profitable and unprofitable.

Following this line of thinking, Schmitt is led to the conclusion that the main distinction of politics is that between friends and enemies.[5] From the very beginning of their formation, nation-states have always grouped themselves according to the friend and enemy antithesis. And this enemy does not exist in the abstract or at the individual or psychological level. Rather, it is a collective understanding that nation-states, as collective actors, decide for themselves. Enmity, or bad feelings as political expression, may lead eventually to actions that justify the taking of lives of those identified as a public enemy. This is war, and this is what states excel at, according to Schmitt.

For Schmitt (2008 [1938]) the nightmare version of liberalism emerges from his fusing a cynical Machiavellianism with the positing of the centrality of power in the formation of the state from Hobbes to Weber. The great strides forward toward enlightenment and emancipation of the citizenry under the liberal constitutional state are a mirage. They are a mirage because even within liberalism and its system of political checks and balances, in times of emergency it is the executive as sovereign who decides on the exception, and it is this extralegal final decisionism which allows totalitarianism and illiberalism to enter through the backdoor (Habermas 1989: 128–139).

Since the friend-enemy distinction is at the heart of politics and the formation and maintenance of the state, it is unlikely we will ever see a global humanity where war as we now know it would be eliminated. As Schmitt (2007: 53) states, "A world state which embraces the entire globe and all of humanity cannot exist." The collection of political entities constitutes a "pluriverse" not a universe. For example, even as President Obama declared in early 2011 that military actions undertaken by American-led coalition forces against Libya were for "humanitarian" reasons, namely, to stop Libyan leader Muammar Gaddafi from attacking self-proclaimed "pro-democracy" Libyan rebels, the invocation of "humanity" in war is a form of cheating.[6] As Schmitt (2007: 54)

---

5 This discussion is taken primarily from Schmitt's book *The Concept of the Political*, first published in German in 1932. The edition being cited here is Schmitt (2007).

6 For more on the issue of the attacks on Libya, see the April 1, 2011 ABC News article posted to correspondent Jake Tapper's Political Punch blog, located at http://blogs.abcnews.com/politicalpunch/2011/04/a-growing-rift-between-the-human-rights-community-and-president-obama.html. Gaddafi was eventually tracked down and killed by Libyan rebel forces on Thursday, October 20, 2011 in his hometown of Sirte near Tripoli. The death of Gaddafi would likely never have occurred had it not been for the US-led NATO bombing campaign.

explains, when a state engages in war against an enemy in the name of humanity, it is more often than not a rhetorical move, justifying its actions as good, just, or humanitarian while simultaneously denying these same lofty attributes could ever apply to the enemy. In taking this position Schmitt rejects the concept of the "just war" (Slomp 2006). The pluriverse of state actors, who sometimes wage war for economic, cultural, or even humanitarian reasons, serve unwittingly to maintain the friend-enemy distinction in shifting configurations across time and into the foreseeable future. It is always a project of imperialism, so argues Schmitt. It is always a raw play for power, just as politics is always a raw play for power.

For Weber politics and the state are based on sovereignty, but Weber does not assume that the powerful are good or true. It is simply the case that within the play of power, especially in the move toward the bureaucratization of government and most other areas of life in modernity, decisions have to be made about how to get things done in the real world. Life is imminent and must be assessed on its own terms. Life is a struggle, and rationality is often invoked to justify who is in power at the moment. But there is always the possibility of a plurality of interests attempting to gain the upper hand in the political realm and beyond. In this sense, Weber's notion of sovereignty and power is virtually the same as that adopted by Schmitt. It is, as William Rasch (2000) has cleverly phrased it, "conflict as a vocation."

This also gives the lie to apoplectic liberal theory conceiving of an inexorable move toward a global order. The nomos of the earth—that is, the claim to distinctive forms of life freely operating within identifiable sovereign borders is, for Schmitt, much to be preferred over the totalizing narrative of universalistic liberalism (Dean 2006). At a minimum, the concept of human freedom translates into an acceptance of the various projects of opinion- and will-formation arising within each distinctive human collectivity (Habermas 1996). The difficult project of humanity is the transition from pure tribalism to an amalgamation of previously hermetically sealed human groupings that eventually come to accept some broader or more general set of values for ordering their lives collectively. Yet, this is rarely done peacefully or harmoniously. At least initially, the amalgamation of smaller collectivities into bigger ones, encompassing sometimes diverse races of people, is accomplished through coercion and conquest as explained by Gumplowicz (1883). Here, again, we see that Schmitt subscribes to a cynical, Machiavellian view of the state and politics. He is also in strong agreement with Tarde over the impossibility of a unified global or world order. In the next section we will examine this issue in somewhat more detail.

The Social Duel as Inimical to a One-World Order

One of the leading trends evident in current philosophy, social science, and political analysis is the shift away from "civilizational analysis"—whereby particular civilizations are studied as autonomous entities for purposes of explaining which features (cultural, economic, political) make them unique—and toward "globalization," namely, the study of the emergence of a homogeneous global unity which, on the way to becoming an empirical reality, systematically renders less meaningful traditional notions of sovereignty, citizenship, borders, and boundaries (see Inglis 2010; Turner 2006).

Many intellectuals holding liberal ideological or political positions welcome the move to internationalization or globalization because it would represent the culmination of the slow and painful attempt to overcome divisive distinctions on the basis of place, nationality, tribe, and tradition. The impetus for this idea was Kant's notion of eternal or perpetual peace (Demenchonok 2007; Fine 2006).[7] This Kantian ideal is evident in the writings of Lester F. Ward, the founder of American sociology, who articulated such a position as far back as 1883. In the deep and dark past human beings were solitary and brutish, and they huddled together in their tribes making war against anyone outside of their group. Slowly, however, human beings learned it was advantageous to set up communitarian and reciprocal relations with other groups, if for no other reason than to avoid an incessant war of all against all. Ward (1883) believed that the development of human society would at some unspecified point in the future take the form of the pantarchic, whereby human beings would be united in a world community as ideals such as altruism, sympathy, and love of humanity would burst beyond the confines of the nation-state, thereby rendering that concept obsolete. Ward was prescient on this point, as he wrote these words well before the development of international organizations such as the World Court, the League of Nations, and the United Nations actually came to fruition.

Likewise, George Herbert Mead's notions of reflexivity, the self, and mindful activity undergirded his own view of a dawning era of ethical reciprocity among human beings even as they were growing more and more dissimilar.

---

7   In actuality the easy equivalence often made between liberalism and peace may be more mythical than real. As Neocleous (2013) argues, upon closer inspection the so-called ideal or pacifistic civil society first emerging out of the eighteenth century Scottish Enlightenment was actually committed to deep and abiding militaristic and masculine values. This finding is more in line with Schmitt and Tarde than with proponents of liberalism, communitarianism, cosmopolitanism, and perpetual peace.

For Mead, role taking is not only something that occurs naturally in the human condition; it also provides a means by which human beings are able to cooperate and ideally realize the democratic ideals of the just and good life. For example, the notion of "rights" makes sense only to the extent that self-consciousness arises as we take on the attitude of others, that is, as we assume the attitude of assent of all members of the community (i.e., the "generalized other"). Like Ward before him, Mead held out hope that this generalized other would expand outward from families, communities, nation-states and eventually to the global level. As Mead (1959: 195) stated, "The Word Court and the League of Nations are other such social objects that sketch out common plans of action if there are national selves that can realize themselves in the collaborating attitudes of others."

The dream of secular humanism is that we are strengthened in our diversity, because as we hold fewer and fewer things in common the one remaining bond shared by all is our humanity (Durkheim 1984 [1893]). A one-world order would be based upon the most general and abstract good which is humanity, and human rights—not national or citizenship rights—would be its major supporting plank. Katz (2001) argues that Tarde was one of the first to point out how media technologies profoundly affect major social institutions. For example, the invention of the printing press and later newspaper contributed greatly to the unseating of the direct rule of kings over their subjects. Later of course more avenues for propagating information to wider audiences emerged, first by radio, then television, and now the Internet. Such new media technologies would appear to accelerate the pace of connecting more and more disparate persons and groups across wider and wider social and physical divides, seemingly also contributing to globalization. Yet critical theorists, especially those of the Frankfurt School, have continued to warn against how the culture industry plays to a lowest common denominator by using mass media to entertain and pacify more than to enlighten, educate, and unify (see especially Gouldner 1976a). It is unclear whether the potentially democratizing impulses of mass electronic media, such as the Internet, can be rectified with the raw calculation of profit underlying the activities and marketing strategies of giant media corporations such as News Corp, Viacom, TimeWarner, General Electric, and Walt Disney.

In any event, the move toward megamergers in the media and entertainment industry, whereby now growing numbers of persons across the globe can receive like stimuli leading to greater possibilities for imitation, does not magically end social duels. If anything, they are accelerated and show up in new configurations, consistent with Tarde's position. Although most modern Western societies have heralded the Internet as a force for democratization and created policies seeking to expand availability to everyone regardless of class standing or ability to pay, a number of countries in Africa, the Middle East, and Asia are curtailing access to the Internet and other popular media for any number of reasons.[8] In Iran and some other Middle Eastern countries, Western fashions, especially women's fashion, are seen as hostile to the teachings of Islam. In Iran, by law while in public women's hair and body are covered (by the *hijab* and *chador*), and many aspects of Western popular culture and fashion are suppressed or censored because of this (see Warf 2011). Interestingly enough, however, because the face is uncovered, Iranian women have experienced few limitations placed on their consumption of Western ideals concerning female facial beauty. As a result, over the last decade an unprecedented number of Iranian women have sought rhinoplasty to correct the ethnic Persian nose (sometimes referred to as the Eurasian "hook nose"). In a 2007 documentary, ABC News proclaimed that Iran is the "nose job capital" of the world.[9] This represents both an individual and social duel that promises to remain active for the foreseeable future.

Research conducted by Elias and Lemish (2011) further illustrates the sorts of duels or conflicts evident even within broader movements toward globalization. Their research keys off their earlier findings (Elias and Lemish 2008) suggesting that immigrant families must make two simultaneous adaptations. One is "outward integration" (or cosmopolitanism) whereby immigrant families seek to blend in with the cultural and social configurations of their new surroundings. The other is "inward integration" (or localism) whereby immigrant families must decide how much of their native culture and activities they should preserve even while consuming host or homeland media. In short, Elias and Lemish (2011: 1246) are concerned with investigating "the roles the mass media are playing in both outward and inward integration processes."

The authors conducted a cross-cultural study of Russian-speaking immigrants in Israel and Germany over the past two decades. They conducted semi-structured in-depth interviews with Russian-speaking immigrant children and their parents in Israel and Germany beginning in 2004. A total of 94 parents and 78 children in 60 families were included in the study. The authors sought to elicit from the informants the extent and type of media use in the family and what conflicts may have arisen as a result. In terms of inward integration, parents in the two countries were concerned about the loss of mastery of the

---

8 More recent curtailment of Internet access by governments has occurred in Egypt and Tunisia following political uprisings in these countries. For the most recent comprehensive study of global access to the Internet, see Kelly et al. (2012).

9 See http://abcnews.go.com/GMA/story?id=2877504.

Russian language by their children and devised strategies to keep this from happening. Examples included forbidding children to speak the host country language at home, or signing up their children for after-school Russian language instruction. For the most part, however, these strategies were not effective because the children resisted attempts by their parents to block access to host language media.

With regard to outward integration, parents in Israel and Germany were concerned with exposing their children to appropriate media for the learning of the host language, even while also seeking to maintain internal integration, that is, proficiency in the Russian language (as discussed above). For younger children, the preferred formats were children's television programming (especially cartoons) and advertising. However older children tended to be somewhat resistant to this sort of blatant assimilation, and this sometimes caused conflicts over adolescent media preferences. For example, adolescent children newly arriving to their host countries were likely to reject watching television programs in the host language and instead favored social networking at various Internet sites (such as Facebook) with their Russian-language friends.

Tarde, Schmitt, and the Civil Sphere

The point of all this is that social and individual duals remain lively and vital even within the alleged movement toward globalization and the growth of humanitarianism. When individual will or agency is challenged or thwarted, even within the context of primary group relations such as the family, duels are likely to arise. These duels are often undergirded with emotionally charged affective states, and these can play out at either the individual or collective levels as both Schmitt and Tarde have argued (see Ost 2004). The march of social evolution and Enlightenment reason—not a contradiction I would contend—has brought with it the conceit that physical aggression will slowly be displaced by more communitarian and peaceful means for organizing our collective lives. According to this line of liberal thinking, the archaic form of conflict resolution—war—gives way to a more "civil" form of freedom in the guise of the free market and the industrial order. Most liberal political theorists, although viewed by Marxists as absolutely inimical to human freedom, saw the rising disparities between the haves and have-nots under capitalism, as simply the cost of social progress (see, e.g., Giddings 1918; Turner 2010). Welfare statism would continue the work of amelioration through juridification of ever expanding areas of life (for example, the idea of healthcare as a right not a privilege), in effect acting to pacify the dislocations and resentments experienced by persons seeking recognition from the state for not having access to full participation in social life. These claims in turn are often based on status (e.g., gender, sexual orientation, class, disability, race or ethnicity, age, and even looks and weight).

The civil or public sphere was the place where modern, enlightened persons living in the urban metropolis could come together and participate in what was ideally envisioned as democratic self-governance (Alexander 2006; Gouldner 1976a). This required heavy doses of imitation among like-minded residents in the shared spaces of neighborhoods, communities, schools, and other voluntary associations. This is Durkheim's "organic solidarity" writ large. This was the outcome of many years of struggle among real flesh-and-blood human beings, whose concerted efforts led to the transition from the eighteenth-century absolute state, to the nineteenth-century noninterventionist state, on through to the total state of the twentieth-century and beyond (Schmitt 2007: 23). But notice something peculiar. The "good society" can never rest on its laurels. The idea of egalitarianism, with which the responsible state wrestles incessantly, must always lead in the direction of repairing those instances in which its ideals are subverted or simply out of reach. This means that the state (or federal government) must intervene, favoring the cosmopolitan over the local (Gouldner 1973a; Schillmeier 2009) and thereby further trivializing the original notion of self-governance along with muting the free play of opinion- and will-formation. In essence, organic solidarity brings with it the colonization of the lifeworld, for good or bad (Habermas 1987).

The friend-enemy distinction, first appearing primordially in tribal conflict and war, becomes a generalized phenomenon as the concept of the political is applied to more and more areas of life. For example, media commentators in the United States complain that political moderates are a dying breed, and that the Democratic and Republican parties have been taken over by extremists on either side. This leads to paralysis in the legislative realm, as bitter political partisanship operates for the purpose of defeating legislation promoted by the other side. The "political" lends itself to extremely polemical uses, in the domestic or private sphere (e.g., "the personal is political"), the economic sphere, the public and civil sphere, and so forth. Where does this leave individuals, battling in the trenches daily deciding which innovations—be it legislation, fashion, dialects, mores, offers of friendship, etc.—to deny or accept?

If too many people retreat from civic participation because of disgust with the choices offered to them in the political realm or elsewhere, they will in effect engage in "inaction" or "indecision," according to Tarde, and if this occurs over a prolonged period of time social stagnation would likely occur. Retreat reduces conflict but also stems the tide of invention and innovation. For Tarde, the duel is necessary for a healthy and vibrant social life, while for Schmitt it is inevitable, appearing under various guises over time and in different contexts.[10]

Conclusion

With the rise of humanism war increasingly is condemned even as it continues to be used as a metaphor in many areas of life, as for example wars on poverty, terrorism, drugs, women, religion, or what have you. Employing the language of medicine is also useful in convincing ourselves that a new era of pacifism is in ascendance, as is obvious in the case of lethal injection as the preferred method of execution for those sentenced to death. "Enemies" disappear and in their place are the disgruntled, the insubordinate, the dispossessed, the disturbed, the dangerous, the confused, the unreliable, and the misguided. But the friend-enemy distinction persists, and it is central to many of the individual and social duels still haunting modern society. Their persistence and durability are due to the fact, as Tarde put it, that "*Society is imitation and imitation is a kind of somnambulism*" (Tarde 1903: 87, emphasis in original). If imitation happens, on some level it is always submission to some ascendancy, be it the proclamation of an eminent thinker, a compelling scientific finding, a religious edict, a new fad or fashion sweeping a nation or even a friendship circle, an invention deemed to be useful for some purpose, a new turn of phrase (for example, "epic fail" rather than "epic failure"), and on and on. On this point, Schmitt converges sharply with Tarde when he stated (circa 1929) that "Great masses of industrialized peoples today still cling to a torpid religion of technicity because they, like all masses, seek radical results and believe subconsciously that the absolute depoliticization sought after four centuries can be found here and that universal peace begins here" (Schmitt 2007: 95). For Schmitt, the psycho-technical machinery of mass suggestion works in such a way as to reflect the sort of somnambulism that is imitation, which is, in turn, society.

Hence, we arrive at a profound ambiguity in Tarde's perspective on the logic of the duel that is absent in Schmitt. As we have seen, for Tarde indecision at the individual level leads to a sort of social paralysis or stagnation if a critical mass is reached of multiple instances of indecision. On the contrary, the lifeblood of social life is the decision to act, to do something as an active agent, to

---

10   Indeed, for Tarde (1897) opposition (or the duel) represents one of three universal forms (the other two being repetition and adaptation) appearing across both the social and non-social realms. For more on Tarde's cosmology, see Barnes (1919) and Giddings (1903).

choose to imitate. Yet, imitation may be seen as largely unconscious, reactive, or somnambulistic. This pushes Tarde perilously close back to the mob psychology of Le Bon. Isn't this an impoverished form of human agency, in essence an embodiment of the defective social psychology against which Durkheim and others so adamantly fought at the end of the nineteenth century? Does this problem lie at the heart of the ultimate rejection of Tarde by the sociological community that solidified into a consensus by the 1930s? Does it reflect a weakness in liberal social theory in general, a weakness exploited by Schmitt early on and which now has been noticed by contemporary left-leaning theorists who have been searching for viable alternatives to liberal theory which do not fall into the collectivist traps of Marxism? Indeed, the logic of the duel may lie at the heart of all our theorizing, leading us to the horrific spectacle of the mob even as we exalt rationality, communitarianism, pacifism, and the (hoped-for) emerging global humanity.

The difficulty in all this, since the time of the French Revolution of 1789, was the attempt to build a political system that was based not on bureaucratic or militaristic principles emphasizing punitiveness, but on the type of cozy, humanistic principles of solidarity and civility modeled on the family and the community (Gouldner 1979a: 199–202). This, again, was and is the project of civil society. This goal, of dealing with people on the most general, cosmopolitan terms possible—that is, the philosophy and practice of global human rights—is difficult to the extent that all actions must by necessity be conducted in some local jurisdiction possibly shot through with traditional cultures and practices, developed and sedimented over a long period of time, which are inimical to ideals of universality and cosmopolitanism. Even Gouldner's two cosmopolitan role types—the outsider and the empire builder—provide no way forward toward the construction of the good and enlightened society through the application of a universalism claiming to maximize humanistic principles of respect, dignity, and recognition untrammeled by localistic influences. Likewise, neither Schmitt's decisionism nor Tarde's imitation are robust enough analytical constructs to escape the gravitational pull of localism.

In the face of this failure to reach the cosmopolitan ideal, the next best thing is to ensure that the local is livable and meets some minimal standards of decency. Always the optimist even in the face of how the metropolis is laced with thick strands of racism, inequality, and violence, Elijah Anderson (2011) still believes that there are oases of cosmopolitanism even in the desert of local urban cityscapes. His "cosmopolitan canopy" consists of the safe spaces where those otherwise relegated to the margins of society—persons of color, homosexuals, immigrants, and others labeled as deviant in some way or another—can participate in social life relatively secure in the belief that they will be treated as fellow human beings. Such safe public spaces—parks, malls, museums, ethnic villages, and town squares—promote diversity and get us close to the cosmopolitan ideal which the cynical localism of a Schmitt or Tarde sees as chimera.

Even with its exalting of rationality, Kantian liberalism produces only a weak and enfeebled cosmopolitanism. This turn of events is congenial to radical social thinkers whose self-assurance is emboldened that historical materialism was the key to the achievement of the good and just society all along. But devout faith in the rightness and inevitability of this theory—or any theory for that matter, as Gouldner warned—can become a pernicious and destructive pursuit. This problem will be explored further in the final chapter.

CHAPTER 9

Mao and the Communist Horizon

Mao and Romantic Millenarianism

In this last chapter I return to issues of communism and new attempts by authors, especially since Gouldner's death, to argue for the continuing resilience of communism even in the face of its world collapse beginning in 1989. I will make the argument that radical intellectuals who sympathized with Mao even as the Cultural Revolution turned unimaginably violent all have blood on their hands, including Gouldner. Gouldner (1977) did indeed refer to Stalinism as a regime of terror, yet acquiesced in the face of the equally bloody and horrific slaughter that took place under Mao in China. In comparing Mao to Stalin, Gouldner (1977: 38) stated "In place of the Stalinist axe, the Maoist carefully slit the vein, letting it bleed for a guarded interval," and that "...Maoism never really succumbed to the extremes of Stalinism." And even with all their vaunted rationality and their culture of critical discourse, Gouldner (1975b: 34) did admit that "...intellectuals can kill; indeed, no little part of modern 'terrorism' is done by middle class intellectuals." By the time of his launching of the Great Leap Forward in 1958, Mao's hunger for domination had grown to gargantuan proportions. Not satisfied merely with the control of China, Mao told his provincial chiefs at a meeting, "In the future we will set up the Earth Control Committee, and make a uniform plan for the Earth" (quoted in Chang and Halliday 2006: 418).

Mao went far beyond merely vein letting during the Great Leap and the Cultural Revolution. State terror under Mao expanded into some of the most brutal and cruel forms imaginable. Mao's need for dominance and command presence meant that anyone showing the slightest hint of disloyalty to the program was to be executed. But mere execution was often not good enough. In 1968 those identified as "class enemies" in Binyang County and Wuxuan were savaged, with some of Mao's officials even resorting to cannibalism. These started as public "denunciation rallies," and after being slaughtered choice body parts—hearts, livers, and genitals—were cut off and eaten before the victims died. Actually the functionaries took time to first cook the body parts in what were known as "human flesh banquets." The justifications for such human slaughter were typified by one person who had carried out a particularly brutal attack against a young peasant boy, explaining that "Didn't Chairman Mao say: It's either we kill them, or they kill us?

You die and I live, this is class struggle!" (quoted in Chang and Halliday 2006: 534). Mao, in fact, is the greatest serial murderer in the history of the world. It has been estimated that 45,000,000 human beings were killed at the hands of Mao, more than the combined mass murders of Hitler and Stalin (Dikötter 2010).

Why did Mao engage in such atrocities, and why do many on the political left sit idly by while rarely denouncing, much less acknowledging, the brutality? It may be the case that Mao was seeking to avoid the death of the revolution through the avoidance of his own death by way of exterminating all those who may have harbored ill will against him or his communist revolution. In other words, the death of the revolution was a kind of millenarianism which, if it were to happen, would signal the death of the world not only the end of Mao's scheme (Lifton 1970). What was being sought was permanent revolution, and one ongoing project folded into Maoism was the overcoming of natural limitations including those of the cycle of life and death. There was an attempt at rebirth, and the agents of that rebirth were the Red Guard, some of whom were as young as thirteen or fourteen years of age (Gouldner and Horowitz 1966). Its launch in 1966 was something akin to the *Triumph of the Will*, the film depicting Hitler at Nuremberg (Lifton 1970: 147). Choosing young students to man the Red Guard is consistent with the idea that death could be defied—or at least staved off—through the use of vibrant youth who could see the revolution through to the end (Gouldner and Horowitz 1966). There is a purification of sorts in experiencing death on behalf of a perceived just cause (Lifton 1970: 152).

Mao's attempt at transcending worldly impediments threatening to derail the revolution meant that, in his most lustful moments near the end, the world's flesh became his flesh, thus marking the transition from "great leader" to despot. It is a type of misguided romantic millenarianism in which Mao the ruler confronts the powers of heaven and earth seeking to defeat all who stand in his way for purposes of rewriting history. Lifton (1970) goes on to suggest that the increasingly enfeebled Mao, beset by sickness and old age, is attempting to stave off the natural loss of potency by transmitting power and force across the generations through the work of all those who understand the goodness and necessity of the revolution. Even so, Lifton continues to romanticize Mao as a "tragic" figure who was indeed a great leader but who gave in to "survival paranoia" and who, dissatisfied with his accomplishments and recognizing his own impending death, sought to transcend worldly limitations to his power and potency by lapsing—ironically enough—into horrific displays of terror and human carnage.

Keeping Communism Going: Public Sociology

Radical intellectuals, especially those of the Marxist persuasion, have been on the run in the face of some of the horrors travelling under the banner of socialism or communism, but also because of the worldwide retreat from communism beginning in the late 1980s. There have been various attempts since the tearing down of the Berlin Wall in 1989 to erect a new, sturdier foundation for historical materialism. But this is not simply the revisionism of a Bernstein or a Mills or even a Lipset, but a complete rebuilding and remodeling guarding against some of the internal contradictions of Marxism, and even attempting to work through the paradox of the Two Marxisms, namely, Scientific and Critical Marxism (Gouldner 1980a; Hamilton 2000). According to apologists, there was a long, historical chain of events from Marx's original development of the method of dialectical materialism to an interpretation of that method in the hands of Engels after Marx's death, and on through to reworkings of communism for political purposes by Lenin, Stalin, Castro, Mao, and others (Grier 1978; Paolucci 2004). Gouldner was prescient in articulating the collapse of world communism a decade before it came to pass. As discussed in Chapter 4, since the time of Hegel, the self-understanding of a community, those symbolic or real attributes of persons that coalesce into systems of solidarity, may become a source of instability and strife in the move from homogeneity to heterogeneity, or from mechanical to organic solidarity (Decker 2012). The development of the early ethnic nation is described by Giddings (1899: 271):

> When patronymic tribes confederate and form the ethnic nation, the agnatic principle and ancestor worship, combined with political and military conditions, confer great authority upon the chief of the confederation. He becomes a military leader, a religious leader or priest, and a supreme judge, all in one. The chief, in a word, becomes a king.

Eventually, over the course of history, the totalitarian state must deal with the disenchantment of a growing mass of former outsiders who came to the homogeneous ethnic nation either through conquest or through the development of a more open and civil state, as for example in the opening up of borders to accommodate the arrival of new immigrants. In the year of his death, in 1980, Gouldner (1980a: 388) noted the following: "As one observes the Russians glumly counting their growing Moslem population, or seized with anger against the Chinese and scanning for a theoretical basis for *détente* with the West, it sometimes seems as if they too may be drawn into this nightmare Marxism."

Recent proponents aiming to reinvigorate public sociology have unabashedly stated, without any hint of irony, that the model for this kind of work is Marxism. The leader of this latest push for public sociology is Michael Burawoy, who attained the presidency of the American Sociological Association in 2004. He took the opportunity to push for a newly emboldened effort to make sociology more pertinent to general publics, and for the last decade he has been preoccupied with seeing this project to fruition. In his 2004 Presidential Address (published in 2005), Burawoy (2005a) presented eleven theses about what he perceives as a new era of public sociology. An opening for public sociology has occurred albeit with cautionary tales as summarized below:

- The fact that over the last 50 years sociology has moved more to the left while the world has moved to the right;
- The existence of multiple publics which can accommodate at least four types of sociology;
- Four basic types of sociology are public sociology, policy sociology, professional sociology, and critical sociology;
- These four types are generated by asking "Knowledge for whom?" and "Knowledge for what?"
- A necessary distinction must be made between sociology as a collective endeavor and the career trajectories of individual sociologists;
- Being overresponsive to different publics can be debilitating and even threatening to the survival of sociology as a collective endeavor;
- Scientific disciplines are fields of power which produce asymmetries between experts and general publics; under this scenario instrumental knowledge tends to prevail over reflexive knowledge;
- Professional sociology with its emphasis on research grants is the model of Big Science within the discipline, and as such tends to overshadow other types of sociology;
- American sociology has dominated other national sociologies oftentimes to their detriment; the ethos of public sociology will help rethink and ameliorate this imbalance;
- The social sciences utilize both reflexive and instrumental knowledge, and this distinguishes them from both the humanities and the natural sciences;
- Sociologists are partisans (a play on Gouldner), and their standpoint is civil society while defending the social in all its vagaries and dimensions (Burawoy 2005a).

In a footnote Burawoy links Gouldner and Bourdieu through the concept of partisanship. Burawoy used a quote from Bourdieu about ethnosociologists as organic intellectuals who can use their culture of critical discourse (a kind of universalism) to guide them in their dealings with any particularities encountered in the field. This is the organic intellectual of either Gramsci or Sartre (or both), so the infrastructure of the entire public sociology enterprise is Marxist. Indeed, critical sociology is the conscience of public sociology according to Burawoy (2005a: 10). But this linking is odd and strained, for Gouldner was railing against the sociologist as partisan of the underdog who, in so doing, is attempting to position professional sociology as the handmaiden of the welfare/warfare state. Bourdieu's purer Marxism would not be as critical of the welfare state as was Gouldner, and he (Bourdieu, in sympathy with Burawoy) would also be less apt to link the welfare state to the warfare state. Gouldner was always wary of partisans and moral entrepreneurs in general, for partisans tend to join together in solidarity such that passions prevail over reason and the intellect. Such solidarity may develop into a vanguard where theory becomes unquestioned doctrine, which in turn can justify terror and other forms of inhumane treatment toward those who disagree with the program. It lends itself to friend-enemy distinctions of the kind Schmitt theorized.

It is interesting to note that Burawoy's (2005a) concept concerning the sociological division of labor is very close to the spirit of Parsons. The fourfold table is produced by asking What type of knowledge? (instrumental or reflexive) and Who is the audience? (academic or extra-academic, or in Parsonian terms, internal or external). According to Parsons (1968), in the system of science, the subsystem of the social sciences lines up functionally in the following manner:

- The A function is fulfilled by economics;
- The G function is fulfilled by political science;
- The I function is fulfilled by sociology;
- The L function is fulfilled by anthropology.

For Parsons (1968: 322), sociology is primarily concerned with "one primary functional aspect of social systems, namely the understanding of the structures and processes especially concerned with the *integration* of social systems." If we look at sociology as the integrative subsystem within the social sciences, we can examine this subsystem one further level down, that is, at the level of the functional elements of sociology. Burawoy's concept of the division of labor of sociology can be plugged into Parsons' analytical framework. This subsystem is depicted in Figure 9.1.

Instrumental knowledge, which is internal to sociology, is professional sociology (L), and that which is external to sociology is policy sociology (A). Reflexive or expressive (or consummatory) knowledge that is internal to sociology is

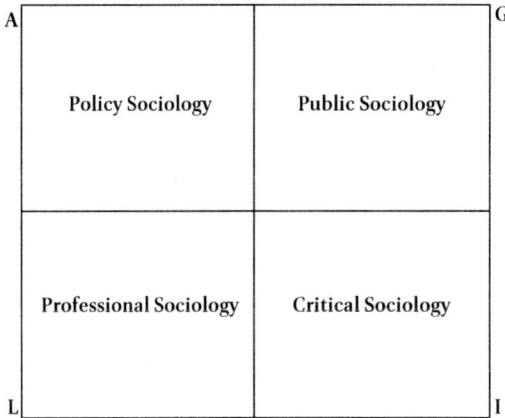

FIGURE 9.1 *The functions of the sociology subsystem (Burawoy's categories)*

critical sociology (I), and that which is external to sociology is public sociology (G). For Burawoy, public sociology can only show up as a public project which contains within its infrastructure a critical sociology that is at heart Marxist (that is, the evaluative paradigm). Yet, the form this takes—Parsonian functionalism—is a nightmare for Burawoy's vision for public sociology because of the deep dissonance between structure and substance contained within it. Although Gouldner saw some of the contradictions of such projects as Burawoyian public sociology from miles away and years apart, later observers have made similar observations concerning the question "Will the center hold?"

For example, Brady (2004) is generally sympathetic to Burawoy's brand of public sociology but lists a few reasons why it may fail. These five reasons are:

- Burawoy's project is theoretically top heavy insofar as concrete proposals for actually achieving public sociology are vague and imprecise;
- There are no incentives listed for doing public sociology, that is, for sociologists to explicitly aim to gear their work toward a more general audience;
- Civil society is not problematized (more on this below);
- The state is demonized, similar to Habermas's conception that systems imperatives permeate and colonize lifeworld activities;
- There is no assessment component insofar as we have no way of knowing what a successful public sociology would look like.

With regard to point three, Burawoy is explicit that public sociology should be aimed not at states or markets—plenty of sociologists study these social arenas—but at the idealistic public sphere of persons communicating and organizing together who along the way form solidary relations. This would not be reflective of, say, public opinion polling, for that endeavor is more closely aligned with dreaded positivism which takes the state for granted as an arena for persons doing things together whether public or private (Mayhew 1997). But also because of its penchant for crunching numbers, such polling thingifies persons and everyday life, thereby doing damage to subjectivity and even fostering false consciousness (a point made repeatedly by Frankfurt School theorists). Yet, Burawoy does not provide much evidence that such a state of affairs exists as an empirical reality. Interestingly enough, though, a good number of Marxists have theorized that the strong capitalist state employs power in such a way that the state and its circulation of elites—politicians, financiers, the military, and so forth—act as a hegemonic force which crushes, cripples, and keeps at bay civil society and all the "off the books" activity that goes on there. So Brady's critique is not quite accurate, for Burawoy is positing the existence of an impaired civil society which his public sociology is equipped to repair and rescue. Garnering a bigger audience beyond the cozy confines of the Ivory Tower for purposes of enhancing one's status as a public intellectual would NOT be a proper motivation for public sociology—and on this point Gouldner would agree—for that would be merely a capitulation to the gravitational pull of capitalism. Yet on the other hand, Gouldner would reject the heroic struggle Burawoy and others of his ilk would claim for themselves in their just cause to right the wrongs of capitalism in the streets and on the ground, at the point of the life experiences of myriad persons suffering various fates not of their own making. Gouldner also would view much more critically than the typical Marxist the easy alignment Burawoy (2005b) makes between professional sociology and the "unconstrained market expansion" of capitalism. In all the years I have been reading and studying Gouldner, I have never had the sense that he was hostile to capitalism, which would of course position him as an outsider to the evaluative paradigm.

Another critique of Burawoy's vision for public sociology worth mentioning is that of McLaughlin et al. (2005). The authors make the point that some of the stridency in Burawoy's position—for example, equating pure or positivist sociology to crass consumerism or implying that quantification is dehumanizing (therefore favoring qualitative over quantitative methods)—has led to a pushback from traditional or conventional sociologists who favor positivistic methods and who fear that public sociology is merely radical sociology in disguise. Hence, there have been movements to "save" sociology from both directions: Either to save sociology from detachment, irrelevance, and naiveté (the public sociology argument), or to save it from lapsing into the crudest form of ideological radicalism which, if allowed to take its course, would damage the professional standing of sociology beyond repair (the defenders of conventional disciplinary sociology).¹ This is doubly troubling for the latter because the architect of this public sociology, Michael Burawoy, received the stamp of approval from the discipline at large as he was named president of the American Sociological Association (ASA) for 2004. This is also ironic insofar as the ASA is the largest organization of professional sociologists in the world. It is the organization for the myriad persons making a living doing sociology, including of course Burawoy. The ascendancy by Burawoy or anybody else for that matter to president is symbolic to the extent that it indicates that there is a critical mass of sociologists who share Burawoy's vision for sociology and how professional sociologists should be spending their time, as Gouldner (1968) explained with regard to the case of the rise of underdog sociology under Howard Becker's tenure as president of the Society for the Study of Social Problems.

McLaughlin et al. (2005) further point out that Burawoy's understanding of reflexivity is far too restrictive, as it implies that reflexivity is associated with political activism, but not just any political activism. The true public sociologist would seek to redistribute wealth and income to repair the damage done to subjectivities and to level the playing field so as to eliminate pernicious forms of inequality and oppression wrought by capitalism. In a word, the public sociologist should show sympathies to the goals of communism and be motivated by this bundle of reflexive values rather than the instrumental values of conventional sociology whether described as market, pure, positivist, policy, or professional. This would also, of course, help to solve the intractable dilemma of the unity of theory and praxis. But could, say, a Tea Party activist be a public sociologist under Burawoy's scheme?² No. How about a proponent of the Occupy movement? Absolutely!

---

1   Actually, realists who are also radicals would admit that the professional status of sociology has always been tenuous, so why keep up the ruse? Instead, embrace the fact that sociology is a value-laden project which is political at heart. Indeed, Jonathan Dean (2014) goes so far as to suggest that the claim of apoliticality is a myth. But throwing up one's hands and claiming "everything is political" denies the multidimensional understanding of a complex social reality. The rub here is that traditional sociologists would favor a multiple-factor approach which, with proper statistical analysis, can disentangle the relative loading of factors contributing to the production of any particular sociological phenomena. Radical sociologists would not favor any of this, but instead would push for central concepts which, it is claimed, ramify through everything of importance in the study of society. Within the evaluative paradigm, for example, favored concepts are labor, gender, sexual orientation, race, and the political.
2   Indeed, it is difficult to imagine a Tea Party public sociologist, just as Gouldner (1970a: 160) once famously averred that the mind boggles at the thought of a "Parsonsian hippie."

Occupy This

Since 2009 two major political movements emerged in the United States, a conservative Tea Party and a progressive Occupy movement. Suffice to say that, given sociology's far left orientation—and indeed, the professoriate's more generally (Gross and Fosse 2012)—scholarly coverage of the Occupy movement has been far more favorable than Tea Party coverage. Indeed, often the Tea Party has been the whipping boy for the righteous indignation of the Left over "ridiculous" claims from traditional media that it was a spontaneous, grassroots, populist movement. Scholarly denunciation of the Tea Party is nearly universal, with the following points most often emphasized:

- Rather than a grassroots, populist movement, the Tea Party is a top-down, well-funded operation of the Koch Brothers and other conservatives with deep pockets;
- Tea Party members are overwhelmingly white, middle-class, nationalistic, sexist, homophobic, and racist (especially with regard to a visceral hatred of Barack Obama, America's first Black President);
- Tea Party members hold an unfavorable, even hostile view of government, and their overweening moralism, elitism, and religiosity are tinged with a Manicheanism that sees the world as divided into "us" (the good) versus "them" (evil outsiders).[3]

A few more nuanced treatments of the Tea Party can be found in the literature, such as the study by McVeigh et al. (2014) that analyzed Tea Party membership by county. Contrary to the standard Left view of Tea Party members as uneducated buffoons protecting against threats to white privilege, McVeigh et al. (2014) found that individuals with a bachelor's degree were more likely to support the Tea Party than persons with no college education, and that the relationship was strongest in areas with high levels of educational segregation. But somewhat in accordance with the negative characterizations of the Tea Party described above, most members were reacting to the economic downturn and to fears that under President Obama, there would be new intrusions into the operation of the free market that would unduly penalize productive members of society. This had to mean that some level of consensus existed among the Right that President Obama is a typical liberal or progressive—or more to the point, a socialist or communist—who believes in an expanded role for

---

3   These three points are derived from Langman (2012), Lundskow (2012), Street and DiMaggio (2012), and Zeskind (2012).

government in the lives of Americans, especially during perceived times of crisis such as the banking crisis and growing concerns over the runaway costs of healthcare and the deleterious impact of growing legions of the uninsured. Hence, conservative political activism embodied in the Tea Party was motivated by similar reasons that animate many other social movements: A concern over distributive justice. Simply, many who joined the Tea Party believed that pending economic policies of the Obama administration in the face of financial crisis were going to hurt their economic interests.

Although they spend more time on the Arab Spring and Occupy, Myers and Estep (2012) nevertheless avoid the kind of invidious distinction many other observers make about the Tea Party as misguided or illegitimate versus the revered Occupy movement. Indeed, according to the authors, the springing up of various protest movements, some of which reach a critical mass and garner the attention of the media and general public over a period of time, is a good sign. That is, it is a sign of a healthy democracy where persons of like mind can band together over shared concerns whether economic, cultural, historical, or in seeking recognition over identity or other group characteristics. From this perspective, then, the Tea Party, the Arab Spring, and the Occupy Movement are understandable within the broad perspective of traditional social movement scholarship, although new developments in technology (such as the Internet and social media) facilitate speedier contact between actors sharing similar concerns (Myers and Estep 2012).

As I mentioned previously, the real darling of social movement scholars is the Occupy movement. Unlike the Tea Party which arose over concerns with government spending that was seen as favoring the "takers" over the "makers," epitomized by CNBC financial reporter Rick Santelli's rant on the trading floor of Wall Street in 2009 over having to bail out homeowners over their bad loans, Occupy emerged several years later as a reaction to bailing out banks that were "too big to fail" (Maxwell and Parent 2012). The Tea Party's animus was not Wall Street but rather government policies aimed at spreading the burden around—this conceptualized as a form of illegitimate wealth redistribution—to those who made bad decisions by taking out home loans that they could not repay or should never have taken out in the first place. However, the Occupy Movement's main animus was Wall Street and fat cat investment brokers who, because of their unconstrained greed, caused a financial collapse which led to austerity measures on the part of government in an attempt to keep the entire financial system from shutting down.

Indeed, in Fall 2011 these austerity policies along with the bank bailouts motivated a group of protesters to assemble in downtown Manhattan. This rather spontaneous, grassroots gathering pitted the 99 percent of average

Americans against the 1 percent affluent class—the mega-rich, the capitalists, the investment bankers, and the crony capitalists within government—represented the beginnings of Occupy Wall Street (Piven 2014). Although starting as an occupation of Wall Street, the movement was flexible as it was able to connect the occupy tag to all manner of targets as segments of the movement saw fit. For example, over the next several years there was Occupy Student Debt, Occupy Sandy, Occupy Davis, Occupy Seattle, and Occupy Cleveland.[4]

Interestingly enough, so far not one scholarly article has noted that in 2012 five Occupy Cleveland members were conspiring to blow up the Ohio 82 Bridge that spans the Cuyahoga Valley National Park. Undercover FBI agents who delivered phony explosives to the group disrupted the plan. Four of the co-conspirators pleaded guilty rather than going to trial. The fifth, Joshua Stafford, stood trial on June 13, 2013 and was convicted on three counts: conspiracy to use a weapon of mass destruction, attempting to use a weapon of mass destruction, and maliciously attempting to destroy a bridge.[5] The silence on the part of the mainstream media over this incident is deafening. However, if a group of Tea Party members had been caught attempting to blow up a bridge or even something far less heinous, the media coverage would have been frenetic and wall-to-wall. It is ironic, for example, that George Lundskow (2012) referred to the "destructiveness" of the Tea Party, but it appears so far the only truly destructive activities or intentions have been on the part of Occupy members.

My intention here is not to take sides. Frankly, I could care less about the Tea Party, the Occupy movement, or the Arab Spring for that matter. But it is important to illustrate the silences and glosses engaged in by true believers—in this case, left academia's fawning over the Occupy movement—and how even violence may be tolerated in pursuit of utopian goals. Indeed, since police are defenders of the status quo, movements like Occupy may embolden its members to confront them and break the law if need be (Pickerill and Krinsky 2012).[6]

---

4 This is only a partial list. For fuller lists and discussions, visit the website at www.occupytogether.org.

5 This information is from the website http://impact.cleveland.com/metro/print.html?entry+/2013/06/federal_jury_convicts_would_be.html.

6 Indeed, breaking the law for a just cause is championed by both the Left and the Right for different reasons. Spiritual guides which are seen as trumping mere manmade law are more likely to motivate perpetrators on the Right, while Left actors may break laws that are interpreted as illegitimate power plays of the status quo who use law to stifle dissent or label deviants. This is seen, for example, with the infatuation of Edward Snowden by the Left for his blowing the lid off the NSA spying program known as Prism (Scheuerman 2014). The Left is more likely to view Snowden as a whistleblowing hero while the Right and persons in positions of authority are apt to condemn him as a traitor.

This also brings us full circle in terms of public sociology, for more recently Michael Burawoy (2014) has admitted that sociology is a "combat sport" (following Bourdieu), and that if the aims of public sociology are met with hostility—for example, Tea Baggers who believe President Obama is a Muslim, a communist, a homosexual, and not even a natural born citizen to boot!—there needs to be a proportionate response. In the case of Burawoy's public sociology, this project of emancipation for the downtrodden while avoiding the traps of coercion and violence in the pursuit of such goals is easier said than done. In a paper titled "What Is to Be Done?" Burawoy (2008) invokes Lenin's words and vanguard organizational framework in the same breath that he calls for the Kantian categorical imperative that persons must be treated as ends and never as means. But what happens when organizational attempts fail to wake persons from their slumber of false consciousness and they are simply apathetic or even hostile in the wake of these public sociologists taking them by the hand and leading them to the Promised Land? True liberalism is hands off to the extent of leaving people to their own devices regardless of the best advice given, while socialism/communism becomes more aggressive in the wake of resistance or reticence. The bottom line is that these two approaches are not easily reconciled. The horrors of Mao, Lenin, Stalin, Castro, and other communist dictators do not much trouble the true believers. This is all extremely nightmarish stuff, the warnings Gouldner tried to give to the Left years ago but which pretty much fell on deaf ears.

Even further to the point, the nightmare might be that terrorism is part and parcel to the operational logic of this sort of political activism. For example, Payne (2011) has illustrated the strong parallels between the insurgency strategies of Che Guevara—another darling of the Left—and the terrorism of Al Qaeda. Che's guerilla warfare was a focoist strategy which emphasized provocation and indoctrination, and instead of taking on a more powerful military directly, Che recommended organized but decentralized violence at the margins of enemy control, and whenever possible slipping behind enemy lines into the urban core to pull off spectacular displays of terror such as suicide bombing missions. Here, the focoist strategy of Che easily turns communist revolution into jihadist terror campaigns. They appear to be cut from the same cloth.

This is the much bigger problem of violence in the pursuit of just goals (Malešević 2009). In his preface to Frantz Fanon's (1968) *Wretched of the Earth*, Sartre (1968) sided with the rebels against the colonial occupiers and administrators, agreeing that a bloody conflict fought to the finish was the only way to eradicate the evil taking up residence there. But do revolutions always have to be violent? Stated differently, is violence built into revolution? Following Arendt, Heller, and Fehér (see below), it may indeed be the case that *political* revolutions assume violence, but many others do not (Auer 2009). Think of scientific or technological or cultural revolutions (although in the hands of Mao even the latter was bloody). Gouldner did not side with Sartre and others who view violence as the *sine qua non* of revolution, political or otherwise. For example, Gouldner's early forays into political activism did not involve violence. He did, however, through much of his life engage in interpersonal bellicosity, which sometimes became physical (as in the famous encounter with Humphreys).

Jodi Dean's Communist Horizon

The Occupy movement is overwhelmingly composed of Millennials, who are Americans born between 1980 and 2000. Another social movement composed of young persons is the Dreamers, who are undocumented immigrants seeking a path to citizenship. Ruth Milkman (2014: 55) says of these two groups "Occupiers and Dreamers are sharply critical of the political establishment, Obama included, and of the explosive growth in inequality since the 1970s." Although there is some truth to this, it should be noted that so far there has been no Occupy the White House, and no taking the president to task for lining the pockets of Wall Street fat cats and investment bankers who have made a killing on the stock market. The Occupy movement will not be taken seriously until its members occupy the White House, and do it while President Obama is still in office. It would be a monumental copout to wait for the Republicans to take the White House to do so, if, that is, the Occupy movement is even around by then (in 2016, 2020, or perhaps 2024?).

The anguish of the far Left is that of a sincere effort to ensure that no one falls through the cracks, that everyone is given a fair shake and that no life is considered unworthy of our attention and compassion. In his 2012 Presidential Address before those assembled at the conference of the American Sociological Association, Erik Olin Wright (2013) sought to provide empirical guidelines for achieving real utopias beyond the capitalist model. He stills believes that compassion for the downtrodden, the dispossessed, and the oppressed can be turned into truly liberative agendas which do not lapse into regimes of terror as has happened in many attempts to institute socialism or communism worldwide. He calls for "transformations"—symbiotic, ruptural, and interstitial—that are aligned respectively with movements of social democracy, revolutionary socialism or communism, and anarchism. Throughout all this, though, there is always the assumption that capitalism is a suboptimal economic system that on balance produces more human suffering than happiness.

Defenders of that which lies beyond capitalism—socialism or communism stripped of the human atrocities that often accompany them—can rationalize the failures of past attempts to forge the good society through collectivism as due either to something faulty within the original Marxist theory, or to the failure to implement it properly. One of the most giddily optimistic defenders of the project of transforming capitalism into a real socialist utopia is Jodi Dean, who published a book in 2012 titled *The Communist Horizon*. The cover depicts the rising red sun (of Mao, or perhaps Soviet communism) with its brilliant rays of light stretching into infinity, the symbol of the continuous revolution. Dean is unapologetic about the goodness of communism, and the fact that it is already here it terms of its being the only viable option to capitalism. She borrowed the phrase "communist horizon" from Bruno Bosteels (2011). Besides Bosteels, Dean is quite enamored of Badiou, Negri, Žižek, and Lukács, all well-known radical intellectuals who any self-respecting communist should be reading.

Dean is convinced that capitalism—or neoliberalism to which it is it now often referred especially as it is wedded to globalization (Habermas 2008: 185–188)—is declining and close to collapse. Communism is depicted as waiting in the wings, ready to be implemented when the time and conditions are right. She sounds really convincing—or at least sincere—when she writes "The communist horizon appears closer than it has in a long time" (Dean 2012: 21). Dean treats communism as a tag for six distinct features of the current age, and dedicates a chapter to each.[7] In good Hegelian fashion, what must be built is scrabbled together from the remnants of the past, both in terms of the symbolic (memories of what worked and what didn't) and the real or physical (the actual organizational tools which are currently available or which are emerging or can be fashioned to fit the particular configuration that communism will take when it arrives). The horizon is distant, but the outlines of what are expected can be ferreted out through the mists and atmospheric distortions. The red sun is rising. Mao would be pleased. The continuing revolution is nigh.

---

7 These six tags are: (1) An image of Soviet communism, successful early and later defeated; (2) An increasingly powerful force in the form of new concerns over communism (such as conservatives thinking Obama is a communist); (3) The sovereignty of the people, where collectivism of the everyday life has always flourished and lies about individualism and privacy are slowly being unmasked; (4) The commons, or the unmasking of communicative capitalism; (5) True desires of egalitarianism and universalism are felt and understood among a critical mass of the body politic; and (6) The organized vanguard party in the form of the Occupy movement, its earlier anarchistic tendencies sublimated and repaired. Indeed, the anarchistic elements of Occupy are one of the main things the movement must resolve in order for it to effect change within the political system (Gitlin 2013).

And by Chapter 6, guess what Dean identifies as the most suitable organizational form for reenergizing the vanguard party when—yes when, not if—that long lost friend, communism, makes its triumphant return? Why the Occupy movement of course! There is such missionary zeal here. It is the same sort of happy sobriety, brimming with confidence and awe that true believers of the Christian faith would no doubt experience with the second coming of Christ.

A Farewell to Marxism

Mao's emphasis on the importance of culture in establishing the permanent revolution was especially influential within the ranks of the New Left in the 1960s and 1970s, and still informs political beliefs of the contemporary Left. Reasons for Mao's continuing popularity among the Left, even in the face of the brutality and terror of his regime, include the following: his emphasis on the questioning of authority; the practice of self-criticism, especially insofar as hidden privileges of race, sex, and class are concerned; the emphasis on therapy, feelings, and self-help; the mobilization of youth into political action (i.e., "the right to rebel"); and consciousness raising as a form of social solidarity (Ross 2005). Mao saw all of these as important precursors to appropriate actions, hence this also held out hope for the unification of theory and practice.

The Left may indeed not be troubled at all by the terrors begotten by socialist and communist projects because rage is acceptable if directed toward a just cause (Sokoloff 2014). This is especially the case when harm is being perpetrated by the system or by the powerful against the relatively powerless, and rage must be made public and focused upon the overturning of the system of privilege that has led to the shabby treatment (or worse) of portions of the population that are being targeted. It is a project of world saving. It is a project of egalitarianism. It is agonistic, representing the contest or struggle.

What I learned from Gouldner the radical sociologist is that missionary zeal is dogmatic and can lead to more harm than good. So all along, Gouldner's critique of all systems of thought—including Marxism and other strains of evaluative theory—was always useful because of how it exposed the nightmare versions of the theories embedded in their infrastructures. But since no person can truly be their own doctor—thereby rejecting self-help and the concept of "physician heal thyself"—Gouldner also admitted that reflexivity has its limits, and may evolve into the "bad infinity" of Hegel. Gouldner's version of reflexive sociology illustrated the contradictions of the entire project, insofar as he lapsed into reverential treatment of the mass murderer Mao. In this scenario, all persons are absolved of the bad things that emerge from their ideas because of the negations—handily hidden in the infrastructure even as they claim keen insights into the social world because of their mastery of reflective practice—which are always part of this kind of work.

For over twenty years now I have been confronting Gouldner, always admiring him for the power and clarity of his thought, but more recently wondering why he directed so much of his energies toward Marxism. I wondered also, for example, why Gouldner's critique of the lack of reflexivity of Marxism did not go into a full denunciation of the nightmarish practices that emerged in a number of real-world attempts to implement the theory (especially in the cases of Stalin and Mao). Ferenc Fehér's (1978) work illustrates the path not taken by Gouldner, even as he (Fehér) cites Gouldner approvingly for noticing that intellectuals can kill and pursue large-scale campaigns of terror. Lukács informed the work of both Fehér and Gouldner, but Fehér linked the critique of fascism with communism and found them to be parallel projects of totalitarianism which seek to crush resistance and opposition and, in so doing, care little about the human suffering they cause.[8] Fehér describes both (communism and fascism) as anti-capitalist formations that emerge as a result of political-military expansion after successful revolutions. In the process of this development, the safeguard which otherwise keeps "good" socialism from going bad, namely self-critique, is extirpated leading instead to a "dictatorship of needs." The loss of self-critique—Gouldner would call it reflexivity—allowed the Jacobin elements already present within radical intellectualism to move unfettered toward an iron-fisted dictatorship which would ensure that the needs of the people be met (at all costs, including their murder if they do not capitulate to the regime). This is bureaucratization run amok, and the Gulag is basically the same as the work or training group. This is not merely a bureaucracy, it is a cadre of planning elites who know what's best for the citizens, and most importantly, understand their *needs*. Eventually, under the brutalism of the project of the dictatorship over needs, put into full force via Marx's theory of the universalization of wage labor, there is a requirement of "complete submission of workers in all aspects of everyday life to the

---

8 Fehér, born in Budapest in 1933, experienced the rise of fascism as a lived conviction, as his father was killed in the concentration camp in Auschwitz. He was married to Agnes Heller and was a member of the Budapest School of György Lukács (Köves 1995). For Fehér, radical politics were always dangerous as they tended toward totalitarianism whether fascism or communism. Gouldner, being also a Lukácsian at heart, agreed with Fehér but did not take the critique as far as Fehér did, very likely because he was born earlier than Fehér and did not personally experience the murder of a family member at the hands of government agents, unlike Fehér who did.

commands of the planning center" (Fehér 1978: 34). Totalizing hyper-rationality turns into irrationality and much worse.

Instead of a happy-go-lucky, idealistic Marxism where oppression is defeated and emancipation prevails—such a wonderful story that tugs at the heartstrings!—sociology students ought to be reading more of Heller and Fehér, perhaps even Schmitt and Arendt. Gouldner is fine too, but he pulled up short where Fehér went the distance in bringing the bad news about communism and its horrors. In bringing an end to this discussion, I have only recently realized that my own need for Gouldner was to maintain my increasingly tenuous connection to Marxism within sociology. In other words, I used Gouldner to maintain some sort of semblance or connection to the world of Marxism and radical sociology. But being this close to Gouldner, I have come to develop a distaste for everything connected with Marxism. The negatives simply outweigh the positivists. Although Gouldner is still worth reading—indeed, he is the key part of whatever critical elements are left in my sociology—with this book I am saying farewell and good riddance to Marxism. You really do not need Marxism at all to appreciate Gouldner's attempt to create a "historically rooted, post traditional normative discourse" (Antonio 2005: 100), which, in no small measure, set out to overcome the provincialism of American sociology.

As a radical sociologist clinging to whatever vestiges of Marxism might still work, Gouldner was trying to figure out a way of retaining the emancipatory potential of critical theory without escaping into the aesthetics of Adorno or the totalizing narrative of Lukács (Piccone 1977).[9] Both in their own way signaled the loss of faith of the critical project, and although Gouldner had also sensed the approaching storm and gave warnings, he hung around somehow believing that Mao or radical intellectuals in general—whom ironically Mao attempted to eradicate—could still deliver the good life in the absence of the proletariat which collectively could not be counted on, especially under the enfeebling conditions of neoliberalism.

This farewell to Marxism won't be a clean break, however. I will still teach Marxism as required whenever I teach sociological theory because I must maintain fidelity to the myth that Marx is a sociologist (but more importantly, because it is a goal explicitly stated in the learning objectives for this course and I don't want to lose my job). Okay, I understand how the game is played. No problem. I'll bite my tongue and get through the material and move on.

---

9   I can read Lenin and agree with Lukács that he was indeed a "superb theorist" (Gouldner 1985: 16). But I also know the kind of destructive, anti-emancipatory practices that emerged from that theory. There is no communist pot of gold at the end of the capitalist rainbow (Piccone 1977).

Gouldner's legacy is assured whether or not Marx remains relevant to contemporary sociology. It would be my hope that when sociologists or other scholars make sojourns back to Gouldner they take his warnings seriously about how dogma and vanguards kill theory and reason, and how the pursuit of the good and the just can turn deadly. More than anything in this so-called postmodern moment, we need reason, and lots of it. It is in the nature of academia that most of us toil in relative obscurity trying to do our best work and somehow hoping to make a difference through our writings and our teachings. My farewell to Marxism is a decision that has been made based upon my own hedonic calculus (and hence Bentham prevails over Marx). So be it. Choices have to be made. You live with them and move on. But there is quite a lot to be said for peace of mind. It really is a beautiful thing.

References

Adler, Alfred. 2009. *Study of Organ Inferiority*. New York: Pranava Books.
Adorno, Theodor W. 1973. *Negative Dialectics*. Translated by E.B. Ashton. New York: Seabury Press.
Adorno, Theodor W. 1978. "Resignation." *Telos* 35:165–168.
Agger, Ben. 1989. *Socio(onto)logy: A Disciplinary Reading*. Urbana: University of Illinois Press.
Agger, Ben. 1992. "The Micro-Macro Nonproblem." In *The Discourse of Domination: From the Frankfurt School to Postmodernism*, 56–72. Evanston, IL: Northwestern University Press.
Agger, Ben. 2007. *Public Sociology: From Social Facts to Literary Acts*, 2nd ed. Lanham, MD: Rowman and Littlefield.
Ahn, Ilsup. 2009. "Decolonization of the Lifeworld by Reconstructing the System: A Critical Dialogue between Jürgen Habermas and Reinhold Niebuhr." *Studies in Christian Ethics* 22 (3):290–313.
Alexander, Jeffrey C. 1982. *Positivism, Presuppositions, and Current Controversies*, Vol. 1 of his *Theoretical Logic in Sociology*. Berkeley: University of California Press.
Alexander, Jeffrey C. 2006. *The Civil Sphere*. Oxford, UK: Oxford University Press.
Alexander, Michael Scott. 2010. "Introduction: The Soviet Romance and Its Demise." *American Jewish History* 96 (1): vii–viii.
Alexopoulos, Golfo. 2008. "Stalin and the Politics of Kinship: Practices of Collective Punishment, 1920s–1940s." *Comparative Studies in Society and History* 50 (1):91–117.
Anderson, Elijah. 2011. *The Cosmopolitan Canopy: Race and Civility in Everyday Life*. New York: Norton.
Antonio, Robert J. 2005. "For Social Theory: Alvin Gouldner's Last Project and Beyond." *Current Perspectives in Social Theory* 23:71–129.
Antonio, Robert J. 2011. "Absolutizing Particularity." In *A Journal of No Illusions: Telos, Paul Piccone, and the Americanization of Critical Theory*, edited by T.W. Luke and B. Agger, 23–46. New York: Telos Press.
Archer, Margaret S. 2007. *Making Our Way through the World*. Cambridge, UK: Cambridge University Press.
Auer, Stefan. 2009. "Violence and the End of Revolution after 1989." *Thesis Eleven* 97:6–25.
Avineri, Shlomo. 1981. *The Making of Modern Zionism: Intellectual Origins of the Jewish State*. New York: Basic Books.
Baehr, Peter R. 2002. *Founders, Classics, Canons: Modern Disputes over Sociology's Heritage*. New Brunswick, NJ: Transaction.

Baert, Patrick. 2011a. "Jean-Paul Sartre's Positioning in *Anti-Semite and Jew*." *Journal of Classical Sociology* 11 (4):378–397.
Baert, Patrick. 2011b. "The Power Struggle of French Intellectuals at the End of the Second World War: A Study in the Sociology of Ideas." *European Journal Social Theory* 14 (4):415–435.
Bagehot, Walter. 1872. *Physics and Politics*. London: Henry S. King.
Barnes, Harry E. 1919. "The Philosophy of the State in the Writings of Gabriel Tarde." *Philosophical Review* 28 (3):248–279.
Barry, Andrew and Nigel Thrift. 2007. "Gabriel Tarde: Imitation, Invention and Economy." *Economy and Society* 36 (4):509–525.
Baudrillard, Jean. 1981. *Simulacres et Simulation*. Paris: Galilée.
Baum, Rainer C. 1976. "On Societal Media Dynamics." In *Explorations in General Theory in Social Science: Essays in Honor of Talcott Parsons*, edited by J.J. Loubser, R.C. Baum, A. Effrat, and V.M. Lidz, 579–608. New York: Free Press.
Baumeister, Roy F. 1998. "The Self." In *Handbook of Social Psychology*, vol. 1, edited by D.T. Gilbert, S.T. Fiske, and G. Lindzey, 680–740. New York: McGraw-Hill.
Beck, Ulrich. 2012. "Redefining the Sociological Project: The Cosmopolitan Challenge." *Sociology* 46 (1):7–12.
Becker, Howard S. 1967. "Who's Side Are We On?" *Social Problems* 14:239–247.
Bell, Daniel. 1980. *The Winding Passage: Essays and Sociological Journeys*. New York: Harper.
Bentham, Jeremy. 1843. *The Works of Jeremy Bentham*, published under the superintendence of his executor, John Bowring. Edinburgh: W. Tait.
Berger, Peter L. and Thomas Luckmann. 1966. *The Social Construction of Reality*. New York: Anchor Doubleday.
Bernal, John D. 1939. *The Social Function of Science*. Cambridge, MA: MIT Press.
Bernstein, Carl. 1989. *Loyalties: A Son's Memoirs*. NY: Simon & Schuster.
Blackburn, Robin, ed. 1972. *Ideology and Social Science: Readings in Critical Social Theory*. London: Fontana.
Bohm, Robert M. 1987. "Comment on 'Traditional Contributions to Radical Criminology' by Groves and Sampson." *Journal of Research in Crime and Delinquency* 24 (4):324–331.
Borch, Christian. 2006. "The Exclusion of the Crowd: The Destiny of a Sociological Figure of the Irrational." *European Journal of Social Theory* 9 (1):83–102.
Borch, Christian. 2009. "Body to Body: On the Political Anatomy of Crowds." *Sociological Theory* 27 (3):271–290.
Bosteels, Bruno. 2011. *The Actuality of Communism*. London: Verso.
Bottomore, Tom. 1984. *The Frankfurt School*. Chichester, UK: Tavistock.
Bourdieu, Pierre. 1984. *Distinction: A Social Critique of the Judgment of Taste*. Translated by R. Nice. Cambridge, MA: Harvard University Press.

Bourdieu, Pierre. 1988. "Vive la Crise! For Heterodoxy in Social Science." *Theory and Society* 17:773–787.
Bourdieu, Pierre. 2004. *Science of Science and Reflexivity*. Translated by R. Nice. Chicago: University of Chicago Press.
Bourdieu, Pierre, Jean-Claude Chamboredon, and Jean-Claude Passeron. 1991. *The Craft of Sociology*. Translated by R. Nice. Berlin: Walter de Gruyter. [First edition published 1968.]
Bourdieu, Pierre and Jean-Claude Passeron. 1977. *Reproduction in Education, Society and Culture*. Translated by R. Nice. Beverly Hills: Sage.
Brady, David. 2004. "Why Public Sociology May Fail." *Social Forces* 82 (4):1629–1638.
Brayne, Sarah. 2014. "Surveillance and System Avoidance: Criminal Justice Contact and Institutional Attachment." *American Sociological Review* 79 (3):367–391.
Breines, Paul. 1990. *Tough Jews: Political Fantasies and the Moral Dilemma of American Jewry*. New York: Basic Books.
Brighenti, Andrea Mubi. 2010. "Tarde, Canetti, and Deleuze on Crowds and Packs." *Journal of Classical Sociology* 10 (4):291–314.
Brown, Carol. 1970. "A History and Analysis of Radical Activism in Sociology, 1967–1969, with Special Reference to the Sociology Liberation Movement, the Black Caucus, the Executive Council, the War in Vietnam and a Few Other Things." *Sociological Inquiry* 40:27–33.
Buhle, Paul. 1980. "Jews and American Communism: The Cultural Question." *Radical History Review* 23:9–33.
Burawoy, Michael. 2005a. "For Public Sociology." *American Sociological Review* 70 (1):4–28.
Burawoy, Michael. 2005b. "Third-Wave Sociology and the End of Pure Science." *American Sociologist* 36 (3–4):152–165.
Burawoy, Michael. 2008. "What Is to Be Done? Theses on the Degradation of Social Existence in a Globalizing World." *Current Sociology* 56 (3):351–359.
Burawoy, Michael. 2014. "Introduction: Sociology as a Combat Sport." *Current Sociology Monograph* 62 (2):140–155.
Cahnman, Werner J. 1976. "Vico and Historical Sociology." *Social Research* 43 (4):826–836.
Cahnman, Werner J. 1981. "Hobbes, Toennies, Vico: Starting Points in Sociology." In *The Future of the Sociological Classics*, edited by B. Rhea, 16–38. Boston: Allen and Unwin.
Cannon, James P. 1972. *The History of American Trotskyism*. New York: Pathfinder Press.
Castells, Manuel. 1997. *The Information Age: Economy, Society and Culture; Volume II: The Power of Identity*. Oxford: Blackwell.
Chambliss, William J. 1975. "Toward a Political Economy of Crime." *Theory and Society* 2:149–170.
Chandler, Bret. 2013. "The Subjectivity of Habitus." *Journal for the Theory of Social Behaviour* 43 (4):469–491.

Chang, Jung and Jon Halliday. 2006. *Mao: The Unknown Story*. New York: Anchor.
Charry, Ellen T. 1992. "The Moral Function of Doctrine." *Theology Today* XLIX (1):31–45.
Cheliotis, Leonidas K. 2011. "For a Freudo-Marxist Critique of Social Domination: Rediscovering Erich Fromm through the Mirror of Pierre Bourdieu." *Journal of Classical Sociology* 11 (4):438–461.
Chilton, Roland. 2001. "Viable Policy: The Impact of Federal Funding and the Need for Independent Research Agendas." *Criminology* 39 (1):1–8.
Chriss, James J. 1993. "Durkheim's Cult of the Individual as Civil Religion: Its Appropriation by Erving Goffman." *Sociological Spectrum* 13 (2):251–275.
Chriss, James J. 1995. "Habermas, Goffman and Communicative Action: Implications for Professional Practice." *American Sociological Review* 60:545–565.
Chriss, James J. 1998. "Review of Habermas's *Between Facts and Norms*." *Theory and Society* 27 (3):417–425.
Chriss, James J. 1999a. "Introduction." In *Counseling and the Therapeutic State*, edited by J.J. Chriss, 1–29. New York: Aldine de Gruyter.
Chriss, James J. 1999b. "The Family under Siege." In *Counseling and the Therapeutic State*, edited by J.J. Chriss, 187–198. New York: Aldine de Gruyter.
Chriss, James J. 1999c. *Alvin W. Gouldner: Sociologist and Outlaw Marxist*. Aldershot: Ashgate.
Chriss, James J. 2001. "Alvin W. Gouldner and Industrial Sociology at Columbia University." *Journal of the Theory of the Behavioral Sciences* 37 (3):241–259.
Chriss, James J. 2002. "Gouldner's Tragic Vision." *Sociological Quarterly* 43 (1):81–96.
Chriss, James J. 2006a. "Giddings and the Social Mind." *Journal of Classical Sociology* 6(1):123–144.
Chriss, James J. 2006b. "The Place of Lester Ward among the Sociological Classics." *Journal of Classical Sociology* 6 (1):5–21.
Chriss, James J. 2013. *Social Control: An Introduction*, 2nd ed. Cambridge, UK: Polity.
Chung, Chen H., Jon M. Shepard, and Marc J. Dollinger. 1989. "Max Weber Revisited: Some Lessons from East Asian Capitalistic Development." *Asia Pacific Journal of Management* 6 (2):307–321.
Cladis, Mark S. 1992. *A Communitarian Defense of Liberalism: Emile Durkheim and Contemporary Social Theory*. Stanford, CA: Stanford University Press.
Clark, Terry N. 1969. "Introduction." In *Gabriel Tarde: On Communication and Social Influence*, edited by T.N. Clark, 1–72. Chicago: University of Chicago Press.
Clark, Terry Nichols. 1973. *Prophets and Patrons: The French University and the Emergence of the Social Sciences*. Cambridge, MA: Harvard University Press.
Cohen, Rich. 1999. *Tough Jews*. New York: Vintage Books.
Collins, Randall. 1992. "The Rise and Fall of Modernism in Politics and Religion." *Acta Sociologica* 35 (3):171–186.
Comte, Auguste. 1830–1842. *System of Positive Philosophy*. Paris: Bachelier.

Connell, R.W. 1997. "Why is Classical Theory Classical?" *American Journal of Sociology* 102(6):1511–1557.

Coser, Lewis A. 1956. *The Functions of Social Conflict*. New York: Free Press.

Cournot, Antoine A. 1956. *An Essay on the Foundations of Our Knowledge*. Translated by M.H. Moore. New York: Liberal Arts Press.

Cullen, Francis T., Cheryl Lero Jonson, Andrew J. Myer, and Freda Adler. 2011. "Introduction: Preserving the Origins of American Criminology." In *The Origins of American Criminology*, edited by F.T. Cullen, C.L. Jonson, A.J. Myer, and F. Adler, 1–14. New Brunswick, NJ: Transaction Publishers.

Davis, James A. 1962. "Rejoinder." *American Journal of Sociology* 67 (5):578.

Dean, Jodi. 2012. *The Communist Horizon*. London: Verso.

Dean, Jonathan. 2014. "Tales of the Apolitical." *Political Studies* 62:452–467.

Dean, Mitchell. 2006. "A Political Mythology of World Order: Carl Schmitt's *Nomos*." *Theory, Culture and Society* 23 (5):1–22.

Deaton, Richard. 1973. "The Fiscal Crisis of the State in Canada." *Our Generation* 8 (4):11–51.

Deaton, Richard. 1989. *The Political Economy of Pensions: Power, Politics and Social Change in Canada, Britain and the United States*. Vancouver: University of British Columbia Press.

Decker, Kevin S. 2012. "Perspectives and Ideologies: A Pragmatic Use for Recognition Theory." *Philosophy and Social Criticism* 38 (2):215–226.

Demenchonok, Edward. 2007. "From a State of War to Perpetual Peace." *American Journal of Economics and Sociology* 66 (1):25–47.

Deutscher, Isaac. 1968. *The Non-Jewish Jew and Other Essays*. London: Oxford University Press.

Dickens, David R. 2011. "*Telos* at Kansas." In *A Journal of No Illusions: Telos, Paul Piccone, and the Americanization of Critical Theory*, edited by T.W. Luke and B. Agger, 62–71. New York: Telos Press.

Dickerson, James, ed. 1999. *North to Canada*. Westport: Praeger.

Dikötter, Frank. 2010. *Mao's Great Famine: The History of China's Most Devastating Catastrophe, 1958–1962*. New York: Walker and Co.

Dilworth, Craig. 1990. "Empiricism vs. Realism: High Points in the Debate during the Past 150 Years." *Studies in the History of Philosophy of Science* 21 (3):431–462.

Dimitriadis, Greg. 2009. "Jean-Paul Sartre and the Moral Authority of the Intellectual." *Cultural Studies ↔ Critical Methodologies* 9 (1):3–13.

Doppelt, Gerald. 1988. "Beyond Liberalism and Communitarianism: Towards a Critical Theory of Social Justice." *Philosophy and Social Criticism* 14 (3/4):271–292.

Durkheim, Emile. 1938 [1895]. *Rules of Sociological Method*. Translated by S.A. Solovay and J.H. Mueller. Chicago, IL: University of Chicago Press.

Durkheim, Emile. 1951 [1897]. *Suicide*. Translated by J. Spaulding and G. Simpson. Glencoe, IL: Free Press.

Durkheim, Emile. 1965 [1915]. *Elementary Forms of the Religious Life*. Translated by J.W. Swain. New York: Free Press.

Durkheim, Emile. 1984 [1893]. *The Division of Labor in Society*. Translated by W.D. Halls. New York: Free Press.

Dyrberg, Torben Bech. 2009. "The Leftist Fascination with Schmitt and the Esoteric Quality of 'the Political.'" *Philosophy and Social Criticism* 35 (6):649–669.

Ebel, Jonathan H. 2012. "Undersold and Oversold: Reinhold Niebuhr and Economic Justice." *Soundings* 95 (4):411–419.

Edwards, Joel. 2008. *An Agenda for Change: A Global Call for Spiritual and Social Transformation*. Grand Rapids, MI: Zondervan.

Eisenstadt, S.N. 1988. "Explorations in the Sociology of Knowledge: The Soteriological Axis in the Construction of Domains of Knowledge." *Knowledge and Society: Studies in the Sociology of Culture Past and Present* 7:1–71.

Elias, Nelly and Dafna Lemish. 2008. "Media Uses in Immigrant Families: Torn between 'Inward' and 'Outward' Paths of Integration." *International Communication Gazette* 70:23–42.

Elias, Nelly and Dafna Lemish. 2011. "Between Three Worlds: Host, Homeland, and Global Media in the Lives of Russian Immigrant Families in Israel and Germany." *Journal of Family Issues* 32 (9):1245–1274.

Ellingsen, Mark. 1988. *The Evangelical Movement: Growth, Impact, Controversy, Dialog*. Minneapolis: Augsburg.

Elliott, Anthony. 2003. "Slavoj Zizek." In *Key Contemporary Social Theorists*, edited by A. Elliott and L. Ray, 273–278. Oxford, UK: Blackwell Publishing.

Ellwood, Charles A. 1901. "The Theory of Imitation in Social Psychology." *American Journal of Sociology* 6 (6):721–741.

Ellwood, Charles A. 1910. *Sociology and Modern Social Problems*. New York: American Book Co.

Ellwood, Charles A. 1921. *An Introduction to Social Psychology*. New York: Appleton.

Ellwood, Charles A. 1925. *The Psychology of Human Society: An Introduction to Sociological Theory*. New York: Appleton.

Engels, Frederick. 1941. *Ludwig Feurbach and the Outcome of Classical German Philosophy*. New York: International Publishers.

Engerman, David C. 2009. *Know Your Enemy: The Rise and Fall of America's Soviet Experts*. Cambridge, UK: Cambridge University Press.

England, Paula and Irene Browne. 1992. "Internalization and Constraint in Theories of Women's Subordination." In *Current Perspectives in Social Theory*, vol. 12, edited by B. Agger, 97–123. Greenwich, CT: JAI Press.

Ephraim, Laura. 2013. "Beyond the Two-Sciences Settlement: Giambattista Vico's Critique of the Nature-Politics Opposition." *Political Theory* 41 (5):710–737.

Espejo, Paulina Ochoa. 2012. "Does Political Theology Entail Decisionism?" *Philosophy and Social Criticism* 38 (7):725–743.

Etzkowitz, Henry. 1988. "The Contradictions of Radical Sociology." *Critical Sociology* 15:95-113.
Etzkowitz, Henry. 1991. "The Contradictions of Radical Sociology: Ideological Purity and Dissensus at Washington University." In *Radical Sociologists and the Movement: Experiences, Lessons, and Legacies*, edited by M. Oppenheimer, M.J. Murray, and R.F. Levine, 74-95. Philadelphia: Temple University Press.
Fanon, Frantz. 1968. *The Wretched of the Earth*. Translated by C. Farrington. New York: Grove Press.
Fehér, Ferenc. 1978. "The Dictatorship over Needs." *Telos* 35:31-42.
Fenyo, Mario D. 1977. "Trotsky and His Heirs: The American Perspective." *Studies in Comparative Communism* 10 (1 & 2):204-215.
Fergusson, Niall. 2005. *The Rise and Decline of the American Empire*. New York: Penguin Books.
Ferrarotti, Franco. 2003. *An Invitation to Classical Sociology*. Lanham: Lexington.
Fine, Robert. 2006. "Cosmopolitanism and Violence: Difficulties of Judgment." *British Journal of Sociology* 57 (1):49-67.
Fischer, George. 1966. "The New Sociology in the Soviet Union." In *Soviet Sociology: Historical Antecedents and Current Appraisals*, edited by A. Simirenko, 275-292. Chicago: Quadrangle Books.
Fitzpatrick, Sheila. 1979. *Education and Social Mobility in the Soviet Union, 1921-1934*. Cambridge, UK: Cambridge University Press.
Flood, Maxwell. 1968. Task Force on Labour Relations. *Wildcat Strike in Lake City*. Study No. 15. Information Canada: 1970.
Foster, William Z. 1952. *History of the Communist Party of the United States*. New York: International Publishers.
Fox, Renee C. 1959. *Experiment Perilous: Physicians and Patients Facing the Unknown*. Philadelphia: University of Pennsylvania Press.
Frankel, Boris. 1974. "Habermas Talking: An Interview." *Theory and Society* 1 (1):37-58.
Fraser, John. 1975. "Soviet Sociology and Its Critics." *Studies in Comparative Communism* 8 (4):370-388.
Fraser, John. 1976. "Rejoinder by John Fraser." *Studies in Comparative Communism* 9 (3):296-298.
Fraser, Nancy. 1989. "Women, Welfare and the Politics of Need Interpretation." In *Politics and Social Theory*, edited by P. Lassman, 104-122. London: Routledge.
Fraser, Nancy. 2001. "Recognition without Ethics?" *Theory, Culture and Society* 18 (2-3):21-42.
Friedrichs, Robert W. 1971. "Friedrichs on Gouldner: The Case for a Plurality of Sociologies of Sociology." *LSU Journal of Sociology* 2 (1):100-107.
Fritz, Jan Marie. 2007. "Clinical Sociology." In *21st Century Sociology*, vol. 2, edited by C.D. Bryant and D.L. Peck, 353-359. Thousand Oaks, CA: Sage.

Fuhrman, Ellsworth R. 1984. "Alvin Gouldner and the Sociology of Knowledge: Three Significant Problem Shifts." *Sociological Quarterly* 25:287–300.
Fukuyama, Francis. 1992. *The End of History and the Last Man*. New York: Free Press.
Fuller, Steve. 1998. "From Content to Context: A Social Epistemology of the Structure—Agency Craze." In *What Is Social Theory?* edited by A. Sica, 92–117. Oxford: Blackwell.
Fuller, Steve. 2006. "Intelligent Design Theory: A Site for Contemporary Sociology of Knowledge." *Canadian Journal of Sociology* 31 (3):277–289.
Furedi, Frank. 2004. *Therapy Culture: Cultivating Vulnerability in an Uncertain Age*. London: Routledge.
Gadamer, Hans-Georg. 2000. *Truth and Method*, 2nd revised ed. Translated by J. Weinsheimer and D.G. Marshall. New York: Continuum.
Gane, Nicholas. 2005. "Max Weber as Social Theorist: 'Class, Status, Party.'" *European Journal of Social Theory* 8 (2):211–226.
Geertz, Clifford. 1973. *The Interpretation of Cultures*. New York: Basic Books.
Gibbs, Jack P. 1989. *Control: Sociology's Central Notion*. Urbana: University of Illinois Press.
Giddens, Anthony. 1970. "Marx, Weber, and the Development of Capitalism." *Sociology* 4 (3):289–310.
Giddings, Franklin H. 1896. *Principles of Sociology*. New York: Macmillan.
Giddings, Franklin H. 1899. *Elements of Sociology*. London: Macmillan.
Giddings, Franklin H. 1903. "Introduction." In *Laws of Imitation*, edited by G. Tarde, iii–vii. New York: Henry Holt and Co.
Giddings, Franklin H. 1908. "Are Contradictions of Ideas and Beliefs Likely to Play an Important Group-Making Role in the Future?" *American Journal of Sociology* 13 (6):784–799.
Giddings, Franklin H. 1918. *The Responsible State*. Boston: Houghton Mifflin.
Gieryn, Thomas F. 1994. "Eloge: Robert K. Merton (1910–2003)." *Isis* 95 (1):91–94.
Gill, Timothy M. 2013. "Why Mills, Not Gouldner? Selective History and Differential Commemoration in Sociology." *American Sociologist* 44 (1):96–115.
Gitlin, Todd. 2013. "Occupy's Predicament: The Moment and the Prospects for the Movement." *British Journal of Sociology* 64 (1):3–25.
Goffman, Erving. 1959. *The Presentation of Self in Everyday Life*. New York: Anchor Books.
Goffman, Erving. 1979. *Gender Advertisements*. New York: Harper.
Gold, Mike. 1948. *Jews without Money*. London: Rita Searl.
Goldberg, Michelle. 2014. "Feminism's Toxic Twitter Wars." *The Nation*, Feb. 17, 2014. Available at http://www.thenation.com/article/178140/feminisms-toxic-twitter-wars#.
Gottfredson, Michael R. and Travis Hirschi. 1990. *A General Theory of Crime*. Stanford, CA: Stanford University Press.
Gould, Rebecca. 2013. "Laws, Exceptions, Norms: Kierkegaard, Schmitt, and Benjamin on the Exception." *Telos* 162:77–96.

Gouldner, Alvin W. (ed.). 1950. *Studies in Leadership: Leadership and Democratic Action*. New York: Harper & Publishers.

Gouldner, Alvin W. 1954a. *Patterns of Industrial Bureaucracy*. Glencoe, IL: Free Press.

Gouldner, Alvin W. 1954b. "The Problem of Loyalty in Groups under Tension." *Social Problems* 2 (2):82–88.

Gouldner, Alvin W. 1954c. *Wildcat Strike*. Yellow Springs, OH: Antioch Press.

Gouldner, Alvin W. 1957a. "Theoretical Requirements of the Applied Social Sciences." *American Sociological Review* 22 (1):92–102.

Gouldner, Alvin W. 1957b. "Cosmopolitans and Locals: Toward an Analysis of Latent Social Roles – I." *Administrative Science Quarterly* 2:281–306.

Gouldner, Alvin W. 1958a. "Introduction." In *Emile Durkheim: Socialism and Saint-Simon*, edited by A.W. Gouldner, v–xxix. Yellow Springs, OH: Antioch Press.

Gouldner, Alvin W. 1958b. "Cosmopolitans and Locals: Toward an Analysis of Latent Social Roles – II." *Administrative Science Quarterly* 2:444–480.

Gouldner, Alvin W. 1962a. "Letter from Gouldner to Irving Horowitz, July 6, 1962." From the Horowitz Transaction Publishers Archives.

Gouldner, Alvin W. 1962b. "Anti-Minotaur: The Myth of a Value-Free Sociology." *Social Problems* 9 (3):199–213.

Gouldner, Alvin W. 1962c. "Letters to the Editor." *American Journal of Sociology* 67 (5):577.

Gouldner, Alvin W. 1963. "The Secrets of Organizations." In *The Social Welfare Forum*, vol. 90, 161–177. New York: Columbia University Press.

Gouldner, Alvin W. 1964a. "Letter from Gouldner to Irving Horowitz, June 15, 1964." From the Horowitz Transaction Publishers Archives.

Gouldner, Alvin W. 1964b. "Taking Over: A Guide to the Anatomy of Succession." *Transaction* 1 (3):23–27.

Gouldner, Alvin W. 1965. *Enter Plato*. New York: Basic Books.

Gouldner, Alvin W. 1966. "Letter from Gouldner to Mary Strong, June 15, 1966." From the Horowitz Transaction Publishers Archives.

Gouldner, Alvin W. 1968. "The Sociologist as Partisan: Sociology and the Welfare State." *American Sociologist* 3 (2):103–116.

Gouldner, Alvin W. 1969a. "Personal Reality, Social Theory, and the Tragic Dimension in Science." In *The Sociology of Research*, edited by G. Boalt, xvii–xxxviii. Carbondale: Southern Illinois University Press.

Gouldner, Alvin W. 1969b. "The Unemployed Self." In *Work*, vol. 2, edited by R. Fraser, 346–365. Harmondsworth, UK: Penguin Books.

Gouldner, Alvin W. 1970a. *Coming Crisis of Western Sociology*. New York: Avon.

Gouldner, Alvin W. 1970b. "Review Symposium." *American Sociological Review* 35 (2):332–334.

Gouldner, Alvin W. 1973a. *For Sociology*. New York: Basic Books.

Gouldner, Alvin W. 1973b. "Foreword." In *The New Criminology: For a Social Theory of Deviance*, edited by I. Taylor, P. Walton, and J. Young, ix–xiv. London: Routledge and Kegan Paul.

Gouldner, Alvin W. 1973c. "Marxism and Mao." *Partisan Review* 15 (2):243–254.

Gouldner, Alvin W. 1974a. "Marxism and Social Theory." *Theory and Society* 1 (1):17–35.

Gouldner, Alvin W. 1974b. "The Metaphoricality of Marxism and the Context-Freeing Grammar of Socialism." *Theory and Society* 1 (4):387–414.

Gouldner, Alvin W. 1975a. "Sociology and the Everyday Life." In *The Idea of Social Structure: Papers in Honor of Robert K. Merton*, edited by L.C. Coser, 417–432. New York: Harcourt, Brace, and Jovanovich.

Gouldner, Alvin W. 1975b. "Prologue to a Theory of Revolutionary Intellectuals." *Telos* 26:3–36.

Gouldner, Alvin W. 1976a. *The Dialectic of Ideology and Technology*. New York: Oxford University Press.

Gouldner, Alvin W. 1976b. "The Dark Side of the Dialectic: Toward a New Objectivity." *Sociological Inquiry* 46 (1):3–15.

Gouldner, Alvin W. 1977. "Stalinism: A Study of Internal Colonialism." *Telos* 34:5–48.

Gouldner, Alvin W. 1978. "News and Social Science as Ideology." *Quarterly Journal of Ideology* 2 (1):4–17.

Gouldner, Alvin W. 1979a. *The Future of Intellectuals and the Rise of the New Class*. New York: Seabury Press.

Gouldner, Alvin. 1979b. "Curriculum Vitae." June: 1

Gouldner, Alvin W. 1980a. *The Two Marxisms*. New York: Seabury Press.

Gouldner, Alvin W. 1980b. "Sartre and the Intellectuals." Talk given at Washington University, St. Louis, November 20, 1980. Washington University Assembly Series Collection (ASL80-15).

Gouldner, Alvin W. 1983. "Artisans and Intellectuals in the German Revolution of 1848." *Theory and Society* 12:521–532.

Gouldner, Alvin W. 1985. *Against Fragmentation: The Origins of Marxism and the Sociology of Intellectuals*. Oxford, UK: Oxford University Press.

Gouldner, Alvin W. and Irving Louis Horowitz. 1966. "The Red Guard." *Society* 4 (1):37–41.

Grier, Philip. 1978. *Marxist Ethical Theory in the Soviet Union*. Dordrecht: Reidel.

Griffin, Donald R. 1976. *The Question of Animal Awareness: Evolutionary Continuity of Mental Experiences*. New York: Rockefeller University Press.

Grosof, Elliott. 1962. "Letters to the Editor." *American Journal of Sociology* 67 (5):577–578.

Gross, Neil and Ethan Fosse. 2012. Why Are Professors Liberal?" *Theory and Society* 41:127–168.

Groves, W. Byron and Robert J. Sampson. 1987. "Traditional Contributions to Radical Criminology." *Journal of Research in Crime and Delinquency* 24 (3):181–214.

Gumplowicz, Ludwig. 1883. *Der Rassenkampf.* Innsbruck: Wagner'sche Univ.-Buchhandlung.

Gupta, Suman. 2000. *Marxism, History, and Intellectuals: Toward a Reconceptualized Transformative Socialism.* Madison, NJ: Fairleigh Dickinson University Press.

Habermas, Jürgen. 1971. *Knowledge and Human Interests.* Translated by J.J. Shapiro. Boston: Beacon Press.

Habermas, Jürgen. 1973. *Theory and Practice.* Translated by J. Viertel. Boston: Beacon Press.

Habermas, Jürgen. 1975. *Legitimation Crisis.* Translated by T. McCarthy. Boston: Beacon Press.

Habermas, Jürgen. 1984. *Theory of Communicative Action,* vol. 1. Translated by T. McCarthy. Boston: Beacon Press.

Habermas, Jürgen. 1987. *Theory of Communicative Action,* vol. 2. Translated by T. McCarthy. Boston: Beacon Press.

Habermas, Jürgen. 1989. *The New Conservatism: Cultural Criticism and the Historians' Debate,* edited and translated by S.W. Nicholson. Cambridge, MA: MIT Press.

Habermas, Jürgen. 1996. *Between Facts and Norms: Contributions to a Discourse Theory of Law and Democracy.* Translated by W. Rehg. Cambridge, MA: MIT Press.

Habermas, Jürgen. 1999. *The Inclusion of the Other: Studies in Political Theory,* edited by C. Cronin and P. De Greiff. Cambridge, MA: MIT Press.

Habermas, Jürgen. 2008. *The Divided West.* Translated by C. Cronin. Cambridge, UK: Polity.

Hacking, Ian. 1983. *Representing and Intervening: Introductory Topics in the Philosophy of Natural Science.* Cambridge: Cambridge University Press.

Haeckel, Ernst. 1866. *Generelle Morphologie der Organismen.* Berlin: Georg Reimer.

Hamblin, Robert, Joseph Kahl, Lee Rainwater, and Rodney Coe. 1968. "Letter to Chancellor Thomas H. Eliot, May 24, 1968." From the Horowitz Transaction Publishers Archives.

Hamilton, Richard E. 2000. *Marxism, Revisionism, and Leninism: Explication, Assessment, and Commentary.* Westport, CT: Praeger.

Hanna, Joseph F. 2004. "The Scope and Limits of Scientific Objectivity." *Philosophy of Science* 71:339–361.

Hempel, Carl G. 1965. *Aspects of Scientific Explanation.* New York: Free Press.

Hobsbawm, Eric. 2003. *Interesting Times: A Twentieth-Century Life.* London: Abacus.

Holland, Ray. 1999. "Reflexivity." *Human Relations* 52 (4):463–484.

Hollander, Paul. 1966. "Models of Behavior in Stalinist Literature: A Case Study of Totalitarian Values and Controls." *American Sociological Review* 31 (3):352–364.

Honneth, Axel. 2001. "Recognition or Redistribution? Changing Perspectives on the Moral Order of Society." *Theory, Culture and Society* 18 (2–3):43–55.

Horowitz, David. 1965. *The Free World Colossus: A Critique of American Foreign Policy in the Cold War.* New York: Hill and Wang.

Horowitz, Irving L. 1978. "Comments." *Current Anthropology* 19 (2):376–377.

Horwitz, Morton J. 1995. "Jews and McCarthyism: A View from the Bronx." In *Secret Agents: The Rosenberg Case, McCarthyism, and Fifties America*, edited by M. Garber and R.L. Walkowitz, 257–263. New York: Routledge.

Howard, Philip K. 1994. *The Death of Common Sense*. New York: Warner Books.

Howe, Irving. 1976. *World of Our Fathers*. New York: Harcourt.

Howe, Irving and Lewis Coser. 1962. *The American Communist Party: A Critical History*. New York: Praeger.

Humphreys, Joshua M. 1999. "Durkheimian Sociology and 20th Century Politics: Célestin Bouglé." *History of the Human Sciences* 12 (3):117–138.

Humphreys, Laud. 1970. *Tearoom Trade: Impersonal Sex in Public Places*. Chicago: Aldine.

Hunter, James Davison. 1983. *American Evangelicalism: Conservative Religion and the Quandary of Modernity*. New Brunswick, NJ: Rutgers University Press.

Hunter, James Davison. 1987. *Evangelicalism: The Coming Generation*. Chicago: University of Chicago Press.

Iggers, Georg G. 1958. *The Doctrine of Saint-Simon: An Exposition, First Year, 1828–1829*. Translated and edited by G.G. Iggers. Boston: Beacon Press.

Inglis, David. 2010. "Civilizations or Globalization(s)? Intellectual Rapprochements and Historical World-Visions." *European Journal of Social Theory* 13 (1):135–152.

Jackson, Kimberly. 2009. "The Resurrection of the Image." *Theory, Culture, and Society* 26 (5):30–43.

Jacobs, Anton K. 1990. "Ideology, Self-esteem, and Religious Doctrine: Toward a Socio-psychological Understanding of the Popularity of Evangelicalism in Modern, Capitalist America." *Ultimate Reality and Meaning* 13 (2):122–133.

Jacoby, Russell. 2009. "Paul Piccone: Outside Academe." *Fast Capitalism* 5 (1).

James, William. 1890. *Principles of Psychology*. New York: Holt. Chicago: University of Chicago Press.

Jasso, Guillermina. 1999. "How Much Injustice Is There in the World? Two New Justice Indexes." *American Sociological Review* 64:133–168.

Jasso, Guillermina. 2007. "Theoretical Unification in Justice and Beyond." *Social Justice Research* 20:336–371.

Jay, Martin 1973. *The Dialectical Imagination*. Boston: Little, Brown and Co.

Jay, Martin. 1982. "For Gouldner: Reflections on an Outlaw Marxist." *Theory and Society* 11 (6):759–778.

Jay, Martin. 1984. *Adorno*. Cambridge, MA: Harvard University Press.

Jelen, Ted G. 1991. *The Political Mobilization of Religious Beliefs*. New York: Praeger.

Johnson, Harry M. 1979. "Religion in Social Change and Social Evolution." *Sociological Inquiry* 49 (2–3):313–339.

Judis, John B. 2000. "The Spiritual Wobbly." *The New York Times Book Review*, July 9.

Karsenti, Bruno. 2012. "Imitation: Returning to the Tarde-Durkheim Debate." In *The Social after Gabriel Tarde: Debates and Assessments*, edited by M. Candea, 44–61. London: Routledge.

Kassof, Allen. 1965. "American Sociology through Soviet Eyes." *American Sociological Review* 30 (1):114–121.

Katz, Elihu. 2001. "Media Technologies, Social Organization and Democratic Polities." In *Identity, Culture and Globalization*, edited by E. Ben-Rafael and Y. Sternberg, 307–318. Leiden: Brill.

Keen, Mike Forest. 2003. *Stalking Sociologists: J. Edgar Hoover's FBI Surveillance of American Sociology*. New Brunswick, NJ: Transaction.

Kelly, Sanja, Sarah Cook, and Mai Truong. 2012. *Freedom on the Net: A Global Assessment of Internet and Digital Media*. A publication of Freedom House (www.freedomhouse.org).

Kierkegaard, Soren. 1964. *Repetition: An Essay in Experimental Psychology*. Translated by W. Lowrie. New York: Harper and Row.

Klapp, Orrin. 1991. *Inflation of Symbols: Loss of Values in American Culture*. New Brunswick, NJ: Transaction Publishers.

Klausner, Samuel Z. 1986. "The Bid to Nationalize American Social Science." In *The Nationalization of the Social Sciences*, edited by S.Z. Klausner and V. Lidz, 3–39. Philadelphia: University of Pennsylvania Press.

Kolaja, Jiri. 1978. "An Observation on Soviet Sociology." *Current Anthropology* 19 (2):373–375.

Köves, Margit. 1995. "Ferenc Fehér (1933–1994): Reflections on a Member of the Lukács School." *Social Scientist* 23 (4/6):98–107.

Kuhn, Thomas S. 1962. *Structure of Scientific Revolutions*. Chicago: University of Chicago Press.

LaFeber, Walter. 1975. *America, Russia and the Cold War 1945–1975*. New York: John Wiley and Sons.

Lane, Tony and Kenneth Roberts. 1971. *[Wildcat] Strike at Pilkingtons*. London: Fontana.

Langman, Lauren. 2012. "Cycles of Contention: The Rise and Fall of the Tea Party." *Critical Sociology* 38 (4):469–494.

Lasch, Christopher. 1968. "The Cultural History of the Cold War: A Shortened History of the Congress of Cultural Freedom." In *Towards a New Past: Dissenting Essays in American History*, edited by Barton Bernstein, 322–360. New York: Pantheon Books.

Lasch, Christopher. 1991. *The True and Only Heaven: Progress and Its Critics*. New York: Norton.

Latour, Bruno. 2002. "Gabriel Tarde and the End of the Social." In *The Social in Question*, edited by P. Joyce, 117–132. London: Routledge.

Laxer, James. 2005. *Red Diaper Baby*. Vancouver: Douglas and McIntyre.

Lazarsfeld, Paul F. and Wagner Thielens, Jr. 1958. *The Academic Mind: Social Scientists in a Time of Crisis*. Glencoe, IL: Free Press.

Le Bon, Gustave. 1896. *The Crowd: A Study of the Popular Mind.* London: Unwin.

Lemert, Charles. 1988. "Future of the Sixties Generation and Social Theory." *Theory and Society* 17:789–807.

Lemert, Charles and Paul Piccone. 1982. "Gouldner's Theoretical Method and Reflexive Sociology." *Theory and Society* 11 (6):733–757.

Lenin, V.I. 1925. "Our Programme." *Selected Works.* London: Lawrence and Wishart, 1968: 34–36.

Lepenies, Wolf. 1988. *Between Literature and Science: The Rise of Sociology.* Cambridge, UK: Cambridge University Press.

Leys, Ruth. 1993. "Mead's Voices: Imitation as Foundation, or the Struggle against Mimesis." *Critical Inquiry* 19 (2):277–307.

Liazos, Alexander. 1972. "The Poverty of the Sociology of Deviance: Nuts, Sluts, and Preverts." *Social Problems* 20:103–120.

Lifton, Robert Jay. 1970. "Mao and the Death of the Revolution." In *America and the Asian Revolutions*, edited by R.J. Lifton, 133–164. New Brunswick, NJ: Transaction.

Lijmbach, Susanne. 1999. "A Hermeneutical Ethology?" In *Hermeneutics and Science*, edited by M. Feher, O. Kiss, and L. Ropolyi, 199–205. Dordrecht: Kluwer Academic Publishers.

Lindholm, Charles. 1992. "Charisma, Crowd Psychology and Altered States of Consciousness." *Culture, Medicine and Psychiatry* 16:287–310.

Lindholm, Jennifer A. 2014. *The Quest for Meaning and Wholeness: Spiritual and Religious Connections in the Lives of College Faculty.* San Francisco: Jossey-Bass.

Lobkowicz, Nikolaus. 1967. *Theory and Practice: History of a Concept from Aristotle to Marx.* Notre Dame, IN: University of Notre Dame Press.

Lowenthal, Richard. 1965. "The Prospects for Pluralistic Communism." In *Marxism in the Modern World*, edited by Milorad M. Drachkovitch, 225–273. Stanford: Stanford University Press.

Luke, Timothy W. 1997. *Ecocritique: Contesting the Politics of Nature, Economy, and Culture.* Minneapolis: University of Minnesota Press.

Luke, Timothy W. 2005. "The Trek with *Telos*: A Remembrance of Paul Piccone (January 19, 1940 – July 12, 2004)." *Fast Capitalism* 1 (2).

Lundskow, George. 2012. "Authoritarianism and Destructiveness in the Tea Party Movement." *Critical Sociology* 38 (4):529–547.

Maine, Henry Sumner. 2002 [1861]. *Ancient Law.* New Brunswick, NJ: Transaction Publishers.

Malešević, Siniša. 2009. "Collective Violence and Power." In *Sage Handbook of Power*, edited by S.R. Clegg and M. Haugaard, 274–290. Los Angeles: Sage.

Mannheim, Karl. 1936. *Ideology and Utopia.* New York: Harvest Books.

Marcuse, Herbert and Franz Neumann. 1994. "A History of the Doctrine of Social Change." *Constellations* 1 (1):116–143.

Marshall, Gordon (ed.). 1994. "Social Justice." In *The Concise Oxford Dictionary of Sociology*, 262–265. Oxford: Oxford University Press.

Marx, Karl and Frederick Engels. 1964 [1848]. *The Communist Manifesto*. New York: Pocket Books.

Maxwell, Angie and T. Wayne Parent. 2012. "The Obama Trigger: Presidential Approval and Tea Party Membership." *Social Science Quarterly* 93 (5):1384–1401.

Mayhew, Bruce H. Jr. n.d. "Grundfragen der Strukturalen Soziologie." Preface to *Das Glucksrad*. Unpublished manuscript.

Mayhew, Leon H. 1997. *The New Public: Professional Communication and the Means of Social Influence*. Cambridge, UK: Cambridge University Press.

Maynard, Fredelle Bruser. 1985. "Jewish Christmas." *Raisins and Almonds*. Toronto: Penguin Books Ltd.

McLaughlin, Neil, Lisa Kowalchuk, and Kerry Turcotte. 2005. "Why Sociology Does Not Need to Be Saved: Analytic Reflections on Public Sociologies." *American Sociologist* 36 (3–4):133–151.

McVeigh, Rory, Kraig Beyerlein, Burrell Van Jr., and Priyamvada Trivedi. 2014. "Educational Segregation, Tea Party Organizations, and Battles over Distributive Justice." *American Sociological Review* 79 (4):630–652.

Mead, George Herbert. 1934. *Mind, Self, and Society*, edited by C.M. Morris. Chicago: University of Chicago Press.

Mead, George Herbert. 1959. *The Philosophy of the Present*, edited by A.E. Murphy. LaSalle, IL: Open Court.

Merton, Robert K. 1968. *Social Theory and Social Structure*, 1968 enlarged edition. New York: Free Press.

Merton, Robert K. and Henry W. Reicken. 1962. "Notes on Sociology in the U.S.S.R." *Current Problems in Social-Behavioral Research* 10:7–14.

Mestrovic, Stjepan G. 1988. "The Social World as Will and Idea: Schopenhauer's Influence upon Durkheim's Thought." *Sociological Review* 36 (4):674–705.

Milkman, Ruth. 2014. "Millennial Movements: Occupy Wall Street and the Dreamers." *Dissent* 61 (3):55–59.

Mills, C. Wright. 1959. *The Sociological Imagination*, New York, NY: Oxford University Press.

Myers, Daniel J. and Kevin Estep. 2012. "Political Renewal: Occupations, Springs, and Tea Parties." *Sociological Focus* 45:274–284.

Naffine, Ngaire. 1996. *Feminism and Criminology*. Philadelphia: Temple University Press.

Nagel, Ernest. 1979. *The Structure of Science*. Indianapolis: Hackett.

Neocleous, Mark. 2013. "'O Effeminacy! Effeminacy!' War, Masculinity and the Myth of Liberal Peace." *European Journal of International Relations* 19 (1):93–113.

Nietzsche, Friedrich. 1954. "Homer's Contest." In *The Portable Nietzsche*. Translated and edited by W. Kaufmann. New York: Viking.

Nietzsche, Friedrich. 1956. *The Birth of Tragedy*. Translated by F. Golffing. New York: Doubleday.
Obituary. 1981. "Alvin Gouldner, 60, A Radical Sociologist, Dead of Heart Attack." *New York Times* January 10.
O'Neill, John. 1976. "On the History of the Human Senses in Vico and Marx." *Social Research* 43 (4):837–844.
O'Neill, John. 1999. "Children and the Civic State: A Covenant Model of Welfare." In *Counseling and the Therapeutic State*, edited by J.J. Chriss, 33–54. New York: Aldine de Gruyter.
Osipov, G. and M. Yokchuk. 1966. "Some Principles of Theory, Problems and Methods of Research in Sociology in the USSR: A Soviet View." In *Soviet Sociology: Historical Antecedents and Current Appraisals*, edited by A. Simirenko, 298–305. Chicago: Quadrangle.
Ossewaarde, Marinus. 2010. "The Continuation of the Dialectic in Sociology." *Critical Sociology* 36 (3):395–413.
Ost, David. 1994. "Search for Balance." *Telos* 101:137–154.
Ost, David. 2004. "Politics as the Mobilization of Anger: Emotions in Movements and in Power." *European Journal of Social Theory* 7 (2):229–244.
Pabst, Adrian. 2013. "The New Evangelicals and the Future of the United States of America." *Telos* 165:179–184.
Pally, Marcia. 2011. *The New Evangelicals: Expanding the Vision of the Common Good*. Grand Rapids, MI: W.B. Eerdmans.
Pankhurst, Jerry G. 1982. "Factors in the Post-Stalin Emergence of Soviet Sociology." *Sociological Inquiry* 52 (3):165–183.
Paolucci, Paul. 2004. "The Discursive Transformation of Marx's Communism into Soviet Diamat." *Critical Sociology* 30 (3):617–667.
Paolucci, Paul. 2011. *Marx and the Politics of Abstraction*. Chicago: Haymarket Books.
Parsons, Talcott. 1937. *Structure of Social Action*. Glencoe, IL: Free Press.
Parsons, Talcott. 1951. *The Social System*. Glencoe, IL: Free Press.
Parsons, Talcott. 1964. "Introduction." In *The Sociology of Religion*, Max Weber, xix–lxvii. Translated by E. Fischoff. Boston: Beacon Press.
Parsons, Talcott. 1965. "An American Impression of Sociology in the Soviet Union." *American Sociological Review* 30 (1):121–125.
Parsons, Talcott. 1968. "An Overview." In *American Sociology: Prospects, Problems, Methods*, edited by T. Parsons, 319–335. New York: Basic Books.
Parsons, Talcott. 1977. *Social Systems and the Evolution of Action Theory*. New York: Free Press.
Parsons, Talcott. 1978. *Action Theory and the Human Condition*. New York: Free Press.
Parsons, Talcott and Gerald M. Platt. 1973. *The American University*. Cambridge: Harvard University Press.

Parsons, Talcott, Edward A. Shils, and James Olds. 1951. "Values, Motives, and Systems of Action." In *Toward a General Theory of Action*, edited by T. Parsons and E.A. Shils, 45–276. Cambridge, MA: Harvard University Press.

Payne, Kenneth. 2011. "Building the Base: Al Qaeda's Focoist Strategy." *Studies in Conflict and Terrorism* 34:124–143.

Pearson, Geoff. 1975. "Misfit Sociology and the Politics of Socialization." In *Critical Criminology*, edited by I. Taylor, P. Walton, and J. Young, 147–166. London: Routledge and Kegan Paul.

Pellicani, Luciano. 2014. "From the Apocalypse to the Revolution." *Telos* 166:25–41.

Pels, Dick. 1998. "The Proletarian as Stranger." *History of the Human Sciences* 11 (1):49–72.

Piccone, Paul. 1975. "Reading the Grundrisse: Beyond 'Orthodox' Marxism." *Theory and Society* 2 (1):235–255.

Piccone, Paul. 1976a. "Beyond Identity Theory." In *On Critical Theory*, edited by J. O'Neill, 129–144. New York: Seabury Press.

Piccone, Paul. 1976b. "Soviet Sociology and Its Apologists." *Studies in Comparative Communism* 9 (3):293–295.

Piccone, Paul. 1976c. "Gramsci's Marxism: Beyond Lenin and Togliatti." *Theory and Society* 3 (4):485–512.

Piccone, Paul. 1977. "The Changing Function of Critical Theory." *New German Critique* 12:29–37.

Piccone, Paul. 1978. "The Crisis of One-Dimensionality." *Telos* 35:43–54.

Piccone, Paul. 1994. "From the New Left to the New Populism." *Telos* 101:173–208.

Pickerill, Jenny and John Krinsky. 2012. "Why Does Occupy Matter?" *Social Movement Studies* 11 (3–4):279–287.

Pittman, David J. and Deirdre Boden. 1989. "Sociology at Washington University in St. Louis: History and Reflections, 1906–1989." *American Sociologist* 20 (4):305–321.

Piven, Frances Fox. 2014. "Interdependent Power: Strategies for the Occupy Movement." *Current Sociology Monograph* 62 (2):223–231.

Platt, Jennifer. 1996. *A History of Sociological Research Methods in America, 1920–1960*. Cambridge, UK: Cambridge University Press.

Poggi, Gianfranco. 1996. "*Lego Quia Inutile*: An Alternative Justification for the Classics." In *Social Theory and Sociology: The Classics and Beyond*, edited by S.P. Turner, 39–47. Oxford, UK: Blackwell.

Pojman, Louis P. 2005. "Kant's Perpetual Peace and Cosmopolitanism." *Journal of Social Philosophy* 36 (1):62–71.

Polanyi, Michael. 1975. *The Contempt of Freedom: The Russian Experiment and After*. New York: Arno Press.

Rasch, William. 2000. "Conflict as a Vocation: Carl Schmitt and the Possibility of Politics." *Theory, Culture and Society* 17 (6):1–32.

Rawls, John. 1971. *A Theory of Justice*. Cambridge: Harvard University Press.

Reiman, Jeffrey. 1989. *Rich Get Richer and the Poor Get Prison: Ideology, Class, and Criminal Justice*. New York: Macmillan.

Richler, Mordecai. 1955. *Son of a Smaller Hero*. New York: Paperback Library Edition.

Robertson, John. 2013. "Sacred History and Political Thought: Neapolitan Responses to the Problem of Sociability after Hobbes." *The Historical Journal* 56 (1):1–29.

Rogers, Richard L. 1992. "The Role of Elites in Setting Agendas for Public Debate: A Historical Case." In *Vocabularies of Public Life: Empirical Essays in Symbolic Structure*, edited by R. Wuthnow, 234–247. London: Routledge.

Ross, Andrew. 2005. "Mao Zedong's Impact on Cultural Politics in the West." *Cultural Politics* 1 (1):5–22.

Rowntree, John and Margaret. 1968. "Youth as a Class." *Our Generation* 6 (1–2):155–190.

Ruggiero, Vincenzo. 2000. "The Fight to Reappear." *Social Justice* 27 (2):45–60.

Runia, Eelco. 2007. "Burying the Dead, Creating the Past." *History and Theory* 46:313–325.

Ryan, James G. 1997. *Earl Browder: The Failure of American Communism*. Tuscaloosa, AL: University of Alabama Press.

Ryan, Kevin. 2009. "Power and Exclusion." In *The Sage Handbook of Power*, edited by S.R. Clegg and M. Haugaard, 348–366. Los Angeles: Sage.

Rytina, Steve. 1986. "Sociology and Justice." In *Justice: Views from the Social Sciences*, edited by R.L. Cohen, 117–151. New York: Plenum Press.

Sartre, Jean-Paul. 1949. *Situations*, vol. 3. Paris: Gallimard.

Sartre, Jean-Paul. 1968a [1948]. *Anti-Semite and Jew*. Translated by G.J. Becker. New York: Schocken Books.

Sartre, Jean-Paul. 1968b. "Preface." In *The Wretched of the Earth*, F. Fanon, 7–31. New York: Grove Press.

Saussure, Ferdinand de. 1966 [1915]. *Course in General Linguistics*. New York: McGraw-Hill.

Savage, Stephen P. 1981. *The Theories of Talcott Parsons*. New York: St. Martin's Press.

Sayer, Derek. 2004. "*Incognito Ergo Sum*: Language, Memory and the Subject." *Theory, Culture and Society* 21 (6):67–89.

Sayles, Leonard R. 1954. "Wildcat Strikes." *Harvard Business Review* 32 (6).

Scheuerman, William E. 2014. "Whistleblowing as Civil Disobedience: The Case of Edward Snowden." *Philosophy and Social Criticism* 40 (7):609–628.

Schillmeier, Michael. 2009. "The Social, Cosmopolitanism and Beyond." *History of the Human Sciences* 22 (2):87–109.

Schmitt, Carl. 1985 [1922]. *Political Theology*. Translated by G. Schwab. Cambridge, MA: MIT Press.

Schmitt, Carl. 2007 [1932]. *The Concept of the Political*. Translated by G. Schwab. Chicago: University of Chicago Press.

Schmitt, Carl. 2008 [1938]. *The Leviathan in the State Theory of Thomas Hobbes*. Translated by G. Schwab and E. Hilfstein. Chicago: University of Chicago Press.

Schoener, Allon, ed. 1967. *Portal to America: The Lower East Side 1870–1925*. New York: Henry & Holt Co.

Schrag, Calvin O. 1989. *Communicative Praxis and the Space of Subjectivity*. Bloomington: Indiana University Press.

Schram, S. 2000. "In the Clinic: The Medicalization of Welfare." *Social Text* 18 (1):81–107.

Schwendinger, Herman and Julia R. Schwendinger. 1974. *The Sociologists of the Chair: A Radical Analysis of the Formative Years of North American Sociology (1883–1922)*. New York: Basic Books.

Scott, James C. 1985. *The Weapons of the Weak: Everyday Forms of Peasant Resistance*. New Haven, CT: Yale University Press.

Scott, James C. 1990. *Domination and the Arts of Resistance*. New Haven: Yale University Press.

Scott, Jerome F. and George C. Homans. 1947. "Reflections on the Wildcat Strikes." *American Sociological Review* 12 (3).

Seidman, Naomi. 1998. "Fag-Hags and Bu-Jews: Toward a (Jewish) Politics of Vicarious Identity." In *Insider/Outsider: American Jews and Multiculturalism*, edited by D. Biale, M. Galchinsky, and S. Heschel, 254–268. Berkeley: University of California Press.

Seidman, Steven. 2013. "Defilement and Disgust: Theorizing the Other." *American Journal of Cultural Sociology* 1 (1):3–25.

Shalin, Dmitri N. 1978. "The Development of Soviet Sociology, 1956–1976." *Annual Review of Sociology* 4:171–191.

Shalin, Dmitri N. 2014. "Interfacing Biography, Theory and History: The Case of Erving Goffman." *Symbolic Interaction* 37 (1):2–40.

Shannon, David A. 1959. *The Decline of American Communism: A History of the Communist Party of the United States since 1945*. New York: Harcourt, Brace and Co.

Shaw, Elizabeth. 2014. "Direct Brain Interventions and Responsibility Enhancement." *Criminal Law and Philosophy* 8:1–20.

Shlapnetokh, Vladimir. 1987. *The Politics of Sociology in the Soviet Union*. Boulder, CO: Westview Press.

Sica, Alan. 1997. "Acclaiming the Reclaimers: The Trials of Writing Sociology's History." In *Reclaiming the Sociological Classics*, edited by C. Camic, 282–298. Oxford, UK: Blackwell.

Simmel, Georg. 1950. *The Sociology of Georg Simmel*. Translated and edited by K.H. Wolff. New York: Free Press.

Sklare, Marshall (ed.). 1958. *The Jews: Social Patterns of an American Group*. New York: The Free Press.

Sklare, Marshall. 1993. *Observing American Jews*. Hanover, NH: Brandeis University Press.

Slomp, Gabriella. 2006. "Carl Schmitt's Five Arguments against the Idea of Just War." *Cambridge Review of International Affairs* 19 (3):435–447.

Small, Albion. 1912. "Socialism in the Light of Social Science." *American Journal of Sociology* 17 (6):804–819.

Sokoloff, William W. 2014. "Frederick Douglass and the Politics of Rage." *New Political Science* 36 (3):330–345.

Sombart, Werner. 1902. *Der moderne Kapitalismus*. Leipzig: Duncker and Humblot.

Sorokin, Pitirim. 1928. *Contemporary Sociological Theories*. New York: Harper and Brothers.

Spencer, Herbert. 1872 [1850]. *Social Statics*. New York: Appleton and Co.

Spencer, Herbert. 1897. *Principles of Sociology*, vols. 1–2. New York: Appleton.

Spiegelberg, Herbert. 1973. "On the Right to Say 'We': A Linguistic and Phenomenological Analysis." In *Phenomenological Sociology*, edited by G. Psathas, 129–156. New York: Wiley.

Srebrnik, Henry F. 2010. *Dreams of Nationhood: American Jewish Communists and the Soviet Birobidzhan Project, 1924–1951*. Boston: Academic Studies Press.

St. Louis *Telos* Group. 1978. "Notes and Commentary: The Totally Administered Society." *Telos* 35:169–185.

Stade, Ronald. 2014. "Citizens of Everything: The Aporetics of Cosmopolitanism." In *We the Cosmopolitans*, edited by L. Josephides and A. Hall, 29–47. New York: Berghahn.

Stark, Evan. 1991. "Talking Sociology: A Sixties Fragment." In *Radical Sociologists and the Movement: Experiences, Lessons, and Legacies*, edited by M. Oppenheimer, M.J. Murray, and R.F. Levine, 54–73. Philadelphia: Temple University Press.

Stark, Rodney. 2001. *One True God: Historical Consequences of Monotheism*. Princeton, NJ: Princeton University Press.

Stark, Rodney. 2003. *For the Glory of God: How Monotheism Led to Reformations, Science, Witch-hunts, and the End of Slavery*. Princeton, NJ: Princeton University Press.

Stark, Werner. 1976. "The Theoretical and Practical Relevance of Vico's Sociology for Today." *Social Research* 43 (4): 818–825.

Street, Paul L. and Anthony R. DiMaggio. 2012. "Beyond the Tea Party: Dismal Democrats, Radical Republicans, Debt Ceiling Drama, and the Long Right Tilt in the Age of Obama." *Critical Sociology* 38 (4):549–563.

Sumner, William Graham. 1906. *Folkways: A Study of the Sociological Importance of Usages, Manners, Customs, Mores, and Morals*. Boston: Ginn and Co.

Sumner, William Graham. 1910. "Religion and the Mores." *American Journal of Sociology* 15 (5):577–591.

Swanson, D.J. 2012. "The Beginning of the End of Robert H. Schuller's Crystal Cathedral Ministry: A Towering Failure in Crisis Management as Reflected through Media Narratives of Financial Crisis, Family Conflict, and Follower Dissent." *Social Science Journal* 49 (4):485–493.

Swartz, David. 1988. "Introduction." *Theory and Society* 17:615–625.

Swartz, David L. and Vera L. Zolberg. 2007. "Sartre for the Twenty-First Century?" *Theory and Society* 36:215–222.

Swindal, James. 2012. "Habermas, Religion, and a Postsecular Society." In *Christianity and Secular Reason*, edited by J. Bloechl, 217-238. Notre Dame, IN: University of Notre Dame Press.

Swinny, S.H. 1914. "Giambattista Vico." *Sociological Review* 7 (1):50-57.

Tannahill, Reay. 1980. *Sex in History*. New York: Stein and Day.

Tarde, Gabriel. 1897. *L'opposition universelle; essai d'une théorie des contraires*. Paris: F. Alcan.

Tarde, Gabriel. 1899. *Social Laws; An Outline of Sociology*. Translated by H.C. Warren. New York: Macmillan.

Tarde, Gabriel. 1903. *Laws of Imitation*. Translated by E.C. Parsons. New York: Henry Holt and Co.

Taylor, Charles. 1994. "The Politics of Recognition." In *Multiculturalism*, edited by A. Gutmann, 25-73. Princeton, NJ: Princeton University Press.

Taylor, Ian, Paul Walton, and Jock Young. 1973. *The New Criminology: For a Social Theory of Deviance*. London: Routledge and Kegan Paul.

Taylor, Ian, Paul Walton, and Jock Young. 1975. "Critical Criminology in Britain: Review and Prospects." In *Critical Criminology*, edited by I. Taylor, P. Walton, and J. Young, 6-62. London: Routledge and Kegan Paul.

Tillich, Paul. 1952. *The Courage to Be*. New Haven: Yale University Press.

Toews, David. 2003. "The New Tarde: Sociology after the End of the Social." *Theory, Culture and Society* 20 (5):81-98.

Toews, David. 2012. "Tarde and Durkheim and the Non-sociological Ground of Sociology." In *The Social after Gabriel Tarde: Debates and Assessments*, edited by M. Candea, 80-92. London: Routledge.

Toscano, Alberto. 2007. "Powers of Pacification: State and Empire in Gabriel Tarde." *Economy and Society* 36 (4):597-613.

Trembath, Kern Robert. 1987. *Evangelical Theories of Biblical Inspiration: A Review and Proposal*. New York: Oxford University Press.

Turner, Bryan S. 2006. "Classical Sociology and Cosmopolitanism: A Critical Defence of the Social." *British Journal of Sociology* 57 (1):133-151.

Turner, Charles. 2010. *Investigating Sociological Theory*. Los Angeles: Sage.

Turner, Jonathan H. 1985. "In Defense of Positivism." *Sociological Theory* 3 (2):24-30.

Turner, Stephen P. 1996. "Introduction: Social Theory and Sociology." In *Social Theory and Sociology*, edited by S.P. Turner, 1-16. Cambridge, MA: Blackwell.

Turner, Stephen P. 2010. *Explaining the Normative*. Cambridge, UK: Polity.

Turner, Stephen P. 2011. "Schmitt, *Telos*, the Collapse of the Weimar Constitution, and the Bad Conscience of the Left." In *A Journal of No Illusions: Telos, Paul Piccone, and the Americanization of Critical Theory*, edited by T.W. Luke and B. Agger, 115-140. New York: Telos Press Publishing.

Van Flandern, Tom. 1993. *Dark Matter, Missing Planets and New Comets*. Berkeley: North Atlantic Books.

Vaughan, Ted R. and Gideon Sjoberg. 1986. "Human Rights Theory and the Classical Sociological Tradition." In *Sociological Theory in Transition*, edited by M.L. Wardell and S.P. Turner, 127–141. London: Allen and Unwin.

Vico, Giambattista. 2002. *The First New Science*. Translated and edited by L. Pompa. Cambridge: Cambridge University Press.

Vucinich, Alexander. 1974. "Marx and Parsons in Soviet Sociology." *Russian Review* 33 (1):1–19.

Wacquant, Loïc J.D. 1996. "Toward a Reflexive Sociology: A Workshop with Pierre Bourdieu." In *Social Theory and Sociology*, edited by S.P. Turner, 213–228. Oxford, UK: Blackwell.

Wagner, Helmut R. 1963. "Types of Sociological Theory: Toward a System of Classification." *American Sociological Review* 28 (5):735–742.

Walby, Sylvia. 2001. "From Community to Coalition: The Politics of Recognition as the Handmaiden of the Politics of Equality in an Era of Globalization." *Theory, Culture and Society* 18 (2–3):113–135.

Wald, Alan M. 1987. *The New York Intellectuals: The Rise and Decline of the Anti-Stalinist Left from the 1930s to the 1980s*. Chapel Hill: University of North Carolina Press.

Wallerstein, Immanuel. 1997. "Social Science and the Quest for a Just Society." *American Journal of Sociology* 102 (5):1241–1257.

Ward, Lester F. 1883. *Dynamic Sociology*, 2 vols. New York: Appleton.

Ward, Lester F. 1903. *Pure Sociology*. New York: Macmillan.

Ward, Lester F. 1906. *Applied Sociology*. New York: Ginn and Co.

Warf, Barney. 2011. "Geographies of Global Internet Censorship." *GeoJournal* 76:1–23.

Watier, Patrick. 2003. "Shifts in Sociological Perspective." *Simmel Studies* 13 (1):302–317.

Watt, David H. 1991. *A Transforming Faith: Explorations of Twentieth-Century American Evangelicalism*. New Brunswick, NJ: Rutgers University Press.

Weber, Max. 1930. *The Protestant Ethic and the Spirit of Capitalism*. Translated by T. Parsons. London: Allen and Unwin.

Weber, Max. 1958. *The Protestant Ethic and the Spirit of Capitalism*. Translated by T. Parsons. New York: Scribner.

Weber, Max. 1963. "Soteriology and Types of Salvation." *The Sociology of Religion, M. Weber*. Translated by E. Fischoff, 184–206. Boston: Beacon Press.

Weber, Max. 1964. *The Theory of Social and Economic Organization*, edited by T. Parsons. New York: Free Press.

Weber, Max. 1968 [1925]. *Economy and Society*. Translated and edited by G. Roth and C. Wittich. New York: Bedminster Press.

Weber, Max. 1978 [1922]. "Excerpts from *Wirtschaft und Gessellschaft*." In *Weber: Selections in Translation*. Translated by E. Matthews, edited by W.G. Runciman, 33–42. Cambridge: Cambridge University Press.

Weinberg, Elizabeth Ann. 1974. *The Development of Sociology in the Soviet Union*. London: Routledge and Kegan Paul.

Wilcox, Clyde and Ted G. Jelen. 1990. "Evangelicals and Political Tolerance." *American Politics Quarterly* 18 (1):25–46.

Wilson, William J. 1987. *The Truly Disadvantaged: The Inner City, the Underclass, and Public Policy*. Chicago: University of Chicago Press.

Winch, Peter. 1958. *The Idea of a Social Science and Its Relation to Philosophy*. London: Kegan & Paul.

Wink, Logan K., Craig A. Erikson, and Christopher J. McDougle. 2010. "Pharmacologic Treatment of Behavioral Symptoms Associated With Autism and Other Pervasive Developmental Disorders." *Current Treatment Options in Neurology* 12:529–538.

Wolfe, Alan. 1989. *Whose Keeper? Social Science and Moral Obligation*. Berkeley: University of California Press.

Wollheim, Richard. 1984. *The Thread of Life*. Cambridge, MA: Harvard University Press.

Wright, Erik Olin. 2013. "Transforming Capitalism through Real Utopias." *American Sociological Review* 78 (1):1–25.

Wrong, Dennis H. 1982. "A Note on Marx and Weber in Gouldner's Thought." *Theory and Society* 11:899–905.

Wuthnow, Robert. 1991. "Understanding Religion and Politics." *Daedalus* 120 (3):1–20.

Yelle, Robert. 2010. "The Trouble with Transcendence: Carl Schmitt's 'Exception' as a Challenge for Religious Studies." *Method and Theory in the Study of Religion* 22:189–206.

Zeskind, Leonard. 2012. "A Nation Dispossessed: The Tea Party Movement and Race." *Critical Sociology* 38 (4):495–509.

Zizek, Slavoj. 1999. *The Ticklish Subject*. London: Verso.

Index

Adorno, Theodor   xxv, 56, 69, 111, 112, 148, 152, 210
Agger, Ben   76, 107, 130
Ahn, Ilsup   149n, 150
Amsterdam   xiii, xiv, xviii, xx, xxiii, xxiv, xxvi, 114n7
American Sociological Association   15, 197, 201, 206
anarchism   206, 207n
Anderson, Elijah   192, 193
Antioch College   xv, xxiii, 46n, 107
Antonio, Robert   107, 210
Arab Spring   203, 204
Archer, Margaret   68, 174, 175
Arendt, Hannah   205, 210

Baehr, Peter   4, 5
Beck, Ulrich   174, 175
Becker, Howard   38, 39, 45, 52, 57, 63–65, 201
Bell, Daniel   xix, xx, xxv, xxvii, 107
Benjamin, Walter   152
Bentham, Jeremy   8, 9, 44, 181, 211
biography   viii–xi, xiv, 4, 7, 22n, 98, 99, 121, 150
Bourdieu, Pierre   33, 68–72, 86–88, 121, 173, 174, 197, 198, 205
  habitus   69–71, 86, 87, 174
Brady, David   199, 200
Breines, Paul   xx, 99
Browder, Earl   91
Burawoy, Michael   197–201, 205

Castro, Fidel   xxxi, 110, 196, 205
Chang, Jung   194, 195
charisma   133, 148, 182, 183
Chicago School of Sociology   41, 42, 45, 65
Chriss, James   vii, xi, xxiv, 15, 39, 60, 77, 80, 84, 87, 97, 99, 109, 122n, 128, 131, 149, 150, 157, 158
City College of New York (CCNY)   xi, xix, xx, 94
civil society   131, 143, 165, 186n, 189, 190, 192, 197, 199, 200
  public sphere   51, 110, 138, 190
  societal community (Parsons)   131

classical sociology   xix, 1–7, 175, 181, 183
Cohen, Jean   108–110
Columbia University   x, xi, xxii, xxv, 11, 18, 47, 94, 98, 99, 104, 108
communism/ist   xxix, 10, 15, 25, 72, 89–91, 96, 105, 120, 122, 126n, 129, 142, 147, 157, 158, 162n, 163, 194, 196, 201, 202, 205
  Communist Party of the US (CPUSA)   xi, xix, xx, xxv, 33, 89–92, 94–97, 115, 123, 128
  factionalism in   89, 90, 94, 96
  FBI surveillance of   95–97, 101, 102
  horizon   206–208
  Italian Communist Party   xxviii
  revolution   xxxi, xxxii, 24, 62, 110, 116, 141, 156n, 158, 195
  Soviet   10, 94, 104, 117, 118
  Young Communist League   xix, xxv
Connell, Raewyn   3, 4
Coser, Lewis   xx, 89, 90, 180
criminology   xii, xxix, 7, 36–40, 43–46, 51–53, 67, 134, 175
  Classical School of Criminology   44, 48
  critical criminology   61, 62, 64, 65

Davis, James   40–43
Dean, Jodi   206–208
Deaton, Alan (Lan)   xi, xvi
Deaton, Emmanuelle   xv
Deaton, Richard   vii–xxxiii, xxxiv, 11, 16n, 94, 95
Deaton, Robert Brooks   xii
Deaton, Shoshanah   xv, xxxiv
Descartes, René   19, 73
Deutscher, Isaac   xvii, xxxi, 96
Dewey, John   74, 97
dialectic   22, 26, 77, 78, 105, 114, 124, 143, 148
  Greek   143, 148
  Hegelian   xxix, 68, 76, 78, 83, 143, 144, 148
  Marxist   xxix, 26, 76, 115, 129, 143, 144, 156, 158n, 196
Dickens, David   107, 108n, 110

INDEX 237

Du Bois, W.E.B.   3, 92
Durkheim, Emile   4, 5, 12–15, 23, 50–52,
  75, 84, 85, 125–127, 131, 144, 175–182, 187,
  190, 192
  mechanical vs. organic
    solidarity   50, 51, 84, 85, 125, 126,
    131, 182, 190, 196

egalitarianism   29, 44, 190, 207n, 208
Elias, Nelly   188, 189
Ellwood, Charles   41, 74, 145, 178n, 179
Engerman, David   101, 104
Enlightenment   13, 14, 32, 87, 124, 158n,
  164, 165, 169, 186n, 189
evolutionism   10, 106, 157, 158, 165, 180, 189

fascism   90, 209
Fehér, Ferenc   205, 209, 210
feminism   12, 25, 26, 43, 56, 64, 79,
  121–123, 132, 134, 172
Ferrarotti, Franco   4, 108
Foster, William   90, 91, 95, 96
foundationalism   87, 123, 151, 166, 196
Frankfurt School of Critical
  Theory   xxvii, 9, 69, 99, 107, 111,
  148, 187, 200
Fraser, John   105, 106
Fraser, Nancy   81–84
Freud, Sigmund   xxx, 23

Garfinkel, Harold   63, 72, 97
  ethnomethodology   12, 63, 71, 72, 75
Giddings, Franklin   6, 70n, 74, 75, 122n,
  178, 189, 191n, 196
globalization   84, 168, 170, 171, 174, 175,
  184–189, 192, 207
Goffman, Erving   xix, 16, 60, 63, 74, 86, 97,
  98, 126, 137, 151
Gouldner, Alessandra   xiv, xviii
Gouldner, Alvin
  and Browderism   xi, xx, xxvii, 94
  on classical sociology   8–15
  and Communist Party (CPUSA)   xi, xix,
    xx, xxv, 33, 92–96, 123
  critical vs. scientific Marxism   37, 106,
    112, 117, 156–160, 196
  culture of critical discourse (CCD)   70,
    116, 117, 141, 166, 167, 194, 198
  and dialectics   22, 26, 77, 78, 105, 114,
    124, 143, 166

European travels   100–102
and family relations   x–xvi, xviii, xxiii,
  xxxiv, 11, 209n
and the Frankfurt School   99
group tensions, theory of   46–48,
  50, 51
Humphreys incident   xxiv, 24, 34, 61
and industrial sociology   xiv,
  xxiv–xxvi, 22, 38, 47, 48, 50, 89, 100,
  103, 104, 141, 155, 171, 174, 175
on intellectuals as a New Class   xxx,
  xxxi, 37n, 38, 63, 87, 108, 109, 113, 167
  ideologues and technologues   22,
    26, 27, 37n, 109, 110, 117, 148
and Judaism   xi, xviii, xix, xxi, xxiii,
  11, 24, 32, 97–99, 121, 127
locals and cosmopolitans, theory
  of   116, 171–173, 175, 190, 192
as Marxologist   x, xxxii
metaphoricality of Marxism   77, 78,
  141–143
Mills poem   17
National Gypsum plant
  (Buffalo)   xxvi, 47, 108, 109
nightmare theory   117, 158, 159, 161,
  164–166, 175, 184, 196, 199, 205, 208
as Non-Jewish Jew   x, xvii, xix, xx,
  96–99
as outlaw Marxist   xi, 52, 94, 97,
  124, 147
his "difficult" personality   ix–xi, xx,
  xxi, 15, 16, 107
on reciprocity   2, 36, 42, 52, 53, 55–57
and reflexivity   xxx, xxxii, 11, 26, 32,
  33, 37, 43, 44, 48, 61, 63–69, 86, 87, 105,
  111, 114, 116, 118, 119, 122, 123, 140, 141, 153,
  154, 156–161, 165–168, 175, 208, 209
Rosenbergs, execution of the   xxiii,
  24, 97, 121, 128
Sartre talk   28–31
as secular humanist   21, 27, 32, 39, 57,
  124, 140
soda jerk incident   xxi
and Soviet sociology   102–105
on starting mechanisms   51, 53–55,
  123, 175
thingification   39, 59–61, 65, 200
as Tough Jew   x, xvii, xx, xxi, 99
on vanguard party   40, 44, 52, 69, 72,
  86, 116, 117, 129, 142, 147, 148, 211

Gouldner, Alvin (cont.)
  on the welfare/warfare state   36, 38,
    39, 41, 42, 45, 46, 57, 61–63, 113, 120, 126,
    147–149, 153, 198
Gouldner, Andrew   xiv, xviii
Gouldner, Helen Pat   xiv, xvi, xviii, xxii,
    xxiii, 127
Gouldner, Janet Walker   xiv, xviii
Gouldner, Louis   xvii
Gramsci, Antonio   xxix, 29, 69, 106, 110,
    111, 115, 198
Great Depression (USA)   xi, xviii, xix, 10,
    90, 150
Groves, Byron   66, 67
Guevara, Che   xxxi, 205

Habermas, Jürgen   21, 59, 74, 76, 79,
    80, 83n, 84, 107, 130, 131, 137, 140, 147–150,
    152, 154, 184, 185, 190, 199, 207
  colonization of the lifeworld   59, 116,
    131, 150, 190, 199
Halliday, Jon   194, 195
Harvard University   xxiii, 10, 11, 22
Hegel, Georg   xxix, 68, 76–78, 82, 83, 110,
    121, 124, 143, 144, 148–150, 155, 158n, 167, 196,
    207, 208
Heller, Agnes   205, 209n, 210
Hitler, Adolf   90, 195
Hobbes, Thomas   180, 181, 184
Hollander, Paul   118, 119
homosexuality   56, 60, 65, 87, 113, 128, 151,
    169, 170, 192, 205
  same sex marriage   53, 55, 139
Hook, Sidney   xxvii, 90, 96
Hoover, J. Edgar   xxii, 92, 95, 96
Horkheimer, Max   99, 148
Horowitz, Irving   16, 24, 34, 97, 100n, 105, 195
Howe, Irving   xviii, xx, xxvii, 89, 90
Humphreys, Laud   24, 25, 34, 61, 206

intellectuals
  organic   29, 198
  New York   viii, xi, xiii, xix, 89, 90, 96, 97
  radical   25, 47, 62, 106, 110, 116, 126,
    159, 194, 196, 207, 209, 210
  revolutionary   xxxi, 25, 28, 97, 112–117
imitation   69, 175–183, 187, 190–192
immigration   xviii, xix, 11, 56, 79, 84, 97,
    98, 106, 140, 188, 192, 196, 206

Jay, Martin   9, 111n, 142

Kant, Immanuel   14, 78, 82, 83, 144, 149,
    150, 173–175, 186, 193, 205
Kassof, Allen   103, 104
Korsch, Karl   110, 111
Kowalchuk, Lisa   200, 201

Lasch, Christopher   xxii, 62n
Lazarsfeld, Paul   xxv, 92n, 98, 99
Le Bon, Gustave   177, 192
Lemert, Charles   87, 121–123
Lemish, Dafna   188, 189
Lenin, Vladimir   xxxi, xxxii, 33, 96,
    101, 102, 105, 114, 117, 126n, 129, 196,
    205, 210n
Lewis, Oscar   xv
Liazos, Alexander   38, 120
liberalism   10n, 11, 39, 41, 85, 107, 112, 138,
    147, 183–186, 193, 205
  neoliberalism   207, 210
linguistic turn   59, 70, 71, 142, 144, 149,
    150, 152
Lipset, Seymour Martin   xix, xx, xxv,
    xxvii, 98, 196
Lowenthal, Richard   xxviii, xxix
Lukács, György   106, 110, 207, 209, 210
Luke, Timothy   81, 106, 107
Lundskow, George   202n, 204

Machiavelli   4, 184, 185
Mao Zedong   xxix, xxxi, 33, 102, 110,
    114–118, 129, 194–196, 205–210
Marcuse, Herbert   19, 69, 106
Marxism/Marxist   xi, xxvii–xxxii, 23,
    45–47, 86, 88, 90, 100, 102, 107, 110, 114,
    115, 122, 126, 129, 144, 148, 156–158, 189,
    192, 200, 207, 210
  Academic vs. Activist   24–26, 111, 128
  alienation   27, 28, 61, 68, 86, 130, 134,
    155, 156
  and capitalism   8–10, 25, 27, 38–40,
    44, 47, 48, 50, 51, 55, 56, 63, 64, 69, 77,
    81, 91, 95, 96, 100, 102–104, 106, 109, 110,
    112, 117, 118, 129, 138, 141, 150, 153–160,
    168, 169, 189, 200, 201, 204, 206, 207,
    209, 210n
  criminology   64–67
  dictatorship   33, 77, 196, 205, 209

INDEX 239

Engels against Marx   32, 33, 129, 196, 207
enslavement   77, 142, 144, 147
false consciousness   8, 25, 67, 69, 77, 102, 104, 115, 117, 123, 156n, 158n, 200, 205
historical materialism   23, 64, 66, 102, 103, 106, 112, 116, 117, 129, 143, 156n, 193, 196
and imperialism   27, 90, 91, 95, 104, 116, 148, 185, 205
and Merton   26, 27, 40, 48
and sociology   8–10, 12, 13, 26, 101, 104–106, 147, 197–200, 208–211
vanguard party   95, 116, 117, 142, 147, 205, 207n, 208
violence in   117, 157, 159, 160, 194, 195, 204–209
McCarthy, Joseph   xv, xxii, xxiii, xxv, 24, 95–97, 104, 128
McIver, Robert   99
McLaughlin, Neil   200, 201
Mead, George   74, 75, 149, 182, 186, 187
Merton, Robert K.   xix, xxii, xxv, 6, 9, 11, 18, 22, 26, 27, 40, 48–50, 52, 57, 94, 97–99, 101–104, 108
Mills, C. Wright   vii, viii, x, xi, xxx, 9, 16, 18, 92, 98, 119, 196
Gouldner's poem about   17
Soviet assessment of   104, 105

naturalism   21, 66, 72, 103
Nietzsche, Friedrich   56, 148, 155, 165

Obama, Barack   170, 184, 202, 203, 205, 206, 207n
Oberlin College   xi, xx, 94
objectivity   x, 13, 39, 63, 70, 73, 75, 76, 86, 87, 102, 106, 161, 169
see also subjectivity
Occupy movement   201–204, 206, 207n, 208
As vanguard party   207n, 208
Ogburn, William   10n, 92
Ost, David   112, 113

Paolucci, Paul   129, 196
paradigms, sociological
evaluative   11–13, 18, 24, 32, 50, 69, 122, 130, 137, 141, 147, 150, 199–201, 208
interpretive   4, 11, 12, 18, 129, 141, 150, 181

positivist   4, 11–14, 18, 21, 42, 43, 66, 70, 76, 119–122, 141, 154, 158n, 162–169, 200, 201, 210
Parsons, Talcott   xxvii, xxviii, xxx, 3, 7, 9–11, 22, 26, 48–51, 53, 59, 68, 72, 92, 100, 101, 103–106, 119, 120, 125–128, 130–133, 136, 137, 139, 149, 181, 198, 199, 201n2
AGIL   131, 132, 138, 198
steering media   131, 180
Pearson, Geoff   62, 63
Piccone, Paul   87, 105–114, 175, 210
Plato   xxiv, xxvi, 5, 48, 143
Polanyi, Michael   102, 103
Pope Francis   168–170
positivism   xxx, 8, 10, 32, 150, 165, 200
and Comte, Auguste   4, 8, 11, 13–15, 21, 22, 125, 126, 164, 169
and Saint Simon, Henri   8, 9, 12–15, 19, 21, 22, 89, 164n
postmodernism   85, 140, 151, 152, 211
public sociology   173, 196–201, 205
and public intellectuals   viii, xi, 31, 33, 200

radical sociology   viii, xxvi, xxix, 8, 11, 18, 57, 62, 66, 92, 105, 114, 121–123, 144, 200, 201n1, 208, 210
Academic vs. Activist Marxists   24, 26
Washington University and   22–25
rationalization   60, 79, 108, 113, 130, 133–136, 139, 140, 144, 147n, 207
standardization   133–136, 139
Rawls, John   52, 82, 153
Reagan, Ronald   41, 96, 136
recognition   60, 69, 78–85, 113, 190, 192, 203
reflexivity   xxx, xxxii, 9, 11, 26, 32, 33, 37, 43, 44, 48, 61, 63–78, 80–87, 105, 111, 111–119, 122, 123, 140, 141, 153–168, 174, 175, 186, 197, 198, 201, 208, 209
religion   xi, xvii, xviii, xxiii, 8, 11, 13, 18, 20, 21, 33, 50, 54, 85, 104, 112–116, 124–137, 139–141, 144–147, 149–153, 157, 164, 165, 168–170, 180, 181, 183, 191, 196, 202
atonement   137–139
the Bible   21, 130, 137, 138, 145, 151
Buddhism   112, 133
burying the dead   20

religion (cont.)
  Catholicism   8, 21, 127, 168, 169
  Christianity   xvii, 48, 55, 112, 114, 128, 130, 132, 135–137, 139, 143–146, 150, 151, 156, 165, 168, 208
  commemoration   20
  Confucianism   115, 133
  evangelicalism   128, 129, 135–140, 150
  Islamic/Muslim   132, 188, 196, 205
  Judaism   vii, x, xi, xvii, xix–xxiii, 11, 24, 32, 89, 95–99, 113, 120, 121, 127, 144
    And Zionism   97, 98
  millenarianism   114, 136n, 194, 195
  Protestantism   106, 127–129, 133, 135, 137, 139, 140, 157
  salvation   115, 128, 130, 132, 133, 135, 137, 139, 140, 157
revolution   xxxi, xxxii, 30, 62, 66, 77, 110, 113, 116, 117, 154, 159, 167, 195, 205–207, 209
  American   80
  cultural   115, 194
  feminist   122
  French   8, 80, 192
  German   28, 31
  vs. reform   24, 25
  scientific   8
Rosenberg, Ethel   xxii, xxiii, 24, 95, 97, 121, 128
Rosenberg, Julius   xxii, xxiii, 24, 95, 97, 121, 128

Sampson, Robert   66, 67
Sartre, Jean-Paul   xvii, 31–33, 115, 198, 205, 206
Sattler, Helen Ruth   xi, xxvi, 94
Schmitt, Carl   107, 111, 112, 147, 175, 176, 182–185, 186n, 189–193, 198, 210
  friend-enemy distinction   151, 176, 182–185, 190, 191, 198
secular humanism   130, 138–140, 144, 145, 150, 151, 165, 170, 187
Shalin, Dmitri   98, 103
Shannon, David   91, 92, 95
Simmel, Georg   5, 85, 173
Sjoberg, Gideon   76, 83, 84
slavery   76, 79, 84, 145–147
Smelser, Neil   40–42
Smith, Adam   6, 100

social justice   75–78, 82, 113, 147, 153–170
social theory vs. sociological theory   6, 7, 121
socialism/ist   8, 13, 27, 62, 77, 89, 94, 95, 101, 104, 110, 112, 116, 118, 122, 141, 142, 144, 147, 157, 158, 196, 202, 205–209
  Fabian   62
  Jacobin   209
  Jewish Socialist Federation   89n
  Socialist Party   89, 90
  Socialist Workers Party   xix, 96
Sorokin, Pitirim   9, 92
Spencer, Herbert   xxviii, 4, 55, 70n, 176, 181
Stalin, Joseph   xx, xxviii, xxix, xxxi, 33, 88, 90, 94, 96, 100, 102–106, 110, 113, 114, 117–119, 129, 160n, 194–196, 205, 209
Stark, Rodney   145, 146, 147n
subjectivity   xxix, 68–78, 82–87, 120, 126, 146, 200, 201
  see also objectivity
Swartz, David   33, 121

Tarde, Gabriel   175–183, 185, 186n, 187, 189–193
Taylor, Ian   36, 37, 39, 61, 62, 64, 65
Tea Party   201–205
Telos   107, 108, 110–114, 117, 175
Tito, Josip   xxviii, xxxi, 94
de Tocqueville, Alexis   4, 6
Togliatti, Palmiero   xxviii
totalitarianism   90, 111, 117, 147, 184, 196, 209
  Totally Administered Society   108–110, 148
Trotsky, Leon   xix, xx, xxvii, xxxi, 90, 94, 96, 97
Truman, Harry   91, 92
Turcotte, Kerry   200, 201
Turner, Bryan   2, 3, 186
Turner, Charles   7
Turner, Jonathan   163
Turner, Stephen   xxxiv, 7, 183n, 189

unity of theory and practice   12, 13, 23, 28, 31, 33, 36, 37, 39, 65, 99, 100–106, 111, 136, 137, 208
University of Buffalo   xx, xxii, 94, 106, 108
University of Illinois, Urbana   xv, xvi, xxiv, xxvi

University of Wisconsin   xii, xxiv, xxvi
utilitarianism   8, 9, 44, 48, 52, 55, 62, 180, 181

Vaughan, Ted   76, 83, 84
Vico, Giambattista   6, 14, 15, 18–22
Vietnam War   xii, xxii, xxviii, 25, 116

Wagner, Helmut   11, 12, 141
Wald, Alan   xx, 96
Wallace, Henry   xx, 91, 92, 94, 95
Walton, Paul   36, 37, 39, 61, 62, 64, 65

Ward, Lester   1, 3, 5, 10n, 22, 26, 70n, 73, 181, 186, 187
Weber, Max   1, 4, 5, 10, 13, 15, 22, 25, 28, 34, 57, 59, 79, 104, 105, 108, 109, 126, 127, 130, 131, 133–137, 145, 147n, 148–150, 181–185
Verstehen   5, 12, 76, 181
World War I   9, 89n, 90, 110
World War II   viii, xix, xxi, xxviii, 10, 90, 99

Young, Jock   36, 37, 39, 61, 62, 64, 65

Zizek, Slavoj   73, 207